Matthew J. and Arlyn Bruccoli in front of the former Dingo Bar in Paris, where F. Scott Fitzgerald and Ernest Hemingway met in the spring of 1925; photograph by John C. Unrue, 1994

ON BOOKS AND WRITERS

Selected Essays

MATTHEW J. BRUCCOLI

Edited by John C. Unrue

*For Dr. Joseph Johnson
with continuing gratitude
and respect
John C. Unrue*

The University of South Carolina Press

© 2010 University of South Carolina

Published by the University of South Carolina Press
Columbia, South Carolina 29208

www.sc.edu/uscpress

Manufactured in the United States of America

19 18 17 16 15 14 13 12 11 10   10 9 8 7 6 5 4 3 2 1

Library of Congress Cataloging-in-Publication Data

Bruccoli, Matthew J. (Matthew Joseph), 1931–2008.
  On books and writers : selected essays / Matthew J. Bruccoli ; edited by John C. Unrue.
    p. cm.
  Includes bibliographical references and index.
  ISBN 978-1-57003-902-7 (cloth : alk. paper)
  1. American literature—20th century—History and criticism. 2. Authors and publishers—United States—History—20th century. 3. Literature publishing—United States—History—20th century. 4. Fitzgerald, F. Scott (Francis Scott), 1896–1940—Criticism and interpretation. I. Unrue, John C. II. Title.
  PS221.B68 2010
  810.9'005—dc22
                                                                                    2009043340

This book was printed on Glatfelter Natures, a recycled paper with 30 percent postconsumer waste content.

"I haven't wasted my life."

M.J.B., comment to
Judith S. Baughman,
2 June 2008

CONTENTS

Preface   ix
Acknowledgments   xiii
Introduction   xv

PART 1. ON FITZGERALD

The Man of Letters as Professional   3
This Side of Paradise: Fitzgerald's Apprentice Novel   15
The Beautiful and Damned: A Warning Prophecy   22
The Great Gatsby: Fitzgerald's Triumph of Genius and Craft   27
Tender Is the Night: From Concept to "The Author's Final Version"   39
The Love of the Last Tycoon: Preparation and Composition   63

PART 2. ON BIBLIOGRAPHY

What Bowers Wrought: An Assessment of the Center for
    Editions of American Authors   83
Textual Variants in Sinclair Lewis's *Babbitt*   91
Hidden Printings in Edith Wharton's *The Children*   97
A Mirror for Bibliographers: Duplicate Plates in Modern Printing   101
Concealed Printings in Hawthorne   106
Notes on the Destruction of *The Scarlet Letter* Manuscript   112

PART 3. ON PUBLISHING AND PUBLISHERS

Getting It Right: The Publishing Process and the Correction
    of Factual Errors—with Reference to *The Great Gatsby*   117
The Profession of Authorship in Twenty-First-Century America   132
What Maxwell Perkins Really Did for *Look Homeward, Angel*   145

PART 4. ON BOOKMEN

Debts   157
Hawthorne as a Collector's Item, 1885–1924   167
George D. Smith and the Anglo-American Book Migration   178
Bookman: Charles Elliot Frazer Clark, Jr., 1925–2001   189

PART 5. ON LIBRARIES AND LIBRARIANS

Mere Collectors' Items   199

Where They Belong: The Acquisition of the F. Scott Fitzgerald Papers   205

John Cook Wyllie   212

Research Libraries without Reference Books   225

PART 6. ON OTHER WRITERS

"The Light of the World": Stan Ketchel as "My Sweet Christ"   231

Thomas Wolfe's "The Four Lost Men"   236

Out of Life: John O'Hara's Character Creation   247

Focus on *Appointment in Samarra:* The Importance of Knowing What You Are Talking About   256

A Reopening of the *By Love Possessed* Case   263

Raymond Chandler and Hollywood   269

Hemingway's Pursuit of Fame   277

Publications by Matthew J. Bruccoli   287

Index   313

PREFACE

On Books and Writers had its genesis in late summer of 2007, when I became aware that despite Matthew J. Bruccoli's writing or editing more than one hundred books and being our foremost F. Scott Fitzgerald scholar, whose importance to American literary scholarship and American literary history can hardly be overstated, no collection of his essays had ever been published. The extraordinary range of Matt's scholarship was acknowledged appropriately in a "Publisher's Note" in *The Profession of Authorship: Essays in Honor of Matthew J. Bruccoli*, a Festschrift edited by Richard Layman and Joel Myerson and published in 1996 by the University of South Carolina Press; the note refers to "Matthew J. Bruccoli's illustrious career as a writer, scholar, textual critic, teacher, bibliophile, and publisher. . . ." He was also a major biographer and the editor of many journals and series, most notably the *Dictionary of Literary Biography*. His knowledge not only about the subjects of his biographies but also about other seemingly countless major and minor writers, and editors as well as nonliterary figures relevant to his work, was encyclopedic. And, of course, his passion for building great book collections and his support for the librarians who shared his passion were legendary.

When I approached Matt with the idea of editing a collection of his essays, I had known him for nearly forty years, having met him in 1968 when I enrolled as a Ph.D. student in his Fitzgerald/Hemingway seminar at the Ohio State University. Being one of his students was most fortunate for me; not only did I have the privilege of studying with the most inspiring teacher I have ever known, but I was also subsequently blessed with a treasured and enduring friendship for which I will always be grateful. From the outset Matt was enthusiastic and supportive of the idea of this collection of his essays, responding to my request to edit the collection in an email on 6 August 2007, saying that he was "delighted and gratified" and adding that I should tell him how "to assist."

During the last several years leading up to his retirement in 2006 from his professorship in the English department at the University of South Carolina, which he joined in 1969 and where he had been Emily Brown Jefferies Professor since 1976, Matt had begun to reflect seriously, sometimes nostalgically, upon his life as a teacher, scholar, editor, publisher, and, as he put it, "bookman." I am convinced that he envisioned a volume that included representative essays from his work for half a century as revealing the course of his career. In fact, that retrospective view probably led to his first and most important suggestion for my consideration—the organization of the collection into six sections or groupings under which his essays could be arranged: "On Fitzgerald," "On Bibliography," "On Publishing and Publishers," "On Bookmen," "On Libraries and Librarians," and "On Other Writers."

Over the next few months I began rereading his essays, and I wrote and submitted a proposal to the University of South Carolina Press, the press that best knew his work and had published or reprinted many of his most important contributions to the study of American literature. From the outset I was so enthralled by the possibility of doing the Bruccoli essay collection that I was unable to resist gathering and tentatively arranging his essays in the six categories long before the press could respond to my proposal. Matt and I spoke often about pieces I was considering for the collection, and, although he remained determined to avoid what he regarded as "intrusion," he must have known that I wanted his observations and suggestions to ensure that I was following the well-known Bruccoli maxim "get it right" as I attempted to find essays that represented the evolution and continuity of his work.

While he never indicated to me that any particular essay be selected, he sent me several offprints that he must have known I could not resist adding. He also sent copies of a couple of essays he said should not be included in the collection, and in a vintage Bruccoli note scrawled on the legal-size lined yellow paper, known to everyone who ever corresponded with him, Matt provided a reason for sending them: "John—I do not recommend these for reprinting. But I am sending to give you an idea of what I did when I was learning my trade." Although I have not selected those articles, they proved valuable because I acquired from them a sense of the almost minimalist focus of Matt's early bibliographical publications that were often the essence of later expanded writings.

Making selections for this volume from such an enormous list of excellent options proved to be my most daunting challenge. In addition to his many periodical publications, Matt's introductions and afterwords, written both for his own books as well as for other authors' books, are some of his finest and most definitive essays, envied models of a rare brand of scholarship founded upon tenacious research and convincing conclusions.

On 23 and 24 April 2008 Matt was in Las Vegas, Nevada, as an invited featured speaker for the library district that was participating in "The Big Read," a program sponsored by the National Endowment for the Humanities. Matt's topic: *The Great Gatsby*. He had actually made several trips to Las Vegas since the mid 1970s, frequently at my invitation during my long tenure as provost and academic vice president at the University of Nevada, Las Vegas. Predictably, our students were astonished by his knowledge and regaled by his wit. They loved him. The casinos held no interest for him, other than as curiosities. However, he never missed going to an antique automobile museum to look at the luxury cars from the 1920s and 1930s, about which he was extremely knowledgeable.

Matt devoted his life to books and writers, and he was reverential about the importance of great literature. And surely everyone who knew him could recall moments during which he demonstrated his commitment to and passion for literature and its makers. One of my most memorable of such moments occurred on the morning of 10 April 2000, as I rushed into my university office in order to answer a ringing telephone. When I picked up the receiver, there was no identification, only Matt's unmistakable voice, solemn, saying: "*The Great Gatsby* is seventy-five years old today." More recently, also during a telephone conversation, he quoted verbatim his favorite passage from Hemingway's *Green Hills of Africa* in which Hemingway expresses his preference for art over fashionable politics, a conviction that Matt not only shared, but also a principle from which he never wavered during his lifetime. Matt said that Hemingway's observations "almost" caused him to forgive Hemingway for some of his cruelties to Fitzgerald.

Matt and I had lunch and our last face-to-face conversation on 24 April 2008, during which I brought him up to date on my plans for the essay collection and sought his suggestions. As we left our table, he reiterated his promise to write an afterword that he said would be an overview of his career. At the airport before boarding a plane for San Francisco to visit his daughter Josie and her family, he said that he would let me know when he learned any news about the status of the proposal for the collection. Ten days later, on Friday, May 4th, Matt called to tell me that he had been diagnosed with an inoperable brain tumor. And he called one last time on 22 May, upbeat and brave, to report that he had been told that the University of South Carolina Press Board had approved the proposal for the Bruccoli essay collection. I recalled soon after Matt's death that he never spoke to me about dying. Rather he said in his last year only that he would like to be able to work ten more years. But, of course, work was his life.

Although my commitment to *On Books and Writers: Selected Essays* had been extremely strong from the book's inception, it increased greatly after Matt's death. In the absence of the afterword he would have written, I hope that these essays achieve my wish for them: that they convey by their arrangement and content their own overview of a remarkable career of one of America's finest scholars whose observations and wisdom cover the full extent of all from which literature is constructed—from the physical production of books to authorial nuance. Written in his clear, spare prose and enlivened always by the colorful Americanisms he favored, these essays will appeal to readers of widely varying perspectives as they provide an indispensable teacher's and scholar's brilliant insider's perspective.

ACKNOWLEDGMENTS

Sweet memories of my son, John Gregory Unrue, who died unexpectedly on 19 September 2008, inspired and sustained me during the last stages of my work on Matt's essays. And his sister, Jane Elizabeth Unrue, provided strength and light in a very dark time. My wife of nearly fifty years, Darlene Harbour Unrue, tirelessly proofread and improved my efforts. Darlene's bravery, wisdom, courage, and love during our most difficult months enabled me to complete this book.

I am indebted most deeply to Matthew J. Bruccoli, preeminent scholar, teacher, and friend whose indefatigable and passionate commitment to his work for more than five decades produced the essays reprinted here. Arlyn Bruccoli, executor of the Matthew J. Bruccoli literary estate, Matt's wife and inspiration, has also my heartfelt gratitude for her support. Judith S. Baughman, frequent collaborator on Bruccoli books and projects, and in her words, Matt's "once and future assistant," responded generously to countless inquiries and made helpful suggestions during the compilation of the essays. I am also deeply indebted to Jennifer Hynes and once again to Judith S. Baughman for permitting me to include here their "Publications by Matthew J. Bruccoli." That Judy was also my copyeditor was a blessing. No other person worked more closely with Matt. Richard Layman, of Bruccoli, Clark, Layman, gave me valuable advice concerning the nebulous location of copyright for the first volume of the *Fitzgerald/Hemingway Annual.* Jan Nordby Gretlund led me to success in gaining permission to reprint from a Scandinavian journal. Beth Alvarez, curator of literary manuscripts at the University of Maryland, College Park, gave me her time and quick access to important materials available in the University of Maryland libraries. My own English department chairperson, Douglas Unger, provided much appreciated teaching schedules beneficial to my work on the collection. Linda Fogle, assistant director for operations of the University of South Carolina Press, has my heartfelt gratitude for her sensitivity and encouragement following the death of my son.

Finally, I thank many of Matt's friends from around the world for their expressions of pleasure and encouragement upon hearing that these essays are being reprinted.

INTRODUCTION

Matthew J. Bruccoli concluded early in his extraordinarily productive and distinguished scholarly career that virtually every aspect of book production, including a thorough knowledge of the history of the transmission of texts, was essential to any serious or credible study of literature and of the authors who produced it. And as essays included in this volume will attest, he held firmly to this conviction as long as he lived. Scholars needed such knowledge and perspective, he was convinced, in order to perform what he regarded as their paramount obligation—the preservation of the author's intention in an accurate text. In fact, Bruccoli frequently described this task not only as a scholar's duty, but rather as a biblical calling, "an act of piety," he said. Scholarship or criticism based upon anything else could yield inaccurate results.

Matthew J. Bruccoli was born in New York City on 21 August 1931. He was the only child of Joseph M. Bruccoli, an intensely patriotic and decorated veteran of the Great War, and Mary Gervasi Bruccoli. In 1996 during a video interview Bruccoli spoke of his childhood: "I grew up in a house without books," he said, and added that his early interest in reading developed from newspapers.[1] Nevertheless, his parents insisted that he pursue his education rigorously in order to be successful, and that, according to Bruccoli, meant that he was to become a medical doctor. With this goal in mind, he attended the Bronx High School of Science and Yale University, where he was a pre-med student, until he became an English major during his junior year. His initial interest in F. Scott Fitzgerald came in 1949 when while driving his parents' car he heard a radio dramatization of "The Diamond as Big as the Ritz."

Following graduation from Yale, he enrolled in the graduate program at the University of Virginia, which, he remained convinced, was "the center of bibliographical scholarship" in the world.[2] There his scholarly interests were nurtured and his career direction determined when he became a student and friend of the revered textual scholar Fredson Bowers. The University of Virginia offered the perfect environment for a serious, dedicated, and gifted twenty-two-year-old graduate student interested in bibliographical studies. There he found a group of highly skilled professionals and experts committed to textual studies and to building collections without which definitive texts could not be established. And there he met Linton Massey, then president of the Bibliographical Society of Virginia, and Charles Feinberg, esteemed Whitman collector. Furthermore, the prestigious *Studies in Bibliography,* edited by Bowers, was housed at Virginia as was a Hinman collator, a technological boon for comparing texts.

Bibliography and textual criticism were gaining an increasing foothold in American literary studies during Bruccoli's time at the University of Virginia as scholars pointed out flaws in texts that often invalidated critical readings lamentably based on those flaws. Perhaps the most memorable of such examples was one well-known to Bruccoli and other graduate students since 1949: the distinguished scholar F. O. Matthiessen's reading of Melville's description in *White Jacket* based on Melville's falling into the sea from the U.S. frigate *Neversink*. Matthiessen had written that Melville's image of a "soiled fish" brushing the author's side was "a *discordia concors*" and that Melville had "created a shudder from calling this frightening vagueness some 'soiled fish of the sea.'" Bruccoli's mentor Bowers was among those who observed that the "shudder" Professor Matthiesssen felt must be attributed not to Melville but to a careless typesetter and that in both the English and American first editions, the adjective was not "soiled," but "coiled."[3]

Bruccoli's graduate work at Virginia focused significantly on his continuing interest in F. Scott Fitzgerald's fiction and further inspired his interest in collecting editions of *The Great Gatsby* and other Fitzgerald works as he had begun to do as a Yale undergraduate. He wrote his M.A. thesis on Fitzgerald's Basil Duke Lee stories (1956) and his notable Ph.D. dissertation on the composition of *Tender Is the Night* (1961). The dissertation was later revised and published as *The Composition of "Tender Is the Night": A Study of the Manuscripts* (1963), and it remains our best work on Fitzgerald's stages of the composition of the novel and reflects Bruccoli's application of what he called "well-defined principles for assessing" Fitzgerald's work.

But he was also assessing the work of such other American authors as Sinclair Lewis, Nathaniel Hawthorne, and Edith Wharton and publishing the results of his scholarship during his graduate student days. Although many of these early textual and bibliographical studies challenge general readers because of their technical nature, Bruccoli regarded them as important in any overview of his career because they showed his work as he was "learning my trade."[4] Consequently, two essays from his graduate student days, "Textual Variants in Sinclair Lewis's *Babbitt*" and "A Mirror for Bibliographers: Duplicate Plates in Modern Printing,"[5] are included in the "On Bibliography" section and illustrate a vital principle of Bruccoli's scholarly approach: that a knowledge of printing and publishing processes is essential for determining textual variants and analyzing textual transmission.

As a graduate student Bruccoli showed convincing evidence of the prolific productivity that characterized his career, publishing in addition to his thesis and dissertation a dozen notes, reviews, and articles. However, despite his work's appearing during an apprentice period, it was superior. In fact, "the great man," as Virginia graduate students called Fredson Bowers, cites two Bruccoli articles in one of his published lectures, *Textual and Literary Criticism*, given while Bowers was Sandars Reader in Bibliography at Cambridge University.[6]

Also included in "On Bibliography" are two additional articles that derive from Bruccoli's continuing examination of printing and publishing practices in order to illustrate the complexity of differentiating printings of texts: "Hidden Printings in Edith Wharton's *The Children*" and "Concealed Printings in Hawthorne." Concluding the bibliography section are: "Notes on the Destruction of *The Scarlet Letter* Manuscript," Bruccoli's presentation of the conflicting accounts of Hawthorne's son, Julian, and Annie Fields, widow of Hawthorn's publisher James T. Fields, and "What Bowers Wrought," an essay delineating Fredson Bowers's major role in establishing standards for editing texts of American authors for the Center for Editions of American Authors (CEAA) and for the Committee on Scholarly Editions (CSE). The essay is particularly important in any overview of Bruccoli's career in that it shows his involvement with a project that not only provided an opportunity to hone further his early training as a bibliographer and textual critic but also helped establish him as a major American literature scholar within a few years of his arrival in 1961 at The Ohio State University, his first academic appointment.

The Department of English at O.S.U. was pleased to find a young textual and bibliographical scholar whose potential was as promising as Bruccoli's. And Professor William Charvat, the coeditor of *The Cost Books of Ticknor and Fields*, then preparing his manuscript of a definitive history of American publishing, was especially pleased to welcome Bruccoli. They shared a commitment to ensuring the accuracy of texts and remained close friends until Charvat's untimely death in 1967, after which Bruccoli edited Charvat's *The Profession of Authorship in America, 1800–1870*. What Howard Mumford Jones observed about Charvat in the foreword to the Bruccoli edition was equally applicable to Bruccoli, who also "grasped almost intuitively the meaning of the triadic relation of the author-publisher-reader in literary history."[7]

Bruccoli quickly exceeded the highest expectations of his colleagues in the English department at Ohio State. His astonishing productivity earned him a promotion to associate professor by 1963, and by 1965, in record time for advancement, to the rank of professor. In addition to writing *The Composition of "Tender Is the Night": A Study of the Manuscripts,* Brucccoli had edited books by Henry James, Jack London, and Stephen Crane; he had edited three books by Nathaniel Hawthorne in *The Centenary Edition of the Works of Nathaniel Hawthorne* series;

he had continued his editorship of the *Fitzgerald Newsletter,* begun in 1958; he had compiled a bibliography for James Branch Cabell and a checklist for F. Scott Fitzgerald; and he had published some thirty-three articles, notes, and reviews. Furthermore, he was contributing markedly to the Fitzgerald revival that had begun in the 1950s.

Just prior to Bruccoli's move to the University of South Carolina in 1969, he addressed an audience at Kent State University on the occasion of the university libraries' acquisition of its 500,000th volume. His strongest praise was directed to Kent State's adding to its special collections. Separately published as *Mere Collectors' Items,* this essay, included in "On Libraries and Librarians," is one of Bruccoli's most passionate and angry defenses on behalf of any library's acquisition of rare books. The inspiration for the address and subsequent article, as well as its strong tone, was motivated by a remark made by a colleague of Bruccoli's at Ohio State who referred derisively to rare books so important to the collections Bruccoli was assiduously building as "mere collectors' items."[8] The moment was never forgotten, and throughout his life the words "mere" and "collectors' items" were often used pejoratively.

"Where They Belong: The Acquisition of the F. Scott Fitzgerald Papers" is another important Bruccoli contribution to American literary history. Based upon primary documents, discussions with Fitzgerald's daughter, Scottie, and interviews, it is the most detailed and accurate account of the nine years of negotiations between representatives of Princeton University Libraries and Scottie Fitzgerald while an agreement was being struck regarding the housing of Fitzgerald's papers at Princeton following Fitzgerald's death on 21 December 1940.

Bruccoli's reverential attitude toward excellent libraries and librarians and his commitment to collections had its strongest inspiration and encouragement at the University of Virginia, where he found an invaluable mentor, resource, and friend in John Cook Wyllie. "Mr. Wyllie," as Bruccoli referred to him, had been curator of rare books, librarian, and ultimately director of libraries at Virginia. For Bruccoli, Wyllie was the best of librarians because he was also a bibliophile who thought, as Bruccoli says in his essay about Wyllie included in "On Libraries and Librarians," rare books were "the unexpendable parts of a library's collection" and because he regarded complete author collections as essential for serious research. The essay "John Cook Wyllie" is Bruccoli's most extensive tribute to Wyllie and reveals the source of many of Bruccoli's own defining views concerning libraries and librarians.

Although Bruccoli never found another John Cook Wyllie, he enjoyed and benefited from his associations with many other librarians. In particular he was especially gratified by his constructive working relationship with George Terry,

Dean of Libraries at the University of South Carolina. Terry, Bruccoli observed, understood the importance of a research library's acquiring major collections and keeping them intact. And he facilitated the acquisition of the Matthew J. and Arlyn Bruccoli Collection of F. Scott Fitzgerald in 1994, enabling the University Libraries at South Carolina to become the second major repository for Fitzgerald materials along with Princeton.

Nevertheless, the final essay in "On Libraries and Librarians," published in Bruccoli's last year, conveys his dismay at librarians who eliminate reference books in deference to data bases during the digital age. Although it is brief, this essay underscores Bruccoli's lifelong commitment to accuracy of information and expresses, once more in Bruccoli's strongest terms, his passion for books, in this case reference books, as personal objects, superior, he argues, because they are validated by the convincing authority of some of the greatest minds of our culture.

By the time he left Ohio State to join the Department of English at the University of South Carolina, Bruccoli had become at age thirty-eight a star among American literary scholars. He was happier at South Carolina, where he found a department less disturbingly political than he had experienced during the turbulent 1960s at Ohio State. At South Carolina his scholarly focus expanded, taking in even more American authors, and he produced standard biographies of John O'Hara, James Gould Cozzens, and F. Scott Fitzgerald. It was his enormous number of books and articles on Fitzgerald, however, that made him our foremost Fitzgerald scholar. Consequently, the section "On Fitzgerald," placed first in *On Books and Writers,* is most extensive. Included are essays on each of Fitzgerald's novels, reflecting Bruccoli's accrued knowledge from his many years of relentless Fitzgerald research. Especially noteworthy are his essays on *The Great Gatsby, Tender Is the Night,* and *The Love of the Last Tycoon,* evolving from his unmatched knowledge concerning their composition. Also included is one of Bruccoli's most informative essays, again on the subject of the profession of authorship—this time as it relates to Fitzgerald. It is one of our best overviews of Fitzgerald's career emphasizing Fitzgerald's struggles to support himself and his family by his writing while attempting to retain his integrity as an artist.[9]

Bruccoli's prolific and distinguished Fitzgerald scholarship led to his becoming founding editor of *The Cambridge Edition of the Works of F. Scott Fitzgerald,* and his Cambridge editions of *The Great Gatsby* (1991) and *The Love of the Last Tycoon: A Western* (1993) are models of scholarly thoroughness and excellence. Nevertheless, his editorship was short-lived. Ultimately, he resigned when he insisted on emending inaccuracies in Fitzgerald's texts and found himself in conflict with the publisher's goals and unsupported by two trustees of the Fitzgerald estate. His essay "Getting It Right," included in "On Publishing and Publishers," addresses his editorial philosophy regarding correcting errors in *The Great Gatsby* and illuminates his decision to resign from the Cambridge series, distinguished by his editorship.

"The Profession of Authorship in the Twenty-First Century," also included in this section, is Bruccoli's true insider's overview of the deterioration of constructive relationships among authors, their publishers, and their editors, and also what he sees as the failure of proliferating creative writing programs to prepare their students for the complexities of an increasingly difficult profession and marketplace and of a diminishing literary culture. Although such programs, he concedes, help support writers who could not otherwise support themselves with income from their writing, they, he believes, offer false hope to students.

Despite the many publishers who were the subjects of Bruccoli's remarkable range of scholarship, the House of Scribner and its legendary editor Maxwell Perkins have always been central to Bruccoli's extensive Fitzgerald and Hemingway scholarship. And at the end of the twentieth century, Bruccoli turned his attention again to Scribners and to Perkins, this time not because of their associations with Fitzgerald or Hemingway but because of his growing interest in Thomas Wolfe. In 2000 Bruccoli and his wife, Arlyn, an independent scholar, edited *O Lost,* the original and complete text of Thomas Wolfe's *Look Homeward, Angel*. The final essay in "On Publishing and Publishers" was derived from this study, and it offers important observations on what Bruccoli found to be wrongful assumptions about Perkins's editorial practices and the extent to which he was, and was not, involved in editing Wolfe's novels.

Because Bruccoli believed that all of the areas represented in this collection are interconnected, there is obvious overlapping throughout the individual sections of the collection. For example, although John Cook Wyllie is included in "Libraries and Librarians," because Wyllie was a librarian by profession, Bruccoli consistently spoke of him also as "the best bookman I ever knew." In fact, librarians and textual scholars whom Bruccoli esteemed were also "bookmen." In his essay "Debts," a particularly nostalgic piece included in the section "Bookmen," Bruccoli acknowledges his indebtedness to Wyllie again and to "bookman" Fredson Bowers, along with rare book dealers and other bibliophiles to whom he was indebted for making him also a "bookman."

In this section appears another "collectors' item" essay—on the importance of "Hawthorne as a Collector's Item," written while Bruccoli was series editor for *The Centenary Editions of the Works of Nathaniel Hawthorne* and surveying the history of Hawthorne's editions and growing popularity among a large group of major collectors and rare-book dealers during the years 1885–1924. This essay further supports Bruccoli's observation on the importance of private collectors in particular, "the best" of whom, he says, "did more than assemble libraries—they promoted Hawthorne scholarship, enlarged the canon of his work, and preserved manuscript material."

The best of all American bookdealers, however, according to Bruccoli, was George D. Smith. Although Smith dealt primarily in English texts purchased for wealthy Americans during the years 1914–1920, Bruccoli found in him heroic bookdealer qualities: the courage to spend whatever was necessary to acquire great collections and the impressive intelligence to beat the British "ring," what Bruccoli defines in his essay as "a conspiracy of bidders to defraud consigners." Furthermore, Smith's "credo," among other book-supporting pronouncements, was that the "collectors' items" Bruccoli defended were "history and sacred history." "George D. Smith and the Anglo-American Book Migration" tells the story of how the Folger and Huntington Libraries acquired many of their greatest literary treasures.

Bruccoli met one of the "best" of the contemporary Hawthorne collectors in 1962 while he was editing Hawthorne: Charles Elliot Frazer Clark, Jr. "Fraze," as Bruccoli called him, became, perhaps, his closest friend, as well as his business partner. Bruccoli reports that Clark built one of the finest Hawthorne collections in America, compiled the standard Hawthorne bibliography, founded and edited the *Nathaniel Hawthorne Journal,* and co-founded the Nathaniel Hawthorne Society. Frazer Clark was the Clark of Bruccoli Clark, the distinguished reference-book publishing house that he founded with Bruccoli in 1977. Bruccoli Clark (which later became Bruccoli Clark Layman) most notably published the *Dictionary of Literary Biography,* the first volume of which appeared in 1978. Roughly four hundred *DLB* volumes were published in Bruccoli's lifetime, and the series continues under the direction of Richard Layman. Bruccoli's memorial essay on Frazer Clark, headed by the label of respect "Bookman," appears here.[10] Few of his writings illustrate more effectively or bluntly Bruccoli's conviction that many of the richest of scholarly resources lie outside the academy and beyond academics.

"On Other Writers" includes essays on some of the major figures in American literature about whom Bruccoli wrote most prolifically and authoritatively. It begins with one of his earliest essays, a reading of the Hemingway story "The Light of the World," and follows what became a familiar approach of Bruccoli's when he ventured into critical analysis: his integration of factual underpinnings, in this instance about the life of the story's central focus, Stan Ketchel, with events conveyed by the narrator. The section concludes with one of Bruccoli's latest essays, also on Hemingway, delineating the method by which the larger-than-life author methodically orchestrated his enormous public fame throughout his lifetime and made himself, as Bruccoli contends, the most famous writer in the world at the time of his death. Admittedly, there is also overlap in this section. Although Bruccoli's essay on Thomas Wolfe's "The Four Lost Men" addresses publishing issues, it is included under "Other Writers" because Bruccoli's intent in the essay is, to great measure, the reaffirmation of Wolfe's literary reputation and his genius, often discredited by facile claims that he was "self-indulgent" and "undisciplined," but, as Bruccoli illustrates, also "impeded by circumstances of publication."

Two essays on John O'Hara appear here. In the first, "Out of Life: John O'Hara's Character Creation," Bruccoli demonstrates that O'Hara was blessed not only with a remarkable ear for language but also with an eye for details that enabled him to develop a fictional technique for creating characters by combining psychological patterns with accurate details of their lives. In "Focus on *Appointment in Samarra:* The Importance of Knowing What You Are Talking About," he considers John O'Hara's memorable novel and O'Hara in the context of hard-boiled writers of the "Black Mask School," acknowledging commonalities while illustrating how O'Hara transcends the limitations of the genre.

"A Reopening of the *By Love Possessed* Case" provides Bruccoli's reexamination of James Gould Cozzens's most successful novel against a backdrop of critics and reviewers who viciously attacked the novel and Cozzens, Bruccoli argues, because they presumed that discourses by the character Julian Penrose were personal pronouncements by Cozzens and failed to see the attendant irony and the self-mockery of Penrose's affectations. This essay, as well as the two O'Hara essays, unites again Bruccoli's command of salient facts concerning authorial intention with his critical prowess.

Bruccoli developed an interest in detective fiction and the "hard-boiled" genre very early in his career, collecting pulp fiction and "dime novels" and subsequently compiling checklists and descriptive bibliographies of works by Raymond Chandler and Ross Macdonald. His 1984 biography of Ross Macdonald attests to his eclectic appreciation of literature. Although he never considered the "hard-boiled" authors major writers, Bruccoli greatly admired their skill, respected their talent, and was convinced that Chandler, as much as anyone else, elevated an essentially "subliterary genre" to literature. The essay on Chandler, included here, provides an overview of Chandler's professional life, with special attention to his years (1944–1951) as a screenwriter in Hollywood and his tortured work on *The Blue Dahlia*.

"Publications by Matthew J. Bruccoli," prepared by Jennifer Hynes and Judith S. Baughman, Bruccoli's long-time assistant, frequent collaborator, and friend, appears as an appendix to this volume.

Throughout these essays, spanning five decades of Matthew J. Bruccoli's career, readers will find, or recognize, the style, irrepressible wit, charm, and spirit of a rare scholar and true man of letters. The voice within these pages is clearly that of authority, derived from and informed by the hallmarks of all of Bruccoli's work—knowledge and facts. Here is a brand of steadfast scholarship, the scope of which has been seldom equaled, scholarship that has endured, or "survived," myriad critical movements, "isms," theories, and trends, preserved in one volume for the instruction and delight of all to whom books and writers matter.

Notes

1. Matthew J. Bruccoli, *Getting It Right: The Craft of Literary Scholarship,* produced by Edwin C. Breland (Columbia: Instructional Services Center, University of South Carolina, 1996), video recording.

2. Ibid.

3. Fredson Bowers, *Textual and Literary Criticism* (Cambridge, England: Cambridge University Press, 1959), p. 30. As Bowers acknowledges in a note, the printing error that caused Matthiessen's flawed reading was pointed out earlier in John W. Nichol, "Melville's 'Soiled' Fish of the Sea," *American Literature* (1949): 338–339.

4. M.J.B. to John Unrue, March 2008.

5. Although Bruccoli's "A Mirror for Bibliographers: Duplicate Plates in Modern Printing" appeared first in *Papers of the Bibliographical Society of America* (Second Quarter 1960): 83–88, I have chosen to use Bruccoli's revision that appears in John Bush Jones, *Readings in Descriptive Bibliography* (Kent, Ohio: Kent State University Press, 1974), pp. 190–195.

6. See Bowers, *Textual and Literary Criticism,* pp. 19–20. Bowers references Bruccoli's "Textual Variants in Sinclair Lewis's *Babbitt,*" *Studies in Bibliography* (1958): 263–268, and Bruccoli's *James Branch Cabell: A Bibliography.* Part II, *Notes on the Cabell Collections at the University of Virginia* (Charlottesville: University of Virginia Press, 1957).

7. William Charvat, *The Profession of Authorship in America, 1800–1870,* edited by Bruccoli (Columbus: Ohio State University Press, 1968), p. xiv.

8. This information was conveyed in an inscription written by M.J.B. in an offprint of *Mere Collectors' Items* sent to John Unrue in 2007.

9. Bruccoli maintained respect for authors as professionals who supported themselves by their writing, and he devoted much of his life, after editing his friend William Charvat's book on this subject, to learning and chronicling the details of their efforts. In particular his scholarship on F. Scott Fitzgerald underscores this interest, and it has never been equaled. In 1996 Bruccoli organized and hosted a centennial celebration in honor of Fitzgerald at the University of South Carolina that included such literary luminaries as James Dickey, Joseph Heller, and Budd Schulberg; that same fall, in honor of Bruccoli's sixty-fifth birthday, *The Professions of Authorship: Essays in Honor of Matthew J. Bruccoli,* a Festschrift edited by Richard Layman and Joel Meyerson, was published by the University of South Carolina Press.

10. As a member of Bruccoli's Fitzgerald/Hemingway seminar in 1968 I had the privilege of visiting Frazer Clark's home with Bruccoli and looking at some of Mr. Clark's

literary treasures, among which, I recall, was Melville's dictionary with marginal comments. On a personal note and as a measure of Bruccoli's friendship with Clark, I reminded him of that visit during our last lunch together in April 2008 and asked him the date of Frazer Clark's death. Bruccoli replied, "I try not to remember the dates of the deaths of my friends."

Part I

On Fitzgerald

"There is no way to explain why the son of a stableman became the finest lyric poet in England or why the son of an unsuccessful manufacturer of wicker furniture wrote the best American prose of his time."
M.J.B., preface to the first edition,
*Some Sort of Epic Grandeur: The Life of
F. Scott Fitzgerald* (1981)

The Man of Letters as Professional

Civilians hold these notions about writers and writing to be self-evident: that it is easy; that there is a trick to it; that writers earn fortunes but that they don't write for money. These assumptions have impeded the proper assessment of F. Scott Fitzgerald as a professional author and distorted his reputation as a man of letters. The professors and the Fitzgerald groupies have collaborated to create an irresponsible writer who sold out to the *Saturday Evening Post.*

Fitzgerald provides a laboratory case for the profession-of-authorship approach to American literary history as formulated by William Charvat in studying the careers of Hawthorne, Melville, and Emerson:

> The terms of professional writing are these: that it provides a living for the author, like any other job; that it is a main and prolonged, rather than intermittent or sporadic, resource for the writer; that it is produced with the hope of extended sale in the open market, like any article of commerce; and that it is written with reference to buyers' tastes and reading habits. The problem of the professional writer is not identical with that of the literary artist; but when a literary artist is also a professional writer, he cannot solve the problems of the one function without reference to the other.[1]

Freud stated that writers write for fame, money, and the love of beautiful women. Dr. Johnson—who combined Grub Street assignments with high scholarship—declared "No man but a blockhead ever wrote except for money." The compulsion to write is concomitant with the compulsion to eat and drink.

Much has been written about Fitzgerald and money—as a subject in his fiction and as a determining factor in his career. The popular notion that he squandered his genius on lavishly paid hackwork persists with the legends of his orgiastic irresponsibility. In actuality Fitzgerald functioned for twenty years as a

---

"The Man of Letters as Professional" appeared as the introductory essay in *F. Scott Fitzgerald: On Authorship,* edited by Matthew J. Bruccoli with Judith S. Baughman (Columbia: University of South Carolina Press, 1996), pp. 11–22. Reprinted with permission of the University of South Carolina Press.

professional writer and as a literary artist—but he did not have two separate careers. He had one career to which everything he wrote connected.

Willa Cather—who should have known better—expressed this lofty position: "Writing ought either to be the manufacture of stories for which there is a market demand—a business as safe and commendable as making soap or breakfast foods—or it should be an art, which is always a search for something for which there is no market demand, something new and untried, when the values are intrinsic and have nothing to do with standardized values."[2] The key word in her pronouncement is *ought*. Geniuses ought not to be concerned with money. Serious writers ought to be able to write what they want to write. But professional writers write for publication. Otherwise they are hobbyists.

During their college days Fitzgerald dumbfounded Edmund Wilson by announcing, "I want to be one of the greatest writers who ever lived, don't you?"[3] He meant it. Moreover, Fitzgerald believed that writers should receive financial rewards commensurate with the quality of their work. He never expected to starve for his art.

One of the enduring myths attached to Fitzgerald is that he made and squandered fortunes. He was extravagant, but he did not earn vast sums from his magazine work or from his books. His total income from 1919 through 1936, before he went to Hollywood, was $374,922.58 (after his agent's commissions) according to his *Ledger*: an average of $20,829.03 over eighteen years.[4]

Many writers think of themselves as good businessmen, and most of them are bad at it. Fitzgerald employed an agent, Harold Ober, for his magazine work but dealt directly with Maxwell Perkins at Scribners for his books. Ober had a good business relationship with the *Post* and was able to negotiate steady raises in Fitzgerald's story payments. Over the years Ober's role altered from that of literary representative to banker as he advanced Fitzgerald the price of written but not-yet-sold stories—and then the price of the stories in progress. From 1927 to mid-1937 Fitzgerald lived from story to story.

The Fitzgerald/Ober correspondence establishes that Ober's function was to sell the stories; he provided no editorial advice until the late Thirties, when Fitzgerald's stories became hard to place. The *Post* editorial archives are lamentably lost, but the skimpy surviving evidence indicates that Fitzgerald had almost no direct contact with the magazine's editors. A few editorial recommendations about material were relayed to Fitzgerald by Ober. It was not until after *Tender Is the Night*, when Fitzgerald's money problems became acute, that he unwisely attempted to interpose in transactions with the *Post*. Fitzgerald dealt directly with editor Arnold Gingrich at *Esquire* during the Thirties, receiving $200 to $300—the magazine's going rate—for the "Crack-Up" essays and the "short-shorts." Ober did not take a commission on these sales.

More is known about the professional life of Fitzgerald than about that of any other major American author because so much of the evidence has been preserved. The year-by-year autobiographical, financial, and bibliographical records he kept in his business ledger include his every sale in the literary market place. The *Ledger* supplements the evidence provided by Fitzgerald's correspondence with Ober[5] and with Perkins at Scribners.[6] Fitzgerald became a full-time professional before his twenty-fourth birthday when Perkins accepted *This Side of Paradise* on 18 September 1919. Six weeks later Fitzgerald wrote his first letter to his agent asking him to place "Head and Shoulders"—which the *Post* took for $400.

When it became clear to Fitzgerald after *The Beautiful and Damned* that his novels would not support his family's habits of living and spending, he tried to strike it rich by writing a play. *The Vegetable* died during its out-of-town try-out in 1923. Thereafter Fitzgerald wrote short stories to buy time for novels in the expectation that his novels would both free him from the need to write stories and establish his permanent literary stature. Fitzgerald's novels were commercial work of a higher order than his magazine stories. He expected them to be critical successes and best-sellers.

The Great Gatsby was written on the $14,700 proceeds from nine stories; but after *Gatsby* the magazine money was often spent before Fitzgerald received it. The composition of *Tender Is the Night* stretched over eight years as he interrupted work on the novel to write stories to pay bills—many of which were for his wife's psychiatric treatment. Fitzgerald's 160 stories during twenty-two years may have required as much writing time as his five novels. Moreover, during his lifetime Fitzgerald was more widely read as a magazine story writer than as a novelist. Although the prominent treatment of his stories in the *Post* and other magazines promoted the recognition of Fitzgerald's name, it does not appear that this exposure significantly increased the sales of his novels. The two novels that sold best predated his peak activity as a *Post* contributor. Fitzgerald never wrote what is now called a blockbuster. *This Side of Paradise* (1920) made the *Publishers Weekly* monthly best-seller list twice, reaching number four; *The Beautiful and Damned* (1922) appeared three times, reaching number six. *The Great Gatsby* never made the best-seller list and did not break 24,000 copies in 1925. *Tender Is the Night* was number ten for April 1934, but did not sell 15,000 copies in that year. In 1929 his royalties on seven books totaled $31.77; and eight *Post* stories brought him $31,000.

The magazines provided most of Fitzgerald's income before he went to work for the movies in 1937: $241,453 for 116 stories. Four short-story collections with royalties of $12,400 increased his cumulative income from short stories to more than $253,800, as against about $41,000 in royalties from four novels.[7] Between 1919 and 1929 Fitzgerald's *Saturday Evening Post* story price rose from

$400 to $4,000. It is impossible to convert 1929 dollars into 1996 dollars, but if the inflation multipliers of eight or ten are used, then a $4,000 Fitzgerald story would be worth between $32,000 and $40,000 in diluted dollars.[8]

The *Post* and other "slick" magazines (so called because they were printed on glossy paper to accommodate advertising art) paid well because pre-television Americans had a large appetite for magazine fiction. In addition to the penny-a-word pulp-paper magazines or dime novels (for which Fitzgerald did not write) there was an array of slicks that competed with the *Post* for fiction. Fitzgerald appeared in *Collier's, Red Book, Ladies Home Journal, McCall's, Metropolitan,* and *Hearst's International.* The *Saturday Evening Post,* with a circulation of 2,750,000, was the most prosperous slick and the most generous to its writers. During the Twenties the *Post*'s circulation and advertising revenues enabled it to provide between 200 and 300 pages each week for a nickel.[9] The hebdomadal mixture of fiction and nonfiction included from six to nine short stories and two or three serialized novels. The 13 July 1929 issue, led by Fitzgerald's "Majesty"—a story about an American girl who makes a king out of a European weakling—had Brooke Hanlon, Almet Jenks, E. Phillips Oppenheim, Octavus Roy Cohen, and Clarence Budington Kelland. The serials were by Gilbert Seldes, Harry Leon Wilson, and Henry C. Rowland. These by-lines are no longer recognized, but in their time Oppenheim (*The Magnificent Impersonation*), Kelland (*Scattergood Baines*), and Wilson (*Ruggles of Red Gap*) were prodigiously popular. The issue's five articles included three by Sir Cecil Spring-Rice and one each by Christopher Morley and Struthers Burt.

Fitzgerald's magazine stories were highly competitive hackwork. His fellow-hacks—as defined by *Post* publication—included William Faulkner, Thomas Wolfe, John P. Marquand,[10] Sir Arthur Conan Doyle, Joseph Hergesheimer, Donn Byrne, Sinclair Lewis, P. G. Wodehouse, Stewart Edward White, Edgar Wallace, Thomas Beer, Earl Derr Biggers, and Don Marquis. Before he won the Nobel Prize in 1951, Faulkner was forced to supplement his novel royalties. He sold fifty-six magazine stories, sixteen of which appeared in the *Post.* He worked for the movies, and there were years when he spent more time in Hollywood than in Yoknapatawpha County. He probably outranked Fitzgerald. Yet Faulkner was respected as a genius who made necessary accommodations for the sake of his art, whereas Fitzgerald was typed as a casualty of materialism and dissipation.

The circumstance that two of Fitzgerald's masterpieces—"May Day" (1920) and "The Diamond as Big as the Ritz" (1922)—appeared in the low-paying *Smart Set* (circulation 22,000) raises futile speculation about the stories he might have written if literary magazines had paid as well as the mass-circulation slicks. Fitzgerald wrote stories to meet market requirements—a matter of material and plot. But he had one style: style, Lionel Trilling observed, is "where eventually all a writer's qualities have their truest existence."[11] The writing in some stories is rushed and flashy, but it unmistakably purveys Fitzgerald's tone and sensibility. The superb "Diamond as Big as the Ritz" was written for the commercial market, and the rejection of this story by half a dozen slicks elicited Fitzgerald's 1922 declaration to his agent: "I am rather discouraged that a cheap story like <u>The Popular Girl</u> [*Saturday Evening Post*, 11 and 18 February 1922] written in one week while the baby was being born brings $1500.00 + a genuinely imaginative thing into which I put three weeks real entheusiasm like <u>The Diamond in the Sky</u> brings not a thing. But, by God + Lorimer,[12] I'm going to make a fortune yet."[13]

At the beginning of his career Fitzgerald was exuberant about the money and exposure generated by his stories. In 1925, following the publication of *Gatsby*, he wrote to H. L. Mencken with a characteristic compound of confession and self-judgment: "My trash for the Post grows worse and worse as there is less and less heart in it. . . . I never really 'wrote down' until after the failing of the <u>Vegetable</u> and that was to make this book possible."[14] The tailoring required for *Post* publication is touched on in a letter wherein Fitzgerald argues that he was in effect a *Post* employee. Having tax problems in 1932, he hoped for a ruling that his earnings from the *Post* be treated as earned income. He asked Ober to provide a document for the Collector of Internal Revenue attesting:

(3.) That you had never considered me a free lance author but that on the contrary my sales were arranged long in advance and that it has been understood for years among editors that my stories were written specificly for the Post by definate arrangment and that I was what is known as a "Post Author." (4.) Moreover that they conform to Post specifications as to length and avoidance of certain themes so that for instance they could not have been published in <u>Liberty</u> which insisted on stories not over 5000 words, + would have been inacceptable to womens magazines since they were told from the male angle. That when I contracted with another magazine such as <u>College Humor</u> the stories were different in tone + theme, half as long, signed in conjunction with my wife. That the <u>Post</u> made it plain that they wanted to be offered all my work of the kind agreed apon; that they always specified that no work of mine should appear in several competing magazines. That during the years 1929 and 1930 no story of mine was rejected by the <u>Post</u>. . . .[15]

The *College Humor* connection requires clarification. During 1929–1930 this magazine published five "Girl" stories by Zelda Fitzgerald with the proviso that Fitzgerald be by-lined as coauthor. The stories were written by her with some polishing by him. The magazine was buying his name for $500 per story. Ober sold one of the stories in the series, "The Millionaire's Girl," to the *Post* for $4,000 as Fitzgerald's solo work.

The greatest change in literary finances between the Twenties and the Nineties involves subsidiary rights. Civilians read current newspaper reports about five-million-dollar book deals and assume that publishing has always been a jackpot business for authors. The newspapers usually fail to make clear that most of the millions derive from subrights (everything except hard-cover publication) in what has become known as "literary property." In the Twenties the standard Scribners contract for Fitzgerald's books disposed of subrights in one gentlemanly sentence because these rights were not lucrative. "It is further agreed that the profits arising from any publication of said work, during the period covered by this agreement, in other than book form shall be divided equally between said Publishers and said Author." Now a book contract devotes a page or pages to reprint, book-club, movie, television, audio, dramatic, and electronic rights. Publishers refer disparagingly to a book as making only a "publishing profit"—that is, from the sale of copies of a publisher's own edition, without ancillary income.

Fitzgerald received no income from paperback rights because there were no paperbacks. There were no book clubs before 1925, and they paid chicken feed during their early years. Fitzgerald's foreign rights were negligible, and he did not have a British readership during his lifetime. Serial rights for *The Beautiful and Damned* brought $7,000 from *Metropolitan Magazine,* and *Scribner's Magazine* paid $10,000 for serializing *Tender Is the Night.* Movie rights to stories brought relatively modest amounts: $2,500 for "Head and Shoulders," $2,500 for *The Beautiful and Damned,* $10,000 for *This Side of Paradise.* The most subsidiary income for a Fitzgerald property derived from *The Great Gatsby:* about $15,000 from the play by Owen Davis; $18,000 for the silent-movie rights; and $1,000 for second serial rights. Apart from occasional windfalls Fitzgerald lived on the sales of his stories and the dwindling royalties from his books until he went on the Metro-Goldwyn-Mayer payroll in 1937. From 1926 to 1933 the royalties on his three novels averaged $2,860 per year.

Like many American writers of varying talents, Fitzgerald regarded Hollywood as an emergency financial resource. When *The Great Gatsby* failed to sell, he wrote to Perkins:

> In all events I have a book of good stories for the fall. Now I shall write some cheap ones until I've accumulated enough for my next novel. When that is finished and published I'll wait and see. If it will support me with no more intervals of trash I'll go on as a novelist. If not I'm going to quit, come home, go to Hollywood and learn the movie business. I can't reduce our scale of living

and I can't stand this financial insecurity. Anyhow there's no point in trying to be an artist if you can't do your best.[16]

His first two Hollywood trips were failures. In 1927 he was paid $3,500 to write an original screen story titled "Lipstick," which was rejected. In 1931 he was paid $6,000 to write a screenplay for *Red-Headed Woman,* which was also rejected. His final California sojourn during 1937–1940 brought him $91,000 for eighteen months at M-G-M and one screen credit for *Three Comrades.* Fitzgerald was unsuccessful as a screenwriter because he resisted collaboration and because the movies could not film the style and voice of his prose.

Satisfying the requirements of the slicks was hard work; it took a lot of fuel to boil the pot. Scholars frequently cite Fitzgerald's denigration of himself as an "old whore" in a 1929 letter to Hemingway:

> Your analysis of my inability to get my serious work done is too kind in that it leaves out dissipation, but among acts of God it is possible that the 5 yrs between my leaving the army + finishing *Gatsby* 1919–1924 which included 3 novels, about 50 popular stories + a play + numerous articles + movies may have taken all I had to say too early, adding that all the time we were living at top speed in the gayest worlds we could find. This <u>au fond</u> is what really worries me—tho the trouble may be my inability to leave anything once started— I have worked for 2 months over a popular short story that was foredoomed to being torn up when completed. . . . Here's a last flicker of the old cheap pride:—the <u>Post</u> now pays the old whore $4000. a screw.

These commentators often omit the next sentence in the passage: "But now its because she's mastered the 40 positions—in her youth one was enough."[17] This complaint makes the point that Fitzgerald's magazine stories required technique and craftsmanship, that early ebullience had given way to mature technique. Hemingway's response clearly identifies the function of Fitzgerald's stories in his working life:

> I wish there was some way that your economic existence would depend on this novel [*Tender Is the Night*] or on novels rather than on the damned stories. Because that is one thing that drives you and gives you an outlet too—the damned stories—. . . .
>
> (They never raise an old whore's price—she may know the 850 positions— they cut her price all the same—so either you aren't old or not a whore or both). The stories aren't whoring They're just bad judgement—You could have and can make enough to live on writing novels.[18]

Fitzgerald could not live on his novels. Neither could Hemingway in 1929; his second wife had a wealthy and generous family.

Fitzgerald's denunciations of his stories become more vociferous during the years when he stalled on the novel that became *Tender Is the Night* and he began to function as a supplier of *Post* stories: the eight Basil Duke Lee stories (1928–1929) and the five Josephine Perry stories (1930–1931). When Ober advised him to make a book out of the Basil stories in 1930, Fitzgerald's response made a firm distinction between reader response to his stories and his novels:

> I could have published four lowsy, half baked books in the last five years + and people would have thought I was at least a worthy young man not drinking myself to pieces in the south seas—but I'd be dead as Michael Arlen, Bromfield, Tom Boyd, Callaghan + the others who think they can trick the world with the hurried and the second rate. These <u>Post</u> stories <u>in</u> the <u>Post</u> are at least not any spot on me—they're honest and if their <u>form</u> is stereotyped people know what to expect when they pick up the <u>Post</u>. The novel is another thing—if, after four years I publish the Basil Lee stories as a book I might as well get tickets for Hollywood immediately.[19]

There was a close—even symbiotic—relationship between Fitzgerald's magazine fiction and his novels because the stories often functioned as tryouts for subjects and themes that were more complexly developed in novels. Thus the cluster of *Gatsby*-related stories: "Winter Dreams," "'The Sensible Thing,'" "Absolution" (cut from an early draft of *Gatsby*), "Dice, Brassknuckles & Guitar," and "The Diamond as Big as the Ritz." Fitzgerald did not have a different style for magazine work. A good writer writes the only way he can write. The writing in the stories is sometimes self-indulgent, the story plots are often too gimmicky, and there is a reliance on the intrusive philosophizing; but the style, tone, voice, and rhythm of the prose are authentic Fitzgerald. He was unable to improve on certain passages that were later required for a novel. It therefore became obligatory for Fitzgerald to maintain a system to prevent himself from using the same passage in a collected story and in a novel—which he considered dishonest. When he classified a story as not worth reprinting in one of his four story collections, he "stripped" passages and phrases for possible use in novels. If material in the story chosen for a collection had been recycled in a novel, he revised the story to remove repetition. During the eight-year evolution of *Tender* he borrowed material from the novel drafts for use in stories.[20] When Perkins advised him not to be overconcerned about duplication of passages in *Taps at Reveille* and *Tender,* citing Hemingway's repetitions, Fitzgerald responded firmly:

The fact that Ernest has let himself repeat here and there a phrase would be no possible justification for my doing the same. Each of us has his own virtues and one of mine happens to be a great sense of exactitude about my work. He might be able to afford a lapse in that line where I wouldn't be and after all I have got to be the final judge of what is appropriate in these cases. . . .

Besides, it is not only the question of the repetitions but there are certain other stories in the collection that I couldn't possibly think of letting go out in their current form. I fully realize that this may be a very serious inconvenience to you but for me to undertake anything like that at this moment would just mean sudden death and nothing less than that.[21]

Writing about Fitzgerald after his death, James Gould Cozzens observed that "writing short stories is living on your capital if you are naturally a novelist—you can get through in a few years all the subjects, even if you have a lot, that you could have written books on."[22] One of the reasons Fitzgerald resented his stories is that they depleted his literary and emotional capital. In 1935 when he was having difficulty writing marketable stories, Fitzgerald explained to his agent that "all my stories are conceived like novels, require a special emotion, a special experience—so that my readers, if such there be, know that each time it'll be something new, not in form but in substance (it'd be far better for me if I could do pattern stories but the pencil just goes dead on me. . . .)"[23]

Largely as a consequence of his reputation as a bad speller, compounded by the factual errors in his published work, Fitzgerald had been classified as a literary ignoramus—as someone who wrote brilliantly without knowing what he was doing. A natural. This condescending view is corrected by his letters, notebooks, book reviews and articles—which establish that Fitzgerald reached usable conclusions about the craft of writing, the discipline of authorship, and the obligations of literature. Fitzgerald wrote perceptively and eloquently when he was analyzing his own work. "Our April Letter," a prose poem in his *Notebooks*, expresses Fitzgerald's sense of his exhausted creative capital: "I have asked a lot of my emotions—one hundred and twenty stories. The price was high, right up with Kipling, because there was one little drop of something not blood, not a tear, not my seed, but me more intimately than these, in every story, it was the extra I had."[24]

There was a time when the appellation "man of letters" would have seemed inappropriate for Fitzgerald; but the evidence of his career establishes that he functioned as a literary personage—not just a literary personality. In 1945 Lionel Trilling provided one of the earliest and best assessments of Fitzgerald as a man of letters.

It is hard to overestimate the benefit which came to Fitzgerald from his having consciously placed himself in the line of the great. . . . To read Fitzgerald's letters to his daughter . . . and to catch the tone in which he speaks about the literature of the past, or to read the notebooks he faithfully kept . . . and to perceive how continuously he thought about literature, is to have some clue to the secret of the continuing power of Fitzgerald's work.[25]

Fitzgerald's conduct as a literary figure was exemplary. He encouraged younger writers and recruited writers—including Hemingway—for Scribners. He did not regard writing as competitive and did not resent the success of other writers. He had firm critical standards and, for example, regarded John Steinbeck's work as bogus. Other writers respected Fitzgerald's literary intelligence—sometimes involuntarily. John Dos Passos recalled, "When he talked about writing his mind, which seemed to me full of preposterous notions about most things, became clear and hard as a diamond. . . . about writing he was a born professional. Everything he said was worth listening to."[26]

From 1920, when he wisecracked that "An author ought to write for the youth of his own generation, the critics of the next, and the schoolmasters of ever afterward,"[27] Fitzgerald was concerned about his permanent stature as a literary figure. Yet it often seemed that he was almost deliberately damaging his literary stature by trading permanent fame for notoriety. Fitzgerald lacked the ruthlessness that normally fosters great literary reputations. He was incapable of sacrificing everything and everybody to his writing—as did Hemingway, Faulkner, and Wolfe. The posthumous Fitzgerald revival was a triumph of genius over misfortune—testimony to the enduring force of words on paper. Although the reviewers of his time—except Gilbert Seldes—did not recognize him as a great writer, other writers understood how important Fitzgerald's writing was. T. S. Eliot orphically pronounced that *Gatsby* was "the first step that American fiction had taken since Henry James."[28] Dos Passos stated of *The Last Tycoon*: "Even in their unfinished state these fragments, I believe, are of sufficient dimensions to raise the level of American fiction to follow in some such way as Marlowe's blank verse line raised the whole level of Elizabethan verse."[29]

Fitzgerald did not play the game of careerism, except by writing. Although he sought the friendship of writers, he belonged to no self-promoting literary-critical groups. During the Thirties he eschewed the mandatory mea culpas and fashionable Marxist conversions by which writers protected themselves. The condescending obituaries in 1940 indicate that Fitzgerald was generally classified as a failure, a writer who had sold out to the slicks and the movies. Inevitably, F. Scott Fitzgerald provided the best epitaph on the mechanism of his professional work and his literary achievements. Writing to his daughter, Scottie, he declared: "I am not a great man, but sometimes I think the impersonal and objective quality of my talent, and the sacrifices of it, in pieces, to preserve its essential value has some sort of epic grandeur."[30] A professional's life is lived most fully in terms of his vocation.

Notes

1. William Charvat, *The Profession of Authorship in America, 1800–1870*, edited by Matthew J. Bruccoli (Columbus: Ohio State University Press, 1968), p. 3.
2. "On the Art of Fiction," *On Writing* (New York: Knopf, 1949), p. 103.
3. Wilson, "Thoughts on Being Bibliographed," *Princeton University Library Chronicle* (February 1944): 54.
4. The buying power of Fitzgerald's dollars is discussed elsewhere in this introduction: but a rough indication of his affluence is provided by the fact that the members of the House of Representatives and the Senate were paid $10,000 per year during the Twenties.
5. *As Ever, Scott Fitz—: Letters Between F. Scott Fitzgerald and His Literary Agent Harold Ober, 1919–1940*, edited by Bruccoli and Jennifer McCabe Atkinson (Philadelphia and New York: Lippincott, 1972).
6. *Dear Scott / Dear Max: The Fitzgerald-Perkins Correspondence*, edited by John Kuehl and Jackson R. Bryer (New York: Scribners, 1971).
7. This figure is approximate because it is impossible to untangle the advances and loans for *Tender Is the Night*.
8. Magazine-fiction rates have not increased since Fitzgerald's time. The *Post's* $4,000 fee represented about eighty cents per word. The top short-story rate in 1996 is one dollar per word, paid by the *New Yorker* and *Esquire; Playboy* pays between $3,000 and $3,500 for a story.
9. In 1996 it is a ninety-six-page monthly selling for $2.95 and bears no resemblance to Fitzgerald's *Post*.
10. Marquand out-published Fitzgerald in the *Post;* between 1921 and 1939, eighty-three Marquand stories appeared there, plus fourteen serials—including *The Late George Apley*.
11. *The Liberal Imagination* (New York: Viking, 1950), p. 344.
12. George Horace Lorimer, the editor of the *Saturday Evening Post*.
13. 7 February 1922. *F. Scott Fitzgerald: A Life in Letters*, edited by Bruccoli with the assistance of Judith S. Baughman (New York: Scribners, 1994).
14. 4 May 1925. Ibid., p. 211.
15. Received 23 April 1932. Ibid., p. 215.
16. Ca. 24 April 1925. Ibid., p. 107.
17. 19 September 1929. Ibid., p. 169.
18. 13 September 1929. Bruccoli, *Fitzgerald and Hemingway: A Dangerous Friendship* (New York: Carroll and Graf, 1994), pp. 135–136.
19. Received 13 May 1930. *Life in Letters*, pp. 182–183.

20. See George Anderson, "Appendix D: F. Scott Fitzgerald's Use of Story Strippings in *Tender Is the Night,*" *Reader's Companion to F. Scott Fitzgerald's* Tender Is the Night, by Bruccoli with Judith S. Baughman (Columbia: University of South Carolina Press, 1996), pp. 213–261.

21. 24 August 1934. *Dear Scott / Dear Max,* p. 207.

22. To Bertha Wood Cozzens, 22 December 1940. Princeton University Library.

23. Received 2 July 1935. *Life in Letters,* p. 284.

24. "Our April Letter," *The Notebooks of F. Scott Fitzgerald,* edited by Bruccoli (New York and London: Harcourt Brace Jovanovich / Bruccoli Clark, 1978), p. 131.

25. *The Liberal Imagination,* p. 243.

26. *The Best Times: An Informal Memoir* (New York: New American Library, 1968), p. 146.

27. "The Author's Apology," *F. Scott Fitzgerald In his Own Time: A Miscellany,* edited by Matthew J. Bruccoli and Jackson R. Bryer (Kent, Ohio: Kent State University Press, 1971), p. 164.

28. *The Crack-Up,* edited by Edmund Wilson (New York: New Directions, 1945), p. 310.

29. Ibid., p. 343.

30. 31 October 1939. *Life in Letters,* p. 419.

This Side of Paradise

Fitzgerald's Apprentice Novel

No reader of *This Side of Paradise* in 1920—except F. Scott Fitzgerald—could have anticipated that his first novel would launch a career of intoxicating success for its twenty-three-year-old author, who had declared as a Princeton undergraduate that he wanted to be "one of the greatest writers who ever lived." It is a flawed novel—episodic, self-indulgent, and loosely structured—written by a young man who didn't know how to plan or write a novel. Five years later the author of *The Great Gatsby* commented on *This Side of Paradise*.

> I like this book for the enormous emotion, mostly immature and bogus, that gives every incident a sort of silly "life."
> F.S.F. 1925
> But the faked references and intellectual reactions + cribs from MacKenzie, Johnson, Wells, Wilde, Tarkington give me the pip.[1]

Timing can be crucial for the success of a novel, and the timing was right for *This Side of Paradise*. America was ready for it. In the spring of the first year of what Fitzgerald christened the Jazz Age, there was a large potential readership for a novel that seriously treated the concerns of youth: ambition, iconoclasm, idealism, and love. *This Side of Paradise* announced a revolt in sexual mores; and it introduced a new heroine to fiction—the brave, independent, intelligent, determined young American woman.

This Side of Paradise was a novel of firsts: the first realistic American college novel and the first in a series of mildly shocking college novels published during the Twenties.[2] Although it ends in 1919, it was the first American novel that examined the impending revolt of youth in the Twenties. *This Side of Paradise* seems tame after eighty-five years, but it was regarded as a sensational document

---

"*This Side of Paradise:* Fitzgerald's Apprentice Novel" was published originally as Matthew J. Bruccoli's introduction to *This Side of Paradise* (New York: Signet Classics, 2006), pp. v–xii. Reprinted with permission of Arlyn Bruccoli for the Matthew J. Bruccoli literary estate.

of social history in 1920 because it published previously undisclosed realities about the generation of the Great War.

On the basis of *This Side of Paradise*, readers would have been justified in expecting Fitzgerald to produce a string of sensational flapper novels or to abandon fiction when he ran out of collegiate material. But examination of *This Side of Paradise* from the perspective of *The Great Gatsby* and *Tender Is the Night* reveals defining elements that were to be developed in Fitzgerald's masterpieces. It was an extraordinarily rapid fulfillment. Within five years after *This Side of Paradise*, Fitzgerald was able to write *The Great Gatsby*, the complexly planned novel that is now contender for "The Great American Novel." There is no promise in *This Side of Paradise* of Fitzgerald's later technical achievements, but the ideas and emotions of his mature novels can be identified in his apprentice novel.

The major themes of Fitzgerald's greatest work are aspiration and commitment to ideas. Lionel Trilling, in *The Liberal Imagination*, described this quality better than any other critic: Fitzgerald "was perhaps the last notable writer to affirm the Romantic fantasy, descended from the Renaissance, of personal ambition or heroism, of life committed to, or thrown away for, some ideal of self." Amory Blaine, like Jay Gatsby and Dick Diver, manifests "a romantic readiness." Fitzgerald's heroes combine a sense of duty with concomitant guilt at their failure to fulfill the requirements of their aristocratic egotism. Fitzgerald, who has been sloppily categorized as the celebrator of hedonism, was a moralist—in fact, a preacher.

The unexpected juxtaposition of characters and material in this novel, and in all of Fitzgerald's major fiction, melds realism and romanticism—accurate social observation combined with a heightened sensitivity to the possibilities of life. *This Side of Paradise* is a love poem to Princeton, and Amory's feelings about his college are documented through the data provided by Fitzgerald: the inside knowledge of the social system, the undergraduate codes of behavior and values. Readers' warm response to *This Side of Paradise* in 1920 was stimulated by their recognition that it was authentic. At the beginning of the great collegiate decade—when the Big Three really were the Big Three—it provided instruction on how to be a big man at Princeton when prominent Ivy Leaguers, not necessarily athletes, achieved national recognition. College success was regarded as preparation for worldly distinction. Amory combines the drive for success and recognition with a sense of his unique destiny. The original title of the novel was "The Romantic Egotist"—which Fitzgerald retained as the title of Book One of *This Side of Paradise*, taking Amory through his departure from Princeton in 1917. Princeton shapes Amory's ambition and ideals. The novel closes with the failed but still-aspiring Amory making a pilgrimage to Princeton, as to a shrine, seeking to renew his faith in his destiny.

This Side of Paradise does not regard Princeton as an educational institution. Nothing worthwhile happens in the classrooms—a Fitzgeraldian judgment that elicited a letter of protest from Princeton president John Grier Hibben after publication of the novel. The faculty is not regarded with respect, and no professor is credited with influencing Amory. Course work and academic requirements interfere with Amory's real education, which he acquires through unassigned reading, writing, and conversation—God, how he talks! For a novel that provides reliable advice on how to flunk out of Princeton, *This Side of Paradise* is a remarkably bookish book. In his *Notebooks,* Fitzgerald identified *This Side of Paradise* as "a romance and a reading list." The titles of sixty-four books and poems and the names of ninety-eight authors are mentioned, and many of them are meaningfully used.[3] The title page epigraphs document Fitzgerald's debts to his reading as well as the influence of English writers on his literary persona at that time. The title of the novel is taken from the poem "Tiare Tahiti," by Rupert Brooke, a romantic figure who died in the Great War. The Oscar Wilde epigram was from his decadent novel *The Picture of Dorian Gray* (1891).

Amory's Princeton career recapitulates Fitzgerald's. There was nothing in math and chemistry courses that Fitzgerald needed or wanted. He served his literary apprenticeship at Princeton by writing for the *Nassau Literary Magazine,* for the *Tiger,* and for the Triangle Club musicals. The reviewer in the *New Republic* described *This Side of Paradise* as "the collected works of F. Scott Fitzgerald," which was more than a wisecrack. The novel is a grab bag and incorporates or recycles one play, one story, and three poems ("The Debutante," "Babes in the Woods," "Princeton—The Last Day," "On a Play Twice Seen," "The Cameo Frame") from the *Nassau Lit.*

Much of the emotional quality of *This Side of Paradise* derives from the conditions of its composition. It was first written in haste as "The Romantic Egotist" in 1917 by an army lieutenant who expected to die in battle and wanted to leave a memorial to himself. Yet the novel omits the shaping event of Fitzgerald's generation. To his lasting regret he did not "get over" during World War I. Since the author who wrote best from the emotions generated by personal experiences had no battle experience to draw upon, *This Side of Paradise* covers Amory's war in two letters and a poem constituting the "Interlude" between Book One and Book Two. Fitzgerald revised "The Romantic Egotist" in 1918 and rewrote it in 1919 as *This Side of Paradise* after a time of misery resulting from his inability to marry Zelda Sayre. The published novel recapitulates the feelings generated in the author by the act of writing.

In the summer of 1919 Fitzgerald provided a preface for *This Side of Paradise,* which he or the publisher sensibly omitted from the book. This self-conscious statement by a self-conscious young writer begins:

Two years ago when I was a very young man indeed, I had an unmistakable urge to write a book. It was to be a picaresque novel, original in form and alternating melancholy, naturalistic egotism with a picture of the generation then hastening to war.

It was to be naive in places and shocking in others, painful to the conventional and not without its touch of ironic sublimity. The "leading character," a loiterer on the borderland of genius, loved many women and gazed on himself in many mirrors—in fact, women and mirrors were preponderant in all the important scenes.

I completed it during the last gasp of a last year at college, and the intricacies of a training camp. Its epigrams were polished by the substitution of the word *one* for the word *you;* its chapter titles were phrased to sound somewhat like the lines from Pre-Raphaelite poems, somewhat like electric signs over musical comedies; the book itself was a tedious casserole of a dozen by MacKenzie, Wells, and Robert Hugh Benson, largely flavored by the great undigested butterball of *Dorian Gray.*

This Side of Paradise was widely read because it was readable. A newspaper ad quoted a letter from Harry Hansen, literary editor of the *Chicago News;* "My, How That Boy Fitzgerald Can Write!" The writing combines clarity with wit, warmth, and charm. Fitzgerald was not an innovative or an experimental writer. The style and narrative of *This Side of Paradise* were based on nineteenth-century English models. Nevertheless it gave the impression of unconventionality or originality because Fitzgerald did not know how to structure a novel and had not yet mastered point of view. *This Side of Paradise* is unfocused. There are at least two points of view—Amory's and Fitzgerald's. The novel is related by the author—there is no narrator—who is mostly indistinguishable from Amory but who also intrudes to comment on Amory and to editorialize on Life. The amateurish interpolations—the scenes in dialogue and poems set in verse or prose—were mistaken for modernism. Yet there is a surprising pre-Joycean stream-of-consciousness passage in "The Egotist Becomes a Personage" (Book Two, Chapter V):

> One Hundred and Twentieth Street? That must have been One Hundred and Twelfth back there. One O Two instead of One Two Seven. Rosalind not like Beatrice, Eleanor like Beatrice, only wilder and brainier. Apartments along here expensive—probably hundred and fifty a month—maybe two hundred. Uncle had only paid hundred a month for whole great big house in Minneapolis. Question—were the stairs on the left or right as you came in? Anyway, in 12 Univee they were straight back and to the left. What a dirty

river—want to go down there and see if it's dirty—French rivers all brown or black, so were Southern rivers.

Readers continue to be puzzled by the two supernatural occurrences in this realistic novel: the apparition of the dead Humbird in the showgirls' apartment and the ghostly presence of Monsignor Darcy in the Atlantic City hotel room. Both connect sex with death, reinforcing Amory's—and Fitzgerald's—sense of evil or corruption; nonetheless, these scenes aren't effective or convincing. In November 1920 Fitzgerald responded to a reader's inquiry:

> Several people have asked me about that chapter + I can only explain it by telling how it came to be written. It was part of my first draft of my novel begun three years ago when I was an ardent supernaturalist + believed that a "personal devil" could and often did materialize before humans. Since then as you can see thru the book I have become practically a materialist so the incident becomes incongruous + out of place. You are right in saying that it was only a delirious apparition conjured up in Amory's drunken mind. Fred [Sloane] would not have seen him. You'll just have to take it as one of the numerous flaws in the book (Sotheby's, 15 December 1998).

This Side of Paradise is an autobiographical novel, as are all of Fitzgerald's novels; but he learned how to disguise or transmute the autobiographical material in his subsequent novels. The obvious—even blatant—personal quality of *This Side of Paradise* was in keeping with the Bildungsroman tradition to which it and many first novels belong: the novel that traces the struggles, sorrows, triumphs, and defeats of a potential genius. It is not the currently popular wishy-washy coming-of-age novel—a label attached to any work of fiction about an unhappy juvenile. Amory aims for and expects greatness: great achievement, great success, great fulfillment, and great love. His epic quest is unfulfilled and unfinished in the novel. It scarcely begins. *This Side of Paradise* doesn't end; it just stops.

This Side of Paradise made Fitzgerald an overweek celebrity. Influential reviewers welcomed him as a bright star of American fiction, praising the brilliance of the writing and its literary quality. H. L. Mencken, the most powerful critic in America, who was hard to please, identified it in the *Smart Set* as "a truly amazing first novel—original in structure, extremely sophisticated in manner and adorned with a brilliancy that is as rare in American writing as honesty is in American statecraft." Robert Benchley wrote in the *New York World* that "in spite of its immaturity, its ingenuousness and its many false notes, it is something new, and for this alone Mr. Fitzgerald deserves a crown of something very expensive."

Fitzgerald's fiction is characterized by rapid changes—up or down—in the careers of his heroes. The fame of *This Side of Paradise* validated the author's conviction of his genius as well as his belief in miracles. The reception of this novel resembled the plot of an F. Scott Fitzgerald story.

There were twelve American printings of *This Side of Paradise* in 1920–1921, totaling 49,075 copies.[4] It made Fitzgerald famous but not rich. The royalty of 10 percent on the first five thousand copies of the $1.75 book and 15 percent thereafter brought the author $12,445—probably $120,000 in 2006 money—enough to launch him and his bride, Zelda, on a life of extravagance and debt. Sinclair Lewis's *Main Street* was a much greater success, selling 295,00 copies in 1920–1921. The real payoff from *This Side of Paradise* was that it made Fitzgerald's short stories salable to the mass-circulation magazines, especially the *Saturday Evening Post*, which shaped his career as a commercial writer.

A side effect of the novel's newspaper reception was to initiate Fitzgerald's reputation as an irresponsible or uneducated writer because the text was carelessly edited at Charles Scribner's Sons; it was pockmarked with risible misusages, misspellings, and factual errors. Fitzgerald later recalled the debacle in a passage that he deleted from "Early Success":

> In a daze I opened the *Tribune* each morning to see if F. P. A. [Franklin P. Adams who conducted "The Conning Tower"] had found any more misspellings in the book. He started with a list of thirty and eager contributors to his column sent in a hundred more. My God—did they expect me to spell? If I was this hot shot couldn't the proofreaders do the spelling?

This 1937 essay explains that the reception of *This Side of Paradise* not only made him famous at twenty-three; it made him a professional: "a sort of stitching together of your whole life into a pattern of work, so that the end of one job is automatically the beginning of another." Fitzgerald concluded: "The compensation of a very early success is the conviction that life is a romantic matter."

It is pointless to speculate about whether *This Side of Paradise* would be in print now if F. Scott Fitzgerald had not subsequently written masterpieces. Beyond its contribution to American social history and to literary biography, this novel has endured because it is not fraudulent: flamboyant, certainly, but truthful.

Notes

1. Compton Mackenzie, author of *Sinister Street* (1913–1914); Owen Johnson, author of *Stover at Yale* (1911); H. G. Wells, author of *The Research Magnificent* (1915); Oscar Wilde, author of *The Picture of Dorian Gray* (1891); Booth Tarkington, author of the Penrod stories (1914 ff.)

2. John F. Kramer's *The American College Novel* (Lanham, Md.: Scarecrow Press, 2004) identifies thirty-two such works published from 1920 through 1929.

3. *This Side of Paradise* is now a historical novel and is as remote to readers as Dickens's or Fielding's novels. An annotated edition is needed to identify and explain all the literary references, songs, college slang, Princeton customs, and topical references. See Dorothy B. Good. "'A Romance and a Reading List': The Literary References in *This Side of Paradise*," *Fitzgerald/Hemingway Annual 1976,* pp. 35–64.

4. The novel was published in England but did not sell well, despite its debts to English authors.

The Beautiful and Damned

A Warning Prophecy

A novel of character deterioration, *The Beautiful and Damned* chronicles Anthony and Gloria Patch as they wait to inherit his grandfather's fortune. It opens in 1913 with Anthony, four years out of Harvard, idling gracefully on his income and fostering his self-image as an immaculate intellectual. He marries Gloria Gilbert, and they both undergo an inexorable decline fueled by alcohol and the spending of capital. Anthony's grandfather, a rabid reformer, invades one of their drunken parties and disinherits him. After the grandfather's death the Patches initiate a long process of breaking the will. Anthony is drafted during the war and has an affair with a lower-class Southern girl. While the inheritance case is being decided after the war, Anthony becomes a sloppy drunk and Gloria's beauty coarsens. They get the money in 1921, but Anthony's mind and health are broken.

Because Fitzgerald did not share the Patches' conviction that the only lesson to be learned from life is that there is no lesson to be learned from life, the novel does not maintain a consistent attitude toward its characters. At times the author seems to credit Anthony and Gloria with a certain integrity of irresponsibility, casting them as victims of philistinism; but Fitzgerald's moralizing compulsion takes over as the novel becomes a warning prophecy for the Fitzgeralds' own marriage. When he began the novel after six months of marriage, Fitzgerald perceived that his wife was not prepared to build her life around his work and that she was the stronger—or less flexible—character. He wrote to Zelda in 1930: "I wish the Beautiful and Damned had been a maturely written book because it was all true. We ruined ourselves—I have never honestly thought that we ruined each other."[1] But in 1940 he told his daughter: "Gloria was a much more trivial and vulgar person than your mother. I can't really say there was any resemblance except in the

"*The Beautiful and Damned:* A Warning Prophecy" is an excerpt from Matthew J. Bruccoli's *Some Sort of Epic Grandeur: The Life of F. Scott Fitzgerald,* second revised edition (Columbia: University of South Carolina Press, 2002), 151–155. Reprinted with permission of the University of South Carolina Press.

beauty and certain terms of expression she used, and also I naturally used many circumstantial events of our early married life. However the emphases were entirely different. We had a much better time than Anthony and Gloria had."[2] Fitzgerald's self-judgment in *The Beautiful and Damned* is divided between Anthony Patch and Dick Caramel, a writer who becomes a supplier of commercial entertainment.[3] Both Anthony and Caramel are projections of what Fitzgerald feared for himself. Another character, Maury Noble, drawn from George Jean Nathan, represents the successful cynic that Anthony cannot become.

Although Fitzgerald's second novel is not structurally distinguished, it marks an improvement over the looseness of *This Side of Paradise*. Nevertheless, he was still relying on subtitles to separate episodes within chapters; and *The Beautiful and Damned* is flawed by sideshows as well as by inconsistencies in tone and style. Fitzgerald was unable to resist interpolating passages of philosophizing—sometimes in playlet form. The "Flash-Back in Paradise," in which Beauty (Gloria) is sent to earth by The Voice, is a violation of the novel's naturalistic approach.

The point-of-view problems in *The Beautiful and Damned* result from Fitzgerald's ambivalent narrative stance as he fluctuates between approval of Anthony's adherence to the doctrine of futility and contempt for Anthony's weakness. The novel is told by the omniscient author, but Fitzgerald does not maintain his perspective. The authorial voice is intrusive and usurps the qualities of a first-person narrator; it analyzes, soliloquizes, and engages in discourses with the reader. This indulgent narrative manner was encouraged by Fitzgerald's magazine-story market. He would not become a complete novelist until he learned the techniques for controlling point of view and disciplining his habit of invading the narrative.

Fitzgerald had proofs of *The Beautiful and Damned* by mid-October [1921]. He regarded proofs as a kind of typescript and used them as an opportunity to make final alterations that went far beyond corrections. Fitzgerald felt he could not make final decisions about his prose until he saw it in print. He told Ober and Wilson that he had "almost completely rewritten parts" of his novel in St. Paul;[4] but it is impossible to be certain about the extent of his proof revisions because the setting typescript and proofs do not survive. The only prepublication form of *The Beautiful and Damned* is Fitzgerald's manuscript with typed inserts at the Princeton University Library.[5] Collation of the book text against the manuscript reveals that he made no proof deletions or additions that change the meaning of the novel—except for the conclusion. There were more cuts than insertions in typescript or proof. Passages were shifted ("A Flash-Back in Paradise," for example), and thousands of spot changes were made as Fitzgerald polished his wording. Maury Noble's account of his education in the "Symposium" chapter was rewritten. Almost every page was revised, but the published novel did not alter the plot or structure of the manuscript. Anthony and Gloria Patch were not significantly changed, although in a few places Fitzgerald made Gloria less culpable for Anthony's deterioration. At the opening of the "Symposium" chapter, after the statement "Gloria had lulled Anthony's mind to sleep," Fitzgerald deleted the manuscript comment: "This, of course, was desperately bad; halting that play and interplay of ideas which is at all times the salvation of such men as he."[6] In the manuscript Anthony urges Gloria to have an abortion during what proves to be a false pregnancy. Fitzgerald also cut the manuscript analysis of Anthony and Gloria's despair after his grandfather's intrusion on their drunken party:

> And then, two evil people finding themselves ringed round by high portentous walls, ran to and fro in a panic, each crying out that the other had built the walls or that this agency and that had built them—then, sitting down to weep, confessed piteously that they had built the walls themselves. Who can doubt that they were wicked people? For if they were not wicked, who is— And what is there we may call evil?[7]

The moralistic tone of this authorial invasion is confusing, for it is not clear whether Fitzgerald intended irony in his application of the word "evil."

One of the chief purposes of Fitzgerald's revisions was to clarify the novel's judgment of Anthony and Gloria. He did not succeed, and his work with the ending reveals his uncertainty about the final impression he wanted to leave with the reader. The manuscript closes with Beauty's return to Paradise:

> "Back again," the voice whispered.
> "Yes."
> "After fifteen years."
> "Yes"
> The voice hesitated.
> "How remote you are," it said, "Unstirred . . . You seem to have no heart. How about the little girl? The glory of her eyes is gone—"
> But Beauty had forgotten long ago.

Fitzgerald replaced this finale with the didactic conclusion of the serial, which unconvincingly pays tribute to Anthony's and Gloria's idealism:

> That exquisite heavenly irony which has tabulated the demise of many generations of sparrows seems to us to be content with the moral judgments of man upon fellow man. If there is a subtler and yet more nebulous ethic somewhere in the mind, one might believe that beneath the sordid dress and near the bruised heart of this transaction there was a motive which was not weak but only futile and sad. In the search for happiness, which search is the greatest and

possibly the only crime of which we in our petty misery are capable, these two people were marked as guilty chiefly by the freshness and fullness of their desire. Their disillusion was always a comparative thing—they had sought glamor and color through their respective worlds with steadfast loyalty—sought it and it alone in kisses and in wine, sought it with the same ingenuousness in the wanton moonlight as under the cold sun of inviolate chastity. Their fault was not that they had doubted but that they had believed.

The exquisite perfection of their boredom, the delicacy of their inattention, the inexhaustibility of their discontent—were disastrous extremes—that was all. And if, before Gloria yielded up her gift of beauty, she shed one bright feather of light so that someone, gazing up from the grey earth, might say, "Look! There is an angel's wing!" perhaps she had given more than enough in exchange for her tinsel joys.

. . . The story ends here.[8]

On 23 December 1921 Fitzgerald wired Perkins: LILDA THINKS BOOK SHOULD END WITH ANTHONY'S LAST SPEECH ON SHIP SHE THINKS NEW ENDING IS A PIECE OF MORALITY LET ME KNOW YOUR ADVICE. . . .[9] Perkins agreed with Zelda. The book text ends with the sardonic view of the broken Anthony whispering to himself: "'I showed them,' he was saying. 'It was a hard fight, but I didn't give up and I came through!'"

Perkins's editorial manner with Fitzgerald is revealed in their disagreement about Maury Noble's account of the Bible as a work of skepticism and irony, which Perkins thought would offend readers unnecessarily. Fitzgerald reacted with an emotional letter invoking Mark Twain, Anatole France, and George Bernard Shaw, charging Perkins with cowardice. On 12 December, Perkins replied: "Don't ever *defer* to my judgment. You won't on any vital point, I know, and I should be ashamed, if it were possible to have made you; for a writer of any account must speak for himself."[10] Fitzgerald then apologized: "The thing *was* flippant—I mean it was the sort of worst of Geo. Jean Nathan. I have changed it now—changed 'godalmighty' to diety, cut out 'bawdy' + changed several other words so I think it is all right."[11] The revised version was included in the novel. Fitzgerald liked Noble's oration so much that he published it in the February *Smart Set*.

In 1922 Perkins was troubled by including "Tarquin of Cheapside" in *Tales of the Jazz Age* because the story presented Shakespeare as a rapist, but he yielded when Fitzgerald reminded him that the story had appeared in the *Nassau Lit* without trouble.[12] Perkins confined himself to offering structural suggestions or spot queries and did not attempt to rewrite Fitzgerald. As their editorial relationship developed, he became the strongest influence on Fitzgerald's professional life. It has been suggested that Perkins, who had five daughters and wanted a son, saw his authors as surrogate sons—of whom Fitzgerald was the firstborn. Despite their mutual affection, they did not reach the Max and Scott stage until 1923.[13]

Notes

1. Ca. summer 1930. Princeton University Library. *F. Scott Fitzgerald: A Life in Letters,* edited by Matthew J. Bruccoli with the assistance of Judith S. Baughman (New York: Scribners, 1994).

2. 14 June 1940. Princeton University Library. Ibid., p. 435.

3. Caramel's complaint about the success of *This Side of Paradise* represents a lapse in Fitzgerald's judgment.

4. To Harold Ober, 29 November 1921. *As Ever, Scott Fitz—*, edited by Bruccoli and Jennifer McCabe Atkinson (Philadelphia and New York: J. B. Lippincott, 1972), p. 31; to Edmund Wilson, postmarked 25 November 1921. *The Letters of F. Scott Fitzgerald,* edited by Andrew Turnbull (New York: Scribners, 1963), p. 327.

5. The manuscript has two title pages. The first has the title "The Beautiful Lady Without Mercy" changed to *The Beautiful and Damned* with a canceled epigraph from Keats's "La Belle Dame Sans Merci" and another epigraph credited to Samuel Butler ("Life is one long process of getting tired."). This page lists seven other possible titles: "The House of Pain," "Misfortune's Street," "O, Beautiful," "The Broken Lute," "The Corruption of Anthony," "A Love Affair," and "Corruption." The second title page uses *The Beautiful and Damned* with the Butler epigraph, which was replaced in the book with "The victor belongs to the spoils.—Anthony Patch." In the manuscript table of contents the three books of the novel are titled "The Pleasant Absurdity of Things," "The Romantic Bitterness of Things," and "The Ironic Tragedy of Things." These headings were not retained in the published volume.

6. Manuscript: book II, chapter 2, p. 1. *The Beautiful and Damned* (New York: Scribners, 1922), p. 191.

7. Manuscript: book II, chapter 3, pp. 338–339. Ibid., p. 276.

8. Manuscript: book III, chapter 3, pp. 93–94. *Metropolitan* (March 1922): 113.

9. Princeton University Library. *Correspondence of F. Scott Fitzgerald,* edited by Bruccoli and Margaret M. Duggan (New York: Random House, 1980), p. 89.

10. Princeton University Library. *Dear Scott / Dear Max: The Fitzgerald-Perkins Correspondence,* edited by John Kuehl and Jackson R. Bryer (New York: Scribners, 1971), pp. 45–47.

11. Ca. 16 December 1921. Princeton University Library. Ibid., p. 49.

12. Princeton University Library. Ibid., pp. 61–62.

13. This process took longer with Harold Ober. In 1925 they dropped "Mr." in their letters and moved to "Dear Ober" / "Dear Fitzgerald"; not until 1927 were they on a first-name basis.

The Great Gatsby

Fitzgerald's Triumph of Genius and Craft

1

The charge that F. Scott Fitzgerald was an irresponsible writer is refuted by the compositional history of *The Great Gatsby*. He began planning the novel during the summer of 1922 as a work set in the Midwest and New York at the end of the nineteenth century. At that time he announced to Maxwell Perkins, his editor: "I want to write something *new* – something extraordinary and beautiful and simple + intricately patterned."[1] He started writing an early version of the novel in the summer of 1923 at Great Neck, Long Island, the locale for the published novel, but serious work did not commence until the summer of 1924 on the Riviera. The typescript was sent to Perkins in November. Prompted by his editor's response, Fitzgerald rewrote and restructured the novel in galley proof during January and February 1925 in Rome.[2]

The rewritten proofs were dispatched to Perkins with Fitzgerald's report that he had solved the problems that bothered both of them:

(1.) I've brought Gatsby to life
(2.) I've accounted for his money
(3.) I've fixed up the two weak chapters (VI and VII)
(4.) I've improved his first party
(5.) I've broken up his long narrative in Chap. VIII[3]

Gatsby achieved its greatness in proof. Fitzgerald's principal concern was to improve the existing plan by shifting the pieces of Gatsby's biography: Gatsby's revelation to Nick of his love for Daisy (originally in Chapter Seven) and the

---

"*The Great Gatsby:* Fitzgerald's Triumph of Genius and Craft" was published originally as the untitled introduction to *New Essays on* The Great Gatsby, edited by Matthew J. Bruccoli (Cambridge, England: Cambridge University Press, 1985), pp. 1–14. Reprinted with permission of Cambridge University Press.

account of Dan Cody and Gatsby (originally in Chapter Eight) were incorporated into Chapter Six. The novel is a work of genius, but it is equally a triumph of craftsmanship.

2

In 1925 Fitzgerald's short novel about a flamboyant racketeer's attempt to recapture the upper-class girl who threw him over seemed an unlikely candidate for masterpiece or world-classic stature. It was a commercial disappointment when it was published in April 1925; the two printings that year totaled 23,870 copies. (*This Side of Paradise* had sold 41,075 copies in 1920).[4] Yet the reviews included the warmest Fitzgerald had received—along with some opaque dismissals. Gilbert Seldes announced that "Fitzgerald has more than matured; he has mastered his talent and gone soaring in a beautiful flight, leaving behind him everything dubious and tricky in his earlier work, and leaving even farther behind all the men of his own generation and most of his elders."[5] This review appeared late in the *Dial,* a small-circulation literary journal. In January 1926 Seldes complained in the English *New Criterion* that the reviews had not been sufficiently enthusiastic, saying that Fitzgerald "stands at this time desperately in need of critical encouragement."[6] Among the prominent receptive critics were William Rose Benét in the *Saturday Review of Literature,* Laurence Stallings in the *New York World* (after an earlier unsigned *World* review was headlined "F. Scott Fitzgerald's Latest a Dud"), Herbert S. Gorman in the *New York Sun,* Harry Hansen in the *Chicago Daily News,* Carl Van Vechten in the *Nation,* and Herschel Brickell in the *New York Evening Post*. Probably the review that most concerned the author was H. L. Mencken's long piece in the *Baltimore Evening Sun,* which expressed reservations about the novel while recognizing Fitzgerald's development as a writer:

> The story is obviously unimportant . . . it is certainly not to be put on the same shelf with, say, *This Side of Paradise*. What ails it, fundamentally, is the plain fact that it is simply a story—that Fitzgerald seems to be far more interested in maintaining its suspense than in getting under the skins of its people. It is not that they are false; it is that they are taken too much for granted. Only Gatsby himself genuinely lives and breathes. The rest are mere marionettes—often astonishingly lifelike, but nevertheless not quite alive.
>
> What gives the story distinction is something quite different from the management of the action or the handling of the characters; it is the charm and beauty of the writing.[7]

Charles Scribner's Sons made a strong effort to promote the book. It was packaged in a striking dust jacket by Francis Cugat, but the jacket copy conveys the impression that the publisher was uncertain about the nature of its product: "It is a magical, living book, blended of irony, romance, and mysticism." The seven ads in the *Saturday Review of Literature* from April to June indicate that Scribners allocated a generous advertising budget to *The Great Gatsby*. The second ad (April 25) was captioned "F. Scott Fitzgerald, Satirist," indicating that the publisher was still looking for the right handle.⁸ The fifth ad (May 23) announced:

"*Mencken is right.*" SAYS JOSEPH HERGESHEIMER

*"It is beautifully written and saturated with a sharp, unforgettable emotion. It gathers up all his early promise surprisingly soon, and what he subsequently does must be of great interest and importance"*⁹

The English impact was negligible. The 1926 Chatto & Windus printing did not sell well, although the reviews were better than those Fitzgerald's previous novels had received in England. The *Times Literary Supplement* called it "undoubtedly a work of art and of great promise"; Edward Shanks in the *London Mercury* commended the author's control over his material. Conrad Aiken, writing in the *New Criterion,* praised the form and originality of the novel but stated that it is not "great," "large," or "strikingly subtle." L. P. Hartley called it "an absurd story" in the *Saturday Review.*¹⁰

The novel was dead in the market before the end of 1925, even though *The Great Gatsby* achieved exposure through the 1926 dramatization by Owen Davis that ran for 112 performances on Broadway and the 1926 silent movie based on the play. This publicity did not sell the book. Copies of the August 1925 second printing were still in the warehouse when Fitzgerald died in 1940. There was one more American printing during the author's lifetime, the 1934 Modern Library volume—discontinued for lack of sales. This reprint added Fitzgerald's introduction replying to the charges of triviality brought against his work in the proletarian Thirties: "But, my God! it was my material, and it was all I had to deal with."¹¹ The only other republications of *Gatsby* during Fitzgerald's lifetime were in two pulp magazines: *Famous Story Magazine* serialized it in 1926, and the English *Argosy* ran it in one 1937 issue.

Fitzgerald's newspaper obituaries revealed no awareness that *The Great Gatsby* was more than a period piece. The *New York Times* devoted a paragraph to the novel:

> The best of his books, the critics said, was *The Great Gatsby.* When it was published in 1925 this ironic tale of life on Long Island at a time when gin was the national drink and sex the national obsession (according to the exponents of Mr. Fitzgerald's school of writers), it received critical acclaim. In it

Mr. Fitzgerald was at his best, which was, according to John Chamberlain, "his ability to catch . . . the flavor of a period, the fragrance of a night, a snatch of old song, in a phrase."[12]

The next day, an editorial stated: "It was not a book for the ages, but it caught superbly the spirit of the decade."[13] James Gray wrote "A Last Salute to the Gayest of Sad Young Men" for the *St. Paul Dispatch* in which he ventured the "heresy" that the Nobel prize had been awarded to writers who had not produced anything as brilliant as *The Great Gatsby:* "Perhaps some day it will be discovered."[14] The *New Yorker*'s comment on the obituaries described *Gatsby* as "one of the most scrupulously observed and beautifully written of American novels."[15]

The 1941 assessments and tributes generally played it safe by viewing Fitzgerald as a writer who had failed to fulfill his promise. Even in the series of reminiscences that appeared in two 1941 issues of the *New Republic,* John Peale Bishop's elegy lamented Fitzgerald's failure. The other contributors included Malcolm Cowley, John Dos Passos, John O'Hara, Budd Schulberg, and Glenway Wescott. Dos Passos challenged the nostalgia or period-flavor critical approach to Fitzgerald and declared that *Gatsby* was "one of the few classic American novels."[16]

Fitzgerald's death triggered a *Gatsby* revival—which triggered the Fitzgerald revival. Unlike the Melville revival, which was the work of academics, the Fitzgerald revival was a popular response resulting from reader demand in the Forties. Critical reassessment of the novel was mainly a process of the Fifties.[17] During the Forties no article devoted to *The Great Gatsby* was published, but there were appraisals or reappraisals of Fitzgerald that singled it out for praise. In 1945 William Troy identified *Gatsby* as Fitzgerald's only completely successful novel, and in 1946 John Berryman declared it a "masterpiece."[18]

Publishers did more than the critics for Fitzgerald. Between 1941 and 1949, seventeen new editions or reprints of *The Great Gatsby* were published. The key event was the inclusion of *Gatsby* with *The Last Tycoon* in 1941, for the respectful posthumous attention attracted by the unfinished novel carried over to *Gatsby.* In 1942 Scribners brought out a small reprint of *Gatsby.*

Three years later, the novel became widely available and widely sold—the surest gauge of a book's influence. In 1945 there were five new editions or reprints—as well as *The Crack-Up,* with its section of letters about *Gatsby* from Edith Wharton, T. S. Eliot, and Gertrude Stein. That year the *Tycoon/Gatsby* edition went into a second printing, the Armed Services Edition was published, the *Viking Portable* Fitzgerald (which included *Gatsby* and *Tender Is the Night*) was published and required a second printing, and the twenty-five-cent Bantam paperback was released. It is impossible to determine the effect of a book giveaway program, but publishing historians have credited the 155,000 copies (nearly eight times the 1925 first printing) of the Armed Services Edition distributed to military personnel with creating a new readership for *The Great Gatsby.*

In 1946 the Bantam paperback was reprinted twice, New Directions published *Gatsby* in the New Classics series—with an introduction by Lionel Trilling—and *Gatsby* was included in *Great American Short Novels* (four printings in the Forties). The *Portable* went into third and fourth printings in 1949, and that year Grosset & Dunlap brought out a tie-in printing for the Alan Ladd movie version.

Before *The Great Gatsby* became a required textbook in the Fifties and Sixties, some half million copies were in the hands of readers who were reading it because they wanted to read it.

3

For a long time, *The Great Gatsby* was classified as "a book about the Roaring Twenties." It is one of those novels that so richly evoke the texture of their time that they become, in the fullness of time, more than literary classics: they become a supplementary or even substitute form of history. It is surprising that this statement should apply to a work by F. Scott Fitzgerald, for in certain ways the historiographer of the Jazz Age (which he named) was ill-equipped for the task.

He was not a documentary writer. John O'Hara paid him the tribute of declaring: "He always knew what he was writing about.... Scott Fitzgerald had the correct impressions because, quite apart from his gifts, the impressions were not those of a man who's never been there."[19] Although O'Hara carefully repeated the word "impressions," the implication that Fitzgerald was a master reporter is overgenerous. His control of detail was never as sharp or comprehensive as O'Hara's. The most famous car in American fiction is never identified. Fitzgerald may have felt that to stipulate its make would render the "circus wagon" / "death car" less extraordinary—it would have become just a Pierce-Arrow or Stutz or Duesenberg. Instead, he treated the vehicle impressionistically: "It was a rich cream color, bright with nickel, swollen here and there in its monstrous length with triumphant hat-boxes and supper-boxes and tool-boxes, terraced with a labyrinth of wind-shields that mirrored a dozen suns" (p. 77).[20] He relied on style to evoke a car appropriate for Gatsby. (Note Fitzgerald's characteristic use of the surprising adjective in *triumphant* hat-boxes.)

The Great Gatsby provides little in the way of sociological or anthropological data. Three cars are identified: Gatsby's Rolls-Royce (not his personal car), Nick's Dodge, and the Ford in Wilson's garage. Three celebrities are named: Joe Frisco, Gilda Grey, and David Belasco—all from show business. Two criminals—Charles Becker and Herman Rosenthal—are mentioned. Yet Fitzgerald's invented list of the attendees at Gatsby's party has become a source for students of Prohibition society. The laureate of the Jazz Age had little interest in jazz. His music was the popular songs of the era, six of which are mentioned in the novel: "The Sheik of Araby," "The Love Nest," "Ain't We Got Fun?" "Three O'clock in the Morning," "The Rosary," and "Beale Street Blues" (a 1917 jazz work by W. C. Handy that was a popular dance tune).

Although he had a keen sense of history, Fitzgerald was indifferent to many of the causes and activities of the Twenties. Despite his call for political and social change annexed to *This Side of Paradise* (1920), he soon abandoned that concern. He ignored the Sacco and Vanzetti case, which enlisted his literary friends. When Fitzgerald came to write his 1931 postmortum, "Echoes of the Jazz Age," he observed: "It was characteristic of the Jazz Age that it had no interest in politics at all."[21] This generalization doesn't hold, but it applies to Fitzgerald. His claim that he had been influenced by *The Decline of the West*—"I read him [Spengler] the same summer I was writing *The Great Gatsby* and I don't think I ever quite recovered from him"[22]—does not bear scrutiny. *The Decline of the West* was not available in English in the summer of 1924.

Another subject of general interest in the Twenties that Fitzgerald was ignorant of was the stock market. Nevertheless, he was able to convey the Eldorado mood that provides the background for *The Great Gatsby*. Nick Carraway decides to enter the investment field because "Everybody I knew was in the bond business" (p. 3). When James B. ("Rot-Gut") Ferret left the gambling table at Gatsby's party, "it meant he was cleaned out and Associated Traction would have to fluctuate profitably next day" (p. 75). Gatsby is involved with Meyer Wolfsheim in a securities swindle, as well as bootlegging, but Fitzgerald was unable to document this activity. When Maxwell Perkins read the unrevised typescript, he noted that Gatsby's criminal activities were vague. Fitzgerald admitted that the flaw resulted from his own ignorance: "But I know now—and as a penalty for not having known first, in other words make sure, I'm going to tell more."[23] Although Fitzgerald subsequently reported to Perkins that "I've accounted for the money,"[24] he only supplied clues that Gatsby was involved in illegal endeavors. His source was a man in Rome who briefed him on the 1922 Fuller-McGee Case, in which the partners in a brokerage firm were charged with misappropriating clients' funds. Arnold Rothstein, the remote source for Wolfsheim, the man who fixed the 1919 World Series, was implicated.

Writing to Corey Ford from Hollywood a dozen years after *The Great Gatsby*, Fitzgerald described his method of treating material:

> In *This Side of Paradise* (in a crude way) and in *Gatsby* I selected the stuff to fit a given mood or "hauntedness" or whatever you might call it, rejecting in

advance in *Gatsby,* for instance, all the ordinary material for Long Island, big crooks, adultery theme and always starting from the *small* focal point that impressed me—my own meeting with Arnold Rothstein, for instance.[25]

Fitzgerald did not work directly from models; he did not attempt to copy life. He transmuted his impressions. "Whether it's something that happened twenty years ago or only yesterday, I must start out with an emotion—one that's close to me and that I can understand."[26]

The figure who controls Gatsby's mysterious wealth is a travesty of Rothstein. Fitzgerald attempted to document Wolfsheim's criminal background through his reminiscences of the 1912 Rosenthal-Becker murder case, but the facts are distorted to accommodate Wolfsheim's sentimentality. Except for the touch of menace provided by his human-molar cufflinks, Wolfsheim is a comic racketeer—as is Gatsby in different ways.[27] O'Hara, one of Fitzgerald's staunchest admirers, commented: "I fully believed Gatsby until I went to NY and met some of those mob people. Gatsby would not have lasted a week with the ones I met, let alone taken control."[28]

Despite inaccuracies and absurdities, *The Great Gatsby* has become a source for historians because of Fitzgerald's sense of time, of the emotions evoked by particular moments. In *This Side of Paradise* he formulated a distinction that he used twice in the novel: "the sentimental person thinks things will last—the romantic person has a desperate confidence that they won't."[29] Many writers have been distinguished by a sense of the past; Fitzgerald possessed a complex and delicate sense of the passing present. Malcolm Cowley has observed that Fitzgerald wrote as if surrounded by clocks and calendars.

Fitzgerald's primary concern was with the rhythms, the colors, the tones associated with time and place—often expressed through synesthesia, as in "yellow cocktail music" (p. 49). Time and place are inseparable in Fitzgerald: not just how it was, but how it felt in "a transitory enchanted moment" (p. 217). He later wrote, "After all, any given moment has its value; it can be questioned in the light of after-events, but the moment remains."[30] His task was to fix and preserve evanescent experience. Fitzgerald's sense of mood was extraordinary: the summer twilight in New York, the riotous Long Island nights, the Chicago railroad station at holiday time (yet he stipulated the wrong station before Ring Lardner corrected it). These passages have become touchstones of American prose.

At the end of "Echoes of the Jazz Age" he observed: "and it all seems rosy and romantic to us who were young then, because we will never feel quite as intensely about our surroundings any more."[31] This theme is not the same as the familiar *ubi sunt* formula. Fitzgerald and his heroes do not yearn for the melted snows of yesteryear; they mourn for their lost capacity to respond to those snows: "the snow of twenty-nine wasn't real snow. If you didn't want it to be snow, you just paid some money."[32]

The strongest feeling generated by *The Great Gatsby* is regret. It is not regret keyed to mutability—which means change. Fitzgerald evokes regret for depleted emotional capacity, a regret as intense as the emotions that inspired it were. While he was writing *The Great Gatsby,* Fitzgerald explained: "That's the whole burden of this novel—the loss of those illusions that give such color to the world that you don't care whether things are true or false as long as they partake of the magical glory."[33]

In "Winter Dreams," the 1922 story that is a miniature of *The Great Gatsby,* poor boy Dexter Green becomes wealthy but loses the rich girl who catalyzed his ambitions. This is his response to her home as published in the magazine text:

> There was a feeling of mystery in it, of bedrooms upstairs more beautiful and strange than other bedrooms, of gay and radiant activities taking place through these deep corridors and of romances that were not musty and laid already in lavender, but were fresh and breathing and set forth in rich motor cars and in great dances whose flowers were scarcely withered.[34]

When Fitzgerald rewrote this passage in Chapter Eight of the novel for Gatsby's response to Daisy Fay's home—scrupulously cutting it from the collected text of the story—"rich motor cars" became "this year's shining motor-cars" (p. 178). Not just expensive cars, but the cars that evoke the aura of a particular time.

At the end of "Winter Dreams," Green is told that the beauty of his dream has "faded."

> For the first time in years the tears were streaming down his face. But they were for himself now. He did not care about mouth and eyes and moving hands. He wanted to care but could not care. For he had gone away and he could never come back anymore. The gates were closed, the sun was gone down, and there was no beauty but the gay beauty of steel that withstands all time. Even the grief he could have borne was left behind in the country of illusion, of youth, of the richness of life, when his winter dreams had flourished.
>
> "Long ago," he said, "long ago, there was something in me, but now that thing is gone. Now that thing is gone, that thing is gone. I cannot cry. I cannot care. That thing will come back no more."[35]

Green grieves for his capacity to respond to "the richness of life," but he nonetheless yields to time and loss. Gatsby doesn't: "'Can't repeat the past?' he cried incredulously. 'Why of course you can!'" (p. 133).

The Great Gatsby is time-haunted from "In my younger and more vulnerable years" to "borne back ceaselessly into the past." There are at least 450 time words in the novel.[36] Exclusive of character names, the second most frequent noun is *time*, with 87 occurrences. (*House* appears 95 times.) *Moment* or *moments* occurs 73 times; *day* or *days*, 70; *minute* or *minutes*, 49; *hour* or *hours*, 47; *o'clock*, 26; *year*, 19; *past*, 18 (as against 5 appearances of *future*); *month* or *months*, 15; *week* or *weeks*, 15; *twilight*, 9; *clock*, 6; *watch* (noun), 5; *time-table*, 3. The first striking image in the novel is the Buchanans' lawn "jumping over sun-dials" (p. 8).

In Chapter 5, the fulcrum of the nine-chapter novel, when Gatsby is reunited with Daisy, his "head leaned back so far that it rested against the face of a defunct mantelpiece clock" (p. 104). A moment later Gatsby almost knocks the clock off the mantle, "whereupon he turned and caught it with trembling fingers, and set it back in place" (p. 105). The irony of this symbolism may be too blatant. Gatsby, the time defier, rescues a defunct timepiece, but time will put him "back in place." When Gatsby takes Daisy to tour his house later in this chapter, Klipspringer plays the piano and Fitzgerald provides the lyric:

> In the morning,
> In the evening,
>   Ain't we got fun—
> . . .
> In the meantime,
> In between time—

And when Daisy leaves Gatsby's party in the next chapter, the orchestra is playing "Three O'Clock in the Morning"—"a neat, sad little waltz of that year" (p. 131).

Fitzgerald's treatment of time with the effect of simultaneous detachment and involvement—what Cowley described as "double vision"[37]—reinforces the permeation of realism and imagination that identifies his best fiction. Thus, Nick jots down the names of the people who came to Gatsby's parties on a time-table headed "This schedule is in effect July 5th, 1922" (p. 73). Such horology fosters the impression of historical truth—which is not the same thing as straight history.

4

The ebullient author of *This Side of Paradise* proclaimed in 1920 that "An author ought to write for the youth of his own generation, the critics of the next, and the schoolmasters of ever afterward."[38] Five years later he achieved those aims—and more. Now the young readers, the scholar-critics, and the schoolmasters are engaged with *Gatsby* and Gatsby. Yet no one in 1925 predicted the present eminence of *The Great Gatsby*—not even Fitzgerald. . . .

Notes

1. *Correspondence of F. Scott Fitzgerald,* edited by Matthew J. Bruccoli and Margaret M. Duggan (New York: Random House, 1980), p. 112.

2. Specimens of the revised galleys are included in *The Great Gatsby: A Facsimile of the Manuscript,* edited by Bruccoli (Washington, D.C.: Bruccoli Clark / Microcard Editions, 1973).

3. *Dear Scott / Dear Max: The Fitzgerald-Perkins Correspondence,* edited by John Kuehl and Jackson R. Bryer (New York: Scribners, 1971), p. 94.

4. The best-selling novels of 1925 were *Soundings* by A. Hamilton Gibbs, *The Constant Nymph* by Margaret Kennedy, *The Keeper of the Bees* by Gene Stratton Porter, *Glorious Apollo* by E. Barrington, *The Green Hat* by Michael Arlen, *The Little French Girl* by Ann Douglas Sedgwick, *Arrowsmith* by Sinclair Lewis, *The Perennial Bachelor* by Anne Parish, *The Carolinian* by Rafael Sabatini, and *Our Increasing Purpose* by A. S. M. Hutchinson.

5. "Spring Flight," *Dial* (August 1925): 162–164.

6. "New York Chronicle," *New Criterion* (January 1926): 170–171.

7. "As H. L. M. Sees It," *Baltimore Evening Sun* (2 May 1925): 9.

8. *Saturday Review of Literature* (25 April 1925): 709.

9. Ibid., p. 777.

10. *TLS* (18 February 1926): 116; *London Mercury* (April 1926): 656–668; *New Criterion* (October 1926): 773–776; *Saturday Review* (20 February 1926): 234–235.

11. (New York: Modern Library, 1934), p. x.

12. (23 December 1940): 19.

13. "Not Wholly Lost" (24 December 1940): 14.

14. (24 December 1940): 4.

15. (4 January 1941): 9.

16. "Fitzgerald and the Press," *New Republic* (17 February 1941): 213.

17. See Jackson R. Bryer and G. T. Tanselle, "*The Great Gatsby*—A Study in Literary Reputation," *New Mexico Quarterly* (Winter 1963–1964): 409–425; also Bryer, *F. Scott Fitzgerald: The Critical Reception* (New York: Franklin, 1978).

18. William Troy, "Scott Fitzgerald—The Authority of Failure," *Accent* (Autumn 1945): 56–60; John Berryman, "F. Scott Fitzgerald," *Kenyon Review* (Winter 1946): 103–112.

19. John O'Hara, introduction, *The Portable F. Scott Fitzgerald* (New York: Viking, 1945), p. xii.

20. All quotations from *The Great Gatsby* are cited from the first printing (New York: Scribners, 1925) as emended in Bruccoli's *Apparatus for F. Scott Fitzgerald's* The Great Gatsby (Columbia: University of South Carolina Press, 1974).

21. *Scribner's Magazine* (November 1931): 459–465. Reprinted in *The Crack-Up,* edited by Edmund Wilson (New York: New Directions, 1945).

22. *The Letters of F. Scott Fitzgerald,* edited by Andrew Turnbull (New York: Scribners, 1963), pp. 289–290.

23. Ibid., p. 173.

24. Ibid., p. 177
25. Ibid., p. 551.
26. "One Hundred False Starts," *Saturday Evening Post* (4 March 1933): 13, 65–66.
27. Bootlegger Max von Gerlach was a partial source for Gatsby. A quarter of a century after the novel was published, the fifty-five-year-old proprietor of a Flushing, Long Island, used-car business shot himself (*New York World-Telegram,* 22 December 1939, p. 4). See Bruccoli, "'How Are You and the Family Old Sport?'—Gerlach and Gatsby," *Fitzgerald/Hemingway Annual 1975,* pp. 33–36.
28. *Selected Letters of John O'Hara,* edited by Bruccoli (New York: Random House, 1978), p. 425.
29. (New York: Scribners, 1920), p. 246.
30. "Six of One—," *Redbook* (February 1932): 22–25, 86, 88. Collected in *The Price Was High,* edited by Bruccoli (New York: Harcourt Brace Jovanovich / Bruccoli Clark, 1979).
31. See note 17.
32. "Babylon Revisited," *Saturday Evening Post* (21 February 1931): 3–5, 82–84. Collected in *Taps at Reveille* (New York: Scribners, 1935).
33. To Ludlow Fowler. *Correspondence of F. Scott Fitzgerald,* p. 145.
34. *Metropolitan Magazine* (December 1921): 11–15, 98, 100–102, 104–107. Collected in *All the Sad Young Men* (New York: Scribners, 1926).
35. *All the Sad Young Men,* p. 90.
36. Andrew T. Crosland, *Concordance to The Great Gatsby* (Detroit: Gale Research, 1975).
37. "Fitzgerald: The Double Man," *Saturday Review of Literature* (24 February 1951): 9–10, 42–44.
38. "The Author's Apology," *This Side of Paradise,* third printing (New York: Scribners, 1920).

Diagram of the Development of *Tender Is the Night*

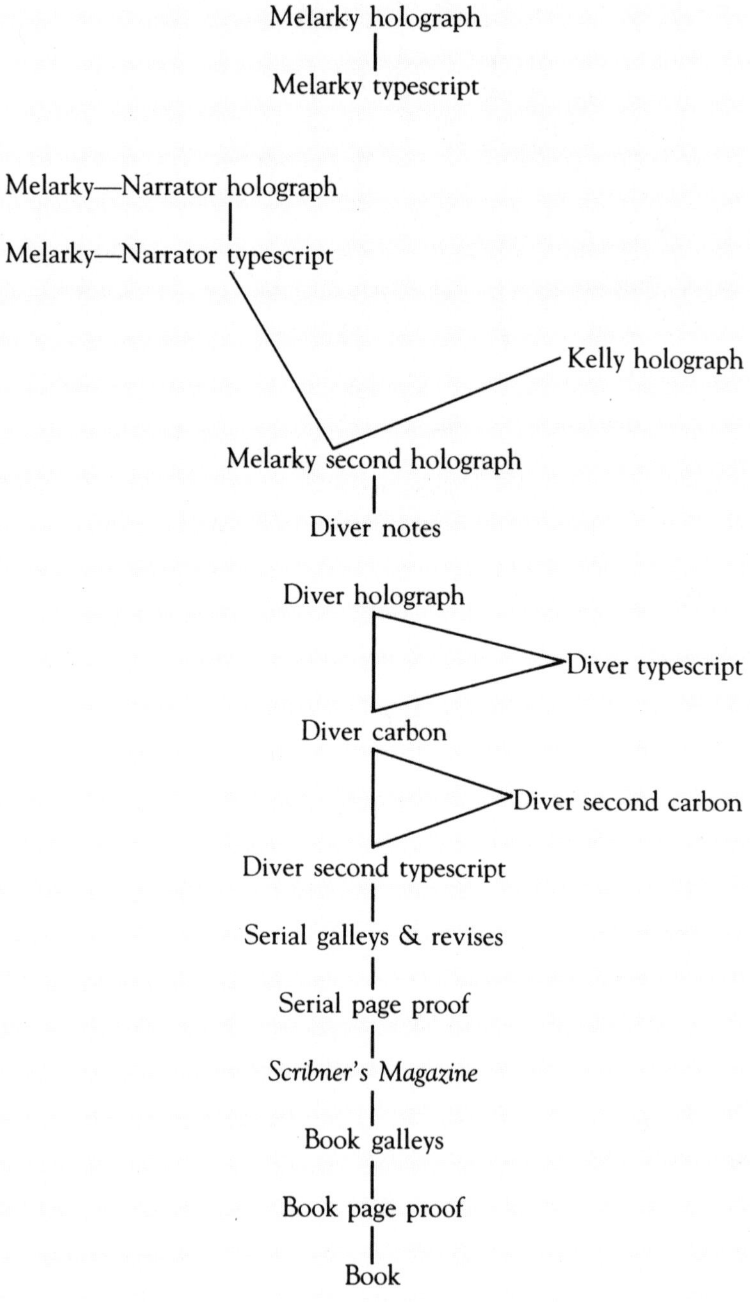

```
                    Melarky holograph
                          |
                    Melarky typescript


  Melarky—Narrator holograph
              |
  Melarky—Narrator typescript
                    \
                     \              ╱— Kelly holograph
                      \            ╱
                    Melarky second holograph
                          |
                      Diver notes

                    Diver holograph
                          ╲
                           ╲——▶ Diver typescript
                      Diver carbon
                           ╲
                            ╲——▶ Diver second carbon
                    Diver second typescript
                          |
                    Serial galleys & revises
                          |
                    Serial page proof
                          |
                    *Scribner's Magazine*
                          |
                      Book galleys
                          |
                    Book page proof
                          |
                         Book
```

Tender Is the Night

From Concept to "The Author's Final Version"

1. Composition

. . . On 1 May 1925, three weeks after the publication of *The Great Gatsby*,[1] F. Scott Fitzgerald wrote to Scribners editor Maxwell Perkins: "The happiest thought I have is of my new novel—it is something really NEW in form, idea, structure—the model for the age that Joyce and Stien are searching for, that Conrad didn't find."[2]

By late April 1926 Fitzgerald informed Harold Ober, his agent: "The novel is about one fourth done and will be delivered for possible serialization about January 1st. It will be about 75,000 words long, divided into 12 chapters, concerning tho this is absolutely confidential such a case as that girl who shot her mother on the Pacific coast last year."[3]

The novel was to be about Francis Melarky, an American in his twenties who murders his domineering mother while they are traveling in Europe. The matricide version occupied Fitzgerald, with many interruptions, from 1925 to 1930. There were five drafts—three in the third person and two with a narrator—but no draft progressed beyond four chapters. Francis Melarky and his mother arrive on the Riviera; he is taken up by attractive American expatriates Seth and Dinah Piper (Roreback) and the alcoholic Abe Grant (Herkimer); Francis, a movie technician, visits a Riviera movie studio, and he acts as a second in a duel; then Melarky, the Grants, and the Pipers go to Paris. There is a flashback opening

---

"*Tender Is the Night:* From Concept through 'The Author's Final Version'" was first published as the introduction to *Reader's Companion to F. Scott Fitzgerald's* Tender Is the Night (Columbia: University of South Carolina Press, 1996), by Matthew J. Bruccoli with Judith S. Baughman. Reprinted with permission of the University of South Carolina Press. This text, Bruccoli says in an introductory note, "draws heavily" upon his *The Composition of* Tender Is the Night (Pittsburgh: University of Pittsburgh Press, 1963).

chapter in which Melarky is beaten by the police in Rome. Many of these incidents are recognizable in *Tender Is the Night*.

The character of Francis Melarky was loosely based on Theodore Chanler, a young expatriate American composer—who was not involved in violent crime. The Pipers are recognizable as Sara and Gerald Murphy. . . ,[4] the Fitzgeralds' close friends at Cap d'Antibes and later. Abe Grant is a portrait of Ring Lardner. . . .[5] The Pipers and Grant were developed into the Divers and Abe North in the published novel.

Trans-Atlantic travel and the effects of Europe on Americans were the subjects of Fitzgerald short stories during the time he was working on the novel. As George Anderson demonstrates. . . ,[6] themes, descriptions, and phrases were transplanted from the novel drafts to stories or from stories to the novel. In June 1929 Fitzgerald reported to Perkins: "I am working night + day on novel from new angle that I think will solve previous difficulties."[7] This "new angle" was a plot utilizing movie director Lew Kelly and his wife, Nicole, who are going to Europe for an extended vacation. Fitzgerald wrote two manuscript chapters set on shipboard. Also aboard the ship is a young actress named Rosemary who hopes to impress Kelly. No typescript survives for the Kelly chapters, which indicates that Fitzgerald abandoned the angle. There is evidence that Fitzgerald returned to Melarky material early in 1930, assembling 127 typescript pages from the previous drafts.

Zelda Fitzgerald's collapse and hospitalization in Switzerland, commencing in April 1930, interrupted work on the novel; and it provided Fitzgerald with material about which he felt strongly, superseding the unfelt Melarky plot. A signal to Fitzgerald's new concerns is provided by "One Trip Abroad," a story written in August 1930, while Zelda was at Les Rives de Prangins clinic on Lake Geneva, Switzerland. The story published in the *Saturday Evening Post* in October is a forecast of *Tender*. An attractive young American couple, Nicole and Nelson Kelly, go to France intending to study music and painting; but they are caught up in dissipation and become patients in a Swiss clinic.

The Fitzgeralds returned to America in September 1931. In January 1932 Fitzgerald reported to Perkins: "At last for the first time in two years + ½ I am going to spend five consecutive months on my novel. I am actually six thousand dollars ahead Am replanning it to include what's good in what I have, adding 41,000 new words + publishing. Don't tell Ernest or anyone—let them think what they want—you're the only one whose ever consistently felt faith in me anyhow."[8] Work was interrupted by Zelda Fitzgerald's February relapse and hospitalization at the Phipps Psychiatric Clinic of Johns Hopkins Hospital in Baltimore. Fitzgerald's plot outline ("Sketch"), chronologies, and character sketches were prepared in Montgomery, Alabama, early in the year or at "La Paix," the house he rented in May 1932 at Towson, Maryland, near Baltimore. In August 1932 he

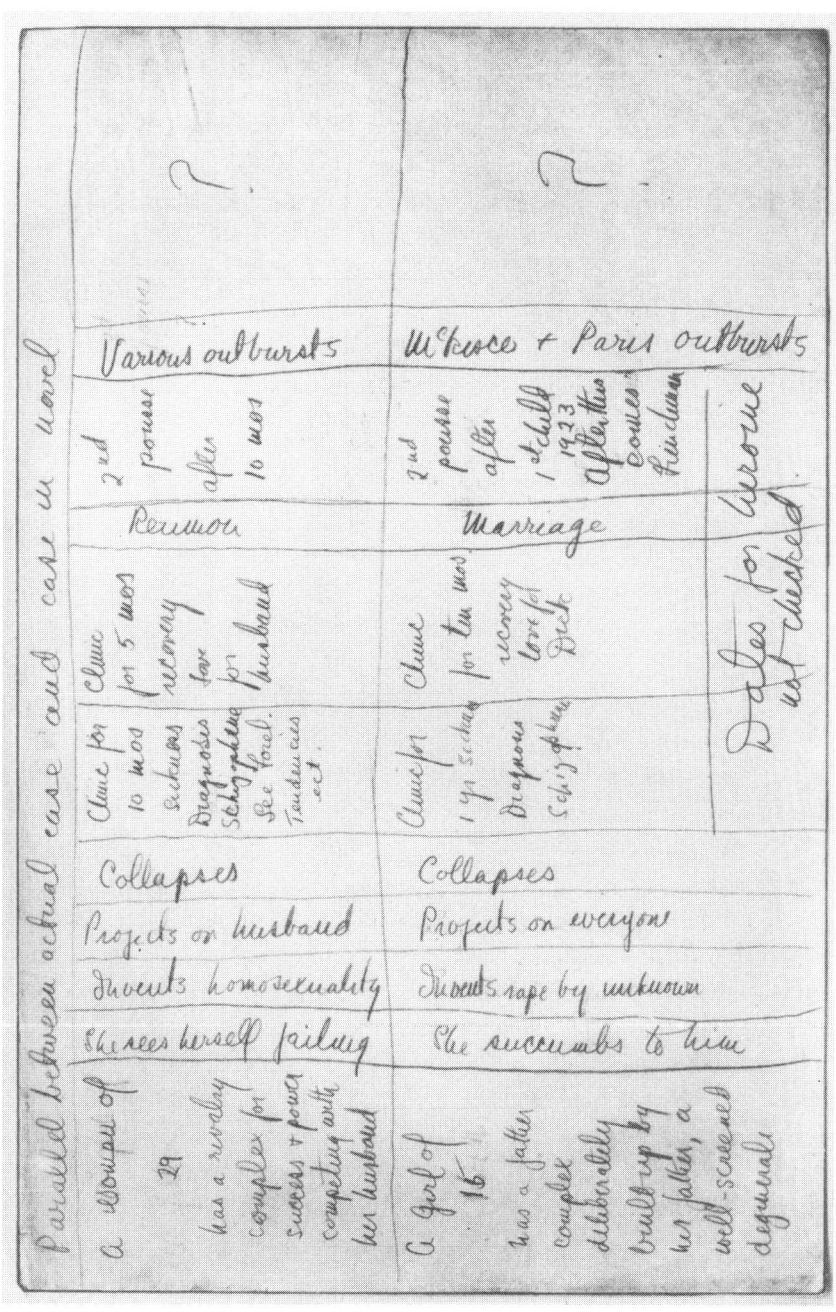

Comparison of Zelda Fitzgerald's and Nicole Diver's case histories

made this entry in his *Ledger:* "The Novel now plotted + planned, never more to be permanently interrupted."9

His wife's illness determined Fitzgerald's final approach to the novel. The details of Nicole Diver's illness were based on Zelda Fitzgerald's illness, as shown by [Fitzgerald's] chart comparing the two case histories, although the incest factor in Nicole's collapse was apparently invention. Zelda Fitzgerald's illness supplied more than factual background for *Tender:* it provided the emotional focus of the novel. Diver's response to Nicole's illness derives from Fitzgerald's feelings about his wife's collapse and relapses.

In the published novel the major departures from the "Sketch" have to do with the nature of Nicole's insanity and with Diver's political ideas. She does not manifest a homicidal mania in *Tender,* nor does she commit a murder that Diver conceals. Diver is not a communist in the novel; he is apolitical. Nothing in the surviving drafts indicates that Fitzgerald tried to develop these ideas.

The criticism has been made that Dick Diver is not a convincing figure as a psychiatrist. It is true that he is not surrounded with medical details, but *Tender* is not about psychiatry. Fitzgerald's note under "Method of Dealing with Sickness Material" indicates that the paucity of medical details was deliberate: "Only suggest from the most remote facts. Not like doctor's stories."

Fitzgerald's memo on the three-part structure establishes that the point-of-view shifts in the novel were planned from the inception of work. Book I shows the Divers through Rosemary's adoring eyes. It is a brilliant surface, with hints of the corruption beneath the façade Diver maintains. "From the outside mostly" provides the rationale for the introductory flashback. Although Fitzgerald reconsidered the flashback structure after the book was published, the plans and drafts show that he did not alter the structural plan during the writing of *Tender.* In Book II the reader is taken behind the barricade of charm to learn Nicole's case history as Diver did. Book III provides Diver's attempts to work out his destiny— to break the bond with Nicole, to cure her, and to save himself.

The preliminary planning material supports the conclusion that *Tender* is not just the result of work Fitzgerald began in 1932; the published novel is the product of a cumulative process salvaging the seemingly wasted work on the Melarky drafts. The dominant theme—the deterioration of a personality under the distractions and dissipations of expatriate life in its most attractive form—endured throughout the process of composition. The treatment of this theme became more penetrating as Fitzgerald worked his way from the matricide plot to the Nicole-Dick material.

The first complete draft of the Dick Diver version—entitled "The Drunkard's Holiday"—was assembled from revised typescripts of the Melarky version (corresponding to Book I, Chapters 1–12; Book II, Chapters 22–23) and from new manuscript for the rest of the novel. Fitzgerald did not type. All of his first drafts were written in holograph and turned over to typists. He revised his work through layers of typescripts and carbon copies. It was not unusual for him to revise retyped drafts for *Tender* three times. Since the manuscript chapters were being typed while Fitzgerald was working ahead, he might be revising typescript and writing new manuscript chapters on the same day.

When Fitzgerald was in the late states of composition—probably during summer 1933—Perkins and Fitzgerald decided to serialize the novel in four monthly installments (January–April 1934) of *Scribner's Magazine*. Serialization would bring Fitzgerald additional income and publicize the forthcoming book. On 25 September Fitzgerald reported to Perkins: ". . . things have gone ahead of my schedule, which you will remember, promised you the whole manuscript for reading November 1, with the first one-fourth ready to shoot into the magazine (in case you can use it) and the other three-fourths to undergo further revision. I now figure that this can be achieved by about the 25th of October. I will appear in person carrying the manuscript and wearing a spiked helmet."[10] The twelve long chapters of the typescript, retitled "Doctor Diver's Holiday A Romance," correspond to the sections of the serial, which were being set in type for *Scribner's Magazine* by 27 October 1933.

In March 1935—nearly a year after the publication of the novel—Fitzgerald wrote to Perkins:

> It has become increasingly plain to me that the very excellent organization of a long book or the finest perceptions and judgment in time of revision do not go well with liquor. A short story can be written on a bottle, but for a novel you need the mental speed that enables you to keep the whole pattern in your head and ruthlessly sacrifice the sideshows as Ernest did in "A Farewell to Arms." If a mind is slowed up ever so little it lives in the individual part of a book rather than in a book as a whole; memory is dulled. I would give anything if I hadn't had to write Part III of "Tender Is the Night" entirely on stimulant. If I had one more crack at it cold sober I believe it might have made a difference. Even Ernest commented on sections that were needlessly included and as an artist he is as near as I know for a final reference.[11]

Fitzgerald's admission about writing Part III (almost certainly referring to the third serial installment) "entirely on stimulant" means that he drank during his work on this section—but not necessarily that he was drunk while writing these chapters or the rest of *Tender Is the Night*.

2. Editing and Publication

The setting copy for the serial galleys consists of revised carbons and revised ribbon-copy typescripts. Fitzgerald revised the serial galleys so extensively that the second, third, and fourth installments were reset. He was a compulsive reviser of his work and defied publishing practice by treating proofs as an opportunity to perfect his prose and especially to alter the effect of his words as they would appear in print. Fitzgerald's proof revisions demonstrate his concern for the details of his text. He enjoined Alfred Dashiell, managing editor of *Scribner's Magazine*, and Perkins against tampering with his system of using italics for emphasis only: "PLEASANT NICE THOUGHTS IT WOULD BREAK MY HEART IF THE PROOF READERS ARE STICKING BACK ALL THOSE ITALICS I TWICE ELIMINATED STOP IN THE FIRST PROOF THEY HAD ALL THE FRENCHMEN TALKING IN ITALICS = SCOTT"[12]

The Dashiell/Fitzgerald correspondence shows that the *Tender* serial was edited on a tight schedule: 29 December 1933—Dashiell sends Fitzgerald second installment proof; 2 January 1934—Dashiell sends revised second installment proof; 12 January—Dashiell sends third installment proof; 6 February—Fitzgerald returns his "first half of Section IV."[13] In addition to queries on the galleys, Dashiell provided editorial queries in letters or in list form. Fitzgerald acted on some of these suggestions and disregarded others. . . .[14] On 13 February Dashiell called attention to word repetition: *reserved* at 333.32/338.1 and *off* at 359.5–6; but Fitzgerald did not alter these readings.

There is surprisingly little editorial correspondence for *Tender;* much of the Fitzgerald-Perkins editorial discussion was probably conducted by phone. On 18 January 1934 Perkins advised omitting the shooting in the Gare Saint-Lazare (serial installment 2) from the book, but Fitzgerald disagreed. . . .[15] When Perkins endorsed Dashiell's decision that the episode in which Dick rescues Mary North Minghetti and Lady Caroline from the Cannes police would have to be cut to eight hundred words in the fourth installment for space reasons, Fitzgerald argued for its retention. . . .[16]

The drafts from manuscript through typescript setting copy for the serial include an account of Tommy Barban and Nicole swimming on the beach of "Monsier Irv," a Chicago gangster living on the Riviera. This material was deleted in the serial galleys and remained unpublished until Malcolm Cowley used it in his 1951 edition.

Three substantial cuts were made between the serial and book publication: The serial includes a fuller account of Abe North's day in the Ritz bar (Book I, Chapter 23). . . .[17] The serial material about the young man who jumps from a ship on which Dick is returning to Europe (Book II, Chapter 19) was omitted. . . .[18] The serial material about Diver's involvement with a woman in Innsbruck (Book II, Chapter 18) was condensed. . . .[19]

Edmund Wilson had read *Tender* in typescript; in a letter postmarked 12 March 1934 Fitzgerald discussed the cuts and revisions:

Despite your intention of mild criticism in our conversation, I felt more elated than otherwise—if the characters got real enough so that you disagreed with what I chose for their manifest destiny the main purpose was accomplished (by the way, your notion that Dick should have faded out as a shyster alienist was in my original design, but I thot of him, in reconsideration, as an "homme épuisé," not only an "homme manqué." I thought that, since his choice of a profession had accidentally wrecked him, he might possibly have walked out on the profession itself.)

Any attempt by an author to explain away a partial failure in a work is of course doomed to absurdity—yet I could wish that you, and others, had read the book version rather than the mag. version which in spots was hastily put together. The last half for example has a <u>much</u> more polished facade now. Oddly enough several people have felt that the surface of the first chapters was <u>too</u> ornate. One man even advised me to "coarsen the texture," as being remote from the speed of the main narrative!

In any case when it appears I hope you'll find time to look it over again. Such irrelevancies as Morton Hoyt's nose dive and Dick's affair in Innsbruck are out, together with the scene of calling on the retired bootlegger at Beaulieu, + innumerable minor details. I have driven the Scribner proofreaders half nuts but I think I've made it incomparably smoother.[20]

The fifth draft of *Tender* conflates serial galleys, revised galleys, revised typescript, and new typescript. These documents representing several layers of revision constituted the latest printer's copy for the serial text. Incomplete marked page proof survives for the *Scribner's Magazine* installments (pp. 168–174, 207–229; corresponding to Book II, Chapters 10–23).

First Installment, January 1934
Pp. [1]-8, [60]-80

Serial section	corresponds to	book
I		I, 1–5
II		I, 6–11
III		I, 12–18

Second Installment. February 1934
Pp. [88]-95, 139–160

Serial section	corresponds to	book
IV		I, 19–25
V		II, 1–9

Third Installment. March 1934
Pp. [169]–174, 207–229

Serial section	corresponds to	book
VI		II, 10–13
VII		II, 14–15
VIII		II, 16–21
IX		II, 22–23

Fourth Installment, April 1934.
Pp. [252]-258, [292]-310

Serial section	corresponds to	book
X		III, 1–3
XI		III, 4–6
XII		III, 7–13

The book galleys were completely reset from the serial installments *without changes,* probably in the naive expectation of expediting book publication, but Fitzgerald revised or rewrote on the proofs anyhow. The surviving galleys for the last third of Book II and all of Book III are covered with revisions; Fitzgerald cut up most of these galleys and patched them together. Galleys for Book II, Chapters 18–22, and III, 2–7, were so densely revised that it was impossible to correct the type; new galleys were set from typescript. There is no complete set of revised book galleys.

3. Reception

Tender Is the Night was published on 12 April 1934; despite the expectation that had been aroused during Fitzgerald's nine-year pause after *The Great Gatsby,* the reviews of the novel were restrained. In the June number of the *North American Review,* Herschell Brickell mentioned "the kind of violent arguments that have been going on about *Tender Is the Night*";[21] since there was no controversy in print—only disagreement—the "violent argument" presumably raged orally among readers. Disagreement about the merits and flaws of the novel has continued since 1934.

Discussions of the novel habitually return to the initial reception of *Tender,* a topic which provides its own controversy. One of the commonplaces of Fitzgerald criticism is that *Tender* failed in 1934 because the critics ganged up on it and dismissed the novel as politically irrelevant. As Cowley explained in 1951, "It dealt with fashionable life in the 1920s at a time when most readers wanted to forget that they had ever been concerned with frivolities; the new fashion was for novels about destitution and revolt. . . . most reviewers implied that it belonged to the bad old days before the crash."[22] John O'Hara shared Cowley's conclusion:

> . . . after *The Great Gatsby* he had toiled and sweated over *Tender Is the Night,* which I considered far and away his best novel. As a favor to Fitzgerald I had read proof on *Tender Is the Night,* galleys and page proofs, and I was shocked and probably frightened by what the critics and the public had done to it and to him. People from whom he had the right to expect respectful treatment were condescending or worse.[23]

According to this influential interpretation the critics compounded their socio-political prejudice with the obtuseness by claiming to find difficulty with the simple flashback structure. The reviewers were allegedly abetted by the reading public, which rejected Fitzgerald in favor of social tracts. Depending upon whether one is listening to a revisionist or anti-revisionist, the accord between the opinion makers and readers either revealed to Fitzgerald what was wrong with the structure of *Tender,* or their response befuddled his critical judgment so that he subsequently attempted to restructure *Tender* in straight chronology.

Like many biographical-critical explanations of Fitzgerald's literary conduct, these alternatives combine fact with romantic invention. Fitzgerald's most ambitious novel sold disappointingly in its own time; yet three printings totaling 14,595 copies was not a catastrophic sale in 1934. The reception hurt and puzzled Fitzgerald, but it is not demonstrable that he was the victim of a critical conspiracy. The majority of the notices were favorable, and there was little complaint about the setting or the flashback. Some of the mainly favorable reviews patronized Fitzgerald, but critics had patronized him in the Twenties.

Examination of the best selling novels of 1934 provides no support for the notion that readers of the Depression rejected *Tender* because they preferred proletarian fiction: Hervey Allen's *Anthony Adverse,* Caroline Miller's *Lamb in His Bosom* (Pulitzer Prize), Stark Young's *So Red the Rose,* James Hilton's *Good-bye, Mr. Chips,* Margaret Ayers Barnes's *Within This Present,* Sinclair Lewis's *Work of Art,* Phyllis Bottome's *Private Worlds,* Mary Ellen Chase's *Mary Peters,* Alice Tisdale Hobart's *Oil for the Lamps of China,* and Isak Dinesen's *Seven Gothic Tales.* The three top sellers of the year were historical novels, and the number-four novel was Hilton's sentimental story about a schoolmaster.

People who lament the commercial failure of *Tender* usually ignore the circumstance that Fitzgerald had never written a prodigious seller: *This Side of Paradise* sold about 41,000 copies in 1920; *The Beautiful and Damned* sold about

50,000 copies in 1922; and *The Great Gatsby* about 23,000 copies in 1925. During his lifetime Fitzgerald was much better known as a magazine story writer than as a novelist.

Four days after publication, John Chamberlain commented in the *New York Times* on the responses of his fellow reviewers:

> The critical reception of F. Scott Fitzgerald's "Tender Is the Night" might serve as the basis for one of those cartoons on "Why Men Go Mad." No two reviews were alike; no two had the same tone. Some seemed to think that Mr. Fitzgerald was writing about his usual jazz age boys and girls; others that he had a "timeless" problem on his hands. And some seemed to think that Doctor Diver's collapse was insufficiently documented.[24]

Of twenty-four reviews by influential critics or by critics appearing in influential American periodicals, nine were favorable, six were unfavorable, and nine were mixed.[25] Gilbert Seldes who was Fitzgerald's friend, recognized *Tender* as "a great novel": "He has gone behind generations, old or new, and created his own image of human beings. And in doing so has stepped again to his natural place at the head of American writers of our time."

Three reviews commented on the flashback:

> C. Harley Grattan, "The integral significance of the opening pages of the book has been missed by most reviewers."
>
> Edward Weeks, "Don't make up your mind until you have read past page 151!"
>
> John Chamberlain, "At this point one could almost guarantee that 'Tender Is the Night' is going to be a failure. But, as a matter of fact, the novel does not really begin until Rosemary is more or less out of the way."

Cowley's *New Republic* review analyzed Fitzgerald's apparent indecision between writing a psychological or a social novel—Fitzgerald thought of it as a dramatic novel. Then Cowley offered a theory that acquired currency: that as the novel developed through its several versions during the years of writing, the early sections crystallized so that Fitzgerald was unable to unify them with later sections.

Two reviews complained about the expatriate material from the Twenties. The unsigned *News-Week* review was headlined "A Sinful, Ginful Tale" and noted that "it is a long time since the decay of American expatriates on the Riviera was hot news." In the *Daily Worker*, the journal of the American Communist Party, Philip Rahv admonished: "Dear Mr. Fitzgerald, you can't hide from a hurricane under a beach umbrella."

Seven reviewers (Mary Colum, Henry Seidel Canby, Clifton Fadiman, J. Donald Adams, Horace Gregory, William Troy, and Edith Walton) expressed reservations about the credibility of Dick Diver and his crack-up. In the *New Yorker* Clifton Fadiman cited the absence of a psychoanalytic approach to Diver:

> Dick's rapid acceptance of his failure, for instance, is not convincing; there must have been some fundamental weakness in his early youth to account for his defeatism. . . . The events of the narrative, tragic as they are, are insufficient to motivate his downfall. It is the failure to reach far, far back into his characters' lives that helps prevent this novel from being the first-rate work of fiction we have been expecting from Mr. Fitzgerald.

Fadiman also complained about the sloppy copy-editing and listed thirteen errors. Henry Seidel Canby in the *Saturday Review of Literature* also criticized Fitzgerald for inadequate or unclear causality:

> What begins as a study of a subtle relationship ends as the accelerating decline into nothingness of Dr. Driver [*sic*]—not for no good reason, but for too many reasons, no one of which is dominant. This book may be life with its veil over causality, but it is not art which should pierce that veil.

J. Donald Adams's review in the Sunday *New York Times Book Review* charged that Nicole and Rosemary were unconvincing and that Dick's collapse was contrived. The following day Chamberlain interrupted his *Times* review of Faulkner's *Dr. Martino* to defend the effectiveness of Diver's characterization:

> It seemed to us that Mr. Fitzgerald proceeded accurately, step by step, with just enough documentation to keep the drama from being misty, but without destroying the suggestiveness that added to the horror lurking behind the surface. . . . And when he does collapse, his youth is gone, it is too late to catch up with the Germans who have been studying new cases for years. This seems to us to be a sufficient exercise in cause-and-effect. Compared to the motivation in Faulkner, it is logic personified.

The two reviews in the papers in Fitzgerald's hometown, St Paul, Minnesota were strongly negative.[26] Both James Gray ("This big, sprawling, undisciplined, badly coordinated book") and H. A. MacMillan ("the obscure manner in which the narrative is developed") denounced the structure. The unsigned review in the *Princeton Alumni Weekly* commented on the structural disagreements engendered by the novel: "*Tender Is the Night* lacks unity in the ordinary sense of the word; the debate of the reviewers is concerned with whether or not Mr. Fitzgerald has achieved a unity less conventional but not less serviceable."[27]

The most thorough defense of Fitzgerald's structure appeared in the *Modern Monthly*, a Marxist journal, some three months after the publication of *Tender*. C. Hartley Grattan observed:

> The integral significance of the opening pages of the book has been missed by most reviewers. Almost to a man they have complained that the stress laid upon Rosemary, the beautiful cinema star, is unjustified by the future action of the story, that the pages devoted to building her up are really wasted effort, and that they "throw the reader off." Rather I should say that in these pages Fitzgerald is presenting the type of girl who, in the past, has always been foreordained to absorption into the world of his characters. . . . Seen through his eyes, however, what glamour remains can legitimately be exploited and by the same token, the tragedy of its actuality can be all the more accentuated.

After quoting Fitzgerald's explication of Nicole's spending habits ("For her sake trains began their run at Chicago . . ."), Grattan concluded his review:

> This is perceptive writing and I should like to stress for the benefit of those austere individuals who see in the bourgeois world nothing but filth and corruption the significance of the words "feverish bloom" and "grace." Only a person utterly insensitive to the grace and beauty of the way of life open to the leisured will fail to see that even in decay these people are infinitely charming, insidiously beguiling to all but sea-green incorruptibles.

The attacks on the verisimilitude of Diver's decline probably troubled Fitzgerald more than anything else the critics wrote. On 23 April he sent H. L. Mencken—who had not reviewed *Tender*—an eloquent defense of the novel's construction.

> . . . I would like to say in regard to my book that there was a deliberate intention in every part of it except the first. The first part, the romantic introduction, was too long and too elaborated, largely because of the fact that it had been written over a series of years with varying plans, but everything else in the book conformed to a <u>definite intention</u> and if I had to start to write it again tomorrow I would adopt the same plan, irrespective of the fact of whether I had, in this case, brought it off or not brought it off. That is what most of the critics fail to understand (outside of the fact that they fail to recognize and identify anything in the book) that the motif of the "dying fall" was absolutely deliberate and did not come from any diminution of vitality, but from a definite plan.
>
> That particular trick is one that Ernest Hemmingway and I worked out—probably from Conrad's preface to "The Nigger"—and it has been the greatest

"credo" in my life, ever since I decided that I would rather be an artist than a careerist. I would rather impress my image (even though an image the size of a nickel) upon the soul of a people than be known, except in so far as I have my natural obligation to my family—to provide for them. I would as soon be anonymous as Rimbaud, if I could feel that I had accomplished that purpose—and that is no sentimental yapping about being disinterested. It is simply that having once found the intensity of art, nothing else that can happen in life can again seem as important as the creative process.[28]

This statement indicates that Fitzgerald's subsequent proposal to reorganize the novel resulted from his desire to reinforce the documentation of Diver's decline by putting together all the information about him—not from his decision that the flashback structure was confusing (see Section 4).

Fitzgerald took satisfaction from the anonymous 1935 review in the *Journal of Nervous and Mental Disease,* which concluded: "an achievement which no student of the psychobiological sources of human behavior, and of its particular social correlates extant today, can afford not to read."[29]

Tender Is the Night was published in England in September 1934, and the located reviews[30] resembled the American reception. D. W. Harding asserted in *Scrutiny* that Fitzgerald had not supplied any cause for Diver's crack-up; yet he admits that he had been moved against his will by Diver's fate, and he concludes by echoing Fitzgerald's style: ". . . I am prepared to be told that this attempt at analysis is itself childish—an attempt to assure myself that the magician really didn't cut the lady's head off, did he? I still believe there was a trick in it." The trick usually goes under the name of genius.

Reviewers who questioned the convincingness of Diver's crack-up may really have been troubled by the chronological flaws in *Tender*. It is difficult for the reader to gauge the step-by-step deterioration of the hero because the time signals are inadequate and contradictory. . . .[31]

4. "The Author's Final Version"

Fitzgerald brooded over the still birth of *Tender Is the Night* and came to blame the opening section written from Rosemary's point of view. Shortly after publication he inscribed a copy for novelist Joseph Hergesheimer:

Dear Joe:

You talked to someone who didn't like this book—I don't know who, or why they didn't. But I could tell in the Stafford Bar that afternoon when you said it was "almost impossible to write a book about an actress" that you hadn't read it thru because the actress fades out of it in the first third + is only a catalytic agent.

Sometime will you open it at the middle, perhaps at page 155 + read on for five or ten minutes—? If it were not for my sincere admiration of your judgement I would forgo this plea. You were not the only one repelled by the apparent triviality of the opening—I.would like this favorite among my books to have another chance in the chrystal light of your taste

Ever yrs

F. Scott Fitzgerald

Page 155—et seq.[32]

In May 1936 Fitzgerald wired publisher Bennett Cerf:

WOULD YOU CONSIDER PUBLISHING TENDER IS THE NIGHT IN THE MODERN LIBRARY IF I MADE CERTAIN CHANGES TOWARD THE END WHICH I SEE NOW ARE ESSENTIAL COMMA IT WOULD MAKE ALL THE DIFFERENCE IN THE SPLIT UP OF THE TWO PRINCIPAL CHARACTERS STOP OR DO YOU THINK THAT ONCE PUBLISHED A NOVEL IS FOREVER CRYSTALIZED PLEASE ANSWER CAMBRIDGE ARMS CHARLES STREET BALTIMORE MARYLAND....[33]

Cerf's response is unknown, but in August Fitzgerald sent him a general explanation of proposed alterations:

Dear Bennett:

The revision job would take the form, to a large extent, of a certain new alignment of the scenes—without changing their order in any case. Some such line as this:

That the parts instead of being one, two, and three (they were one, two, three, and four in the magazine serial) would include in several cases sudden stops and part headings which would be to some extent explanatory; certain pages would have to be inserted bearing merely heads. Part two, for example, should say in a terse and graceful way that the scene is now back on the Riviera in the fall after these events have taken place, or that, This brings us up to where Rosemary first encounters the Divers. Those examples are not accurate to my intention nor are they at all couched as I would have them, but that's the general idea. (Do you remember the number of subheads I used in "This Side of Paradise"—at that time a novel experiment, the germ of which I borrowed from Bernard Shaw's preface headings to his plays; indeed that was one of the few consciously original things in "This Side of Paradise.")

There would be certain changes but I would supply the equivalent line lengths. I have not my plan with me; it seems to be in Baltimore. But I know how printing costs are. It was evolved to have a very minimum of replacement.

There is not more than one complete sentence that I want to eliminate, one that has offended many people and that I admit is out of Dick's character: "I never did go in for making love to dry loins." It is a strong line but definitely offensive. These are all the changes I contemplated with in addition some minor spelling corrections such as would disturb nothing but what was within the printed line. There will be no pushing over of paragraphs or disorganization of the present set-up except in the aforesaid inserted pages. I don't want to change anything in the book but sometimes by a single word change one can throw a new emphasis or give a new value to the exact same scene or setting.[34]

At this point he intended to retain the flashback structure but wanted to insert signals alerting the reader to narrative shifts. Again, Cerf's response has not been located, but he obviously did not encourage the project.

When Fitzgerald knew that his Metro-Goldwyn-Mayer contract would not be renewed, he wrote Perkins in December 1938 proposing several publishing ideas intended to revive his reputation—including an omnibus volume of three novels:

> But I am especially concerned about <u>Tender</u>—that book is not dead. The <u>depth</u> of its appeal exists—I meet people constantly who have the same exclusive attachment to it as others had to <u>Gatsby</u> and <u>Paradise</u>, people who identified themselves with Dick Diver. It's great fault is that the <u>true</u> beginning—the young psychiatrist in Switzerland—is tucked away in the middle of the book. If pages 151–212 were taken from their present place and put at the start the improvement in appeal would be enormous. In fact the mistake was noted and suggested by a dozen reviewers. To shape up the ends of that change would, of course, require changes in half a dozen other pages.[35]

Perkins tactfully declined, and there was no further discussion of the revision.

At the time of Fitzgerald's death on 21 December 1940 his books included a copy of *Tender Is the Night* in which he had written on the front endpaper: "This is the <u>final version</u> of the book as I would like it." This disbound book reorders the chapters in straight chronological order, beginning with Dick Diver's arrival at Zurich in 1917. The plan for restructuring the novel into five sections is in Fitzgerald's *Notebooks*:

Analysis of Tender:
  I. Case History 151–212 61 pps. (change moon) p. 212
  II. Rosemary's Angle 3–104 101 pps. P. 3
  III. Casualties 104–148, 213–224 55 pps. (-2) (120 + 121)
  IV. Escape 225–306 82 pps.
  V. The Way Home 306–408 103 pps. (-8) (332–341)[36]

Plan of Cowley's Restructured Edition

First Edition Corresponds to "The Author's Final Version"

Book I:	1	Book II:	2
	2		3
	3		4
	4		5
	5		6
	6		7
	7		8
	8		9
	9		10
	10		11
	11		12
	12		13
	13	Book III:	1
	14		2
	15		3
	16		4
	17		5
	18		6
	19		7
	20		8
	21		9
	22		10
	23		11
	24	Book III:	12
	25		13
Book II:	1	Book I:	1
	2		2
	3		3
	4		4
	5		5
	6		6
	7		7
	8		8
	9		9
	10	Book II:	1
	11	Book III:	14

	12	Book III 15 & Book IV:1
	13	Book IV 1
	14	2
	15	3
	16	4
	17	5
	18	6
	19	7
	20	8
	21	9
	22	10
	23	11
Book III:	1	Book V: 1
	2	2
	3	3
	4	4
	5	5
	6	6
	7	7
	8	8
	9	9
	10	10
	11	11
	12	12
	13	13

Fitzgerald made some forty corrections or revisions in this copy. . . .[37] On p. 160 of Book II, Chapter 5, Fitzgerald wrote: "This is my mark to say that I have made final corrections up to this point."[38] The note suggests that he lost interest in the endeavor—or at least that he broke off revising and never resumed.

In 1951, during the early stage of the Fitzgerald revival, Scribners published Malcolm Cowley's edition of *Tender* "With the Author's Final Revisions." In addition to Fitzgerald's revisions, Cowley corrected scores of proofreading errors, stating rightly that the errors in the first edition "had a cumulative effect on the readers and ended by distracting their attention. . . ."[39]

In his 1951 introduction Cowley claimed that the revised edition improved *Tender:* "By rearranging the story in chronological order Fitzgerald tied it together. He sacrificed a brilliant beginning and all the element of mystery, but there is no escaping the judgment that he ended with a better constructed and more effective novel."[40] The revised edition had a limited impact, receiving a few unenthusiastic reviews. Charles Poore commented in the *New York Times* that "It takes a case history that he had transmuted into art and prosaically tries to bring it back closer to what might be a case historian's heart's desire."[41] Budd Schulberg concurred in the *New York Times Book Review:* "Logic and clarity have been gained, but at the cost of irony, beauty and a dramatic suspense. . . . I believe that Fitzgerald's first esthetic instincts were sound, as usual, and that he was panicked by failure and disappointment."[42] John Chamberlain, who had defended the novel in 1934, gave the Cowley redaction one sentence: "The reshuffling of the components of 'Tender is the Night' into more strictly chronological order does improve the novel."[43] The publication of "The Author's Final Version" was not a literary event.

Although Ernest Hemingway had expressed strong criticism of *Tender* in 1934, he had come to admire the "magic" of the prose. When he read the revised edition in 1951, he wrote Cowley:

> Scribner's sent the new edition of Tender Is The Night yesterday and I have read it until page 206.
>
> Truly I did not want the reforms to turn out as I was afraid they might. But I am afraid the whole idea was just a bad idea of Scott's.
>
> In straight chronological order the book loses the magic completely. Starting off with a case history there is no secret to discover and no mystery and all sense of a seemingly magical world (the world of Sara and Gerald Murphy) being destroyed by something that is unknown and lost.
>
> By the time the bath-room incident comes off the reader knows everything which was to come as a shock. In the form it is now it is simply a pathological and not a nice one at that. It has all the dullness of all stories of the insane and where it had the charm of the strange mixture that was Scott it is now about as much fun to read as The Snake Pit.
>
> I know you did it for Scott and it was what he wanted. But I think if he had been completely sane I could have argued him out of it.
>
> It is just like takeing the wings off a butterfly and arrangeing them so he can fly straight as the bee flies and loseing all the dust that makes the colors that makes the butterfly magical in the process.[44]

In the once-influential *The Rhetoric of Fiction* (1961), Wayne C. Booth made a case for restructuring *Tender:*

> The achievement of the revision is, in short, to correct a fault of over-distancing, a fault that springs from a method appropriate to other works at other times but not to the tragedy Fitzgerald wanted to write. His true effect could be obtained only by repudiating much of what was being said by important

critics of fiction about point of view and developing a clean, direct, old-fashioned presentation of his hero's initial pre-eminence and gradual decline.[45]

The defenders of the revised version miss the point about how *Tender Is the Night* was written—how every serious work of fiction is written. As Fitzgerald wrote he knew what he had already written and what he intended to write next. The circuitry of the novel became fixed as it grew on paper. Everything connected. To shuffle the chapters is to break the circuits.

When Fredson Bowers and Matthew J. Bruccoli were planning their interrupted critical edition of *Tender Is the Night* in 1989, Bowers prepared an evaluation of the claims that "The Author's Final Version" embodied Fitzgerald's best and final intentions. The Bowers document was not written for publication, but it is so powerfully reasoned that sections merit inclusion here:

> Literary history has other instances of authors being influenced by outside opinion to change their original conceptions of the presentation or content of a work. It is interesting that not one of these has gone unchallenged by posterity. Self-censorship is sometimes a prominent reason for a change in authorial expression, but closely related to this is influence of outside opinion that has succeeded in convincing an author, however reluctantly, that if his book is to succeed to his hopes it must undergo some major alteration. An author's reliance on such outside opinion as to a book's reception instead of his own creative force that produced the version under criticism has not always been found—as remarked—to be in his ultimate best interest. Most authors are right in the end when they trust to their instincts and their original creative plan. We may take this as applying with particular weight to Fitzgerald's acceptance of what the critics believed to be a serious flaw. The depth of his acceptance of the flashback as "a serious fault" cannot be estimated—how much he convinced himself in his desire for a reversal of the book's initial reception remains unknowable. What is of textual importance to an editor is the distinction between the internal forces that generated Fitzgerald's recognition of the desirability of removing the lengthy incident of the governess at Innsbruck and the external forces that (post-creation) led him to want to ensure the future success of the novel by convincing himself that the critics' view of the flashback was correct. . . .
>
> One other consideration is appropriate. When a narrative has been structured in a particular way, the balance of the treatment rests on it accordingly. The account of the earlier events in Switzerland and of the ironic consequences up to the opening on the beach is written with the technique of a catching-up of the narrative. Merely to rearrange the sequence of events to a chronological order does violence to the balance of the opening and then in

a sense réprise in the original book. There can be little question that if Fitzgerald had reordered the events at some stage in the composition, even so late as the book's galley proofs, the early events would have been differently narrated, since there would be no reliance on the reader's understanding of them resulting from his view of the Divers in their introduction on the Riviera. *Tender* is not so mechanically conceived and executed as to yield to post-creation restructuring in such an important matter that has dictated the treatment both of start and of middle. In the sense of "might-have-been" we can envisage a novel that Fitzgerald himself had composed, or revised, to read in chronological order, but it would be a fundamentally different novel from what results in the Cowley edition when the middle is bodily transferred to the beginning without the necessary reworking. This is no doubt special pleading, but the concept is true. Scribners exhibited the right attitude when the firm re-issued in paperback the originally conceived (and in fact the only published) version as a substitute for Cowley's extrapolation of Fitzgerald's letter to Perkins and his note in his private copy. This is one instance where an author's own version must be respected despite his after-the-event wishes. To choose the Cowley ordering as the base-text for a critical edition would be an act of violence to the inner coherence of authorial conception and execution. The pressure that Fitzgerald felt to popularize his novel was illegitimate. His capitulation to what he conceived of as public opinion, no matter how rationalized, should not be permitted to tear apart the living fabric of the novel as he wrote it.[46]

The longevity of "The Author's Final Version" was decided by reader preference. Scribners reprinted it through 1959 but let it go out of print to no outcry.[47] Cowley's edition was first published in England in 1953 and reprinted in the widely distributed Penguin paperbacks between 1955 and 1978. "The Author's Final Version" is out of print in America and England in 1995.

Notes

1. Here a brief introductory paragraph, referencing the purpose and functions of the volume, has been deleted. Ed.

2. 1 May 1925. *F. Scott Fitzgerald: A Life in Letters,* edited by Matthew J. Bruccoli with the assistance of Judith S. Baughman (New York: Scribners, 1994), p. 108. Fitzgerald's letters and manuscripts are transcribed here as written.

3. Ibid., pp. 140–141. In January 1925 Dorothy Ellingson, a sixteen-year-old San Francisco girl, murdered her mother; Fitzgerald knew of this crime only from newspaper reports.

4. American expatriates Gerald (1888–1964) and Sara (1883–1975) Murphy owned "Villa America" at Cap d'Antibes, a partial model for Diver's "Villa Diana." Some of the Divers' "social qualities" were inspired by the Murphys; however, "the circumstances of the

Divers' lives" were drawn from the Fitzgeralds. Here and in subsequent sections of this essay M.J.B. directs readers' attention to explanatory notes, appendices, or other sections within the volume for additional information. I have examined such notes, appendices, or sections, and I have provided brief summaries of essential content in Bruccoli's words as much as possible. Ed.

5. The American humorist and short story-writer Ring W. Lardner (1885–1933), like Abe Grant, was an alcoholic. Bruccoli notes that Fitzgerald's memorial essay "Ring" (*New Republic* [11 October 1933]: 254–255) "expresses regret that Lardner undervalued and partly wasted his genius." Ed.

6. In appendix D (pp. 213–261) of *Reader's Companion,* George Anderson's "F. Scott Fitzgerald's Use of Story Strippings in *Tender Is the Night*" lists thirty-seven stories from which Fitzgerald stripped themes, descriptions, or phrases that he included in *Tender Is the Night.* Among the most memorable is his description of Paris, where in the twilight "the fire-red, gas-blue, ghost-green signs began to shine smokily through the tranquil rain," a passage taken from "Babylon Revisited" (1931). Ed.

7. Ca. June 1929. *Dear Scott / Dear Max: The Fitzgerald-Perkins Correspondence.*, edited by John Kuehl and Jackson R. Bryer (New York: Scribners, 1971), p. 156.

8. Ca. 15 January 1932. *Life in Letters,* p. 208.

9. *F. Scott Fitzgerald's Ledger: A Facimile,* introduction by Bruccoli (Washington, D.C.: Bruccoli Clark / NCR Microcard Editions, 1972), p. 186.

10. *Life in Letters,* p. 235.

11. 11 March 1935. *Life in Letters,* pp. 277–278.

12. To Maxwell Perkins, 15 March 1934. *Correspondence of F. Scott Fitzgerald,* edited by Bruccoli and Margaret M. Duggan (New York: Random House, 1980), p. 332.

13. Scribners Archives, Princeton University Library.

14. Here M.J.B. has directed the reader to the "Emendations" section of the *Reader's Companion* volume (pp. 159–185). Included there are emended readings for the 1934 edited text; rejected readings in the 1934 first printing (the base text); readings that have not been emended (identified by *stet*) for which textual notes or cross references are provided; omitted punctuation marks; and unchanged words. Emended readings that have explanatory notes are also indicated, and Malcolm Cowley's emendations in his 1951 "Author's Final Version" are so identified. Ed.

15. M.J.B. refers readers to an explanatory note offering Perkins's rationale for suggesting Fitzgerald consider cutting the shooting in Gare Saint-Lazare: "I thought you might conceivably cut out the shooting in the station. The purpose would be only that as soon as people get to Dick Diver their interest in the book, and the perception of its importance increases some thirty to forty percent. People do read a book differently from a serial though...." Fitzgerald saw the scene as an important part to his originally conceived plan. Ed.

16. A Bruccoli note explains Fitzgerald's rejection of Perkins's request to cut the Minghetti-Lady Caroline episode. Fitzgerald considered it "absolutely necessary for the unity of the book" and to show that although Diver was ruined, he should not be made

to appear "ineffectual." This scene was essential, Fitzgerald believed, to reconstruct Diver's personality that should "be viewed as a unit throughout." Ed.

17. M.J.B. refers the reader to Appendix C of the *Reader's Companion,* which includes material Fitzgerald deleted from his magazine account of Abe in the Ritz Bar after he returns to Paris rather than continuing his journey to America. The magazine gives a fuller sense of Abe's time in the bar from morning until late afternoon or early evening, replete with descriptions of the physical appearance of the famous bar, specific drinks (even a derivation of Abe's "Dashdeller" pick-me-up), diverse patrons, the conduct of the bartender and waiters and Collis Clay, and the onset of Abe's drunkenness as the day tends toward evening. According to M.J.B. Fitzgerald made this and subsequent excisions because he thought "they slowed the narrative." Ed.

18. Fitzgerald deleted a scene, printed in Appendix C of the *Reader's Companion,* that occurs during Diver's return voyage to Europe, following his father's funeral. When a young man jumps from the ship into the cold sea, the act does not surprise Diver, who had predicted to Albert McKisco that the man would likely "commit a crime of violence." The young man is rescued, relatively unharmed, and returns to the ship's lounge, where he is joined by Diver. Because the young man is denied alcohol by the lounge bartender, Diver, despite his attempts to recover from a "bender," promises to have sent to his own cabin a drink that he will send on to the young man. There is another deleted scene in which McKisco showily works on deck in front of other passengers and is disturbed by the presence of "a well-known woman novelist." Fitzgerald likely saw both scenes as what he often termed "side shows." Ed.

19. Fitzgerald greatly condensed a scene from the magazine version (printed in Appendix C of the *Reader's Companion*) in which Dick encounters a woman in Innsbruck, "Alice," a presumed governess of the children of Barker McKibben, who had been with Tommy Barban during Dick's reunion with Tommy in Munich. He had included in the magazine version Dick's thoughts about the seemingly prescribed conventions with which he and "Alice" conducted their conversation, an intimate scene during which McKibben discovers Dick and Alice kissing and reveals that Alice is, in fact, his mistress. In this version Alice chides McKibben for his jealousy and threatens to return to America, as their argument continues in the presence of McKibben's wife, whom Dick attempts to comfort, ultimately concluding that such scenes as he witnesses played by the McKibbens "were only pale reflections of what had been played many times with much more poignancy in their hearts." Ed.

20. *Life in Letters,* p. 250.

21. Pp. 569–570.

22. Introduction, *Tender Is the Night: With the Author's Final Revisions* (New York: Scribners, 1951), p. x.

23. "Hello Hollywood Good-Bye," *Holiday* (May 1968): 54–55, 125–126, 128–129.

24. "Books of the Times" (16 April 1934): 15.

25. – Mary M. Colum, *Forum and Century* (April 1934): 219–223; + Burton Rascoe, *Esquire* (April 1934): 133, 159; + Edward Weeks, *Atlantic Monthly* (April 1934): 17; +

Harry Hanson, *New York World-Telegram* (12 April 1934): 25; + Gilbert Seldes, *New York Evening Journal* (12 April 1934): 23; ± Hal Borland, *Philadelphia Public Ledger* (13 April 1934): 9; + John Chamberlain, *New York Times* (13 April 1934): 17; ± Lewis Gannett, *New York Herald Tribune* (13 April 1934): 15; ± Fanny Butcher, *Chicago Tribune* (14 April 1934): 10; – Henry Seidel Canby, *Saturday Review of Literature* (14 April 1934): 630–631; ± Clifton Fadiman, *New Yorker* (14 April 1934): 112–115; – Edith H. Walton, *New York Sun* (14 April 1934): 30; ± J. Donald Adams, *New York Times Book Review* (15 April 1934): 7; ± Horace Gregory, *New York Herald Tribune Books* (15 April 1934): 5; + Cameron Rogers, *San Francisco Chronicle* (15 April 1934): 4D; + John Chamberlain, *New York Times* (16 April 1934): 15; ± *Time* (16 April 1934): 77; – Philip Rahv, *Daily Worker* (5 May 1934): 7; – William Troy, *Nation* (9 May 1934): 539–540; + Herschel Brickell, *North American Review* (June 1934): 569–570; ± Edith H. Walton, *Forum and Century* (June 1934): iv–v; ± Malcolm Cowley, *New Republic* (6 June 1934): 105–106; + C. Hartley Grattan, *Modern Monthly* (July 1934): 375–377; – Gertrude Diamant, *American Mercury* (October 1934): 249–251; – *NewsWeek* (14 April 1934): 39–40. Most of these reviews are reprinted in *F. Scott Fitzgerald: The Critical Reception,* edited by Jackson R. Bryer (New York: Franklin, 1978).

26. Gray, *St. Paul Daily News* (12 April 1934): 1, 8; MacMillan, *St. Paul Daily News* (22 April 1934), magazine section, 4.

27. (4 May 1934): 665.

28. *Life in Letters,* pp. 255–256.

29. (July 1935): 115–117.

30. Peter Quennell, *New Statesman & Nation* (28 April 1934): 642; E. B. C. Jones, *New Statesman & Nation* (22 September 1934): 364–366; D. W. Harding, *Scrutiny* (December 1934): 316–319; *Spectator* (21 September 1934): 410; *Times Literary Supplement* (27 September 1934): 652.

31. M.J.B. suggests in the "Time Scheme" section of *Reader's Companion* that despite the debate over the 1925–1917–1925 flashback, "the structural flaw in *Tender* is the blurred time scheme from summer 1925 to summer 1929." Therefore, he contends, an editor of a critical edition must emend the errors and inconsistencies of time in order to ensure that events of the text clearly conform to the 1925–1929 chronology Fitzgerald stipulated in the first edition. "The key time signals," Bruccoli says, "are 236.18 ("this past year and a half on the Zugersee") and 238.3–4 ("For eighteen months now he lived at the clinic"). Eighteen months after Christmas 1925 in the previous chapter places the time of Book II, Chapter 14, in summer 1927, allowing a month or two for the Divers' move to Switzerland. This calculation fits the 1928 date, M.J.B. adds, "that Fitzgerald stipulates in the Rome chapters." He argues also that those readers who believe that Diver departs the Riviera in 1930 ignore the fact "that the crash (29 October 1929) is never mentioned in the novel" and that "the financial data in the closing chapters are all related to the boom. . . . The story," he adds, "ends in July 1929." Ed.

32. University of Virginia Library. See *in their time / 1920–1940* (Bloomfield Hills, Mich.: and Columbia, S.C.: Bruccoli Clark, 1977), # 118.

33. 16 May 1936. *Life in Letters,* pp. 300–301. See Andrew B. Myers, "'I Am Used to Being Dunned': F. Scott Fitzgerald and the Modern Library," *Columbia Library Columns* (February 1976): 28–39.

34. 13 August 1936. *Life in Letters,* pp. 306–307.

35. 24 December 1938. Ibid., p. 374.

36. P. 212 of the first edition is the last page of Book II, chapter 10, and is marked for deletion in Fitzgerald's copy. Pages 332–341 describe the Divers' visit to the Minghetti establishment at Book III, chapter 4, but are not marked for deletion in Fitzgerald's copy. The only *moon* between page 151 and page 212 is at 158.11: "moon over the mountain."

37. Here Bruccoli directs the reader to Appendix B that includes Fitzgerald's revisions of his marked copy for "The Author's Final Version." See pp. 198–200 of *Reader's Companion*. Ed.

38. Princeton University Library.

39. Introduction, p. xiii.

40. Ibid., p. xiv-xv.

41. "Books of the Times" (15 November 1951): 26.

42. "Prodded by Pride and Desperation" (18 November 1951): 5, 38.

43. "A Reviewer's Notebook," *Freeman* (19 November 1951): 121–122.

44. 10 November 1951. Bruccoli, *Fitzgerald and Hemingway: A Dangerous Friendship* (New York: Carroll and Graf, 1994), p. 224.

45. (Chicago: University of Chicago Press, 1961), p. 195.

46. Bruccoli Collection, Thomas Cooper Library, University of South Carolina.

47. The plates for the revised edition were inadvertently used for three printings in the Contemporary Classic / Scribner Library series in 1970–1971.

The Love of the Last Tycoon

Preparation and Composition

Screenwriting never satisfied Fitzgerald—even at $1,250 per week—and in 1938 he began writing Maxwell Perkins about two possible book projects: a "modern novel" and an expansion of the four medieval "Count of Darkness" stories.[1] On 4 January 1939—after he knew that MGM would not renew his contract—Fitzgerald wrote Perkins about his writing plans for 1939: "if periods of three or four months are going to be possible in the next year or so I would much rather do a modern novel. One of those novels that can only be written at the moment and when one is full of the idea. . . . I think it would be a quicker job to write a novel like that between 50 and 60,000 words long than to do a thorough revision job with an addition of 15,000 words on 'Phillipe.'"[2]

In April 1939 Fitzgerald took Zelda on a disastrous trip to Cuba, and ended up drying out in a New York hospital. At this time he discussed his writing plans with Maxwell Perkins, Harold Ober, and Charles Scribner. The earliest clear evidence that Fitzgerald was working on the novel that became *The Last Tycoon* is his 22 May 1939 letter to Perkins, five months after the termination of his MGM contract, although the purpose of this letter was to insist that he was *not* writing a Hollywood novel: "Just had a letter from Charlie Scribner. . . . He seemed under the full conviction that the novel was about Hollywood and I am in terror that

---

"*The Love of the Last Tycoon*: Preparation and Composition" is chapter 3 in Matthew J. Bruccoli's *"The Last of the Novelists": F. Scott Fitzgerald and* The Last Tycoon (Carbondale & Edwardsville: Southern Illinois University Press / London & Amsterdam: Feffer and Simons, 1977), pp. 22–39; 158–160. Reprinted with permission of Arlyn Bruccoli for the Matthew J. Bruccoli literary estate. The definitive edition (and study) of Fitzgerald's *Tycoon* is F. Scott Fitzgerald, *The Love of the Last Tycoon: A Western*, edited by Matthew J. Bruccoli., volume 2 of *The Cambridge Edition of the Works of F. Scott Fitzgerald* (Cambridge, New York, & Melbourne: Cambridge University Press, 1993). Bruccoli concluded that Fitzgerald's preferred title for his "work in progress" was *The Love of the Last Tycoon: A Western*, the only title on a page of holograph notes headed *Title* that Fitzgerald did not cross out.

this mis-information may have been disseminated to the literary columns. If I ever gave any such impression it is entirely false: I said that the novel was about some things that had happened to me in the last two years. It is distinctly *not* about Hollywood (and if it were it is the last impression that I would want to get about.)"[3] The novel was, of course, about Hollywood; but Fitzgerald was concerned that an announcement of his material would make it difficult for him to find movie work. A week later Fitzgerald informed Ober of his plans.

First, I *have* blocked out my novel completely with a rough sketch of every episode and event and character so that under proper circumstances I could begin writing it tomorrow. It is a short novel about fifty thousand words long and should take me three to four months.

However, for reasons of income tax I feel I should be more secure before I launch into such a venture—*but* it will divide easily into five thousand word lengths and *Collier's* might take a chance on it where the *Post* would not. They might at least be promised a first look at it when it's finished—possibly some time late in the Fall.[4]

The idea that *Collier's* might be interested in serializing the novel resulted from the circumstance that in May 1939 Fitzgerald had satisfactorily revised an old story, "Thumbs Up," for *Collier's* and had corresponded with Kenneth Littauer, the fiction editor, about a story Sheilah Graham had written.

In July 1939 Ober declined to make an advance against an unsold story, and Fitzgerald broke with him. There is no further correspondence between them about the novel, and Fitzgerald pressed Perkins into service as his New York spokesman in his dealings with Littauer. On 18 July Fitzgerald wrote to Littauer proposing an advance of $750 for first refusal on the novel and some short stories.

I was of course delighted to finish off the Civil War story ["Thumbs Up"] to your satisfaction at last—I may say to my satisfaction also, because the last version *felt* right. And after twenty months of moving pictures it was fun to be back at prose writing again. That has been the one bright spot in a situation you may have heard of from Harold Ober: that I have been laid up and writing in bed since the first of May, and I am only just up and dressed.

As I told your Mr. Wilkinson when he telephoned, the first thing I did when I had to quit pictures for awhile was to block out my novel (a short one the size of *Gatsby*) and made the plan on a basis of 2500 word units. The block-out is to be sure that I can take it up or put it down in as much time as is allowed between picture work and short stories. I will never again sign a long picture contract, no matter *what* the inducement: most of the profit when one overworks goes to doctors and nurses.

Meanwhile I am finishing a 4500 word piece designed for your pages. It should go off to you airmail Saturday night, because I am going back to the studios for a short repair job Monday.

I would like to send the story *directly to you,* which amounts to a virtual split with Ober. This is regrettable after twenty years of association but it had better be masked under the anonymity of "one of those things." Harold is a fine man and has been a fine agent and the fault is mine. Through one illness he backed me with a substantial amount of money (all paid back to him now with Hollywood gold), but he is not prepared to do that again with growing boys to educate—and failing this, I would rather act for a while as my own agent in the short story, just as I always have with Scribner's. But I much prefer, both for his sake and mine, that my sending you the story direct should be a matter *between you and me.* For the fact to reach him through your office might lead to an unpleasant rather than a pleasant cleavage of an old relationship. I am writing him *later in the week* making the formal break on terms that will be understood between us, and I have no doubt that in some ways he will probably welcome it. Relationships have an unfortunate way of wearing out, like most things in this world.

Would you be prepared, in return for an agreement or contract for *first look at the novel* and at *a specified number of short stories in a certain time,* to advance me $750., by wire on receipt of this letter—which will be even before the story reaches you Monday? This is a principal factor in the matter at the moment as these three months of illness have got me into a mess with income tax and insurance problems. When you get this will you wire me Yes or No, because if you can't, I can probably start studio work Friday. This may be against your general principles—from my angle I am offering you rather a lot for no great sum.

P.S. If this meets your favorable consideration the money should be wired to the Bank of America, Culver City. If not would you wire me an answer anyhow because my determination to handle my magazine relationship myself is quite final.

The novel will be just short of 50,000 words.[5]

Littauer's reply has not been located, but he obviously rejected Fitzgerald's proposition. (Some of the gaps in the Fitzgerald/Littauer correspondence can be accounted for by telephone calls.) The short story has not been identified, but was probably "Discard," which Littauer declined on 28 July as "too elliptical or something." During the summer and fall of 1939 Fitzgerald unsuccessfully submitted other stories to *Collier's*, of which only "Three Hours between Planes" and "Mike Van Dyke's Christmas Wish" are named; but it seems likely that "Last Kiss" was also submitted. The time when "Last Kiss" was written cannot be determined—ironically, it was finally published in *Collier's* in 1949—but it has a significant relationship to the material of the novel. Although the hero is a producer, he is nothing like Stahr; however, the heroine resembles Sheilah Graham and anticipates Kathleen. Like Kathleen and Miss Graham, Sybil Higgins is an English girl with an unusual background—she admits to having been "an old man's darling." The mood of "Last Kiss" is tragic, for Sybil is defeated by Hollywood and dies.

In June 1939 Fitzgerald told Zelda that he had "blocked out a novel," but not until 31 October did he inform Scottie that he was writing a novel, being careful to tell her nothing about the material.

> Look! I have begun to write something that is maybe great, and I'm going to be absorbed in it four or six months. It may not *make* us a cent but it will pay expenses and it is the first labor of love I've undertaken since the first part of *Infidelity*. . . .
>
> Anyhow I am alive again—getting by that October did something—with all its strains and necessities and humiliations and struggles. I don't drink. I am not a great man, but sometimes I think the impersonal and objective quality of my talent and the sacrifices of it, in pieces, to preserve its essential value has some sort of epic grandeur. Anyhow after hours I nurse myself with delusions of that sort.
>
> And I think when you read this book, which will encompass the time when you knew me as an adult, you will understand how intensively I knew your world—not *ex*tensively because I was so ill and unable to get about.[6]

The first dated synopsis for the novel was sent to Littauer (with copy to Perkins) on 29 September 1939.

> This will be difficult for two reasons. First that there is one fact about my novel, which, if it were known, would be immediately and unscrupulously plagiarized by the George Kaufmans, etc., of this world.[7] Second, that I live always in deadly fear that I will take the edge off an idea for myself by summarizing or talking about it in advance. But, with these limitations, here goes:
>
> The novel will be fifty thousand words long. As I will have to write sixty thousand words to make room for cutting I have figured it as a four months job—three months for the writing—one month for revision. The thinking, according to my conscience and the evidence of sixty pages of outline and notes, *has already been done*. I would infinitely rather do it, now that I am well again, than take hack jobs out here.

The Story occurs during four or five months in the year 1935. It is told by Cecelia,[8] the daughter of a producer named Bradogue in Hollywood. Cecelia is a pretty, modern girl neither good or bad, tremendously human. Her father is also an important character. A shrewd man, a gentile, and a scoundrel of the lowest variety. A self-made man, he has brought up Cecelia to be a princess, sent her East to college, made of her rather a snob, though, in the course of the story, her character evolves *away from this,* That is, she was twenty when the events that she tells occurred, but she is twenty-five when she tells about the events, and of course many of them appear to her in a different light.

Cecelia is the narrator because I think I know exactly how such a person would react to my story. She is *of* the movies but not *in* them. She probably was born the day "The Birth of a Nation" was previewed and Rudolf Valentino came to her fifth birthday party. So she is, all at once, intelligent, cynical but understanding and kindly toward the people, great or small, who are of Hollywood.

She focuses our attention upon two principal characters—Milton Stahr (who is Irving Thalberg—and *this is my great secret*) and Thalia [who later becomes Kathleen], the girl he loves. Thalberg has always fascinated me. His peculiar charm, his extraordinary good looks, his bountiful success, the tragic end of his great adventure. The events I have built around him are fiction, but all of them are things which might very well have happened, and I am pretty sure that I saw deep enough into the character of the man so that his reactions are authentically what they would have been in life. So much so that he may be recognized—but it will also be recognized that *no single fact is actually true.* For example, in my story he is unmarried or a widower, leaving out completely any complication with Norma.

In the beginning of the book I want to pour out my whole impression of this man Stahr as he is seen during an airplane trip from New York to the coast—of course, through Cecelia's eyes. She has been hopelessly in love with him for a long time. She is never going to win anything more from him than an affectionate regard, even that tainted by his dislike of her father (parallel the deadly dislike of each other between Thalberg and Louis B. Mayer). Stahr is over-worked and deathly tired, ruling with a radiance that is almost moribund in its phosphorescence. He has been warned that his health is undermined, but being afraid of nothing the warning is unheeded. He has had everything in life except the privilege of giving himself unselfishly to another human being. This he finds on the night of a semi-serious earthquake (like in 1935) a few days after the opening of the story.

It has been a very full day even for Stahr—the bursted water mains, which cover the whole ground space of the lot to the depth of several feet, seems to release something in him. Called over to the outer lot to supervise the salvation of the electrical plant (for like Thalberg, he has a finger in every pie of the vast bakery) he finds two women stranded on the roof of a property farmhouse and goes to their rescue.

Thalia Taylor is a twenty-six year old widow, and my present conception of her should make her the most glamorous and sympathetic of my heroines. Glamorous in a new way because I am in secret agreement with the public in detesting the type of feminine arrogance that has been pushed into prominence in the case of Brenda Frazier, etc.[9] People simply do not sympathize deeply with those who have had *all* the breaks, and I am going to dower this girl, like Rosalba in Thackeray's "Rose and the Ring" with "a little misfortune." She and the woman with her (to whom she is serving as companion) have come secretly on the lot through the other woman's curiosity. They have been caught there when the catastrophe occurred.

Now we have a love affair between Stahr and Thalia, an immediate, dynamic, unusual, physical love affair—and I will write it so that you can publish it. At the same time I will send you a copy of how it will appear in book form somewhat stronger in tone.

This love affair is the meat of the book—though I am going to treat it, remember, as it comes through to Cecelia. That is to say by making Cecelia at the moment of her telling the story, an intelligent and observant woman, I shall grant myself the privilege, as Conrad did, of letting her imagine the actions of the characters. Thus, I hope to get the verisimilitude of a first person narrative, combined with a Godlike knowledge of all events that happen to my characters.[10]

Two events beside the love affair bulk large in the intermediary chapters. There is a definite plot on the part of Bradogue, Cecelia's father, to get Stahr out of the company. He has even actually and factually considered having him murdered. Bradogue is the monopolist at its worst—Stahr, in spite of the inevitable conservatism of the self-made man, is a paternalistic employer. Success came to him young, at twenty-three, and left certain idealisms of his youth unscarred. Moreover, he is a worker. Figuratively he takes off his coat and pitches in, while Bradogue is not interested in the making of pictures save as it will benefit his bank account.

The second incident is how young Cecelia herself, in her desperate love for Stahr, throws herself at his head. In her reaction at his indifference she gives herself to a man whom she does not love. This episode is *not* absolutely necessary to the serial. It could be tempered but it might be best to eliminate it altogether.

Back to the main theme, Stahr cannot bring himself to marry Thalia. It simply doesn't seem part of his life. He doesn't realize that she has become necessary to him. Previously his name has been associated with this or that well-known actress or society personality and Thalia is poor, unfortunate, and tagged with a middle class exterior which doesn't fit in with the grandeur Stahr demands of life. When she realizes this she leaves him temporarily, leaves him not because he has no legal intentions toward her but because of the hurt of it, the remainder of a vanity from which she had considered herself free.

Stahr is now plunged directly into the fight to keep control of the company. His health breaks down very suddenly while he is on a trip to New York to see the stockholders. He almost dies in New York and comes back to find that Bradogue has seized upon his absence to take steps which Stahr considers unthinkable. He plunges back into work again to straighten things out.

Now, realizing how much he needs Thalia, things are patched up between them. For a day or two they are ideally happy. They are going to marry, but he must take one more trip East to clinch the victory which he has conciliated in the affairs of the company.

Now occurs the final episode which should give the novel its quality—its unusualness. Do you remember about 1933 when a transport plane was wrecked on a mountain-side in the Southwest, and a Senator was killed? The thing that struck me about it was that the country people rifled the bodies of the dead.[11] That is just what happens to this plane which is bearing Stahr from Hollywood. The angle is that of three children who, on a Sunday picnic, are the first to discover the wreckage. Among those killed in the accident besides Stahr are the two other characters we have met. (I have not been able to go into the minor characters in this short summary.) Of the three children, two boys and a girl, who find the bodies, one boy rifled Stahr's possessions; another the body of a ruined ex-producer; and the girl, those of a moving picture actress. The possessions which the children find, symbolically determine their attitude toward their act of theft. The possessions of the motion picture actress tend the young girl to selfish possessiveness: those of the unsuccessful producer sway one of the boys toward an irresolute attitude; while the boy who finds Stahr's briefcase is the one who, after a week, saves and redeems all three by going to a local judge and making full confession.

The story swings once more back to Hollywood for its finale. During the story *Thalia has never once been inside a studio.* After Stahr's death as she stands in front of the great plant which he created, she realizes now that she never will. She knows only that he loved her and that he was a great man and that he died for what he believed in.

This is a novel—not even faintly of the propaganda type. Indeed, Thalberg's opinions were entirely different from mine in many respects that I will not go into. I've long chosen him for a hero (this has been in my mind for three years) because he is one of the half-dozen men I have known who were built on the grand scale. That it happens to coincide with a period in which the American Jews are somewhat uncertain in their morale, is for me merely a fortuitous coincidence. The racial angle shall scarcely be touched on at all. Certainly if Ziegfield could be made into an epic figure than what about Thalberg who was literally everything that Ziegfield wasn't?

There is nothing that worries me in the novel, nothing that seems uncertain. Unlike *Tender Is the Night* it is not the story of deterioration—it is not depressing and not morbid in spite of the tragic ending. If one book could ever be "like" another I should say it is more "like" *The Great Gatsby* than any other of my books. But I hope it will be entirely different—I hope it will be something new, arouse new emotions perhaps even a new way of looking at certain phenomena. I have set it safely in a period of five years ago to obtain detachment, but now that Europe is tumbling about our ears this also seems to be for the best. It is an escape into a lavish, romantic past that perhaps will not come again into our time. It is certainly a novel I would like to read. Shall I write it?[12]

The letter sent to Littauer and the copy sent to Perkins have not been located. A four-page carbon copy—with the bottom of page four torn off—is with the notes for *The Last Tycoon*. Another carbon of page four has Fitzgerald's note "Orig Sent thru here" after "Shall I write it?" The rest of page four reads:

> As I said, I would rather do this for a minimum price than continue this in-and-out business with the moving pictures where the rewards are great, but the satisfaction unsatisfactory and the income tax always mopping one up after the battle.
>
> The minimum I would need to do this with peace of mind would be $15,000., payable $3000. in advance and $3000. on the first of November, the first of December, the first of January and the first of February, on delivery of the last installment. For this I would guarantee to do no other work, specifically pictures, to make any changes in the manuscript (but not to having them made for me) and to begin to deliver the copy the first of November, that is to give you fifteen thousand words by that date.

Unless these advances are compatible with your economy, Kenneth, the deal would be financially impossible for me under the present line up. Four months of sickness completely stripped me and until your telegram came I had counted on a buildup of many months work here before I could *consider* beginning the novel. Once again a telegram would help tremendously, as I am naturally on my toes and [*The rest of the letter is missing.*]

Fitzgerald either decided that the $15,000 figure was too low or that he wanted to have Littauer make the opening bid. In any case, Fitzgerald later declined to write the serial for $15,000.

The 29 September synopsis represents an early form of the story—without the double blackmail and murder plots, or Kathleen's past as the mistress of a king and her commitment to marry another man. Of particular significance is Fitzgerald's analysis of the narrator. Although he compares this novel to *The Great Gatsby*, it is clear—from both the synopsis and the sections he wrote—that Fitzgerald intended a more flexible role for Cecelia than he had permitted Nick Carraway. Nick either witnesses or documents every scene in the novel (except Gatsby's murder); but Cecelia was to be allowed "to imagine the actions of the characters"—thereby providing the double viewpoint of narrator and omniscient author.

Littauer responded on 10 October, saying that *Collier's* could not make an advance without seeing a "substantial sample of the finished product"—15,000 words.[13] If the sample was sufficiently promising, *Collier's* was prepared to advance $5,000, with a second advance of $5,000 for the next 20,000 words—"against a total purchase price which remains to be negotiated." Littauer suggested that the purchase price be based on the rate of $2,500 per 7,000–8,000–word installment, with a bonus of $5,000. Therefore the talking figure for serial rights to a 50,000-word novel was at least $20,000. But *Collier's* was not prepared to consider an advance before seeing a 15,000-word sample, and Fitzgerald needed an advance with which to write the sample. Fitzgerald then wired Perkins to negotiate with Littauer for him. On 16 October 1939 Perkins wrote a memo for Charles Scribner indicating his concern that Fitzgerald would turn to Scribners for backing.

Collier's are quite keen about Scott's idea, but they have a natural suspicion of his reliability. They are willing to pay him approximately $30,000 for the serial if they agree to take it after seeing 15,000 words.—And if they do see that number of words, and if they like them, they will advance him two installments of $5,000 each. The trouble is Scott has such extravagant ideas of what he needs that he says he must have $3,000 a month. I am afraid he will now turn to us to help him do the 15,000. I believe he could on this present basis turn to Harold Ober, whose debt he has entirely cleared up, and who has made plenty of money out of his movie contracts, etc. too. Harold refused to lend him any more, thinking it would do him good, and this made Scott mad, and all this new plan is supposed to be a complete secret from Harold.[14]

While these negotiations were going on—by letter, wire, and phone—Fitzgerald sent Littauer a story called "Mike Van Dyke's Christmas Wish," which was declined because it was "not a rounded story."[15] Fitzgerald changed the character's name to Pat Hobby, and wrote seventeen sketches about him for *Esquire* in 1939 and 1940. At $250 each, Pat Hobby helped finance the writing of *The Last Tycoon*.

The Pat Hobby stories, which appeared in *Esquire* from January 1940 to May 1941, are uneven, and their relationship to *The Last Tycoon* has been distorted by readers who see them as a quasi-autobiographical account of Fitzgerald in Hollywood. About the only thing that these stories have in common with the novel is the Hollywood setting; the intention, the tone, the themes, are entirely different. Fitzgerald did not write the Pat Hobby series until after he had started work on *The Last Tycoon,* and he wrote them only for money—using Hobby to finance Stahr. It is obvious that Fitzgerald was careful not to waste any *Last Tycoon* material on the Hobby stories. One way he was able to keep the two projects distinct while working on both simultaneously was by sharply differentiating his attitude toward the characters. Pat Hobby is contemptible; Monroe Stahr is heroic. Rarely did Fitzgerald allow Hobby to be sympathetic—as in "Two Old Timers" and "A Patriotic Short." Elsewhere Pat is ignorant, mean, and dishonest. Because critics and students have been conditioned to regard Hollywood as a concentration camp for writers, judgments of the Hobby stories have been influenced by presuppositional responses to Hobby—and Fitzgerald—as victims of Hollywood. But Hobby is only a victim of his own dishonesty and lack of ability.

The Pat Hobby stories were simply an undemanding way to make a little money—$4,250—while Fitzgerald was saving himself for work on *The Last Tycoon*. It is absurd to regard Pat Hobby as a self-portrait of Fitzgerald. Hobby is an illiterate who never had any talent—a cliché-infested dope—with whom Fitzgerald did not identify. Fitzgerald can be connected to Hobby only by viewing Hobby as Fitzgerald's self-warning—an exaggerated depiction of what Fitzgerald was afraid of becoming. Even if Fitzgerald identified with Hobby, then he was using Hobby to dissipate resentments that he did not want to intrude into the novel. The only viewpoint that *The Last Tycoon* and the Hobby stories have in common is contempt for the incompetents.

Fitzgerald fulfilled Perkins's prophecy on 20 October 1939, asking if Scribners could subvene the writing of "the first ten thousand words":

I have your telegram but meanwhile I found that Collier's proposition was less liberal than I had expected. They want to pay $15,000 for the serial. But (without taking such steps as reneging on my income tax, letting go my life insurance for its surrender value, taking Scottie from college and putting Zelda in a public asylum) I couldn't last four months on that. Certain debts have been run up so that the larger part of the $15,000. has been, so to speak, spent already. A contraction of my own living expenses to the barest minimum, that is to say a room in a boarding house, abandonment of all medical attention (I still see a doctor once a week) would still leave me at the end not merely penniless but even more in debt than I am now.[16]

On the same day that he wrote to Perkins, Fitzgerald wrote to Littauer reviewing the terms of the proposition:

I was disappointed in our conversation the other day—I am no good on long distance and should have had notes in my hand.
I want to make plain how my proposition differs from yours. First there is the question of the *total* payment; second, the *terms* of payment, which would enable me to finish it in these straightened circumstances.
In any case I shall probably attack the novel. I have about decided to make a last liquidation of assets, put my wife in a public place, and my daughter to work and concentrate on it—simply take a furnished room and live on canned goods.
But writing it under such conditions I should want to market it with the chance of getting a higher price for it.
It was to avoid doing all this, that I took you up on the idea of writing it on installments. I too had figured on the same price per installment you had paid for a story, but I had no idea that you would want to pack more into an installment than your five thousand word maximum for a story. So the fifty thousand words at $2500. for each 5000 word installment would have come to $25,000. In addition, I had figured that a consecutive story is *eas*ier rather than harder to write than the same number of words divided into short stories because the characters and settings are determined in advance, so my idea had been to ask you $20,000. for the whole job. But $15,000.—that would be much too marginal. It would be better to write the whole thing in poverty and freedom of movement with the finished product. Fifteen thousand would leave me more in debt than I am now.
On the question of the terms of payment, my proposition was to include the exact amount which you offer in your letter only I had divided it, so that the

money would come in batches of $3000. every four weeks, or something like that.

When we had our first phone conversation the fact that I did not have enough to start on, further complicated the matter, I have hoped that perhaps that's where Scribner's would come in. A telegram from Max told me he was going to see you again but I've heard nothing further.

I hope that this will at least clear up any ambiguity. If the proposition is all off, I am very sorry. I regret now that I did not go on with the novel last April when I had some money, instead of floundering around with a lot of dissociated ideas that were half-heartedly attempted and did not really come to anything. I know you are really interested, and thank you for the trouble you have taken.[17]

Like most writers who think of themselves as good businessmen, Fitzgerald was a bad one. He was spoiling a deal over the question of a payment that could not be resolved until he had submitted a sample. Moreover, Perkins was under the impression that *Collier's* was prepared to go as high as $30,000. The thing for Fitzgerald to do was submit the sample. It was clear that Littauer favored the project, and he had agreed to "shorter installments."[18] On 2 November Littauer made a further concession: "We are willing to make you a small advance on the basis of six thousand words of manuscript in hand—provided, of course, that much of the story seems to us promising."[19]

A key factor in Fitzgerald's negotiations with Littauer was that he wanted an expression of confidence. Fitzgerald always needed money, but at this stage he was also seeking a sign that *Collier's* believed in him. He felt forgotten and worried that his friends had given up on him. Ober's refusal to advance him money on stories had hurt Fitzgerald, and it was apparent that Scribners was not offering to back the new novel. Perkins clearly understood that Fitzgerald expected Scribners to underwrite the novel, but Perkins did not feel that he could justify committing the firm.

At this time Fitzgerald sent a 6,000–word sample to both Littauer and Perkins. The actual material has not been identified, but it is virtually certain that Fitzgerald sent an early draft of the opening of the novel—the plane trip to California. The first chapter is a superb opening for the novel—introducing Stahr and foreshadowing major themes—but it was not an ideal sample *as a sample* to submit because much of what Fitzgerald is doing does not become clear until the reader has absorbed more of the novel. Fitzgerald's case would have been much stronger had he been able to send Littauer the first two chapters, including Stahr's initial encounter with Kathleen during the studio flood. Littauer responded by wire on

28 November: "FIRST SIX THOUSAND PRETTY CRYPTIC THEREFORE DISAPPOINTING. BUT YOU WARNED US THIS MIGHT BE SO. CAN WE DEFER VERDICT UNTIL FURTHER DEVELOPMENT OF STORY? IF IT HAS TO BE NOW IT HAS TO BE NO. REGARDS."[20] Fitzgerald immediately reacted telegraphically. To Littauer: "NO HARD FEELINGS THERE HAS NEVER BEEN AN EDITOR WITH PANTS ON SINCE GEORGE LORIMER"[21]—thereby effectively cutting off further negotiations. To Perkins: "PLEASE RUSH THE COPY AIR MAIL TO SATURDAY EVENING POST ATTENTION TO JOE BRUAN STOP I GUESS THERE ARE NO GREAT MAGAZINES EDITORS LEFT."[22]

"Joe Bruan" was Joseph Bryan III, an associate editor at the *Post*. Fitzgerald and Bryan had never met or corresponded when Fitzgerald phoned him to ask if he would read a sample of the novel. Bryan was excited by the chance: he had gone to Princeton largely because of reading Fitzgerald and had lived in Fitzgerald's room at 15 University Place. Bryan does not know why Fitzgerald decided to call him, but guesses that their mutual friend Donald Ogden Stewart told Fitzgerald about him. (Stewart has no recollection of this.) When he read the material Bryan was deeply disappointed to find that it was too "broad" for the *Post*. He circulated it to the other editors, but the decision was unanimous: the *Post* could not publish the novel.[23]

Concerned about the effect Littauer's decision would have on Fitzgerald, Perkins wired on 29 November: "A BEAUTIFUL START. STIRRING AND NEW. CAN WIRE YOU TWO HUNDRED FIFTY AND A THOUSAND BY JANUARY."[24] He was acting in a private capacity, not on behalf of Scribners. Perkins—who was not a rich man—had come into a small inheritance and was prepared to gamble some of it on Fitzgerald. On the same day Fitzgerald wired Perkins to show the synopsis to agent Leland Hayward, with the idea that Hayward could get a movie studio to underwrite his work on the novel in return for the movie rights—a reversal of Fitzgerald's earlier anxiety that the movie people might learn about his novel.[25] Hayward told Perkins that he could not handle the property until it was written.

One of the results of Littauer's decision was that Fitzgerald fell off the wagon temporarily. When *Collier's* editor Max Wilkinson called on him in December 1939 he found Fitzgerald drunk and abusive.[26] On 7 December, Fitzgerald sent Perkins "a little more, introducing the character of the heroine"—part at least, of Chapter 2.[27] Fitzgerald made no further attempts to deal with *Collier's;* and between the end of 1939 and the fall of 1940 there were no progress reports to Perkins. Nevertheless, *Collier's* appears to have retained an interest in the novel after Fitzgerald broke off negotiations, for on 7 December 1940 he wrote Scottie that he had recently seen Littauer in Los Angeles. On 23 February 1940 Fitzgerald submitted a short-short, "Dearly Beloved," to *Esquire,* which Arnold Gingrich declined.[28] This story marks a stage in the gestation of *The Last Tycoon,* for it is about a Negro who is interested in the Rosicrucians. Although February was too early for Fitzgerald to be working on episode 14 in the novel—where Stahr and Kathleen meet the Negro gathering grunion—the existence of "Dearly Beloved" in February suggests that Fitzgerald had such a character in mind. In March 1940 Fitzgerald took an assignment to adapt "Babylon Revisited" for independent producer Lester Cowan, for which he earned something between $2,300 and $5,000.[29]

Frances Kroll Ring, Fitzgerald's secretary, reports that he was not able to devote full attention to his novel until after he moved to the Laurel Avenue apartment in May/June 1940. "Concerning the constant revisions of the early chapters of the Last Tycoon: Scott made so many starts before he got into working on the book full time, that he necessarily made changes with each new start. In Encino, he worked mostly on notes interrupted by turning out the Pat Hobby stories for bucks. When he moved to Laurel, he began to work on LT again. This time, the interruption was the Babylon Revisited screenplay. He didn't begin writing the book in a continuous stream until after the screenplay was done."[30] This chronology indicates that Fitzgerald made rapid progress on the novel, writing much of the seventeen episodes in less than six months.

The first evidence of substantial progress on the novel comes in Perkins's 19 September 1940 letter to Fitzgerald expressing pleasure in John O'Hara's report that he had read 25,000 words. A great admirer of Fitzgerald's work, O'Hara told him, "Scott, don't take any more movie jobs till you've finished this. You work so slowly and this is so good, you've got to finish it. It's real Fitzgerald."[31] In the fall of 1940 Fitzgerald stayed on the wagon and worked steadily on the novel, interrupting it only to write an adaptation of Emlyn Williams's *The Light of Heart* for Twentieth Century-Fox in October. From October 1940 Fitzgerald included progress reports in his weekly letters to Zelda: "I expect to be back on my novel any day and this time to finish a two months' job" (11 October); "I'm trying desperately to finish my novel by the middle of December and it's a little like working on 'Tender is the Night' at the end—I think of nothing else.... My room is covered with charts like it used to be for 'Tender is the Night' telling the different movements of the characters and their histories" (19 October); "I am deep in the novel, living in it, and it makes me happy. It is a *constructed* novel like *Gatsby,* with passages of poetic prose when it fits the action, but no ruminations or sideshows like *Tender.* Everything must contribute to the dramatic movement. ... Two thousand words today and all good" (23 October); "The novel is hard as pulling teeth but that is because it is in the early character-planting phase. I feel people so less intently than I did once that this is harder. It means welding together hundreds of stray impressions and incidents to form the fabric of entire personalities" (2 November); "No news except that the novel progresses and I am angry that this little illness has slowed me up. I've had trouble with my heart before but never anything organic. This is not a major attack but seems to have come on gradually and luckily a cardiogram showed it up in time" (6 December); "The novel is about three-quarters through and I think I can go on till January 12 without doing any stories or going back to the studio. I couldn't go back to the studio anyhow in my present condition as I have to spend most of the time in bed where I write on a wooden desk . . ." (13 December).[32]

To Edmund Wilson—who would edit the novel for posthumous publication—Fitzgerald reported on 25 November 1940: "I think my novel is good. I've written it with difficulty. It is completely upstream in mood and will get a certain amount of abuse but is first hand and I am trying a little harder than I ever have to be exact and honest emotionally. I honestly hoped somebody else would write it but nobody seems to be going to." The letter has a postscript. "This sounds like such a bitter letter—I'd rewrite it except for a horrible paucity of time. Not even time to be bitter."[33]

F. Scott Fitzgerald died of a heart attack on 21 December 1940, leaving 44,000 words of the latest working draft of the novel.

Notes

1. An excellent study of possible connections between these two projects is Kermit W. Moyer's "F. Scott Fitzgerald's Two Unfinished Novels: The Count and the Tycoon in Spenglerian Perspective," *Contemporary Literature* (Spring 1974): 238–56. Professor Moyer argues that both works should be read in light of the impression *The Decline of the West* made on Fitzgerald and that Kathleen's explanation that she was being educated to read Spengler is a clue to the meaning of the novel. In his essay on *The Great Gatsby* included in this collection, Bruccoli refuted Fitzgerald's contenion that he had read Spengler's *The Decline of the West;* however, Bruccoli appears to have become receptive to the possibility of Spenglerian influence on Fitzgerald. Ed.

2. *Dear Scott / Dear Max: The Fitzgerald-Perkins Correspondence,* edited by John Kuehl and Jackson R. Bryer (New York: Scribners, 1971), pp. 253–254.

3. Ibid., p. 256.

4. *As Ever Scott Fitz—: Letters Between F. Scott Fitzgerald and His Literary Agent Harold Ober, 1919–1940,* edited by Matthew J. Bruccoli and Jennifer McCabe Atkinson (Philadelphia and New York: Lippincott, 1972).

5. New York Public Library

6. *The Letters of F. Scott Fitzgerald,* edited by Andrew Turnbull (New York: Scribners, 1963), pp. 61–62.

7. Bruccoli included notes in his Cambridge edition of *The Love of the Last Tycoon: A Western* (p. xxx) and in *The Love of the Last Tycoon: A Western* (New York: Scribners, 1994), p. ix, indicating Fitzgerald believed that playwright George S. Kaufman had taken the idea for *Of Thee I Sing* (1931) from his play *The Vegetable*. Ed.

8. Fitzgerald consistently spelled this name *Cecelia*. His form has been retained in this study—except when quoting from Edmund Wilson's edition of *The Last Tycoon*, where it was emended to *Cecilia*. The character was named for Fitzgerald's cousin, Cecilia Delihant Taylor, whom he addressed as "Cousin Ceci." It is impossible to determine whether Fitzgerald simply didn't know the correct spelling for *Cecilia*, or whether the spelling *Cecelia* was deliberate. Fitzgerald's spellings for the names of his characters have been followed in this study. His spelling inconsistencies and idiosyncracies have been preserved when quoting the manuscript.

9. Brenda Frazier was a New York celebrity and debutante. Ed.

10. Bruccoli noted in his Scribners edition of *Tycoon* (p. xi) that from early stages of composition Fitzgerald was concerned about point-of-view. Ed.

11. This incident is described in notes in the Cambridge (p. xxxiii) and Scribners (p. xii) editions of *Tycoon:* "On 6 May 1935 Senator Bronson M. Cutting and four others were killed when a passenger plane crashed at Atlanta, Missouri. Also aboard were members of a Paramount film crew. The local people aided in rescuing the injured; the wreckage was not plundered. See Richard Lowitt, *Bronson M. Cutting* (Albuquerque: University of New Mexico Press, 1992)." Ed.

12. *Last Tycoon* notes, Fitzgerald Papers, Princeton University Library.

13. Fitzgerald Papers, Princeton University Library.

14. Scribners Archives, Princeton University Library.

15. 19 October 1939. New York Public Library.

16. *Dear Scott / Dear Max*, p. 258.

17. Fitzgerald Papers, Princeton University Library.

18. Wire, 31 October 1939. New York Public Library.

19. Fitzgerald Papers, Princeton University Library.

20. New York Public Library.

21. New York Public Library.

22. Scribners Archives, Princeton University Library.

23. Joseph Bryan, III to Bruccoli, 9 September 1975. "There is a 1 December 1931 wire from the *Post* to Fitzgerald in the Fitzgerald Papers at Princeton: FIRST INSTALLMENT RECEIVED FROM SCRIBNERS BUT SECOND HAS NOT ARRIVED. EXPECT MONDAY. WILL COMMUNICATE IMMEDIATELY AFTER READING="

24. Fitzgerald Papers, Princeton University Library.

25. Scribners Archives, Princeton University Library.

26. A carbon copy of Fitzgerald's letter of apology is with the Fitzgerald Papers at Princeton University Library.

27. Scribners Archives, Princeton University Library.

28. "Dearly Beloved" was posthumously published in the *Fitzgerald/Hemingway Annual 1969* and collected in *Bits of Paradise: 21 Uncollected Stories by F. Scott and Zelda Fitzgerald,* edited by Scottie Fitzgerald Smith and Bruccoli (London: Bodley Head, 1973; New York: Scribners, 1974).

29. On 20 May 1940 Fitzgerald supplied the $2,300 figure to Perkins, but Sheilah Graham reports in *The Real F. Scott Fitzgerald: Thirty-Five Years Later* (New York: Grosset and Dunlap, 1976) that he received $1,000 for rights to the story plus $400 a week for ten weeks. The duration of Fitzgerald's work on the "Babylon Revisited" screenplay—which was also called "Honoria" or "Cosmopolitan"—is not clear; there are scripts dated August 1940. It appears that he worked on it intermittently during the spring and summer.

30. Frances Kroll Ring to Bruccoli, 22 April 1975.

31. O'Hara's account of reading Fitzgerald's working draft is in "Certain Aspects," *New Republic* (3 March 1941): 311.

32. Fitzgerald Papers, Princeton University Library.

33. *Letters of F. Scott Fitzgerald,* p. 349.

Part 2

On Bibliography

"Fredson Bowers was a good master, and I was a fortunate apprentice."
M.J.B., "Working with Fredson Bowers,"
DLB Yearbook 1991

"A bibliography is outdated the day it is published."
M.J.B., introduction, *F. Scott Fitzgerald:
A Descriptive Bibliography* (1974)

What Bowers Wrought

*An Assessment of the Center for
Editions of American Authors*

The Center for Editions of American Authors (CEAA) of the Modern Language Association (MLA) was constituted in 1963 and reconstituted in 1976 as the Committee on Scholarly Editions (CSE). During its ten years of operation with funding from the National Endowment for the Humanities (NEH), the CEAA established the standards for editing the texts of American literature. More than that, it made the editing of American literature a serious professional endeavor. Before the CEAA—before Fredson Bowers—academicians were still assuring students of American literature that "the last edition in the author's lifetime" provided the best text of a work. Before Bowers promulgated the principles for the *Centenary Edition of the Works of Nathaniel Hawthorne* in 1961, there were only two completed editions of American authors that aspired to textual reliability: *The Poems of Emily Dickinson* and *The Letters of Emily Dickinson* (Harvard University Press, 1955 and 1958)—a transcription from the manuscripts—and the ten-volume Sidney Lanier (Johns Hopkins University Press, 1945). Other editions-in-progress in 1961 were the *Works of Jonathan Edwards* (Yale University Press), the Emerson *Journals and Miscellaneous Notebooks* (Harvard University Press), and the New York University edition of Walt Whitman.

Although the Lanier editors assembled his manuscripts, there is no clear explanation of how the documents were used. The following statement may be taken as representative of editorial thinking as applied to American literature during the 1940s and 1950s: "The authoritative text for the poetry and prose has been established by a rule of thumb as that text which last passed under Lanier's eyes and

---

"What Bowers Wrought: An Assessment of the Center for Editions of American Authors" was first published in *The Culture of Collected Editions,* edited by Andrew Nash (Houndmills, Basingstoke, Hampshire, UK, and New York: Palgrave Macmillan, 2003), pp. 237–244. Reprinted with permission of Arlyn Bruccoli for the Matthew J. Bruccoli literary estate.

met with his approval . . . whether found in book, periodical, or manuscript."[1] The Lanier apparatus is incomplete and inadequate: "the variants for 29 of his lesser poems seemed too insignificant to be recorded. For 30 more, in which the variants were few in number or could be adequately represented by samples, the treatment is confined to a line or so in the notes. . . . Variants in mechanical matters, such as punctuation, capitalization and spelling have not been noted except when especially significant."[2] That was before W. W. Greg's "The Rationale of Copy-Text"—orally delivered in 1949 and published in 1950.

Bowers's declared purpose was to apply to American literature the same standards accorded to works of English literature: "When scholars editing American literature will bring to their tasks the careful effort that has been established for English Renaissance texts, say, then the editing of American texts will become a respectable occupation at long last, and not a piece of hack work for the paperbacks."[3] This crusade was initiated by a scholar who, at that time, had almost no interest in American literature and commented that American authors provided dissertation subjects for graduate students who weren't good enough to work in the English Renaissance. Moreover, the author of *Principles of Bibliographical Description* remarked that "Book collectors are crazy."

Bowers became involved with American literature—he later served as textual editor for the Stephen Crane edition, as well as acting in editorial capacities for the John Dewey and William James editions—when he was asked to advise Ohio State University on an edition of Nathaniel Hawthorne. Ohio State was then the right place for the edition because William Charvat was the senior American literature man there. He had edited the *Cost-Books of Ticknor & Fields,* Hawthorne's publisher; and he was working on his unfinished history, *The Profession of Authorship in America.* Charvat was not a bibliographer or a textual editor or even a bookman; but he recognized the need for accurate, trustworthy texts of the nineteenth-century American authors. He is left out of the official accounts of the *Centenary Edition of the Works of Nathaniel Hawthorne*—one of his colleagues claimed the credit—but the history of that endeavor would have been very different without Bill's backing. Bowers offered to take textual responsibility—meaning control—for the whole Hawthorne project and seconded me to Columbus in 1961 to set up and manage the editorial operation. *The Scarlet Letter*—the first "definitive edition" of a classic American literary work—was published in 1962. Another non-Americanist, John Hurt Fisher, a medievalist who became secretary—that meant the head—of the MLA in 1961, was responsible for convening the 1962 planning sessions that culminated in the CEAA and for supporting the grant applications that resulted in NEH subventions.

The CEAA was headquartered at New York University under its first director William Gibson from 1962 to 1969 and at the University of South Carolina under me from 1969 to 1976. There was a revolving advisory committee consisting of textual editors, nonbibliographical scholars, and university press directors. The chief duties of the CEAA director and the advisory committee were to obtain annual grants from NEH, to parcel out the grants, and to enforce textual/editorial standards by awarding or withholding the CEAA "Approved Text" seal after 1967.

For a time it became a badge of academic respectability for an English department to have a definitive edition, and the CEAA was besieged by applicants seeking encouragement and guidance. Most of these projected editions were nonstarters. A couple died after one or two volumes. The home institutions weren't equipped to do the work because of inadequate library holdings or inadequate funding—but usually because of the absence of trained or experienced editors. They didn't know how to do it.

When Bowers established the principles and procedures for editing and publishing the Gregian edition of Hawthorne, half a dozen editions—Emerson, Mark Twain, Irving, Thoreau, Melville—were being discussed or planned. Some volumes were in progress, but they were not "definitive editions" (which soon became a junk term). The editorial/textual policies varied from edition to edition, volume to volume, and editor to editor. Typically ten volumes would be parceled out to ten different scholars in ten different locations—without uniform textual standards or uniform editorial procedures or any boss. In some cases the volumes were regarded as vehicles for critical or historical introductions and historical or explanatory notes.

The Scarlet Letter (1962), the first volume in the Hawthorne edition, Bowers's first American-author edition, established the basic elements of a CEAA edition:

1. The general editorial plan for the edition.
2. The editorial plan for the volume.
3. The established text.
4. Editorial emendations in the copy-text (substantives and accidentals).
5. Textual notes.
6. Historical collations.
7. Word-division (end-of-line hyphenation). This one aroused incredulity and risibility.

Other Hawthorne volumes included complete lists of alterations in the manuscripts and special collations as required by evidence for that work. Bowers's explanation of the apparatus concludes: "All the cards are on the table, face up." He reiterated that if the apparatus was complete and trustworthy, the collating would never have to be redone by subsequent editors who were re-editing the text.

Two of the most powerful Bowers-CEAA influences on American literary scholarship were (1) the protection of authorial punctuation, spelling, capitalization—what W. W. Greg unhappily classified as *accidentals*—and (2) the scrupulous recording of manuscript alterations. Before CEAA, editors of what were alleged to be scholarly texts customarily "cleaned up" the punctuation—silently. There was little recognition that "an author's accidentals are an important part of his total style by which he conveys meaning." The critical value of manuscript revisions was understood, but the chore of recording them fully was considered unnecessary. It was also a lot of work. The Bowers edition of *The House of Seven Gables* was the first CEAA edition to record the author's manuscript deletions, insertions, revisions, and corrections.

Bowers's "Preface to the Text" for the Hawthorne edition stated:

> The text itself is a critical unmodernized reconstruction. It is critical in that it is not necessarily an exact reprint of any individual document: the print or manuscript chosen as copy-text (that is, as the basis for this edition) [*copy-text* became a fighting term] may be emended by reference to other authorities or by editorial decision. (p. xxix)

And later:

> the purpose of the Centenary Edition is to establish the text in as close a form, in all details, to Hawthorne's *final intentions* [another fighting term] as the preserved documents of each separate work permit. (p. xxxv)

A key element in the organization of the Hawthorne edition is that there was an editorial center, which I ran at OSU. All the bibliographical research, collating, transcribing, and proofing was performed at what became known—with an element of derision—as the "Hawthorne Factory." Bowers remained in Virginia, but he was the editorial czar. The evidence was fed to him; he prepared working texts which were checked and perfected at the editorial center. The editions that aborted or that experienced infant mortality were the ones that were decentralized: each volume had its own textual editor, and the evidence was scattered. In the 1970s Bowers urged me to join him in a plan to assemble the CEAA bibliographical/editorial teams as one big operation; but I stupidly declined.

In 1967 the CEAA instituted the seal that was awarded to an "Approved Text." The seal meant that the volume had been vetted and blessed by a competent scholar who was not associated with the edition and that the published text—

without front or back matter—would be made available for reprinting on a nonexclusive basis for a reasonable fee. The sealing process was mandatory for volumes funded by the CEAA, but optional for nonfunded "associated editions." The seal generated strong protests about "violating the traditions of scholarship," as did the CEAA/NEH policy of requiring evidence of satisfactory work-in-progress by grantees. Some of the grantees accomplished nothing and declined to account for the grants they had received. I was not allowed to recover this squandered money: there are more accurate terms than "squandered."

Beginning in 1966–1967 the CEAA received annual grants through MLA from the NEH averaging $300,000 per year—roughly three million dollars over the course of ten years. These funds were restricted to the original ten CEAA editions. Other editions were "associated," meaning that they qualified for the seal and received aid and comfort—but no money—from the CEAA. Probably another two million came from the editors' home universities in the form of released time from teaching and student help. All publication costs were borne by the university presses, and no royalties were paid.

When the CEAA was transmogrified into the CSE in 1976 there were 144 sealed volumes—of which 101 were in the 9 remaining funded editions and 43 volumes in the 5 associated editions. Deducting administrative costs and aborted volumes, the 101 funded volumes averaged $20,000 in NEH support for *editorial work only.*

At the time of the initial CEAA grant application to the NEH there was a competing application from Jason Epstein of Random House, fronting for Edmund Wilson, for an American version of the French Pléiade editions. The Epstein-Wilson application was denied. In 1968 Wilson published a long article, "The Fruits of the MLA," in the *New York Review of Books,* edited by Epstein's wife, denouncing the CEAA and its volumes. Wilson charged that the volumes were unattractive, expensive, and burdened with unnecessary editorial apparatus that was termed "barbed wire" by his supporters. Wilson did not discuss textual theory or editorial standards and said nothing about how his envisioned volumes were to be edited. At the same time so-called "younger scholars" in the squalid 1960s were denouncing textual work as "irrelevant" and demanding that the CEAA be terminated and the money transferred to relevant projects. In 1979 Epstein was instrumental in obtaining $1,800,000 from the Ford Foundation and NEH to tool up the Library of America, a nonprofit commercial operation that has published 124 volumes—24 of which use CEAA or CSE texts.

The CEAA made enduring contributions to the study and teaching of American literature. It provided the first established critical editions for classic works of American literature. Too much money was wasted. Too much time was wasted.

Yet there were long-lasting benefits from the CEAA endeavor—in addition to the published volumes. The work of the CEAA led to refinements of copy-text theory and editorial practice by working on literary forms and methods of publication that had not been previously examined—such as newspaper syndication. The CEAA editors also drove unlocated manuscripts out of hiding and corrected or augmented the existing author bibliographies. The CEAA stimulated work on author/editor/publisher relationships in America; but more should have been done in this field. Many of the CEAA editors were not bookmen and regarded the business of publishing with fastidious condescension.

The editorial centers hired and trained graduate students. There were jobs for bibliographers with brand-new degrees. Junior faculty members were able to utilize their participation in the editorials as career launching pads—sometimes deserting after tenure or promotion. Some of the old boys regarded their grants as prizes in recognition of long service to their authors and did little or nothing to earn them. I learned to interpret the words "my shack in the mountains"— always *mountains,* never *seashore*—to mean that the CEAA would get nothing for the grant money. Somehow I was supposed to believe that demanding scholarship could be best performed in the before-the-computer years without access to libraries, books, manuscripts, or colleagues. It bears repeating that I was forbidden to attempt recovery of the wasted money.

There is no complete inventory of the leasing of CEAA-sealed texts, but the textbook publishers did not line up to obtain reprint rights. The most widely-used American literature college text, the *Norton Anthology,* prints pieces of four CEAA editions. The trendy *Heath Anthology* uses four Melville short stories from the CEAA edition. The reprinting publishers were expected to perform scrupulous multiple proofings of reset texts to ensure their trustworthiness, but it was impossible to enforce this expectation. There is no way, short of multiple collations, to check the reliability of reset texts; but no one took this responsibility. My experience with the Cambridge University Press critical edition of *The Great Gatsby* inspires dubiety about the reliability of reprinted or reset texts—even in the age of electronic publishing. It always comes down to who is responsible for maintaining the chastity of the text. The answer is usually Bert Williams's "Nobody."

After fourteen years with the Hawthorne edition and the CEAA I was determined to apply Bowers's practice and standards to twentieth-century American literature. F. Scott Fitzgerald's daughter, Scottie, endorsed my plan for a "Daddy edition"; but Charles Scribner, Jr., who controlled Fitzgerald's American publication rights, was incredulously opposed. When I became a trustee of Fitzgerald's literary properties after Scottie's death, I was able to obtain permission from the new proprietors of the Scribners imprint to negotiate with Cambridge University Press for publication of a Fitzgerald edition in return for exclusive USA reprint rights to the texts—without editorial apparatus. The NEH declined to make a grant for the Fitzgerald editorial work, but I funded the editorial work with my father's money. Bowers came on board as textual consultant. Editorial Paradise.

The project soon turned rotten when Andrew Brown of CUP tampered with my text of *The Great Gatsby* and persuaded two of the trustees—Scottie's daughter and Scottie's corrupt ex-husband, S. J. Lanahan—to support him in cancelling two emendations: my correct description of the *retinas* of the eyes on Dr. Eckleburg's billboard, and my correction of the location of the Queens end of the Queensboro Bridge from *Astoria* to *Long Island City*.[4] After further interference in my edition of *The Love of the Last Tycoon* by Brown, the other trustees, and a shiten shepherde, I quit in shame and disgust.

The CUP *Gatsby* was published in 1991. By the seventh CUP printing in 1996 three substantive variants had been introduced. The 1991 trade *Gatsby* published in the UK by Scribner's/Macdonald introduced three substantive variants—one of them the loss of a meaningful structural space break. In 1995 CUP published a flawed text of *Gatsby* in its "Cambridge Literature" series. The Fitzgerald trustees at first supported my insistence that all copies be destroyed, but then two-thirds of them yielded to CUP and allowed the books to be sold. This text was reprinted in 1998 as a "Special Edition for sale in South Asia only." Presumably it didn't matter what the natives read.

In the United States the CUP *Gatsby* text was incorporated in the "Scribner Classics" series in 1992. The enmity among the Fitzgerald trustees and the interference of S. J. Lanahan in textual concerns resulted in the contradictory use of *Astoria* and *Long Island City* for the location of the Queens end of the Queensboro Bridge in the first printing. The crux was resolved in subsequent printings of the Scribner "Authorized Text." Eternal vigilance is the price of textual accuracy.

In 1996 I celebrated the F. Scott Fitzgerald centenary by publishing a critical text of *Tender Is the Night* with Everyman. By then *Tender* was out of copyright in the UK. There was no editorial interference from Upper St. Martin's Lane. This is what I learned: stick to works in public domain, and keep the hell away from the CUP.

The funded CEAA editions as of 1976:

Works of Stephen Crane (University Press of Virginia). Completed.
The Journals and Miscellaneous Notebooks of Ralph Waldo Emerson (Harvard University Press). 8 volumes.
The Collected Works of Ralph Waldo Emerson (Harvard University Press). 1 volume.
The Works of Nathaniel Hawthorne (Ohio State University). 14 volumes.

The Selected Edition of William Dean Howells (Indiana University Press). 26 volumes.
Washington Irving (University of Wisconsin Press and Twayne). 19 volumes.
The Writings of Henry David Thoreau (Princeton University Press). 5 volumes.
The Works of Mark Twain and *Mark Twain Papers* (University of California Press). 14 volumes.
Collected Writings of Walt Whitman (New York University Press). 2 volumes.

The associated editions:

James Fenimore Cooper (State University of New York Press). 2 volumes.
John Dewey (Southern Illinois University Press). 11 volumes.
Herman Melville (Northwestern University Press). 9 volumes.
William Gilmore Simms (University of South Carolina Press). 4 volumes.
Charles Brockden Brown (Kent State university Press). 2 volumes.
Harold Frederic (Texas Christian University Press). 1 volume.
William James (Harvard University Press). 5 volumes.

There were also sealed one-shot volumes:

The Bigelow Papers
The Autobiography of Benjamin Franklin
Cotton Mather's *Paterna*
Sealed manuscript facsimiles for *The Red Badge of Courage* and *The Great Gatsby*.

Notes

1. *The Centennial Edition of Sidney Lanier,* 10 volumes, edited by Charles R. Anderson (Baltimore: Johns Hopkins University Press, 1945), vol. 1, p. x.

2. Ibid., vol. 1, p. 287.

3. Lecture to the American Literature section of the South Atlantic Modern Language Association, 22 November 1962, and published in *Studies in Bibliography* (1964): 223–228.

4. Matthew J. Bruccoli, "Getting It Right: The Publishing Process and the Correction of Factual Errors—with Reference to *The Great Gatsby,*" p. 117 in this book. Originally published in *Essays in Honor of William B. Todd,* edited by Dave Oliphant, compiled by Warner Barnes and Larry Carver (Austin: Harry Ransom Humanities Research Center, University of Texas at Austin, 1991), pp. 40–59. Revised and separately published (Columbia, S.C.: [n.p.], 1994).

Textual Variants in Sinclair Lewis's *Babbitt*

For students of modern bibliography Sinclair Lewis's *Babbitt* offers worthwhile evidence about textual variation, and its problems, in present day printing from plates. The facts of variation are in themselves of no particular significance (save that they occur); but the implications that can be drawn from a study of *Babbitt*'s printing history as revealed by these facts are of real moment to critics of contemporary texts and to scholars who must quote from texts produced by the twentieth-century printing shops. Of more specialized interest is the appearance of two bibliographical problems, for one of which, at least, no certain solution is available.

The variants in question appear in a table at the end of this note. They were discovered by examining copies of different printings on the Hinman Collating Machine owned by the University of Virginia Library.[1]

In all, five states of variation may be found between the original state of the plates and the state represented by current reprints in the Modern Library and Harbrace Modern Classics editions (both printed from the same plates). The first stage of correction occurs during the initial printing published on September 14, 1922, by Harcourt, Brace & Co. Here the substitution of *Lyte* for *Purdy*, and of *any* for *my* on p. 49 is of some seriousness since the original reading had misnamed the character. The problem is in two parts, of course: (1) to determine whether the error was corrected by stop press or by cancellation within a single impression, or whether the error was confined to the whole first impression, and the corrected state of page 49 to a different impression of the book; and (2) who caught the error and when, and how it was corrected.

Because stop-press alteration of plates is expensive in lost press-time when undertaken by modern printing establishments, absolutely attested cases have not, apparently, found their way into published bibliographical investigation. Hence one's first impulse might be to conjecture that there were two pre-publication printings of *Babbitt* and that the changes on p. 49 were made between the two

---

This essay first appeared in *Studies in Bibliography* 11 (1958): 263–268. Reprinted with permission of the Bibliographical Society of the University of Virginia.

impressions. There were indeed two pre-publication printings. The Harcourt, Brace records[2] show that the first printing bill for 80,500 copies of *Babbitt* was dated July 27, 1922; and the second press bill for 20,000 copies September 23, 1922. The first plate correction bill was September 23, 1922. Since publication date was September 14, it is clear that the second impression had been ordered before publication and may even have been run off the presses by that date although (see below) not released until October.

However, this impression can be identified, and it is not the same as the impression in which the only variants are those on page 49, for in this second printing the Hinman Collator discloses some evidence of slight plate damage that would occur through storage of plates between impressions. Moreover, additional plate corrections were made, on pages 75, 85, and 271, not present in the various copies containing only the page 49 altered readings. Doubtless because the order for the second printing of 20,000 copies was placed before publication as a supplement to the original printing, no change from the first-impression date was made on the verso of the title-page for these copies; hence they can be distinguished from first-printing copies only by the presence of the corrected readings on pages 75, 85, and 271. However, on the title-page verso of the third impression this second printing is given belated recognition as *Second Printing, October 1922,* followed by the line *Third Printing, October, 1922.*[3]

To sum up. The publisher's records list between the first and third printings a second of 20,000 billed on September 23, 1922. By some slight plate damage and by alterations to the plates of pages 75, 85 and 271 (accounting for the September 23 bill for plate corrections) this impression differentiates itself from the impression with the original states of the plates and (on the evidence of the Hinman Collator in the lack of plate damage) from the same first impression though with the two alterations on p. 49. This second printing is subsequently numerated on the title-page verso of the third and fourth impressions, although not on its own title-page verso. The *Lyte-any* variants on page 49, therefore, were not made in the interval between two impressions but instead are present within the original first impression.

As to the exact circumstances of these page 49 alterations within the first printing we have no information and at this late date are unlikely to secure any. On some occasions a modern pressman at the start of printing will scan an early copy of a sheet for mechanical errors; but that such a workman would be so intimately concerned with the sense as to catch the mistake in a name, as here, is scarcely credible. It would be possible to conceive on other occasions that delay in the delivery of author's corrected proof for final revises, or some error in failing to make final corrections, might inadvertently extend even to the early stages of printing. No precise decision seems possible here, although conjecture may be allowed. It would seem most probable that by some accident, the details of which cannot be recovered, these two page 49 corrections ordered for the text in linotype form had not been made before casting of the plate; and the failure to correct was then discovered by comparison of such proof with the foundry proof (pulled from the plates) only after printing of the forme had started. We know that Lewis had partly relied upon the professional proofreaders in the Quinn & Boden printing establishment. Hence, as an alternative theory we might guess that someone, perhaps interested in the story, took it upon himself to read the whole collection of foundry proofs and in this process came upon the page 49 errors.[4]

Thus we are faced with the simple proposition, either (1) the case is one of stop-press correction, or (2) the case is one of sheet cancellation. That the *Lyteany* sheets of the first printing represent completely reimposed and newly imprinted sheets at a later time is possible but not probable on the evidence. If a cancellans sheet had been manufactured before binding had started, the *Purdy-my* sheets would need to represent faulty copies which had been ordered destroyed but by some error found their way to the bindery along with corrected sheets. Such a theory cannot be maintained in view of the evidence that substantial numbers of the original state are in existence (6 of the original against 8 of the corrected in the 14 copies I have checked).

As an alternative we should need to suppose that binding had started before the error was discovered and the cancellans sheets provided; in such a case the *Purdy-my* copies would represent copies initially bound before the cancellans sheets arrived. There is no positive evidence for this theory, and some rather slight evidence against it. In the first place, no records of a cancellans sheet exist. In the second, I am inclined to lean some weight on the fact that at the time the alterations were made in the original set of plates, a duplicate set of shells (unbacked plates) that had also been cast were similarly altered. The argument is not strong, but on the evidence that later plate alterations were not (except for two anomalous pages) simultaneously transferred to the shells, there may be reason to associate the page 49 corrections as near as possible to the original casting and checking of both original plate and shell, since changes made in the one seem to have been made simultaneously in the other. The odds are, therefore, that in the page 49 variants we have an example of comparatively rare modern stop-press correction.[5]

In the unnumbered second printing (not distinguished from the first but subsequently listed as the second, and as distributed in October), the page 49 alterations are found, of course, and in addition errors of pages 75, 85, and 271 were corrected in the plates; and in the numbered third printing (October) a further necessary change was made, on page 397, from *against the Open Shop* to *for the Open Shop*. In large part as the result of Mr. Louis Feipel's suggestion,[6] twelve further corrections were made in the fourth printing distributed in November of the same year. This state of the plates also machined the Grosset & Dunlap movie reprint edition of 1924.

An immediate anomaly appears when the series of printings are collated as represented by the Harbrace Modern Classics, post-1942 cheap edition Grosset & Dunlap editions, and the Modern Library reprints, for with the exception of the two corrections on page 49 stemming from the plate alteration to this single page during the first impression, and the variants on pages 188 and 196 first found in the fourth printing, the remaining fourteen alterations revert to their original faulty readings as present in the first-impression plates. Duplicate plates provide the explanation. The Harcourt, Brace & Co. records show that on July 1, 1922, one set of plates and a duplicate set of shells (unbacked plates) were manufactured (information again by the courtesy of Mr. Gerald Gross). On December 20, 1941, the original set of plates was melted, and on January 7, 1942, the duplicates, or shells, were backed up to make them into printing plates. From this second set, therefore, were printed all the Harbrace Modern Classics and Modern Library editions.

That page 49 in these duplicate plates appears in the corrected state is explicable in the normal course provided the stop-press alterations were made from foundry proof and thus in both sets at the same time, plates and shells. However, the seemingly arbitrary selection only of pages 188 and 196 to bring into conformity with the first-set alterations in the fourth impression is very puzzling. Both pages are in the outer forme of the same sheet, but the significance of this fact is difficult to apply.[7]

From this history of the plates we learn that the Lewis who sneered at an English Rotarian for speaking of "Bertrand Shaw" was not himself so scrupulous as he might have been about the accuracy of his references to the fraternal organizations that he was satirizing. The *B.* in *B.P.O.E* he twice expanded in error as *Brotherly* (pp. 9, 165, corrected in the fourth printing) although once correctly as *Benevolent* (p. 55). The forms *Oddfellows* (p. 203) and *Redmen* (p. 188 but correctly on p. 203) might seem as ignorant to members of these orders as "Bertrand" Shaw to a literary man.

But the really interesting conclusion from this plate study, outside of the two bibliographical problems involved, is the evidence that in modern textual transmission one cannot necessarily trust the latest editions of plated books to be the most correct. Before the institution of the duplicate plates the history of *Babbitt* was one of steady improvement in the state of the text through the fourth printing, although no evidence is present to suggest authorial correction at any stage. But beginning with 1942 editions, the almost wholly uncorrected second set of plates reverted to a state of textual error that wiped out substantially all the results of the improvements in the second, third, and fourth impressions. As a result, the only reading texts now being printed are more corrupt than any impression after the original; and a textual critic of the future will need to search out either the fourth impression or some reprint before 1942 since only these represent the most highly corrected state of *Babbitt*'s readings.[8]

Notes

1. The two variants on page 49 were first discovered by Mr. Jacob Blanck (see *Sinclair Lewis: A Biographical Sketch,* by Carl Van Doren, with a bibliography by Harvey Taylor [1953], pp. 102–103); the rest, I believe, have not been recognized. I am grateful to Mr. John Wyllie, University of Virginia Librarian, for suggesting this study to me and for helping me to work out the evidence, and to Professor Fredson Bowers for assistance in the preparation of this account of my findings.

2. *Teste* Mr. Gerald Gross of Harcourt, Brace and Co., to whom I am particularly indebted for much valuable information. I am also grateful to Mr. James T. Quinn of Quinn and Boden Co. (the original printers of the book), and to Mr. William Simon, Jr., of H. Wolff Co (printers of the Modern Library edition), for answering questions about the printing of *Babbitt.*

3. Extended search has failed to turn up any copy listing itself as the second printing on the title-page verso. It is not likely that one will be found since the time interval between this recorded second printing and the third printing is very likely too narrow for still another to exist.

4. The possibility that this stage of the plate alteration resulted from some error in the printing plant might be argued since it would seem that these particular plate alterations were never billed to Harcourt, Brace.

5. A collector concerned with "points" will, of course, choose the *Purdy-my* state as the earlier. There is no validity whatever to the arguments of the bookseller Robert K. Black that since the *Lyte-any* readings are found in a copy autographed by Lewis on the day after publication (the copy is now in the University of Virginia Library), they must represent the state found in the author's advance copies and thus must be considered as "gathered and bound before any of the so called 'first-state' copies, so that in terms of priority of issue, though not of printing, it actually precedes them and is therefore more desirable" (See Mr. Black's *List Number Forty-Five* issued ca. March 1956 from Upper Montclair, N.J.). In the first place, the copy cannot be proved to be from the advance copies sent Lewis. In the second place, the assumption that an author's advance copies represent the first copies off the binding machines is ordinarily wrong: it supposes that copies are shipped to the publisher in driblets from the bindery and that the publisher immediately breaks open a case and sends out the author's copies. In the third place, the order of

pre-publication distribution of copies can have no bearing on questions of "issue," especially when mere press variants are involved. For a full discussion of this matter, see Bowers, *Principles of Bibliographical Description* (1949), pp. 409–411.

6. Mr Feipel, who makes a hobby of proofreading published books to note their errors and inconsistencies, wrote Harcourt, Brace on 6 November 1922, enclosing a list of over seventy readings that in his view required alteration for consistency of usage or because of real error. In response to the question whether the spelling *areoplane* on pp. 19 and 85 was intentional, Mr. Donald C. Brace of Harcourt, Brace, acknowledging on 9 November Mr. Feipel's list, replied that the spelling was intentional, and added, "It may interest you to know that it was an effort, each time the proof was read, to keep the proof reader from changing it." Lewis's response to the list was in character: "J. Henry! This man Feipel is a wonder—to catch all these after rather unusually careful proofreading not only by myself and my wife but also by two or three professionals at Quinn's! . . . (Gawd, Feipel has me nervous about hyphens!)" (Lewis to Donald Brace, 10 November 1922, quoted from Harrison Smith, editor, *From Main Street to Stockholm* [1952], pp. 113–114.) The change from *benny* (i.e., overcoat) to *kelly* (i.e., hat) was suggested by Keith Preston in his column "Hit or Miss" in the Chicago *Daily News* for 4 November 1922, on p. 8, in connection with a note, signed "XYLOID," about the glossary in the British edition of *Babbitt*.

7. The Hinman Collator discloses that type wear on pp. 188 and 196 present in the fourth impression does not appear in the later printings that were made from the duplicate plates of these pages. Hence one is barred from conjecturing that for some reason the original plates for these pages were held over for use in later impressions: it is certain that pp. 188 and 196 were printed from the duplicate plates, which must therefore have been altered. But why other plates were not also altered at the same time to conform to the fourth-impression corrections cannot be explained.

8. As a pendant to this commentary on modern textual transmission, one might point out that the single really substantive alteration that corrects something not clearly a misprint (except for the *Purdy-Lyte* alteration) was in fact made on the suggestion of an outsider (i.e., *kelly* for *benny* on p. 121).

Hidden Printings in Edith Wharton's *The Children*

The Children (1928) is a minor novel in the Edith Wharton canon, but it is an intriguing bibliographical item. Although corroborative details from the publisher's records are incomplete, physical evidence in copies of the book reveals that what has passed for the first printing of *The Children* actually consists of two printings from duplicate plates; furthermore, both these printings include two states. Subsequent production of the novel introduced more hidden printings. It seems extremely unlikely, though, that there was any attempt by the publisher to mislead the public.

Even though the text of the novel is not altered, *The Children* points a lesson for all who are professionally concerned with books printed from plates: modern printing methods are not to be taken as guaranteeing uniformity in all copies included within a single impression. Moreover, an attempt to differentiate printings cannot be restricted to an examination of the publisher's code or the information supplied on the copyright page. Although in most cases there is no intentional deception, the information too frequently turns out to be erroneous or misleading. In some instances the publisher is simply not interested in the strict accuracy of this information; in other cases the divorce between the editorial office and the printing plant makes the correct facts unavailable.

It has been a rule for collectors and cataloguers to differentiate printings of an Appleton book by the numeral in parentheses at the foot of the last page of text. A "(2)," for example, indicates that the book in hand is a second printing. Undoubtedly, collectors have noticed that the first printing is sometimes designated by a roman "(I)" and sometimes by an Arabic "(1)"; but since both forms were never reported in the same title, this distinction apparently occasioned no speculation. In *The Children,* however, both "(I)" and "(1)" occur.[1] Copies with "(1)" have also the statement "*First Printing, September, 1928*" on the copyright page—which is contrary to Appleton practice—whereas "(I)" copies lack

---

"Hidden Printings in Edith Wharton's *The Children*" was originally published in *Studies in Bibliography* 15 (1962): 269–273. Reprinted with permission of the Bibliographical Society of the University of Virginia.

this legend.² When queried, Appleton-Century-Crofts, Inc. (the successor firm to D. Appleton & Co.) replied: "The reason for this [the two sets of markings in *The Children*] was to distinguish between our copies for trade distribution and those supplied to the Book-of-the-Month Club for their use. We can only *assume* that the copies with the legend 'First Printing, September, 1928' on the title pages verso were the first copies run off on the original printing, and the balance of the copies were for the Book-of-the-Month Club."³ This explanation would seem to indicate either a stop-press revision or two printings. On the other hand, neither of these alternatives will satisfactorily account for the variants within the printings. That *The Children* was a book-club selection suggests the possibility of duplicate plates, which provides the key to the problem.

Collation on the Hinman Machine at the University of Virginia reveals that pages 122 and 135 of *The Children* were reset without textual revision. Both forms of each page appear in "(I)" copies and in "(1)" copies, thus producing four states of the "first printing." Since page 122 was not reset line-for-line, the two forms of the page are readily distinguished. Page 135 was reset line-for-line—although the lengths of short lines 8 and 15 were not kept uniform—but there is a typo in one form of page 135, where "moters" appears for "motors." But it is doubtful that page 135 was reset just to correct "moters," for this correction could have been made with a plate patch. Rather, "moters" appears to be a typo which was introduced when the page was reset for another reason, which is detailed below.

The Children was published on 1 September 1928, and on 22 September Appleton advertised in *Publishers' Weekly* that more than 100,000 copies were in print. The book was a sleeper, and the necessity for producing a large number of copies in some haste plus Book-of-the-Month Club distribution made duplicate plates practicable. The Book-of-the-Month Club at that time purchased copies from the original publisher, rather than leasing plates for separate publication, as is its practice now.⁴

Although there is an ingenious way to account for the four states of the "first printing" by postulating stop-press revisions of the code number and copyright page in both sets of plates, what follows is a more reasonable explanation. Two sets of plates were prepared at the beginning of production. In one of these sets the copyright page and the code number were altered to distinguish the Book-of-the-Month Club copies. From the fact that the "(1)" is tilted and badly printed, it is probable that the "(1)" was mortised in to replace the "(I)," and that "*First Printing, September, 1928*" was added to the copyright page of the "(1)" set of plates to make it doubly distinguishable. Both sets of plates were machined at about the same time; but in one set the inner forme of the ninth gathering sustained serious damage or batter in the area of pages 122 and 135 (these are adjacent in standard octavo impositions), necessitating resetting and replating of the two pages. In this resetting the typo "moters" was introduced.

That the "(I)" copies were distributed by Appleton and the "(1)" copies by the Book-of-the-Month Club is indicated by the locations of certain copies. Both Library of Congress copyright deposit copies (A 1054115, deposited 6 September 1928) have "(I)," whereas the Book-of-the-Month Club file copy has "(1)." Two inscribed copies in the Yale University Library, dated August 1928 and 14 August 1928, have "(I)"—and it is certain that the author's advance copies would have come from the publisher rather than a book club.

The only available printing information in the Appleton-Century-Crofts files clearly supports the theory that there were two separate printings included within the "first printing."

ptg # 1   ptg # 1
14182   14221
6/19/28 30,740   7/23/28 55,000

Here the five-digit number is the job or order identification number.

The foregoing account identifies two printings from duplicate plates, but not the four states that have been noted. These were created when the sheets were bound. Except for the first and last gatherings, no attempt would have been made to segregate the sheets printed from the two sets of plates; consequently the sheets for the ninth gathering (containing pages 122 and 135) were integrated when they came off the presses and were moved to the bindery. This statement is at least partially substantiated by the gutter markings in *The Children*. Throughout the book the letter "I" or "N" appears in the gutters. These are identification marks inserted by the stonemen or pressmen in the dead areas of the formes so as to print on the spines of the gatherings or deep in the gutters.[5] Most likely, these particular letters are the initials of the men, who for our purposes may be dubbed Isaac on press # 1 and Newton on press # 2. A tabulation of these initials in twelve copies—one of which was cut apart—revealed no discernible pattern, a finding that lends further support to the idea that the sheets were mixed in the bindery. This theory would be neatly substantiated were freak copies with "(I)" and "*First Printing, September, 1928*" or "(1)" and no legend to turn up.

The most curious point about this problem is the fact that although two printings from duplicates are clearly indicated, these two printings cannot be isolated—except for the first and last gatherings—because the sheets were scrambled. In any case, the Edith Wharton collector will need all four states of the first two printings.

In 1928 it was not the practice of the Book-of-the-Month Club to reorder; it placed just one order for the quantity of a title needed for distribution.[6] Yet Appleton continued to print *The Children* from both sets of plates. This statement contradicts the printing records:

ptg # 2	ptg # 3
14274	14294
8/23/28 10,000	9/13 15,170

But on the evidence of the variant pages 122 and 135, the copies marked "(2)" include two printings; and there is no other way to account for these variants. The same is true for copies marked "(3)." Moreover, the two sets of plates were shuffled before the "(3)" copies were printed, a procedure that introduced two new combinations of pages 122 and 135—the combination of the "is . . . most" form of 122 with the "motors" form of 135, and the combination of "is . . . sen-" with "moters." The Grosset & Dunlap copies—printed from one set of plates leased from Appleton[7]—were a new impression, although this fact is obscured by the retention of the "(3)" in these copies.[8]

Notes

1. This information was communicated to me by Hendon Chubb II, a collector who urged me to pursue the matter further.

2. The standard bibliography, Lavinia R. Davis, *A Bibliography of the Writings of Edith Wharton* (1933), mentions only copies with "(1)" and "*First Printing, September, 1928.*" Merle Johnson's *American First Editions,* Fourth Edition (1947) mentions only the "(I)."

3. Miss Helen Cohan to M. J. Bruccoli, 18 April 1958.

4. *Teste* Harry S. Dale, Vice President and Production Manager.

5. These gutter markings are not to be confused with the various systems of collating marks put on the spines of gatherings as an aid to bindery workers.

6. *Teste* Harry S. Dale.

7. *Teste* Irving B. Simon, Production Manager.

8. I am indebted to the following friends for checking copies: Robert Turner, J. M. Edelstein, Roger Stoddard, Donald Gallup, and Mrs. Neal E. Firkins. I am also obligated to Frank Gil and Robert Chapman of Appleton-Century-Crofts, Inc. for responding to my queries. This article was discussed with John Cook Wyllie and Oliver Steele whose suggestions were extremely helpful. Frank Tofano, Charles Moran, and Mark Rinker supplied me with information about printing methods.

A Mirror for Bibliographers

Duplicate Plates in Modern Printing

The achievements in the biographical study of the hand-press period have been mainly won by inference from such evidence as can be found in the books themselves. No printer of 1480 or 1580 has bequeathed to us a primer of his craft. Moxon, our earliest eyewitness, is as late as 1680; and he is often unsatisfactory—for example, on press figures. Today, when printing is evolving so rapidly, bibliographers must not all be archeologists; some must accept the duty of recording present-day practice, both for contemporary studies and as an archive for future scholars. Unless the facts of current publishing and printing practice are organized, the bibliographers of the twenty-third century will curse us when they work on the masterpieces of this century. In all conscience, our branch of scholarship cannot study Thomas Creede's shop of 1599 and neglect Kingsport Press in 1973.

Such neglect has been rationalized in two ways. First there is the usual academic apathy toward contemporary literature, the attitude that a twentieth-century novel just isn't worth the trouble of painstaking bibliographical investigation: what does it matter if the text of a modern novel is foul? It does matter. It does matter whether one of the most delicate passages in American fiction has the correct reading *orgastic* or the incorrect *orgiastic:* "Gatsby believed in the green light, the orgastic future that year by year recedes before us." Second, it is asserted that modern technology has perfected printing—there are no more problems. And, anyway, if it isn't perfect, it is certainly so complex that a bibliographer simply can't learn enough about it. A most pernicious and false doctrine, this. Each new development in printing introduces new problems which bibliography must recognize.

This essay appeared in *Readings in Descriptive Bibliography,* edited by John Bush Jones (Kent, Ohio: Kent State University Press, 1974), pp. 190–195. Reprinted with permission of the Kent State University Press. It is a revision of an essay published originally in *Papers of the Bibliographical Society of America* 54 (Second Quarter 1960): 83–88.

I have chosen the problem of duplicate plates to illustrate my contention that the advance of bibliography can proceed only from a familiarity with printing and publishing practices. In so doing, I must also make a plea for conservative use of bibliographical terminology—for precise usage which relates the published text to the facts of printing.

Printing from duplicate plates is not an esoteric problem; it is standard practice, and a rudimentary knowledge of the use of duplicate plates is requisite for any bibliographer working with machine-printed books. The bibliographical stakes involved can be high indeed. For example, when Houghton Mifflin decided to publish a new edition of *The Scarlet Letter* in 1959, the Riverside Edition—which had been kept in print since 1883, partly by the use of duplicate plates—was collated against the first edition. Nearly 900 variants were found.[1]

Virtually all trade books are printed from plates—stereotypes, electrotypes, plastic or rubber plates, as well as offset plates. Duplicate plates may be prepared for immediate use, or the mats may be stored against the time when the originals wear out. Metal plates are surprisingly fragile, and shop handling or the strains of normal use frequently result in batter. Plates can be repaired, corrected, or revised by cutting out a section and replacing it with a patch of the same material. Metal plates are sometimes altered by the insertion of linotype, and the new material will initially print more boldly or more sharply because it has not experienced as much wear as the original section. In most cases the only method for differentiating sets of duplicate plates is by collating copies of the book for evidence of emendation, repair, or batter.

Oliver Steele has demonstrated that the English plates of *The Miller of Old Church* were cast from the corrected American plates.[2] The American plates contained inserted linotype corrections which, being softer than the plate metal, spread during printing. But the English plates—though they included the corrections—did not show this spreading, indicating that the English plates were cast from the corrected American plates *before* the American plates were used. By rigorously applying *edition* as all the copies of a book printed from one setting of type or from plates made from that setting, and *impression* or *printing* as all the copies of a book printed at one time without removing the type or plates from the press, it is clear that nothing more than reimpression was involved in the English and American copies of *The Miller of Old Church*. The case is clearer for Cozzens's *By Love Possessed*: after 50,000 copies were printed from flat plastic plates, curved electros were made from the original molds. Again, only reimpression is involved.

It is incorrect to apply the term *state* to the products of duplicate plates unless within an impression there are alterations which, in Fredson Bowers's words "are attempts to create a form of ideal copy."³ An example would be a stop-press plate correction made within an impression, as is the case in the first printing of *Babbitt*.⁴

If the working set of plates is revised and the stored duplicates are not, the anomalous situation of a late printing reverting to an earlier form of the text will result. This also occurred in *Babbitt*. The Modern Library and Harbrace Modern Classics copies currently for sale are less corrected than certain 1922 copies—yet all these copies represent the same original settings of type.

An instructive problem is presented by Edith Wharton's *The Children*.⁵ Plate batter repair indicates that two sets of plates were used throughout the career of this novel. Perhaps Appleton was caught short by the inexplicable success of this novel and was compelled to print from two sets of plates for the sake of speed, or perhaps the Appleton and Book-of-the-Month Club copies were printed separately from duplicate plates. When the so-called third printing was required, the two sets of plates were scrambled, thereby creating two new textually indistinguishable forms of the novel. Since the Appleton code designates each of the double impressions as one single impression, what the publisher designates as the third impression actually includes the fifth and sixth impressions. Is a bibliographer to classify these as separate impressions or as two "states of a general impression"? Strictly speaking, they are separate impressions. When a publisher persists in numbering simultaneous impressions as single impressions, however, and when there is no way to differentiate the impressions, then it is convenient—if less accurate—to resort to some such terminology as "states of a general impression."

Mention of the Book-of-the-Month Club introduces another problem. When the Club selects a title at present, it contracts with the original publisher for three sets of plates, which are run in different plants. The publisher of the book will have one or more sets made for his own use. As a result, Hemingway collectors, desperate for a first first, have been reduced to competing for a dust-jacket point in *The Old Man and the Sea*. It would be instructive to collate the four original impressions of this book against each other and then against the three simultaneously printed regional "editions" of *Life* magazine in which the novel was pre-published.

Although letterpress plates can be produced from photographs of a book, photo-offset has established itself as less expensive. If a publisher decides to reprint a work for which he does not own plates or mats from which plates can be cast, planographic duplicates of the original typesetting can be made by photographing the book itself. Since it is a trade practice to use an early impression of the book as offset copy for the sake of sharpness, it is not uncommon for a late photo-offset reprint to revert to an earlier form of the text. Moreover, since it is also common practice to mount the pages from two copies of the work for photocopying—although a single copy can be used—it is not difficult to predict what results when one copy is from the first printing and the other is from a later revised printing. My example for the snares of the photo-offset is *The Beautiful and Damned*, which was reprinted by offset thirty-six years after it had gone out of print.[6] First the printed novel was proofread and some eighty corrections were made by pasting printed lines over the original lines before the book was photographed. Most of these corrections deal with the system of hyphenation; and nine of the would-be corrections actually introduce fresh hyphen errors into the text. Therefore the impression of the novel currently on sale as part of a uniform edition corresponds to no authorized text; and although it reproduces the original setting of type, it introduces new errors. My preference would be to describe this as merely another impression; but more liberal bibliographers might classify this as a sub-edition, since it will probably father a new line—albeit on the wrong side of the sheets.

A related problem is simultaneous printing from standing type and from plates made from that type. This usually occurs in the production of a limited printing sold in conjunction with the regular trade printing. It is sometimes asserted that the limited or deluxe impression is printed from the type before the plates are made, but it is almost certain that in order to minimize the risk of type batter the plates are made before the deluxe impression is printed. This can be demonstrated in *Something About Eve*.[7] The subtitle in the deluxe impression reads "A Comedy of Fig-leaves," but the first trade impression has "A Comedy of Fig-Leaves." Since later impressions have the lower-case l, the title page must have been revised after the plates were made, but before the deluxe impression was printed.

Another interesting area is monotype composition. Theoretically, a monotype tape can be rerun through a type-casting machine again and again to reproduce duplicate type-settings from which plates can be made; another font of type may even be used while retaining every other characteristic of the original setting. Paper tapes are easier to store than plates or molds, and the tapes can be mailed cheaply from one plant to another. In practice, however, there appears to be considerable variation in the use of monotype in America. Kingsport Press reports an error factor of .28 per 1,000 ems, which necessitates thorough proofreading every time a type is run through a caster; but the Plimpton Press reports no error factor.[8] There is also reason to suspect that monotype procedure varies between England and America. Further investigation is indicated.

A useful bibliography must provide material for analysis of textual transmission, which requires that the bibliographer have an understanding of the processes involved in perpetuating a text. It is folly to persuade ourselves that modern literature constitutes a separate bibliographical domain in which we can waive the requisite knowledge of printing practice.

Postscript, 1973

Thirteen years after this article was written I can report that the techniques of bibliographical description for plated books are significantly improved over 1960. Perhaps the chief cause for this improvement is the Center for Editions of American Authors (CEAA), whose work on definitive editions of nineteenth-century American authors has refined bibliographical theory and practice and has added to our knowledge of book production for the stereotype-linotype period. This refinement is also reflected in certain recent bibliographies, notably the volumes in the Pittsburgh Series in Bibliography. Nonetheless, "bibliographies" are still being published that barely merit the appellation of "Checklists"—works that claim to be permanent reference tools and yet misuse bibliographical language and fail to retrace the typographical transmission of texts. The need for true and thorough bibliographies remains great. Bad bibliographies impede good scholarship.

Notes

1. This information was made available to me by Henry Thoma of Houghton Mifflin Company and Prof. Harry Levin, the editor of the new Riverside edition of *The Scarlet Letter*.

2. William W. Kelly, *Ellen Glasgow: A Bibliography*, edited by Oliver Steele (Charlottesville: Bibliographical Society of the University of Virginia, 1964).

3. Fredson Bowers, *Principles of Bibliographical Description* (Princeton: Princeton University Press, 1949), pp. 393–426.

4. Matthew J. Bruccoli, "Textual Variants in Sinclair Lewis's *Babbitt*," *Studies in Bibliography* (1958): 263–268. Included in this chapter of the collection—Ed.

5. Bruccoli, "Hidden Printings in Edith Wharton's *The Children*," *Studies in Bibliography*, (1962): 269–273. Included in this chapter of the collection—Ed.

6. Bruccoli, "Bibliographical Notes on F. Scott Fitzgerald's *The Beautiful and Damned*," *Studies in Bibliography* (1960): 258–261.

7. Bruccoli, *James Branch Cabell: A Bibliography*. Part II, *Notes on the Cabell Collection at the University of Virginia* (Charlottesville: University of Virginia Press, 1957), pp. 42–43.

8. The Kingsport Press data is based on a letter to me from Mr. William C. Hagan, the composing room superintendent, 3 November 1958; the information about Plimpton Press is based on personal interviews with composing room personnel, August 1959.

Concealed Printings in Hawthorne

The following work-in-progress report from the Centenary Editions of the Works of Nathaniel Hawthorne is published in the hope that it will uncover still more concealed printings in Hawthorne. The editors of the Centenary Hawthorne will be grateful for communications on this subject.[1]

The differentiating of concealed printings which have resulted from the reimpression of stereotype or electrotype plates is a wide-open subject. Much of the work that has already been done has been performed by point-hunters, and these investigators have frequently been satisfied with flimsy evidence, such as binding variants or non-integral bound-in advertisements. But the binding or inserted advertisements of a book have no relation to the printing of the sheets and cannot be used to establish textual priority.[2] Many old-line bookmen have shown an abhorrence for the Hinman Collating Machine, but with it the job of comparing a suspected late printing with a suspected early printing can be done with great accuracy and comparative speed.

Although the researcher engaged in work on concealed printings runs the risk of becoming involved in a kind of bibliographical solitaire—that is, he may find himself playing a game in which there are no textual stakes—unsuspected (or, at least undifferentiated) printings abound in nineteenth-century American literature; and there is always the possibility that significant emendations are hidden in the plates of a work. In bibliography you never know what you are going to find until you find it.

As has been mentioned, the best way to attack concealed printings is by collating multiple copies on the Hinman Machine for textual variants or resettings. Since plate alteration normally occurs between printings, it is a good working rule that evidence of plate alteration is evidence of reimpression. The Hinman Machine will also reveal type batter, but batter—if it really is batter and not bad impression or bad inking—may occur in press as well as in storage and can only

---

"Concealed Printings in Hawthorne" was first published in *Papers of the Bibliographical Society of America* 57 (First Quarter 1963): 42–49. Reprinted with the permission of the Bibliographical Society of America.

be used to distinguish late copies from earlier copies. Another method for identifying printings is gutter measurement. Since the two facing pages where a book is sewn had to be adjacent in the imposition of the plates on the press, any significant variation in the width of a given gutter in two copies may be taken as evidence of reimposition. Allowing for paper shrinkage, a significant difference would be three or more centimeters.

Since Nathaniel Hawthorne is a major figure in our literature, *The House of Seven Gables* (1851), *The Blithedale Romance* (1852), and *The Marble Faun* (1860)—all printed in first editions from stereotype plates—will serve as examples of jobs worth doing. *The Scarlet Letter* (1850) was not plated until its third edition, but there are unrecorded states of the two editions from type, which are discussed by Fredson Bowers in the Centenary Hawthorne edition of *The Scarlet Letter*. Loosely speaking, up to now a "first edition" or even a "first printing" of *Seven Gables, Blithedale*, or the *Faun* has been an edition bearing the year of first publication on its title-page—although some firsts have been considered "firster" than others on the basis of dated advertisements or gilt stamping. However, *The Cost Books of Ticknor and Fields* reveals that there were four printings of *Seven Gables* in 1851, two printings of *Blithedale* in 1852, and seven printings of the *Faun* in 1860.³

Machine collations reveals no textual variants in the 1851 *Seven Gables,* but there are three resettings which mark four printings:

A	B	C	D
57.32–34			reset
58		reset	
149.1–3	reset		

In the earliest form of the plates the first three lines of page 149 are battered on the right-hand margin, and this area of the page is reset in the second printing. In the third printing page 58 is completely reset: the clearest difference is that in the earlier printings the question mark in line 17 is to the left of the *y* in *lady,* but in the reset page the question mark is directly beneath the *y.* The resetting of the last three lines on page 57 in the fourth printing can be readily detected on the machine; the eye may be able to tell that in line 33 of the original setting the *c* in *child* is slightly to the right of the *f* in *for,* but in the resetting the *c* is directly beneath the *f.* This division into four printings is supported by gutter measurements. The *Cost Books* also list an 1852 reprint of *Seven Gables*. Since no copy with this date has been found, it is almost certain that the 1852 reprint is hidden among the 1851 copies; and this fifth printing can be isolated by gutter measurement:

	D	E
120/121	3.3 cm.	3.8 cm.
216/217	3.3 cm.	3.7 cm.

There are two textual changes resulting from type damage in *Seven Gables*. In the second printing *apparent* becomes *apparen* (50.25) and *or* becomes *o* (278.25); only the latter was revised during the life of the plates, when *o* was incorrectly emended to *of* in 1866.

An intriguing possibility for further work on *Seven Gables* is suggested by the *Cost Books* entries showing that the first printing was imposed in 22 formes and that the next four printings were imposed in 11 formes. Applying a technique developed by Oliver Steele,[4] it should be possible to reconstruct the imposition of a copy of *Seven Gables* from the pattern of its rough and smooth edges—but all 15 copies I have examined are trimmed. Imposition of inner and outer formes of 32 pages each, producing four different 16-page gatherings, would result in rough side edges on leaves 2, 3, 5–8 of each gathering, and rough bottom edges on leaves 3–6. Imposition of inner and outer formes of 16 pages each, producing two different 16-page gatherings, would result in rough side edges on leaves 5–8, and rough bottom edges on leaves 3–6. Imposition of one 16-page forme printed work-and-turn, producing two copies of the same 16-page gathering, would result in rough side edges on leaves 1–4, and rough bottom edges on leaves 1–8.

There are no resettings in the 1852 *Blithedale*—and I am morally certain of this because I have machined C. Waller Barrett's proof copy against an 1855 reprint. Neither are there significant gutter variations, so it has been impossible to differentiate the two printings listed in the *Cost Books*. But there is a neat pattern of progressive type batter that shows five states of the plates:

	A	B	C	D	E
vi.14			x	x	x
16.15					x
57.26				x	x
69.6					x
97 r.t			x	x	x
97.1			x	x	x
108.28		x	x	x	x
229.2			x	x	x

Thus far the textual pickings have been lean; but with *The Marble Faun* we hit pay dirt, for there are 30 unrecorded textual variants in the 1860 printings of this romance.

As first issued on 7 March 1860 the ending of the *Faun* baffled its readers, and a 5-page "Conclusion" subscribed "LEAMINGTON, March 14, 1860." was added to a later printing in that year. This conclusion has made the distinction between the "first edition" and the "second edition" and has discouraged closer scrutiny of the book. The *Cost Books* show that the problem is considerably more complicated than has been thought: three printings were on sale during the first week of publication (all three may, in fact, have been pre-publication printings), and four more printings were required later in the year. In addition, there were two printings in 1864 and one in 1865, all three of which may have carried the 1860 date on their title-pages. Although the *Cost Books* usually manifest puritanical thrift in their attention to small charges, they unaccountably include no entry for setting and plating the conclusion; and they offer no other clue about which 1860 printing first added the conclusion. However, since the conclusion was written on 14 March in England, it could not have appeared in Boston before the fourth printing of about 7 April.[5]

Although I have not been able to differentiate all seven 1860 printings on the basis of a 50-copy sample, there is clear-cut evidence for identifying four printings of volume I and five printings of volume II—and each volume must be considered separately because there is no guarantee that any two volumes now mated are not living in sin.

The most striking thing about the 1860 printings of the *Faun* is that there were three make-ups of volume I and two of volume II before the conclusion was added—a fact that I have found noted in print only three times.[6] Both volumes are signed in twelves, but the suspected first printing of each is gathered in eights. The suspected second printing is gathered in twelves, but the misimposition of the contents before the preface produces a hiatus in the pagination of volume I. I call the order of these printings suspected because it is reversible, although some slight batter evidence supports the ordering on the chart. The third printing—that is, the third printing I have been able to identify—is gathered in twelves, and volume I has the preliminary matter correctly ordered. That this printing is later than the other two is established by the appearance of two plate changes in volume I and twelve plate changes in volume II. The fourth printing of volume II—which marks the first appearance of the conclusion—includes six errors, of which five on page 98 almost certainly resulted from hasty repair of shop damage. Only one of these errors was corrected during the life of plates, when 98.3 was changed in 1865.

I can speak with some confidence about the first three printings of volume I and the first four of volume II; but beyond this point I am in trouble because I have not isolated all seven of the 1860 printings listed in the *Cost Books*. I strongly suspect that I have not found the printing of volume I that corresponds to the fourth printing of volume II; and I further suspect that this undiscovered printing has the ten plate changes which appear in the fifth printing. It is, however, unlikely that there are any undiscovered textual variants in the missing printings of the *Faun*, for the copies bearing the legend "SEVENTEENTH THOUSAND." were printed late in 1860. Indeed, if the figure is honest—and it probably is not—it could not apply to any 1860 printings because the *Cost Books* show that only 14,500 sets were printed in 1860. However, on 2 November 1860 Ticknor & Fields advertised in the *Boston Evening Transcript*, "Eighteenth Thousand. Now Ready.", so that the "SEVENTEENTH THOUSAND." legend probably marks the seventh printing of September 1860, the last printing of the year.

Of the *Faun* variants, only the one at 199.13 of volume II is of critical significance. Here Kenyon, the artist, who has been "stood up" by Hilda at the Vatican galleries thinks in the first printing that it was a "very cold heart to which he had devoted himself." The correction to a "very cold art" obviously changes the meaning of the passage from a lover's lament to a statement of Hawthorne's prejudice against the pictorial arts.[7]

Notes

1. A slightly different version of this paper was read before General Topics 8: Bibliographical Evidence, at the December 1962 meeting of the Modern Language Association of America—M.J.B. Soon after his arrival as an assistant professor at the Ohio State University in 1961, Bruccoli began setting up and managing the Centenary Hawthorne Project for which Fredson Bowers had assumed textual responsibility. He continued his work on the Centenary Edition of the Works of Nathaniel Hawthorne throughout the life of the series (1962–1970)—Ed.

2. For the record: on the spine of *The House of Seven Gables* some copies have a straight ampersand and a large *O* in *Ticknor & CO.*; others have a crooked ampersand and a small *o*. On the spine of *The Blithedale Romance* some copies have a large *O* in *CO.*; others have a small *o*.

3. *The Cost Books of Ticknor and Fields,* edited by Warren S. Tryon and William Charvat (New York: Bibliographical Society of America, 1949).

4. See *The Library,* 5th Series (September 1962). I am grateful to Mr. Steele for other information which he has communicated to me.

5. A letter from Hawthorne to Smith, Elder & Co., the publisher of *Transformation,* the English edition of *The Marble Fawn,* reveals that he returned the proof of the conclusion to the printer on 16 March. I am deeply grateful to Norman Holmes Pearson for allowing me to see his transcription of this letter, which is in the collection of Mrs. Reginald Smith.

6. Jacob Blanck, "Nathaniel Hawthorne," *News Sheet of the Bibliographical Society of America* No. 67 (1 March 1946). Lyle H. Wright, *American Fiction 1851–1875: A Contribution Toward a Bibliography* (San Marino, Calif.: Huntington Library, 1957). Fredson Bowers has commented on the make-ups of *The Marble Faun* in his *Principles of Bibliographical Description* (Princeton: Princeton University Press, 1949), pp 386–387, 390, 433.

7. Although I have limited my discussion to the American edition of *The Marble Faun*, I have included the first printing of *Transformation* in the table of variants because *The Marble Faun* was set from advance sheets of *Transformation*. On 7 March 1860 Hawthorne wrote to Smith, Elder & Co., calling attention to two errors in the text of *Transformation:* II-9.7 *with foot;* II-30.17 *literary.* In the third printing of *Transformation*, *literary* was corrected to *literally*, but *with foot* was left unchanged. All the 1860 printings of *The Marble Faun* have *with foot* at I-198.9 and *literally* at I-212.16. Hawthorne's letter is in the collection of Mrs. Reginald Smith, and again I am indebted to Norman Holmes Pearson for allowing me to see his transcription.

Notes on the Destruction of
The Scarlet Letter Manuscript

All that survives of *The Scarlet Letter* manuscript is the title leaf with the table of contents on its verso.[1] There are two explanations of how the manuscript was destroyed: Hawthorne's obscure—in both senses—statement, and his son Julian's commonly-accepted but apparently untrue account.

On 3 November 1850, Hawthorne added this postscript to a letter to his bibliophilic publisher James T. Fields: "The MS. of the Scarlet Letter was burnt long ago."[2] Although the part of this letter dealing with *The House of Seven Gables*— then in progress—has been printed, the postscript has remained unpublished.[3]

Julian Hawthorne's version first appeared in print in *Hawthorne and His Circle* (1903): "I have seen the manuscripts of all his tales except *The Scarlet Letter,* which was destroyed by James T. Fields's printers—Fields having at that time no notion of the fame the romance was to achieve, or of the value that would attach to every scrap of Hawthorne's writing" (p. 52). Julian does not absolutely contradict his father, for Hawthorne did not say who did the burning, himself or the printers; nevertheless it seems unlikely that Fields would have asked Hawthorne for a manuscript that had been destroyed by the publisher's own workmen. It does, however, appear that Julian was right in stating that Fields came to a late acquisitive appreciation of *The Scarlet Letter,* for the manuscript went through the press early in 1850.

Yet, it is unwise to place total faith in Julian's testimony, for he was a confirmed feuder and something of a con-man; and there had been bad feeling between Fields and him. Indeed, his statement about *The Scarlet Letter* manuscript merits less than complete belief because of its curious tone of personal injury. Julian seems, somehow, to feel that he had been deprived of a manuscript he could have sold. He did, in fact, make a good thing of selling his father's papers.

"Notes on the Destruction of *The Scarlet Letter* Manuscript" was first published in *Studies in Bibliography* 20 (1967): 257–259. Reprinted with permission of the Bibliographical Society of the University of Virginia.

The publication of *Hawthorne and His Circle* brought a protest from Fields's widow, Annie, in a letter to Julian which has not previously been printed:

> There is one passage which I think it would be well for you to omit in a reprinting of your last book.
>
> I refer to the one in which you speak of Mr. Fields as inappreciative of the "Scarlet Letter," and for that reason having burned the manuscript. If you will re-read what your father himself published upon the subject of being appreciated and helped by his publisher I think you will cross out of your mind as well as off the printed page any such thought or remark.
>
> Your father told me one day, after saying that he was glad to have me accept and treasure the manuscript of "The House of The Seven Gables",—"I wish I had the manuscript of "The Scarlet Letter" to give you also, but I put it up the chimney."
>
> You may imagine, having heard this from his own lips, how the passage in your book amazed me.
>
> Nothing is of much moment now, except the truth for your own sake, therefore you will, I am sure, cross off the passage in question and publish this brief note wherever and whenever it shall seem to you appropriate.[4]

In fairness to Julian, it should be noted that he had not charged Fields with "having burned the manuscript." What reply he made to Mrs. Fields is not known: and since *Hawthorne and His Circle* was not reprinted, he did not have the opportunity to revise it. Mrs. Fields, meanwhile, repeated her claim—and her defense of Fields—later in the year in a letter to Robert S. Rantoul.[5]

It is unlikely, though, that Julian would have changed his story, for he repeated it—with embellishments—as late as 1931 in what has become the best-known account of the destruction of the manuscript:

> By the way, I was lately in contact with a gentleman who, in the fervour of the moment, said he would pay Twenty Thousand Dollars, cash or certified check, for the original manuscript of *The Scarlet Letter,* to him in hand delivered. I was obliged to decline; not from any foolish pride of possession, nor because no such manuscript ever existed; but because my father, after he had written the thing, delivered it to young Mr. James T. Fields, who, not to be too late for the Spring Book Market, promptly passed it on to the printers; and they, after they had set it up, dropped the sheets into the waste-basket, or used them for pipe-lighters. I have heard Fields, in later and wiser years, bitterly lament this indiscretion. But the rash deed was committed four-score-and-one years ago, and is irrevocable.

Possibly the eager virtuoso mentioned above, before making his proposition, may have been aware of its futility. Nevertheless, it was a gallant and eloquent gesture, and helps the trade.[6]

And again one is struck by Julian Hawthorne's irrational sense of outraged wallet.[7]

Notes

1. Now in the Pierpont Morgan Library, this leaf was formerly owned by Stephen H. Wakeman but was not included in the Wakeman sale catalogue (American Art Association, 28–29 April 1924). See the Centenary Hawthorne volume of *The Scarlet Letter* (1962) for a facsimile of the title page. See also W. H. Cathcart, *A Bibliography of the Works of Nathaniel Hawthorne* (Cleveland: Rowfant Club, 1905), p. 33.

2. Possibly dated 5 November. Houghton Library, Harvard University, MS. My colleague Professor William Charvat told me about the postscript.

3. James T. Fields, *Yesterdays with Authors* (Boston: J. R. Osgood, 1872), pp. 55–56.

4. Rome, 27 February 1904. Houghton Library, Harvard University, MS Am. 1745.1 (4). My thanks to Dr. William Bond and Professor Fredson Bowers for calling this document to my attention.

5. *First Editions of Ten American Authors Collected by J. Chester Chamberlain . . . February 16 and 17, 1909 . . . The Anderson Auction Company . . .* Part I, #170: "An interesting fact about 'The Scarlet Letter' is that the original MS. (with the exception of the title) was destroyed by Hawthorne. In a letter from Mrs. Annie Fields to Robert S. Rantoul, June 13th, 1904, she says in part: '. . . *Hawthorne himself told me that he put the manuscript of "The Scarlet Letter" up the chimney, never thinking that it would be of any value.*'"

6. "The Making of 'The Scarlet Letter,'" *Bookman* (December 1931): 401–402.

7. I am indebted to C. E. Frazer Clark, Jr., for the use of his books and brains.

Part 3

On Publishing and Publishers

"Publication is the mandatory act of authorship. A book is not a book until it is published. The teaching and study of modern literature are flawed because the circumstances of publication for books are ignored; therefore, the profession of authorship is ignored."

M.J.B., preface, *The Sons of Maxwell Perkins: Letters of F. Scott Fitzgerald, Ernest Hemingway, Thomas Wolfe, and Their Editor* (2004)

Getting It Right

The Publishing Process and the Correction of Factual Errors—with Reference to The Great Gatsby

> I take it that the business of an editor is to edit. If he is unprepared to take the risks of backing his own judgments, he should peddle another line of goods.
>
> Fredson Bowers

A sense of the fundamental textual decencies is parceled out unequally at birth. Editors who are otherwise sound oppose the correction of factual errors in critical editions. Factors affecting the decision to emend authorial errors in works of fiction include the nature of the work, the author's commitment to accuracy, the author-editor relationship, the conditions of publication, and the proper functioning of editorial intervention. Most of the examples discussed here are from *The Great Gatsby* because it is a widely published masterpiece with a history of textual maladies.[1]

F. Scott Fitzgerald advised his daughter that it is the writer's task to "make even a forlorn Laplander feel the importance of a trip to Cartier's."[2] Cartier is an upscale jeweler with branches throughout the world, but not in Lapland.[3] A deliberate writer will endeavor to convey to readers the ambience, the sense of elegance and affluence at the Cartier establishment; but the reader who has been there and understands Cartier's ranking in the hierarchy of jewelers will respond more complexly. The material of fiction is always more meaningful to initiated readers, and social realists build recognition effects into their fiction.

This text of "Getting It Right" is revised from an earlier essay of the same title published in *Essays in Honor of William B Todd*, edited by Dave Oliphant and compiled by Warner Barnes and Larry Carver (Austin: Harry Ransom Humanities Research Center, University of Texas at Austin, 1991). The revision was privately printed—Columbia, S.C.: [n.p.], 1994. Reprinted here with permission of Arlyn Bruccoli for the Matthew J. Bruccoli literary estate.

The author of realistic fiction is committed to the way it was or the way it is. He gets facts and details right for the sake of accuracy itself and because the associations of the real place or real event enlarge the meanings of fiction. He does not restrict himself to actual settings or artifacts; but when he utilizes the real thing, some readers are expected to recognize it. Accuracy stimulates the pleasure of recognition and reinforces reader trust. The writer who knows what he is writing about assigns a car make to a character because it helps define the owner.[4] The writer who knows what he is doing sets a scene in an actual hotel because it is an establishment where the action is plausible and because the characters are the sort of people who patronize that hotel: thus the Plaza Hotel in *The Great Gatsby*. The fiction writer is free to invent a setting; but when he stipulates a real place it ought to be all right.

James Gould Cozzens wrote about characters whose lives were shaped by their professions; he had certain of his novels vetted by a doctor, an attorney, and an Air Force general because the validity of the characters and the truth of fiction would have been damaged by errors in professional activities. When a realist blunders, the error reveals something about the author's command of his material; but a correctable error requires editorial attention because it damages the work. That Sinclair Lewis erred in the names of three fraternal organizations (Elks, Red Men, and Odd Fellows) in *Babbit* is of biographical interest, but the errors are non-functional in the novel; the correct forms are necessary in a properly edited text.[5] (A non-functional error is unintentional and serves no purpose in the work.) Theodore Dreiser was a great social historian and a great outsider. The impossible tennis score "twenty love" in *An American Tragedy* is easily remedied; but the description of Sondra "running to serve him" in the preceding sentence must be retained because correction would necessitate rewriting (that is, running to return his serve).

Careful readers and certain writers hold that an author who cannot be trusted in details may not be trustworthy at all. This doctrine has been declared by Nelson Algren:

> You have to know how many bars there are in a jail cell. You can't just say, "The guy's in jail." You've got to *know*. You've got to know there are different doors—there are solid doors, doors without bars. Some cells have one bar left out in the middle for a little shelf there. You have to know what the shelf is for.... You're talking about a jail in Texas—well, how do you know if the cot is iron or not, or if the blankets are cotton, or whether you get a mattress or not. Some jails have mattresses. The reason I've never read Jack Kerouac is because the first book of his I picked up says in the first sentence that the guy

was lying in a gondola. Well, I stopped to think: a gondola is a coal car and the bottom opens. You can't lie in a gondola; you'll hit the track. He doesn't know. He doesn't know what he talks about, so why read him?⁶

Many critics and teachers of literature are disdainful of what they call "surface realism." Saul Bellow has defended this aberration:

> The demands, editorial and public, for certified realities in fiction sometimes appear barbarous to the writer. Why this terrible insistence on factual accuracy? . . . How many stories does the Ansonia Hotel really have; and can one see its television antennae from the corner of West End Avenue and Seventy-second street? What do drugstores charge for Librium? What sort of mustard is used at Nedick's? Is it squeezed from a plastic bottle or applied with a wooden spoon?
>
> These cranky questions will be asked by readers, compulsively. Publishers know they must expect their errors to be detected. They will hear not only from the lunatic fringe and from pedants but from specialists, from scholars, from people with experience "in the field," from protective organizations and from public relations agencies, from people who have taken upon themselves the protection of the purity of facts.⁷

Bellow states that "Publishers know they must expect *their errors* to be detected." But the errors are not the publishers'. They are authorial errors that the editorial staff failed to detect or which the author refused to correct. While dismissing the literary value of "the purity of facts" and presumably expressing his superiority to factual accuracy in his own fiction, Bellow nonetheless assigns responsibility for correctness to the publisher in order to forestall complaints from lunatics, pedants, specialists, scholars, and other self-appointed guardians of factual purity. If correctness is the publisher's responsibility when the work is initially published, then it is the textual editor's concern when the work is subsequently deemed worthy of a critical edition or a "definitive edition" or a textbook edition.

The editor of a critical edition is not compelled to retain a factual error because it derives from an authoritative document—not even if it is present in the manuscript. An accurate transcription of a text is useful—and a facsimile is more useful—but a transcription does not serve the purpose of a critical edition: to provide an emended text that is as close to the published work the author intended as the evidence and the editor's abilities permit.

The concept of intention (original intention? final intention?) causes more vexation than any other term in the editorial lexicon. Editorial decisions based on the attempt to fulfill authorial intention may partake of the psychic. The editor claims to know what the author really meant while writing something else. Or the editor claims to have recovered what the author wrote in a lost document. The emendation process always involves the judgment, knowledge, and experience of each editor. The editor who knows nothing about cars will not notice a wrong model or a wrong mechanical detail. There are editors, critics, readers, teachers, and authors who believe that such things do not matter: that they have nothing to do with the meanings of the work and that people who care about them are "limited to facts." In the case of an author who is on record as indifferent or opposed to factual accuracy—often qualified by "mere"—it may well be best to leave published errors alone; but they should be identified in the apparatus of a critical edition.

Since the uninformed reader is not aware of being misinformed by incorrect details, it is possible to argue that such errors do not affect his response to the work of fiction. Most readers are indifferent to the correctness of details: people who do not notice much in life do not notice much in fiction. The noticer's creed has been expressed in a movie review by Donald Barthelme:

> Some of the duffelbags carried by the soldiers in *Yanks,* which has to do with Americans billeted outside a small English town in 1942–44, dangle limply from their owners' shoulders as if containing maybe a couple of shirts or something, like no duffelbag that ever was. The duffelbag is always fatly packed. And Richard Gere, as a mess sergeant, wears his SFC's stripes sewn to his cook's whites, which is like having them sewn to his arms—are we to assume he's insecure? And the trucks are wrong, Korean-era trucks rather than Second World War trucks, and the trumpet solo played on "I'll Be Seeing You" at the film's big New Year's Eve dance couldn't have been phrased before Art Farmer. God is in the details, as Mies van der Rohe put it.[8]

The publisher has a stake in the correctness and polish of the printed book; nevertheless, the publishing contract does not normally stipulate the extent of editing and checking to be provided. Editorial participation is largely a matter of custom and differs for every author, book, editor, and publisher. Certain authors come to depend on certain editors. Two Random House authors insisted on contracts permitting them to leave the publisher if their editor left the firm. The proliferation of "personal imprints"—for example, A Helen and Kurt Wolff Book—has resulted from close author-editor relationships.

Maxwell Perkins provided the role model for the collaborating editor; but the legendary editorial relationships he developed at Charles Scribner's Sons with Fitzgerald, Hemingway, and Wolfe were personal—not contractual. Moreover, his working procedures with these authors varied. Wolfe was the only one of the three who required or permitted Perkins's intervention in content and structure. Perkins's authority—and that of any house editor—was and remains a matter of custom or informal understanding. The contract between Scribners and Fitzgerald for *The Great Gatsby* does not mention authorial or editorial responsibility for the correctness of the text.[9] Unlike standard publishing agreements now in use, it does not include wording about "Delivery of Satisfactory Copy."

The initial publishing process includes some or all of these pre-galley stages:

1) Reading of a proposal or work in progress by an acquisitions editor—who may not become the in-house editor responsible for seeing the book through publication. This submission step is usually restricted to young writers or nonprofessional authors such as public figures.
2) Editorial review of the complete typescript by the in-house editor, who may recommend revision or rewriting.
3) Line-editing of the final draft: word-by-word editing—ideally performed by the in-house editor. Queries are referred to the author. This step is now customarily omitted or combined with copy-editing.
4) Copy-editing (house-styling) of the setting copy. This step is now routinely assigned to free-lance editors. The author should have the opportunity to check the copy-edited typescript before it goes to the printer.

From the evidence of books published during the last decade, it is clear that editorial stages have been skipped.

The editor of a critical edition occupies the position of the original publisher's editor and is obliged to do what the in-house editor should have done. The principal impediment to this arrogation of responsibility is, obviously, that the textual editor acts on the words of dead and defenseless authors, whereas the in-house editor was expected to query the author.

It is useful to consider the editorial treatment of William Faulkner's Snopes trilogy by Random House. *The Hamlet* was first published in 1940; *The Town* in 1957; and *The Mansion* in 1959. When the three volumes were posthumously published as a set in 1964, *The Hamlet* carried the "Publisher's Note" explaining that "a number of errors that occurred in either or both of the earlier editions" of that novel, as well as discrepancies among the three novels, had been corrected. Some of these emendations made by Random House editor Albert Erskine had been approved by Faulkner, though not published during his lifetime. Erskine's statement of his policy for editing Faulkner is instructive: "I know that he did not wish to have carried through from typescript to printed book his typing mistakes, misspellings (as opposed to coinages), faulty punctuation and accidental repetition. He depended on my predecessors, and later on me, to point out such errors and correct them; and though we never achieved anything like a perfect performance, we tried."[10] Faulkner was a Nobel laureate, and his works merited special consideration at Random House.

Authorial errors can be usefully categorized as internal errors (within the invented world of a work) or external errors (with reference to the real world which provides the setting for fictional events).[11] There are borderline or overlapping cases, of course. In *The Great Gatsby,* East Egg and West Egg are invented (although based on Great Neck and Manhasset Neck); therefore, the reader or editor is not concerned with the accuracy of Fitzgerald's descriptions of East Egg and West Egg—even though their relative locations on Long Island seem to shift. Such matters should be noted in the editorial apparatus. But when the characters enter New York City the details should be right: the Queensboro Bridge and Central Park should be situated where they actually are.

The decision to emend an internal error can be especially difficult because the distinction between intentional and unintentional inconsistencies may not be as clear for verifiable external errors. In Chapter I of *Gatsby,* set in June 1922, Nick records Daisy's statement that her daughter is three years old. Daisy married Tom Buchanan in June 1919. If her child is indeed three, then Daisy was nine months pregnant at her wedding. Fitzgerald fumbled his chronology or his arithmetic. The emendation of Pammy Buchanan's age to two is necessary in Chapter I. Determined exegetes might challenge this correction by arguing that the age of the child is a clue, planted by Fitzgerald, to Daisy's premarital promiscuity or even an indication that Pammy is Gatsby's child. Gatsby was sent overseas in 1917 after he "took Daisy one still October night," and Tom did not meet Daisy until 1919; therefore, the father of her three-year-old child would have to be some unidentified lover—perhaps the man who sired Miss Quentin in Faulkner's *The Sound and the Fury.* It might also be asserted that Daisy's mistake in Pammy's age was intended by Fitzgerald to indicate her indifference to the child. It is not the function of a critical edition to accommodate promiscuous speculation.

Further evidence for assigning this crux to authorial inadvertence is provided by Nick's indication in Chapter IV that, in the summer of 1922, Daisy has been married for five years ("He had waited five years and bought a mansion") and for four years in Chapter VI ("After she had obliterated four years"). Retaining such inconsistencies for the sake of fidelity to the text that Fitzgerald did not see through the press—because he was in Europe—is misplaced piety. Even if he had had the opportunity to approve final proofs, the chronological inconsistencies would still require editorial correction.

The good editor restricts intervention to treatable cruces. Possible internal discrepancies which can be accounted for by sensible readers are best left alone.

In Chapter I Nick states that he "came back from the East last autumn"—that is, after Gatsby's murder which occurred around Labor Day 1922. At the end of the novel Nick remarks that he remembers the events of the day of the murder "after two years." This inconsistency is probably Fitzgerald's lapse; but it is possible that he added a year to the time scheme to account for the time Nick was writing the book. It can therefore be retained.

External errors include details that are wrong without reference to the work of fiction. The textual editor has the responsibility to emend obvious factual blunders that can be corrected by simple substitution. The oculist's billboard in *Gatsby*'s valley of ashes was presumably invented, but Fitzgerald's description includes a correctable error: "The eyes of Doctor T. J. Eckleburg are blue and gigantic—their retinas are one yard high." Impossible—the retina is at the back of the eye. Fitzgerald meant *pupils* or *irises*—probably irises. It has been objected that emendation here is improper because the editor is required to decide between two possible corrections—*pupils* or *irisis*. Surely the selection of either correct reading is preferable to perpetuating a distracting error. It has also been claimed that since the novel is narrated by Nick Carraway, this and other factual errors characterize him and bear on the question of his reliability. According to this perverse argument, some of Nick's errors may have been deliberately planted by Fitzgerald and should therefore be retained. Even so, it is impossible to explain why Nick's misuse of *retinas* would have been meaningfully intended by Fitzgerald. The claim that the author liked the sound of *retinas* is unsatisfactory.

Nonetheless, putative authorial errors can be deliberate and meaningful. A geographical crux in *Gatsby* involves the character named Biloxi who is "from Biloxi, Tennessee." There is no Biloxi in Tennessee, although there is a Biloxi in Mississippi. It is remotely possible that Fitzgerald was characterizing this rather grotesque figure by means of geographical absurdity. Such problems are especially tricky in editing Fitzgerald. Because he had trouble getting things right, it is difficult to credit him with purposefully getting things wrong. Gatsby's claim to be a midwesterner from San Francisco indicates his autobiographical unreliability; but many readers have regarded it as Fitzgerald's blunder.

F. Scott Fitzgerald's classic fictions are accepted as documents of American social history by readers all over the world in every printed language. *The Great Gatsby* is read as a record of American life at a certain time and place. Gatsby is more real than Calvin Coolidge. Much of the force of Fitzgerald's fiction results from his delicate sense of time and place and from his ability to evoke them. Yet his fiction is peppered with errors of geography, errors of chronology, errors of arithmetic, and inconsistencies. John O'Hara was overgenerous in crediting Fitzgerald with the qualities of his own fiction: "F. Scott Fitzgerald was a *right* writer.... The people were right, the talk was right, the clothes, the cars were real. ..."[12] Fitzgerald knew very little about cars; the most famous vehicle in American fiction, Gatsby's car, is not identified. Fitzgerald's reputation as the historiographer of the Twenties is distorted. He was a social novelist whose work became social history, but he was not a documentary or reportorial realist.

It is misleading to assign Fitzgerald's errors to simple carelessness or indifference to factual accuracy. His fiction provides ample evidence of his deliberate use of selected data, and his working drafts reveal a controlled concern for correct detail. For the account of Nicole's Paris shopping expedition in *Tender Is the Night*, the typed draft reads "jackets of kingfisher blue and autumnal red from (name)"; Fitzgerald inserted "Hermes"—the appropriate store for such purchases. The errors in Fitzgerald's published texts resulted from complicated factors having to do with the conditions of his writing and the pressure of publication, as well as his memory.

Fitzgerald was an impressionistic realist who evoked, by means of style and tone, the emotions or sensory responses associated with places and events. Note that he specified the requirement of making the Laplander "*feel* the importance." He explained that "in *Gatsby* I selected the stuff to fit a given mood of 'hauntedness' or whatever you might call it, rejecting in advance in *Gatsby*, for instance, all the ordinary material of Long Island, big crooks, adultery theme and always starting from the *small* focal point that impressed me—my own meeting with Arnold Rothstein for instance."[13] Racketeer Rothstein was the source—not the model—for Meyer Wolfshiem, and the novel refers to events and personages that 1925 readers were expected to recognize. The references to the Rosenthal murder are right—Fitzgerald correctly identifies Becker and the Metropole—but the novel is not a register of Twenties celebrities. Only three other well-known figures of the time are mentioned in the text, none of whom actually appears in the novel: Joe Frisco, Gilda Gray, and David Belasco.

Fitzgerald did attempt to verify certain details he needed for *Gatsby*. In December 1924 he asked Maxwell Perkins for factual help:

Montenegro has an order called *The Order of Danilo*. Is there any possible way you could find out for me there what it would look like—whether a courtesy decoration given to an American would bear an English inscription—or anything to give verisimilitude to the medal which sounds horribly amateurish.[14]

Perkins's reply has not been found. There is no place on the actual medal for engraving, but in the novel it has to be engraved to establish Gatsby's war record. No sane editor would now attempt to emend the printed description of Gatsby's medal. In the same letter to Perkins from Rome discussing revision plans, Fitzgerald boasted: "Anyhow after careful searching of the files (of a man's mind here) for the Fuller Magee case and after having had Zelda draw pictures until her fingers ache I know Gatsby better than I know my own child." Gatsby's unspecified financial activities were loosely based on the 1922 collapse of the brokerage firm of E. M. Fuller and William F. McGee. Fitzgerald did not have access to newspaper files at Valescure and Rome when he wrote and revised *Gatsby*. Even if they had been available, it probably would not have made a difference. He was not a born researcher or compulsive checker; his notion of research was to talk to someone. He clearly expected and needed more editorial vetting than he received. Whether the editor of a critical edition now has the duty to perform Perkins's work properly is more a matter of conviction than of theory. It may well be impossible to rescue inexperienced critics and inattentive readers from the licentious embrace of error.

Nevertheless, it is reckless to assume that an author does not know what he is doing. The revised typescript for "The Captured Shadow" has a note in Fitzgerald's hand: "Please follow all spelling throughout, even when wrong." The instruction refers to passages from the juvenile hero's writings, which include deliberate Fitzgerald misspellings. Such evidence provides a corrective to groupies who find gratification in the image of Fitzgerald as an irresponsible (that is, drunk) writer who spontaneously generated flawed masterpieces.

Fitzgerald's reputation for ignorance and carelessness has fostered two pernicious editorial-critical positions. The first of these is that since he did not strive for factual accuracy, the correctness of his texts does not matter. The second position—which compounds error—is that editors are free to alter anything in Fitzgerald's work that seems problematical. Thus when Edmund Wilson edited *The Great Gatsby* in 1941 he emended the celebrated line "Gatsby believed in the green light, the orgastic future, that year by year recedes before us." He subsequently explained: "The word *orgastic*, on the last page I took to be Scott's mistake for *orgiastic*—he was very unreliable about words."[15] But Fitzgerald's intention is certain. Perkins had queried *orgastic,* and Fitzgerald replied that "it expresses exactly the intended ecstasy."[16] Wilson's emendation to "orgiastic future" became the standard reading in later editions of the novel.

Fitzgerald is regarded as an orthographic phenomenon on the basis of his manuscripts ("yatch," "apon," "facinating"); but he not unreasonably expected proofreaders to do their job. Because of the scores of misspellings and usage errors printed in *This Side of Paradise* (1920), Fitzgerald's career was launched with the stigma of irresponsibility that remained attached to him and has influenced editorial thinking about his work. Wilson described that first novel as "one of the most illiterate books of any merit ever published (a fault which the publisher's wretched proof-reading apparently made no effort to correct)."[17] Assessing the extent of Scribners' responsibility for textual details is crucial to establishing policy for re-editing Fitzgerald. Wilson's application of *illiterate* is hyperbolic; nevertheless, Fitzgerald never developed the habit of accuracy. His sense of direction was unreliable, and his arithmetic was approximate—especially in calculating the ages of characters. These handicaps do not diminish his genius—which did not depend on navigation or mathematics—but they blemished his texts and provided ammunition for detractors. Fitzgerald was not indifferent to the errors in his published work and their effect on his reputation. In 1920 he urged Perkins to provide corrections for the London edition of *This Side of Paridise,* and in 1938 he proposed a new edition of the novel with a "glossary of absurdities and inaccuracies."[18]

Despite the close personal and literary relationship between Fitzgerald and Perkins, the now-legendary editor did not take responsibility for vetting Fitzgerald's facts. Charles Scribner, Jr., the former head of the house, has written: "Perkins was totally useless when it came to copy editing or correcting a text. Such details meant very little to him. Consequently, the early editions of books such as Scott Fitzgerald's *The Great Gatsby* were textually corrupt to a nauseating degree."[19] Since the edited setting-copy typescript and the master galleys for *Gatsby* have not survived, there is no record of the queries Perkins or other Scribners editors may have made for Fitzgerald to consider. After noting Perkins's "aristocratic disregard for details so long as a book was right in its feeling for life," Malcolm Cowley concluded that the errors in *Tender Is the Night* (1934) "had a cumulative effect on readers and ended by distracting their attention."[20] In editing the 1951 restructured edition, Cowley made some ninety corrections of spelling, usage, geography, and fact. When Hemingway read the emended edition he noted errors that Cowley had not caught, commenting that: "None of the above is important unless everything is important in writing."[21]

Fitzgerald was a painstaking reviser who polished his work through multiple drafts and layers of typescript; but because of his custom of revising and rewriting in proof, the production stages of *Gatsby* and *Tender* were rushed. In *Gatsby,* which was rewritten in galleys, Scribners' ability to make proof queries and Fitzgerald's power to make final corrections were restricted by the time required for boat mail between New York and Rome or Capri. If Fitzgerald received the reset galleys or page proofs, it was after the book had been published.

It would be perjury to testify that Fitzgerald was committed to minute particularity, but he was not indifferent to the errors in his books. His own annotated copy of *Gatsby* includes some forty revisions and corrections; the military units in which Nick and Gatsby served are altered; the hotel in Louisville is corrected from the *Muhlbach* to the *Sealbach* (that is, the *Seelbach*).[22] Corrections were made in the second printing of the novel at Fitzgerald's instruction: St Olaf's (that is, St. Olaf) was moved from *northern* to *southern* Minnesota.

Fitzgerald's and Perkins's policies on factual errors in *Gatsby* are revealed by their responses to the errors spotted before publication by Ring and Rex Lardner.[23] In March 1925, Perkins informed Fitzgerald:

I had to make two little changes: there are no tides in Lake Superior, as Rex Lardner told me and I have verified the fact, and this made it necessary to attribute the danger of the yacht to wind. The other change was where in describing the dead Gatsby in the swimming pool, you speak of "the leg of transept." I ought to have caught this on the galleys. The transept is the cross formation in a church and surely you could not figuratively have referred to this. I think you must have been thinking of a transit, which is an engineer's instrument. It is really not like compasses, for it rests upon a tripod, but I think the use of the word transit would be psychologically correct in giving the impression of the circle being drawn. I think this must be what you meant, but anyway it could not have been transept. You will now have page proofs and you ought to deal with these two points and make them as you want them, and I will have them changed in the next printing.[24]

Perkins's remark that he "ought to have caught this on the galleys" probably indicates that the first set of galleys sent to Fitzgerald had editorial queries.

Ring Lardner sent Fitzgerald corrections on 24 March:

... I acted as volunteer proof reader and gave Max a brief list of what I thought were errata. On Pages 31 and 46 you spoke of the newsstand on the *lower level* of the Pennsylvania station and I suggested substitute terms for same. On Page 82, you had the guy driving his car under the elevated at Astoria, which isn't Astoria, but Long Island City. On Page 118 you had a tide in Lake Superior and on Page 209 you had the Chicago, Milwaukee & St. Paul running out of the La Salle Street Station. These things are trivial, but some of the critics pick on trivial errors for lack of anything else to pick on.[25]

Fitzgerald probably received this letter on Capri around 1 April—ten days before publication at the earliest—by which time the book was printed. His response to Lardner's list was sent to Perkins on publication day:

Now as to the changes I don't think I'll make any more for the present. Ring suggested the correction of certain errata—if you make the changes all right—if not let them go. Except on p. 209 old dim La Salle Street Station should be old dim Union Station and should be changed in the second edition. Transit will do fine though of course I really meant compass.[26]

—*if not let them go* indicates that Fitzgerald was not opposed to making these corrections, but he did not regard them as crucial. Had he been sufficiently concerned, he would have cabled spot-corrections.

The identification of the Chicago railroad station was mis-corrected at Scribners to "Union Street station" in the first printing—and was re-corrected to "Union Station" in the second printing of August 1925. It is characteristic of Fitzgerald that he set one of his most admired passages in the wrong station. He brilliantly evoked the sense of the station at Christmas time, the emotions Nick associated with "One of my most vivid memories"; but he did not remember which Chicago station it was.

The "Astoria" reading is a laboratory specimen of Fitzgerald's geographical lapses and provides a test case for the rationale of factual emendation in his work. The Queensboro Bridge crosses the East River between Manhattan's 59th Street and Long Island City (which is not a city, but a section of the borough of Queens). The Queensboro Bridge does not connect with Astoria (another section of Queens). It might be imagined that Fitzgerald liked the sound of "Astoria" and deliberately substituted "Astoria" for "Long Island City"; or that "Astoria" was an oblique reference to John Jacob Astor and therefore to the history of great American fortunes. Other frivolous suppositions might be offered. The best explanation is that Fitzgerald did not know the name of the section of Queens he had frequently driven through between fall 1922 and spring 1924—an explanation that is consistent with other place-name confusions in his work. There is no evidence that Fitzgerald purposefully moved the bridge or meaningfully renamed the sections of Queens. The fictional characters are in the real borough of Queens crossing the real Queensboro Bridge into the real borough of Manhattan.[27] Fitzgerald did not make the correction in his marked copy of the novel.

Lardner's recommended relocation of the waiting room in Manhattan's Pennsylvania Station is not mandatory. The main waiting room was on the street level; but the Long Island Railroad had a ticket counter below the main waiting room, which Nick refers to as "the lower level." Moreover, correction here cannot be accomplished by simple substitution. Errors integral to syntax or action are unemendable. Gatsby is described as "beating his way along the south shore of Lake Superior as a clam-digger and a salmon-fisher." There are no clams or salmon in Lake Superior, but emendation to "a deck-hand and trout fisher" would be improper. Fitzgerald's readings must be retained here at the risk of misinforming readers about the fishery resources of the Great Lakes.[28]

The textual editor's responsibility is to *preserve* the author's intention: to forego the enticements of emendation. The rule that he edits best who emends least is generally sound. However, this conservative rationale is vitiated by editors who, in the cause of textual fealty, prohibit emendation of correctable factual errors when based on editorial inference. But what is the basis for correcting "obvious misprints"? The detection of a typo often requires editorial inference.

Fidelity to errors because they have become part of the fabric of a classic work is simplistic. The anti-emendation school argues that it is sufficient to report factual errors in the textual apparatus of a critical edition—in the back of the book. But a minuscule portion of the readers of any classic reads it in a critical edition. Virtually all readers—and most teachers—are tranquilly unaware that there are good or bad, emended or unemended texts. Nonspecialists assume that all copies are created equal. These innocents require a properly corrected text because they do not recognize errors when they read them; and even if they are puzzled by what they read, they do not know what to do. Textual apparatus is no help to a reader who does not have access to it or does not even know that it exists. An edited text—especially for a popular classic—should be potentially useful to all readers. The current protocol for the publication of critical editions is to format them so that the text pages can be reprinted without apparatus in affordable "clear texts" or "readers' editions." Consequently, when the text alone—omitting all notes—is reprinted without back matter, readers are unable to determine if errors have been corrected or retained.

The best policy is to include, in all printings of the edited text, concise textual notes at the bottom of the pages identifying the most troublesome cruces. Yet publishers fear that this procedure scares off readers. So we beat on, goats against the current. . . .

Notes

1. See the introduction and back matter in the critical edition of F. Scott Fitzgerald's *The Great Gatsby*, edited by Matthew J. Bruccoli (Cambridge and New York: Cambridge University Press, 1991).

2. Undated letter to Scottie Fitzgerald, *The Letters of F. Scott Fitzgerald*, edited by Andrew Turnbull (New York: Scribners, 1963), p. 101.

3. Fitzgerald was probably referring to the original Paris store on the Rue de la Paix or to the Manhattan store on Fifth Avenue.

4. For John O'Hara on Buicks and Franklins, see "The Rider College Lectures," *"An Artist Is His Own Fault": John O'Hara on Writers and Writing*, edited by Bruccoli (Carbondale and Edwardsville: Southern Illinois University Press / London and Amsterdam: Feffer and Simons, 1977), pp. 14–15.

5. The corrections were made in the fourth printing with Lewis's approval after a reader sent Harcourt, Brace a list of errors and inconsistencies. However, errors tend to perpetuate themselves, and these errors reappeared in subsequent editions. See p. 91, this book. Orig. published as Bruccoli, "Textual Variants in Sinclair Lewis's *Babbit*," *Studies in Bibliography* (1958): 263–268.

6. *Conversations with Nelson Algren*, edited by H. E. F. Donohue (New York: Hill and Wang, 1964), p. 154.

7. Saul Bellow, "Facts that Put Fancy to Flight," *New York Times Book Review* (11 February 1962): 1.

8. Donald Barthelme, "The Current Cinema," *New Yorker* (1 October 1979): 104.

9. This contract is facsimiled in Bruccoli, *F. Scott Fitzgerald: A Descriptive Bibliography* (Pittsburgh: University of Pittsburgh Press, 1972), pp. 336–337.

10. *The Faulkner Concordance Newsletter* (May 1974): 2–3. See also Erskine to Faulkner, 6 February 1959. *Faulkner: A Comprehensive Guide to the Brodsky Collection, Volume II: The Letters*, edited by Louis Daniel Brodsky and Robert W. Hamblin (Jackson: University Press of Mississippi, 1984), pp. 250–251.

11. See G. T. Tanselle, "External Fact as an Editorial Problem," *Studies in Bibliography* (1979): 1–47.

12. John O'Hara, "In Memory of F. Scott Fitzgerald: Certain Aspects," *New Republic* (3 March 1941): 311.

13. 1937 letter to Corey Ford. *The Letters of F. Scott Fitzgerald*, pp. 550–551.

14. *F. Scott Fitzgerald: A Life in Letters*, edited by Bruccoli with the assistance of Judith S. Baughman (New York: Scribners, 1994), p. 92,

15. To George M. Schieffelin, 26 February 1965; see Bruccoli, "The Perkins/Wilson Correspondence about Publication of *The Last Tycoon*," *Fitzgerald/Hemingway Annual 1978*, pp. 63–66.

16. 24 January 1925. *Life in Letters*, p. 94.

17. Edmund Wilson, "The Literary Spotlight," *Bookman* (March 1922): 22.

18. See letters of July 1920 and 24 December 1938. *Dear Scott / Dear Max*, edited by John Kuehl and Jackson R. Bryer (New York: Scribners, 1971), p. 31 and pp. 250–252.

19. Charles Scribner, Jr., *In the Company of Writers* (New York: Scribners, 1991), p. 44.

20. F. Scott Fitzgerald, *Tender Is the Night: With the Author's Final Revisions*, edited by Malcolm Cowley (New York: Scribners, 1951), p. xiii.

21. 10 November 1951. Neville Collection.

22. *The Great Gatsby*, edited by Bruccoli, pp. 143–154.

23. Rex Lardner was a *Liberty* editor and read the novel in typescript when it was being considered for serialization; the *Liberty* letter declining serial rights is dated 4 December 1924. Ring Lardner read *Gatsby* in proof as a matter of friendship.

24. *Dear Scott / Dear Max*, p. 97.

25. *Correspondence of F. Scott Fitzgerald*, edited by Bruccoli and Margaret M. Duggan (New York: Random House, 1970), pp. 154–155.

26. 10 April 1925. *Dear Scott / Dear Max,* pp. 99–100.

27. The Cambridge University Press critical edition of *The Great Gatsby* retains the unemended readings "retinas" and "Astoria" because two of the trustees of the Fitzgerald Estate exercised their contractual right of approval and overruled the third trustee, the general editor. He became increasingly ashamed of his capitulation and subsequently resigned as editor of the edition.

28. In 1926 Ernest Hemingway sent Fitzgerald a parody description of *The Sun Also Rises:* "The hero, like Gatsby, is a Lake Superior Salmon Fisherman. (There are no salmon in Lake Superior)." See Bruccoli, *Fitzgerald and Hemingway: A Dangerous Friendship* (New York: Carroll and Graf, 1994), p. 59. But the lake trout may have been known as "landlocked salmon."

The Profession of Authorship in Twenty-First-Century America

This is William Charvat's definition of "the profession of authorship":

> The terms of professional writing are these: that it provides a living for the author, like any other job; that it is a main and prolonged, rather than intermittent or sporadic, resource for the writer; that it is produced with the hope of extended sale in the open market, like any article of commerce; and that it is written with reference to buyers' tastes and reading habits. The problem of the professional writer is not identical with that of the literary artist; but when a literary artist is also a professional writer, he cannot solve the problems of the one function without reference to the other.[1]

But I disagree with my friend's distinction between the literary artist and the professional writer in his otherwise admirable statement. All literary artists who publish their work through the book trade are professional writers. I am concerned here with literary trade books—not with text books, reference books, cookbooks, how-to-do-its, sex manuals, or technical books.

The profession of authorship refers to how writers get published and how they make a living. Literature runs on money—although a small share of the money generated accrues to the authors. Accordingly the profession of authorship can be examined in terms of author-editor-publisher-agent relationships.

These are the factors determining the state of American authorship in 2004:

Sales are down.
Readership is down.
Revenues are up.
Book prices are up.
Library circulation is up.

"The Profession of Authorship in Twenty-First Century America" was first published in *American Studies in Scandinavia* 37, no. 1 (2005): 1–15. It was revised from a presentation Bruccoli gave at the September 2004 ASANOR Conference in Oslo. Reprinted with permission of *American Studies in Scandinavia*.

The chain stores dominate book selling.
Books are easy to acquire online: Amazon.
The book clubs are losing ground.
American publishing houses continue to be combined—notably through acquisitions by foreign-owned conglomerates.
Publishing houses are run by corporate officers, not editors.
Agents are increasingly powerful.
Subsidiary rights are crucial in determining publishing decisions.
The author's ability to self-promote himself and his work especially on television has become a significant element in publishing decisions.
Literary editors are less influential and do less editing.
More than ever, writing is a feast-or-famine endeavor for writers.

Here are some numbers for American book sales in 2003:

- 128 works of adult fiction sold more than 100,000 clothbound copies.
- 121 works of adult nonfiction sold more than 100,000 clothbound copies.
- *The DaVinci Code* sold 5,724,750 hardback copies.
- *The Purpose-Driven Life* sold 11,300,000 copies.

Authorship and publishing are jackpot endeavors. In most cases writing is not the writer's main or sole occupation. The proliferating college creative-writing programs provide security for thousands of American writers who would otherwise give up or beg. These programs damage the teachers and harm their students. The teachers—usually second-raters—write less; and the students are given false expectations. Failed writers are teaching writing courses. The virgins are running the brothels. George V. Higgins acknowledged that teaching writing made it possible for him to keep writing while living comfortably.

> But were it not for the fact that I am employed by Boston University, I would have been in serious financial trouble. There are such things as medical insurance and the necessity for pensions and that sort of thing, that you don't think about a lot when you're in your twenties, and your thirties, and even in your forties. It's a good thing for me that when I was in my late forties somebody else thought of it and got me into this line of work, which I love to do, because it does provide an anchor to windward. Being a free-lance writer today doesn't. . . .
>
> It is awfully nice to know that when the mortgage comes due each month, you will have the money to pay it and your health insurance too, most of it. And there will be something set aside for your old age, when you become completely

toothless and your imagination runs out. Otherwise it's very hard to work solely as a writer in the United States today, if you want to enjoy a nice life.

When you're in your twenties and your thirties, well, maybe not in your thirties, but when you're young, you don't think of that. You can say, "I will give all for art. And when I'm in my fifties I won't have a nice house. So what. Unless I strike it rich, which most writers don't, I won't have a nice car and I won't have a beach house and I won't have vacations in Europe, nice dinners in restaurants, all the fine things that your average stock broker who's forty years old takes as a matter of course. . . .

I managed to get most of those things, but it was because I was practicing law, and I did have some good fortune now and again with book sales, *and I have worked like a horse.*[2]

Higgins published thirty books between 1972 and 2000.

Writing students are given false expectations and are set up for disappointment or worse by the unwarranted encouragement provided by their teachers, who are required to lie in order to maintain the enrollments needed to keep their jobs. The graduate writing programs provide fellowships or assistantships for their students. These students are usually assigned to teach freshman writing classes. The deaf leading the blind.

When Sinclair Lewis, the first American to receive the Nobel Prize for Literature, was invited to speak to a group of Yale students who professed their desires to become writers, he asked them, "Why the hell aren't you home writing?" There are at least 540 American colleges and universities offering undergraduate degrees (including 39 Ph.D. programs) in writing—plus some 250 conferences, colonies, and centers. The doctorates qualify their holders for tenure-track jobs teaching writing. Higgins again:

> I generally discourage my undergraduate students from getting into graduate programs in writing. . . . The reason that I generally discourage them is because it can become a dependency. And now you must keep in mind that I have a bias here. I realize that we're not supposed to speak ill of the deceased, especially the recently deceased, but I studied creative writing at Wallace Stegner's center at Stanford. I became convinced that what Mr. Stegner wanted was not writers but acolytes. He had his devotees, his disciples, who'd follow him around campus like he fed them, following him home. I think that's a dependency, and of all the people in the world who should not have dependencies on other people or on instructions, are writers. If you can't do your own thinking, you're in the wrong line of work.[3]

Novelist R. H. W. Dillard, who headed the writing program at Hollins College for thirty-two years, believes that "the teaching of creative writing, when it is done in a supportive and sensitive manner, without any false promises or the building of false hopes, is a very valuable thing for the future of literature and the profession of authorship." But he deplores the "cancerous over-proliferation" of creative-writing programs: "Greedy universities, looking for cash cows, have leapt into the game, lowering the value of a writing degree by accepting students who never would have been accepted even ten years ago and seeing to it that they get their degrees as long as their tuition is paid." Moreover, Dillard states that "it is immoral for universities to promise prospective students that a degree from their program will gain them a writing career and a teaching job."[4] Betrayal, debt, and heartbreak on the New Grub Street.

Professional writing can't be taught. Gifted or promising writers can be advised, but the untalented ones are doomed. The good ones are born that way. The more they write, the better they get. Dr. Johnson was partly right when he declared that no one but a blockhead ever wrote except for money. Freud was closer to the truth when he observed that writers write for three things: money, fame, and the love of beautiful women. Most writers write because they can't help themselves. This compulsion afflicts the talented and the untalented, the promising and the unpromising. The no-talent failures as well as the best-selling junk writers are convinced of their literary merit.

The creative-writing boom has resulted in the lowering of literary standards. About 175,000 new titles were published in 2003, but it is impossible to determine how many qualify as literature. It is estimated that 20,000 trade books were published in cloth or paperback in 2003: 55 per day for 365 days or 7 per hour during a working day. If half of them—10,000—were fiction, that makes it 27 per day. Most of these are "genre" or "category" books: romance and bodice-rippers, sci-fi and fantasy, mystery and crime. Publishers admit that too many books are now being published; they agree that the other publishers should cut back. The reason for the spewing-forth of unnecessary books is that they feed the editorial machine and contribute to the overhead. Apart from manufacturing, it costs relatively little to add 5 or 10 books to the list of a large house. Editors no longer edit, except for their star authors. The line-editing and copy-editing that were once routinely performed in-house are now farmed out to free-lancers who are really proof-readers. The current crop of American volumes provides dismaying evidence that unedited books are being routinely published.

The continuity of the author's relationship with an editor and a house—before and after the book is published—now rarely obtains. John Jakes—a blockbuster author if there ever was one—who ought to command editorial attention, isn't getting what he used to get:

> It's a truism in the business that so-called line editing is a thing of the past (editors now specialize in "acquisition"). Whether this is 100 percent true, or not, I act as though it is, and spend far more time combing through a manuscript line editing than I did even fifteen years ago. [Julian] Muller, [Joe] Fox, and [Herman] Gollob were all superb experienced editors who not only corrected line by line, word by word, but often suggested new directions for a scene, or the entire story.[5]

A personal note: Albert Erskine of Random House required me to defend single words and punctuation marks in my typescripts. It is reported that authors who can afford to do so are hiring their own "personal editors" because their publishers do not provide the help they formerly expected and received. The increase in personal imprints, invented by William Jovanovich—"A Helen and Kurt Wolff Book"—within large houses is a response to authors' needs for editorial guidance and attention. As authors move from publisher to publisher in their quest of better deals, the author/editor relationships become one-night stands or one-lunch stands. The author/agent relationship is replacing the author/editor relationship.

In the twenty-first century and in every other century since the beginnings of professional authorship in eighteenth–century England, literary publishing has been supported by the authors. Authors underwrite literature. The authors get the small piece of the publishing pie. For a so-called "mid-list" novel that sells 5,000 copies at $30, the money pie is $150,000. The author gets 10 percent of the list price: $3 X 5,000 = $15,000—of which an agent takes 15 percent; the retailer gets at least a 40 percent discount, which is $12 X 5,000 = $60,000. That leaves $75,000 for printing, binding, distribution, promotion, overhead, and the publisher's profit. If the manufacturing price per book is $5 per copy—$25,000 for 5,000 copies—the publisher is left with $50,000 to cover promotion, distribution, overhead, and profit. Overhead—including $100 lunches—involves creative accounting. The corporate officers do better than the authors. Publishing houses claim that their return-on-investment is only 2 percent or 3 percent. They must be altruists, bad businessmen, or liars.

In an unfinished fictional treatment of his publisher, Charles Scribner's Sons, Thomas Wolfe ironically observed:

> The mythology of publishing was this:
> That publishing was different from any other forms of capitalistic enterprise in that it was not influenced by the profit motive. True, an author's works occasionally sold in sufficient quantities to reward the publisher with a

profit—a very modest one, one was told, in no ways commensurate with the outlay of time, expense, labor, care and risk that had been involved. But even when this happened, and there was a small profit, it was used mainly for the purpose of making up the deficits incurred by the publication of scores of books which had not sold at all. Indeed, one was told that "the average book" did not even pay for itself; if a publisher could just break even on the cost of publication, he was lucky. If one enquired why the publisher published so many books with no hope of selling them, the publisher replied he published them because of his interest in literature, because he took pride in the publication of good books, regardless of whether they sold or not; publishing thus became a kind of handmaiden to the fine arts.[6]

The author who is not a star usually—not always—receives an advance against royalties ranging from $10,000 to $40,000—which doesn't support him during the year or two or three while the book is being written and produced. The first printing for a mid-list novel ranges from 5,000 to 20,000 copies—the high figure for a novel the publisher had decided to push. Publishers over-print because it is cheaper to remainder or destroy unsold copies than to order a second printing. The usual time from delivery of typescript to book publication is nine months. The publisher retains all royalty earnings until the advance has been earned back. The author is therefore broke when the book is published and stays broke for at least another year unless he gets an advance for another book.

"Gone today, here tomorrow," Alfred Knopf remarked about returns. The bookstores are permitted to return unsold copies for full credit. This system may benefit the publishers—which I don't believe—but it does not benefit the writers.[7] The returns system encourages over-printing and probably increases the selling price of the book. Clothbound returns average at least 30 percent; paperback returns are in the 50-percent range. Authors receive no income from returned books. Returns delay royalty payments because publishers withhold a portion of the authors' royalties in anticipation of returns. By the way, there is no good reason why, in the age of computers, royalties are calculated twice a year. The bad reason is that publishers collect interest on unpaid royalties, referred to as "the float." The author does not earn interest on his money; the publisher does.

Writers cannot make a living from book sales alone except for the so-called blockbuster books. Library circulation is up in America. There are 9,129 public libraries spending $1,125,000,000 on books per year. There are 3,527 academic libraries and 93,861 school libraries; it is impossible to determine how much they spend on literature acquisitions. American authors do not benefit from library readership, apart from the copies bought by libraries. There is no other occupation in which the maker's product is given away. In the UK and certain other

European countries, the Public Lending Right brings authors a minuscule royalty based on library circulation.[8] George V. Higgins was ungracious to readers who told that they had reserved his new novel at the library. He rightly felt that they had just informed him that his novel wasn't worth buying. I concur: readers should support authors by buying their books. Libraries are for scholars or paupers.

The figures on authorial earnings provided by the 1994 survey of Authors Guild and Dramatists Guild members disclosed that of the 637 responders, 24 percent received no income during the first half of 1993, and 16 percent earned less than $1,000. These figures are useless because the sample was meaningless. The 2004 survey by Poets & Writers disclosed that on average 14 percent of creative writers' annual income came from writing; but 54 percent of the respondents earned nothing from writing. These failures are not professional writers. They are hobbyists. A writer lives by writing or tries to. A better survey published by Columbia University in 1986 revealed that most American authors were unable to support themselves from their writing. The median annual income from writing was $4,775 or $4.90 per hour for 20 hours per week. Two percent of American authors earned more than $80,000 in 1979. Why should we expend sympathy on these people who obviously aren't sensible about their career choices? The answer is that despite—or maybe because of—their folly, they provide the most precious and enduring thing in America: our national literature. Major writers matter more than anyone else. Yet there is no correlation between writing a masterpiece—or just writing well—and the income the work brings. The first printing of *The Great Gatsby* sold 20,870 copies and brought Fitzgerald about $6,260. Indeed, the big money is most often earned by the writers whose books are justly doomed to be forgotten. Nonetheless, civilians nurture outlandish notions about writers, believing that all published books make a great deal of money. This misapprehension probably results from media reports about huge advances for ghosted books by politicians and sex objects.

The celebrated paperback editor/publisher Patrick O'Connor told me that "the hardcover business is in the business of collecting paperback royalties—and has been for years." The hardback publisher shares in the subsidiary rights: paperbacks, movies, television, and other media. F. Scott Fitzgerald's two-page 1919 contract with Charles Scribner's Sons for *This Side of Paradise* covered subsidiary rights in one sentence: "It is further agreed that the profits arising from the publication of said work, during the period covered by this agreement, in other than book form shall be divided equally between Publisher and said Author." The current Scribner contract requires twenty-seven pages and includes clauses for the division of these secondary rights or sub-rights:

The Profession of Authorship

- Dramatic Rights
- Movie Rights
- Theme Park Rights!
- Radio Rights
- Television Rights
- First Periodical Rights
- Commercial Rights
- Foreign-Language Rights
- British Commonwealth Rights
- Book Club Rights
- Mass Market and Trade Paperback
- Calendar Rights
- Textbook Rights
- Abridgment or Condensation Rights
- Second Periodical Rights
- Transcription Rights
- Electronic Rights
- Audio Rights
- Video Rights
- Digest Rights

The two hundred book clubs—fifty of which are owned by Bookspan and have ten million members—account for 5 percent of the books sold in America. There was a time when bidding wars between the Book-of-the-Month-Club and the Literary Guild were a potential bonanza for authors and publishers; but now they are both owned by Bookspan and do not bid against each other.

The division of the sub-rights spoils is a matter of negotiation, depending on the author's fame and ability to promote himself. Celebrity writers get a bigger cut than literary figures. For the anticipated best-seller of a celebrity writer, the "hard-soft deal" is normal: the cloth publisher acquires all book rights and sells the paperback rights to another publisher or to his own paperback imprint, if there is one. But it can work the other way, and the paperback publisher acquires all publishing rights up front.

Thomas Whiteside argued in *The Blockbuster Complex* (1981) that publishers are looking for the big book with lots of sub-rights income. Agent Eugene Winick believes that during the past twenty years publishers have been giving marketing support to best-selling authors and denying support to other writers. My position is that best-seller lists—which began in America in 1895—are pernicious and should be abolished because they substitute fashion for individual judgment. "In the past the literary potential of the author was considered," Winick comments, adding that the conglomerate control of publishing houses "may not tolerate the publication of non-commercial literary books, though nonetheless deserving of publication. If something does not jump off the page for an editor, reflecting commercial possibilities, it would probably be ignored and passed over." Well, why not? Is publishing business, or isn't it? Yes: but the discovery of genius and the publication of enduring books set it apart from other businesses. That's what the money-men tell the authors when negotiating contracts.

Authors' opportunities for non-book or between-books earnings have been greatly reduced by the shrinkage of the magazine fiction market. The slicks—so-called because they were printed on slick paper—have closed down or cut back on fiction. *The Saturday Evening Post* once supported a tribe of good professionals, including F. Scott Fitzgerald, who earned $4,000 per story at his peak (perhaps $40,000 in 2004 dollars), and the magazine maintained a huge readership for fiction at five cents and ten cents a copy. The pulp magazines of the Twenties and Thirties were printed on wood-pulp paper and sold for a dime. At a penny or two cents per word they kept writers alive during the Depression and produced a place for them to learn their trades. The pulps were mostly genre-focused and produced Hammett and Chandler, as well as a flock of notable sci-fi writers. The once-flourishing mass-market paperback originals that provided a training-ground for writers—including Kurt Vonnegut—have dried up.[9]

Authors can supplement their incomes on the lecture or reading circuit—usually at colleges and universities. The remunerations range from $3,000 for minor poets and one-book novelists to $40,000 for literary stars and celebrities. These personal appearances are normally combined with book-signings, which increase royalties.

The main problem for a writer—apart from eating and drinking—has never changed: how to get published. My publisher friends assure me that "good books always get published." How do they know about the good books that don't get published? It is my impression that the odds against the publication of literature have increased. One guess is that one out of 15,000 unsolicited submissions is accepted. Self-publishing—as opposed to vanity publishing—is becoming an increasingly viable option for writers who lack trade connections. A writer can arrange to print 500 paperback copies of a book for $3,500–$4,000 and then self-promote and self-market them. Apart from providing the satisfaction of seeing the book, self-publishing may help the writer to find an agent or publisher. Self-publishing is related to on-demand printing, which permits a publisher to reprint a back-list book a few copies at a time—thereby keeping it in print. Lightening

Source, the largest provider of print-on-demand titles, produced nine million copies in 2002–2003. The average print run at the Digital Book Center (Edwards Brothers) is twelve to fifteen copies.

Long ago people presumably became publishers and editors because they cherished literature and wanted to be associated with writers. Bennett Cerf and William Jovanovich were proud of their authors and maintained warm relationships with them. Maxwell Perkins's devotion to authors was once regarded as an ideal for editorial conduct. In this century writers have become a necessary nuisance. The process of publishing excludes authors unless they are needed to peddle books. National Book Award winner Mary Lee Settle has elegantly observed that "a whole industry depends on us and treats us like shit."[10]

The personal literary culture of American publishing has diminished. Increasingly I deal with un-read book-dopes who are making publishing decisions. It offends them if I refer to any work of literature published before 1990. An editor at Scribner—once the noblest name in American publishing—angrily asked me, "How do you know about the books you keep talking about?" Publishing values and standards are shaped by what sociologists call the publishers' "reference groups." The book-dopes pal around together and make publishing decisions on the basis of what people like them like. There used to be the shared conviction that the author's job was to write masterpieces and that the publishers' job was to publish masterpieces. I have known editors and publishers who believed it. They are all dead. Writers don't set out to write masterpieces. They write books that somebody else—beginning with the editor—recognizes as masterpieces. Now America is in an era of no great books. I walk the display aisles at BookExpo, the annual American publishers' launch meeting—at which the chief business is selling rights—and conclude that American publishing is dominated by the quest for best-selling ghost-written memoirs of meretricious celebrities. For whom are the publishers publishing? The First Amendment does not require them to publish junk books.

An unpublished writer isn't a writer. The hardest part of the writing life—apart from writing—is breaking into print. Talent or even genius is not enough. It requires determination or even ruthlessness, luck, and connections. Never underestimate the force of luck in literary careers. The writing courses may help in providing connections with editors who sometimes serve as visiting lecturers. Anything a writer does to achieve publication is understandable and even forgivable. Since most of these writing programs have their own little—very little—journals, they provide places for their students to have their work printed—not the same thing as publication. And maybe, somebody with influence may read it. Maybe. . . .

George Garrett, the distinguished novelist and Hoyns Professor of Writing, Emeritus, at the University of Virginia—who has done more for other writers than any writer I know—provided this evaluation of the subsidized journals:

> The colleges want maximum visibility from their writers. To gain this they need places to publish.
>
> The whole setup is a DISINCENTIVE to adventurous or experimental work. Likewise for any ideas that are not comfortably trendy and safe.
>
> Thus so much recent American writing is so bland and insignificant.[11]

The Directory of Literary Magazines for 2001 lists 408 in America—probably a low figure—exclusive of uncountable on-line endeavors. Most of them are university-sponsored, and most of them publish poetry. How else can a poet get published? The 125 university presses in America published 12,000 new titles in 2003. Of these 125 presses, 21 publish volumes of original fiction and 34 publish books of verse. University presses don't sell many copies of new literary works—or of anything else—but they provide exposure. Louisiana State University Press hit the jackpot with *A Confederacy of Dunces,* but that was a happy fluke.

When Elmore Leonard asked his agent to name the most lucrative kind of writing, H. N. Swanson told him, "Ransom notes." He was wrong. The most lucrative kind of writing is scholarly books published by university presses for junior faculty—who are not professional writers. University presses publish books written by academic types who are rewarded by promotion and tenure. A scholarly book that may bring an assistant professor a couple of hundred bucks in royalties can be worth hundreds of thousands of dollars to him or her in promotion, tenure, and lifetime salary increases.

After a young writer achieves the miracle of publication, he needs more luck to get his book noticed and sold. Pat O'Connor flatly states that "in books, everything is distribution. There is nothing but distribution."[12] Obviously publishers can't devote equal effort to the marketing and distribution of all their books. Most books are published in obscurity and vanish. Book-review venues have shrunk. There are in 2004 four newspaper book-review supplements in America—in New York, Washington, San Francisco, and Los Angeles. A handful of newspapers have weekly book-review pages. Most newspapers do not even review books. The great-god-telly competes for reading time, but it can sell books. The Oprah Book Club selected forty-eight titles in six years—all of which became best-sellers. Her 2003 selection of Steinbeck's *East of Eden,* originally published in 1952, sold 1,700,000 trade-paperback copies.

There is a critical establishment—largely operating in the groves of academe—that can make an author's reputation.[13] Reviewing and criticism in American literary journals is controlled by and addressed to constituencies of politics, gender, race, and sexuality. They write for each other. Authors who are connected are rewarded with praise, prizes, recognition, promotion and tenure, contracts, and even book sales. It is hard for a writer who is just a writer to get inducted into this mafia. In moments of disgust I seek comfort in Samuel Johnson:

> Of the innumerable authors whose performances are thus treasured up in magnificent obscurity, most are forgotten, because they never deserved to be remembered, and owed the Honour which they once obtained, not to judgment or to genius, to Labour or to art, but to the prejudice of faction, the stratagem of intrigue, or the servility of adulation.[14]

If the chain stores—Barnes & Noble, Borders, Books-a Million—don't order a book, it is stillborn. They charge $10,000 per month for displaying a book front-out at the end of the shelf and at eye-level. It costs the publisher $3,500 to $5,000 per week for front-of-store placement. Apart from the mystery of why publishers should accede to this extortion, the lesson is that the chains control the market; and publishers can only pay the bribes for sure winners. Moreover, publishers routinely submit proposals or typescripts to the chain buyers for guidance in making publishing decisions. If publishers and editors don't have confidence in their own judgment, they are in the wrong line of work.[15]

Publishers have always insisted that books sell by word-of-mouth—not by advertising. In 2004 that means getting on television. Not only does the author have to write well: now he is expected to sell himself and his book. This factor has always operated: think of Mark Twain and Ernest Hemingway, who mastered the fame game. But their fame had something to do with literature; the current celebrity writers are celebrated for being celebrities—not for their words on paper.

There are now two cultures: the print culture and the electronic culture. A 2004 survey determined that half of Americans do not read one book a year—which I suspect is an inflated figure. This is not a shocking revelation. There have always been nonreaders, but the new threat is that reading time has more competition than ever before: television and then computers. There is a population of people who prefer to get their information on the screen. The libraries are full of them.

The principal uncertainties about the conditions of authorship in the twenty-first century are connected with the expansion of "electronic publishing"—which isn't publishing. More and more books are available gratis on-line—some of them in violation of copyright. Apparently there are a couple of generations who find it comfortable to read this way and even prefer to read newspapers on the screen. No decent comment seems possible. A larger threat to the print book is the E-Book—the book-format electronic reading device which holds the texts of five hundred real books and permits 10,000 page-views. The Scribner experiment of making all of Hemingway's books available by E-Book was a commercial failure, probably because the device is still clumsy and expensive ($370). The price will come down, and the mechanism will be improved. Authors require readers. Books require readers. "Nothing can replace the book! Nothing will replace the book!" So proclaim readers born before 1960 or 1970. Judging from my students, book readers are a perishing breed.

Publication is the essential act of authorship. The ways in which new and old literary works are produced and published will change in the twenty-first century. So will the Profession of Authorship in America. The only certainty is that writers will go on writing.

Every great book is a miracle. We try not to think about the unpublished masterpieces.

Notes

1. William Charvat, *The Profession of Authorship in America*, edited by Matthew J. Bruccoli (Columbus: Ohio State University Press, 1968), p. [3].

2. *Dictionary of Literary Biography Yearbook 1998*, edited by Bruccoli (Detroit: Bruccoli Clark Layman / Gale, 1999), p. 174.

3. *Dictionary of Literary Biography Yearbook 2002*, edited by Bruccoli and George Garrett (Detroit: Bruccoli Clark Layman / Gale, 2003), pp. 356–357.

4. Letter to Bruccoli.

5. Letter to Bruccoli.

6. Wisdom Collection, Houghton Library, Harvard University.

7. In 1981 William Jovanovich attempted to buck the returns practice. The booksellers refused to order the non-return books, and other publishers did not join Harcourt Brace Jovanovich's effort.

8. The American tax laws also are not kind to writers. For example, a writer cannot claim tax relief for donating his papers to a library; but his widow can.

9. Commentators with steady incomes denounce writers who "sell out." One of the putative forms of selling out is writing for the movies or television. An additional chapter is required to discuss this aspect of authorship.

10. Letter to Bruccoli.

11. Letter to Bruccoli.

12. Letter to Bruccoli.

13. A separate chapter on how literary reputations are made is required. Who are the opinion-makers or taste-makers? Who has the clout? Is there a lit-crit establishment?

14. *Rambler* 106 (23 March 1751).

15. Barnes and Noble has commenced publishing books—now usually reprints or coffee-table volumes. It seems inevitable that with hundreds of outlets the book chain will enter trade publishing—unless the Feds interfere.

What Maxwell Perkins Really Did for *Look Homeward, Angel*

Maxwell Perkins of Charles Scribner's Sons is the only literary editor serious readers and teachers of literature know about, because of his work with F. Scott Fitzgerald, Ernest Hemingway, and—especially—Thomas Wolfe. Certainly there have been other great trade editors with great authorial stables—such as Albert Erskine at Random House, with whom I worked—but Perkins, who died in 1947, continues to be perceived as the model for what an editor should do. Yet Perkins didn't do what he is alleged to have done for Wolfe. Literary history is mainly literary gossip. The career of Maxwell Perkins is now legendary, and like all legends it has been fictionalized. Perkins has been canonized as the ultimate collaborative editor who recognized unpublishable manuscripts as potential works of genius and transformed them into masterpieces. Nevertheless, he was not a collaborative editor. His rule was: "The book belongs to the author."

Because of our editorial work on *O Lost*,[1] reviewers and journalist have endeavored to stage a fight between the Bruccolis and Maxwell Perkins. For the record: No Perkins, no *Look Homeward, Angel*—and very likely no Wolfe. Our intention was not to diminish Perkins's stature. He merits all the respect and fame accorded to him. But what he really did for his authors was different—and better—than what has been attributed to him. He did not revise or rewrite Fitzgerald, Hemingway, or Wolfe. Perkins advised them, encouraged them, and supported them financially and artistically.

Perkins's most renowned editorial relationship was with Thomas Wolfe. The official apocryphal story repeated by generations of English majors and Wolfe buffs goes like this: a huge pile of unpublishable manuscript (typescript) entitled *O Lost* was delivered to Charles Scribner's Sons in 1928, and Perkins recognized

---

"What Maxwell Perkins Really Did for *Look Homeward, Angel*" was originally published in *Look Homeward and Forward: Thomas Wolfe, an American Voice across Modern and Contemporary Culture*, edited by Agostino Lombardo, Mario Faraone, Monica Melloni, and Igina Tattoni (Rome, Italy: Casa Editrice Università degli Studi di Roma La Sapienza, 2003), pp. 221–230. Reprinted with permission of Casa Editrice Università La Sapienza.

that it was a work of genius; he proceeded to cut it, reorganize it, and tell Wolfe how to rewrite it—thereby rendering the volume published in 1929 as *Look Homeward, Angel* a masterpiece. Versions of this story sometimes claim that Perkins reworked Wolfe's prose. The setting copy and revised galleys do not survive; but there is no page of *Look Homeward, Angel* work-in-progress with Perkins's rewriting.

Perkins's chief editorial miracle was holding this pathologically suspicious author for eight years and publishing four of his books. This is what Perkins did to launch Wolfe's career and then see through press all the books Wolfe published during his lifetime:—

When the six-inch-high, 1,100-page typescript of *O Lost* arrived at Scribers, Perkins did not immediately read it and recognize its brilliance. He was not even the first reader. It was read by Charles Dunn—the Scribners first reader—who recommended it to editor John Hall Wheelock, who read it and recommended it to Perkins. But Perkins later credited another Scribners editor, Wallace Meyer, with calling his attention to *O Lost*. When Perkins read it, he wrote Wolfe on 22 October 1928:

I do not know whether it would be possible to work out a plan by which it might be worked into a form publishable by us, but I do know that setting the practical aspects of the matter aside, it is a very remarkable thing, and that no editor could read it without being excited by it, and filled with admiration by many passages in it, and sections of it.[2]

Author and editor had their first meeting on 2 January 1929, which Wolfe reported to Margaret Roberts:

Then he began cautiously on the book. Of course, he said, he didn't know about its present form—somewhat incoherent and very long. When I saw now that he was really interested, I burst out wildly saying that I would throw out this, that, and the other—at every point he stopped me quickly saying, "No, no—you must let that stay word for word—that scene's simply magnificent." It became apparent at once that these people were willing to go far farther than I had dared hope—that, in fact, they were afraid I would injure the book by doing too much to it. I saw now that Perkins had a great batch of notes in his hand and that on the desk was a great stack of handwritten paper—a complete summary of my whole enormous book.[3] I was so moved and touched to think that someone at length had thought enough of my work to sweat over it in this way that I almost wept. When I spoke to him of this, he smiled and said everyone in the place had read it. Then he went over the book scene by scene—I found he was more familiar with the scenes and the names of characters than

I was—I had not looked at the thing in over six months. For the first time in my life I was getting criticism I could really use. The scenes he wanted cut or changed were invariably the least essential and least interesting; all the scenes that I had thought too coarse, vulgar, profane, or obscene for publication he forbade me to touch save for a word or two. There was one as rough as anything in Elizabethan drama—when I spoke of this he said it was a masterpiece, and that he had been reading it to Hemingway. He told me I must change a few words. He said the book was new and original, and because of its form could have no formal and orthodox unity, but that what unity it did have came from the strange wild people—the family—it wrote about, as seen through the eyes of a strange wild boy. These people, with relatives, friends, townspeople, he said were "magnificent"—as real as any people he had ever read of. He wanted me to keep these people and the boy at all times foremost—other business, such as courses at state university, etc., to be shortened or subordinated. Said finally if I was hard up he thought Scribners would advance money.[4]

The reasons for the required cutting were matters of business as well as propriety. At 294,000 words it was an expensive project at a time when novels were priced at $2.50; and there was probably concern that readers and reviewers would boycott a very long first novel. The typescript was rich in bawdry, sexual data, and religious iconoclasm unpublishable by Scribners in 1929—the year when Perkins required Hemingway to replace vulgar words with dashes in *A Farewell to Arms.* The gossip about the cutting of *O Lost* has triggered the application of "shapeless," "formless," and "undisciplined" to all of Wolfe's work. Nonetheless, *O Lost* was a planned and organized novel publishable as Wolfe wrote it—as established by the University of South Carolina Press edition of the complete novel in 658 pages of 10.75/13 Granjon type.

When Wolfe was unable to cut *O Lost,* Perkins recommended passages to be cut and may have also suggested new connecting passages to bridge the cuts. Perkins performed no unilateral amputations: Nothing was cut without Wolfe's grudging capitulation. The result was that 60,000 words (147 passages) of the 294,000 words were removed from *O Lost:* 20 percent. And 5,000 words (16 passages) were added to *Look Homeward, Angel.* The title change was recommended by Scribners salesmen who complained that *O Lost* was not what is known in the trade as "a selling title." (These were the salesmen who had previously pressured Fitzgerald to retitle *Trimalchio* to *The Great Gatsby.*) Wolfe and Perkins settled on *Look Homeward, Angel* from a list of titles provided by Wolfe. The 1929 Scribners first edition of *Look Homeward, Angel* had 626 printed pages; the 2000 USC Press edition of *O Lost* has 658 text pages in larger type on larger pages. It was publishable in 1929—if Perkins had wanted to publish it uncut.

Principal Cuts

Pett Pentland and orphans
Henry Pentland
Roseberry equestrian episode
Judge Sondley's demonology
Eugene's trips with mother
Final encounter between Ben and Eugene on porch at Gant's shop: 78 lines cut
Young Leonard
Norfolk work episodes—16 pages
Italian woman on ship in Norfolk
Visit to Effie in Henderson
Pulpit Hill material
Visit to North Carolina girls' school
    Patriotic fervor at Pulpit Hill: "O brave young galahad of the majorities, who in time of peril came so boldly out with the mob. . . ."
Brothel scenes
Account of debate
Poem about Ben in graveyard scene
Medical school cadavers
Fat Jack Harvey at Pulpit Hill
Prof. Randolph Ware
Folk plays at Pulpit Hill

Among the 147 casualties was the 21,400-word opening describing young W. O. Gant and the Battle of Gettysburg. It is painful to lose any of W. O.—the richest comic figure in American literature. Thousands of words were excised from Eugene Gant's college years at Pulpit Hill. The apparent rationale for cutting *O Lost* was to keep the focus on Eugene and the Gant family while sacrificing material about Altamont/Asheville and Pulpit Hill/Chapel Hill. Perhaps the most ill-considered excision in the book occurs in the Pulpit Hill section.

    As he went up the path he heard the mellow class bell ringing jubilantly. Then the son of the registrar, Billy Watson, bounded down the broad stone steps of Faculty Hall and ran towards him with high leaping stride.
    "What are the bugles blowing for?" said Eugene.
    "You've made the first One that Vergil Weldon has given in Logic for eighteen years!" screamed Billy Watson. "And your essay has won the Ramsay Prize. It will be published."

Then other boys rushed at him from all sides, yelling: "You made a One on Logic, 'Gene!"

"O Christ! O God!" Eugene screamed, casting his arms up. "I feel so good I could die."⁵

That is a golden passage in Wolfe. It is puzzling that Perkins and Wolfe deleted other passages that emphasize Eugene's singularity: *Look Homeward, Angel*—like *O Lost*—is a Bildungsroman or Kunstleroman, a novel about the apprenticeship of a genius. Another consequence of the surgery—"They're cutting my balls off!" Wolfe proclaimed—was to deprive Wolfe of his proper recognition as a humorist, particularly as a parodist. Much of the bawdy humor was removed. Two of the deleted parodies are the twenty-line T. S. Eliot parody, "Mose Extinct," and the parody of English renaissance prose showing off Wolfe's mastery of food and early English literature:

"Marry!" exclaimed the host proudly. "An I fail to cram your worship's gullet with the daintiest cates that ever graced a table since Lucullus drank his mother's milk, then the devil's an ass, and they may put a hempen collar round my neck on Tyburn Hill.

"Ye shall have three quarts of sack and a butt of ale to river your thirst down, and a charger of salted herring, sprats, dace, pickled hake, carps' tongues, smoked sturgeon, lamprey godwits, and calvered salmon to spur Bacchus up if he grows jaded."⁶

Perkins explained after Wolfe's death:

The extent of cutting in that book has somehow come to be greatly exaggerated. Really, it was more a matter of reorganization. [Not accurate—there was little reorganization between *O Lost* and *Look Homeward, Angel*. M.J.B.] For instance, Tom had that wonderful episode when Gant came back from his far wandering and rode in early morning on the trolley car. . . . This was immediately followed by an episode of a similar kind where Eugene, with his friends, walked home from school through the town of Asheville. . . . By putting these episodes next to each other the effect of each was greatly diminished, and I think we gave both much greater value by separating them.⁷

This was the *only* significant structural alteration made during the editorial process: but Perkins misremembered the ordering of the episodes. In *O Lost*, Gant's return is a flashback in Chapter 11, pp. 183–192—separated by 150 pages from Chapter 23—not "immediately followed by" the boys' walk. (In *Look Homeward, Angel* Gant's return is chronologically positioned in Chapter 7, pp. 70–80—240 pages from the boys' walk in Chapter 24.) Moreover, the placement of Gant's return in *O Lost* has a contrapuntal purpose: it comes between two early-morning scenes featuring Ben in the newspaper office and then the all-night diner.

After the charge that Wolfe could not write or finish a novel without Perkins became critical gospel—largely resulting from Wolfe's declaration of his debts to Perkins in the dedication to *Of Time and the River* and in *The Story of a Novel*—Wolfe wrote to his editor in 1936:

> So far from needing any outside aid "to help me write my books," the very book which my detractors now eagerly seize on as my best one, the gauge by which the others must be measured, and itself the proof and demonstration of my subsequent decline, had been utterly finished and completed to the final period, in utter isolation, without a word of criticism or advice from any one, before my publisher ever saw it; and that whatever changes were finally made were almost entirely changes in form of omission and of cuts in view of bringing the book down to a more publishable and condensed form. That book, of course, was "Look Homeward Angel."

Wolfe's testimony continues:

> But what you gave me, what in my acknowledgment I tried to give expression to, was so much more than this technical assistance—an aid of spiritual sustenance, of personal faith, of high purpose, of profound and sensitive understanding, of utter loyalty and staunch support, at a time when many people had no belief at all in me, or when what little belief they had was colored by serious doubt that I would ever be able to continue or achieve my purpose, fulfill my "promise"—all of this was a help of such priceless and incalculable value, of such spiritual magnitude, that it made any other kind of help seem paltry by comparison. And for that reason mainly I have resented the contemptible insinuations of my enemies that I have to have you "to help me with my books." As you know, I don't have to have you or any other man alive to help me with my books. I do not even have to have technical help or advice, although I need it badly, and have been so immensely grateful for it. But if the worst came to the worst—and of course the worst does and will come to the worst—all this I could and will and do learn for myself, as all hard things are learned, with blood-sweat, anguish and despair.[8]

Editorial Method

The University of South Carolina Press edition of *O Lost* is not a conflation of *O Lost* and *Look Homeward Angel*. An editor may decide to edit either work, but the tasks are separate. The reader of *O Lost* gains 60,000 Wolfe words but loses 5,000 words of bridging material written into *Look Homeward, Angel.*

The full text of *O Lost* testifies that Wolfe's first novel as submitted by him was a completed novel. It is possible to argue about the necessity for certain episodes or events in *O Lost,* but they are mainly purposeful. The parodies of low and high literature establish the influence of young Eugene's prodigious reading as well as the retrospective point-of-view of Eugene Gant / Thomas Wolfe.

The published text of *O Lost* was established by collating Wolfe's manuscript written in 17 ledgers against the typist's transcription—Wolfe could not master the typewriter—to determine what he wrote. Wolfean errors and inconsistencies in this recovered text were then emended by the editors—after checking possible corrections against *Look Homeward, Angel.* The USC Press *O Lost* makes some 630 substantive (word) emendations in the carbon-copy of the novel—the only surviving typescript—of which some 390 are corrections of the typist's misreadings of Wolfe's manuscript, and some 165 are editorial corrections of errors of fact and inconsistencies in the manuscript. All substantive emendations are stipulated. Some 140 of these *O Lost* errors were—and still are—perpetuated in the Scribner edition of *Look Homeward, Angel.* An emended *Look Homeward, Angel* is seventy years overdue; nevertheless, Scribner has declined to correct the text. Perkins was an indifferent proofreader with what Malcolm Cowley described as an aristocratic indifference to details if the rest of the work was right. The proofing of *Look Homeward, Angel* was turned over to John Hall Wheelock, who was responsible for seeing the novel through the press. James Dickey, who was later published by Wheelock, told me that Wheelock remarked that he had done more work on Wolfe's books than Perkins had—meaning more line-editing and proofing. After hundreds of errors and inconsistencies were reported in the published *Look Homeward, Angel,* Wheelock comforted Wolfe by explaining that: "I don't doubt that one of the tribe who make a profession of this sort of thing could find a great many errors, typographical and other, if he went over the book with a fine-tooth comb; but then this much could be said of any book, however carefully edited."[9] Since Wolfe's marked proofs do not survive, his proofing practices are unknown, but he seems to have proofed from memory—not against setting copy.

"Correct Thomas Wolfe! How dare you desecrate a masterpiece!" I experienced outraged denunciations from civilians and amateurs when I emended *The Great Gatsby*—another sloppy text published by Perkins. Correcting is not rewriting. Substituting the right word for the wrong word or the correct detail for the incorrect detail is not rewriting. The purpose of editorial emendation is to fulfill the author's desire for accuracy. Getting it right is the responsibility for the editor of any author who worked close to life—especially for Wolfe. Factual errors distract good readers and damage the book by eroding reader trust in the author. Wolfe's factual errors are infrequent, and therefore require emendation because he dearly cared about accuracy. *O Lost* is an attempt to preserve Asheville through filtered memory.

Great writers return to the places of their youth with a compound of bitterness, love, sentiment, regret, and fidelity to the way it was. They write about their differentness. No community in American fiction is richer than Altamont. Wolfe's endeavors to evoke Altamont/Asheville resulted from his determination to preserve his memories of the lost life. The past is not dead; life is not buried while writers remember it. The cuts of Altamont social data in *Look Homeward, Angel* modify the purpose of *O Lost*. For example, the pruning of about 3,700 words from chapter 23, the account of the boys' after-school walk through the town, damages the clear intention of this chapter as a social panorama and as a sustained exercise in what has become known as intertextuality.

The next necessary project is a reader's companion or an annotated edition of *O Lost*, identifying sources, historical references, factual details, and literary references. Wolfe was so steeped in literature that he naturally wrote into his own prose phrases and lines from the range of English literature. He may have expected good readers to recognize many, or even most, of these unquoted quotations. The complete Chapter 23 of *O Lost* has 138 literary references or echoes as identified by Arlyn Bruccoli.[10] No reader can understand fully Wolfe's intentions and meanings in *O Lost*—or in *Look Homeward, Angel*—without help. The more the reader understands about Wolfe's intentions and methods, the richer the reading experience.

The standard anti-Wolfean slander/libel is that "he worked too close to life"—implying an insufficiency of inventive power. This charge is also expressed as "surface realism"—usually preceded by "mere." A writer who can't be trusted to get the details right can't be trusted with anything else. Of course *O Lost* is autobiographical. All serious fiction is autobiographical. Wolfe made this note: "The artist—keeping himself out of his work—like keeping water out of rain." Wolfe's writings constitute the greatest autobiographical saga in American fiction. Wolfe anticipated these objections in his preface to *Look Homeward, Angel* addressed "To the Reader":

> The writer's main concern was to give fullness, life, and intensity to the actions and people in the book he was creating. Now that it is to be published, he would insist that this book is a fiction, and that he mediated no man's portrait here. [Not true. M.J.B.]

Fiction is not fact, but fiction is fact selected and understood, fiction is fact arranged and charged with purpose. [True. M.J.B.][11]

Notes

1. The reference here is to *O Lost: A Story of the Buried Life,* the original, uncut version of *Look Homeward, Angel*. *O Lost* was edited by Arlyn and Matthew J. Bruccoli and published by the University of South Carolina Press in 2000. Ed.

2. *To Loot My Life Clean: The Thomas Wolfe–Maxwell Perkins Correspondence,* edited by Matthew J. Bruccoli and Park Bucker (Columbia: University of South Carolina Press, 2000), p. 3.

3. Perkins's notes have not been found

4. *The Letters of Thomas Wolfe,* edited by Elizabeth Nowell (New York: Scribners, 1956), p. 169.

5. *O Lost,* pp. 628–629.

6. Ibid., p. 338.

7. "Thomas Wolfe," *Harvard Library Bulletin* (August 1947): 269–277.

8. *To Loot My Life Clean,* pp. 205–206.

9. Ibid., p. 48.

10. *An Annotated Chapter from* O Lost, explanatory notes by Arlyn Bruccoli (Columbia: University of South Carolina Press, 2000).

11. *Look Homeward, Angel* (New York: Scribners, 1929), p. vii.

Part 4

On Bookmen

"Everything you do connects if you are good at what you do. One of the ways you establish your values is by what you spend your money on. Book collecting is an expression of the bookman's taste, judgment, determination, and knowledge. Bookmanship is not a hobby: it is a way of life."

    M.J.B., *22 Collections: An Exhibition from the Matthew J. and Arlyn Bruccoli Collections 27 October 2005–3 January 2006* (Thomas Cooper Library, University of South Carolina, 2005)

Debts

> I hold every man a debtor to his profession, from the which, as men of course do seek to receive countenance and profit, so ought they of duty to endeavor themselves, by way of amends, to be a help and ornament thereunto.
>
> Francis Bacon, preface, *The Elements of the Common Laws of England*

These remarks put on record my debts to the bookmen who trained me and befriended me. There are no textbooks for bookmanship. I learned from apprenticeship to generous masters.

I became a bookman in the fall of 1954, when, as a graduate student, I met John Cook Wyllie, the curator of rare books at the University of Virginia. He was the best bookman I have known. At that time I had graduated from Yale, where I had taken a bibliography course for which the textbook was McKerrow. But none of my professors had suggested that there was a mandatory connection between bookmanship and the proper study of literature. My favorite undergraduate teacher had discouraged me from collecting Hemingway because *Three Stories and Ten Poems* and *In Our Time* would cost me $200 or $300 each—which, he indicated, was more than I would want to spend. Indeed I did not even know that I wanted to be a bibliographer until I found Mr. Wyllie, and I did not know that the University of Virginia was the best place in America to learn bibliography. I got there by luck.

Mr. Wyllie was a librarian without a library-school degree, and he had created the University's rare-book collection by gleaning it book-by-book from the general stacks. He devoted many days over the course of five years to teaching me what he had taught himself. I never took a formal course with him. He showed

---

"Debts," which began as a paper delivered at the 1990 meeting of the Private Libraries Association in London, was published originally in *The Private Library*, 4th series, 4 (Winter 1991): 133–145. Reprinted with permission of Arlyn Bruccoli for the Matthew J. Bruccoli literary estate and with permission of the Private Library Association.

me things. He taught me how to look at a book, and he taught me the techniques that he had worked out for differentiating concealed printings. When the Hinman Collator arrived at the Library he asked me to try it out. I put F. Scott Fitzgerald's *This Side of Paradise* on it, and Mr. Wyllie arranged for Fredson Bowers to publish the result in *Studies in Bibliography*. Mainly Mr. Wyllie encouraged me to handle the books, which is the only proper training for a bookman or bibliographer or scholar.

In those days many curators of rare books were chronic unemployables. They discouraged people from touching the books and endeavored to impede the acquisition of more material. These types did not understand the purpose of rare-book or special-collection libraries. Mr. Wyllie knew what the books were for: they were to be used. His stacks were populated by multiple copies because his rule was that no book was a duplicate until proven so.

Mr. Wyllie cared nothing for "countenance and profit." Because he was a diffident man—I am certain that he never recognized his own brilliance—he declined to publish his most interesting work. There is no copy of his Grolier Club talk on the bibliographical significance of second editions. Two of his three Rosenbach Lectures on the uses of type as bibliographical evidence survive only in working drafts—and the third seems lost. In 1964 Mr. Wyllie addressed the Bibliographical Society of America on the subject of "The Bibliographer and the Collecting of Historical Materials." These sentences indicate the force of his mind:

> With eighty-five per cent of the collectors who have ever lived still alive today, and with ninety-five per cent of the bibliographers who have ever lived still stalking the land, how do we create the conditions to get the two populations into useful juxtaposition for this presumably desirable heat transfer? How do we bring about the set of circumstances that will put great collections to great uses? How can great needs be supplied with great means?

His answer to these questions—before the personal computer or the CD-ROM—was that "we are living in an age of machines, and we ought to learn to use them. . . . The great and solitary heroes like Bradshaw and De Ricci are gone, and we must all soon follow."

Mr. Wyllie helped me to develop a rationale for a private collector, based on the test of utility. He taught me to ask, "What is the purpose of this effort?" These principles apply to single-author collections because that is the focus of my work.

The purpose of an author collection is to yield a bibliography—either by the collector or by someone with whom the collector shares his books and knowledge—and to assemble material for textual scholars. Mr. Wyllie and I agreed that the high-spot collectors or firsts-only collectors were not contemptible, for they acquired books that would eventually go to a research library or become available for re-acquisition; but we differentiated bookmen from collectors. It was clear to us that advanced bookmanship involved the discovery and systematic assembling of all the forms of republication that do not appear in dealers' catalogues because these reprints are not worth the trouble and expense of listing them. Bookmanship requires more than the ability to write checks. It was our conviction that an author collection should aim for *every printing of every edition in the English language*. (I am unable to muster enthusiasm for translations: we all have our flaws.) Ostensibly worthless reprints are where you find them: junk shops, attics, basements, charity bazaars.

The every-printing requirement serves two goals: to establish a physical history of the author's career and the book's reputation; and to provide the evidence for a textual pedigree.

The first goal meets the needs of that branch of literary history that my friend William Charvat called "The Profession of Authorship." The cheap reprints, the book-club editions, the depth of dust-jacket cleavage, the blurbs, the movie tie-in editions—these all document the way the book and author are presented to the readership and trace the fluctuations of reputations. For example, the first paperback of *The Great Gatsby* in 1945 had a cover with the obligatory cocktail art—which didn't lure buyers; four years later a dust-jacket was provided—a rare publishing occurrence—showing a bare-chested Alan Ladd. Or compare the pre-Nobel Faulkner paperbacks with the post-Nobel treatment for the metamorphosis of yokel gothic fiction into classic literature.

The second object of the every-printing commandment is to provide the evidence of the transmission of the text and textual variants introduced intentionally or inadvertently, authorially or editorially or compositorially. The words—the author's words—are why literature matters. The words themselves—as well as the forms of the words and the punctuation by which the author controls the rhythms of his style—undergo a process of corruption or departure from the manuscript expression. Books may be silently abridged or censored. The author may introduce postpublication revisions or corrections into the texts; these late emendations are of the greatest importance because they represent the writer in the act of editing himself after the work was presumably in final form. Thus the second printing of *The Great Gatsby* with Fitzgerald's five plate spot-changes is as textually valuable as the first printing. British editions (from reset type) of American books may embody crucial textual evidence because, in the preelectronic composition era, authors took advantage of a British resetting that followed the American edition to make textual alterations that go beyond the simple spot-corrections that are feasible in printing plates. Apart from the emendations made by an American author in a trans-Atlantic resetting, there are sometimes amusing, sometime injurious unauthorial alterations introduced in a British edition for the fancied convenience of British readers. It is disconcerting to find American low-life characters speaking the Queen's English; but it is far more serious when British editors or typesetters unilaterally improve the American language. In a Raymond Chandler text the British edition changes the Americanism *vag* (for vagrant or vagrancy) to *wag*. Yet British publication for three of Chandler's novels—*The Little Sister, The Long Goodbye*, and *Playback*—preceded American publication; the Hamish Hamilton texts are ones that he proof-read. Apart from chronological precedence, these British editions possess special authority.

The collector who fulfills the every-printing requirement may have to confront the problem of how to maintain the collection as a working collection. Some—and I fear that the correct word is *most*—libraries will not accept such a collection as a gift with the proviso that it must be kept together in the rare-book or special-collections department. The blame must be divided between librarians and faculty members who know nothing about books and are therefore incapable of formulating collection policies for their institutions.

I am compelled to believe that I eventually would have become some sort of bookman, but the University of Virginia accelerated and enriched the process. In addition to Mr. Wyllie, there was Fredson Bowers—the greatest textual scholar—who published *Principles of Bibliographical Description* in 1949 and was promulgating and refining textual theory and procedure in a series of brilliant studies and superb editions. Bibliographical and textual scholarship was the most important activity at the University, and Charlottesville seemed like the center of the bibliographical world. Maybe it was. I worked with Fred for thirty years, and we became collaborators. He never gave me orders; he trained me by inviting me to undertake pieces of his editions.

Linton Massey, the President of the Bibliographical Society of the University of Virginia, which sponsored *Studies in Bibliography*, was a man of independent means who enjoyed encouraging students. At that time he was the leading William Faulkner collector. He let me use his books, and he introduced me to his book friends. The Bibliographical Society had an active program of visiting speakers, one of whom was Charles Feinberg, the greatest Walt Whitman collector, who became my friend. Charles taught me the two best rules for collecting: "Buy it—you may never get another chance at another copy" and "Books cost more today than they did yesterday; but tomorrow they'll cost even more." When other big-time collectors were warning me that book-collection was a rich man's game, Charles told me that he had bought his first books with money he earned as a shoe-shine boy. He liked to say: "Without books my life would have been a desert." I must emend that to: "Without books and bookmen my life would have been a desert." Charles gave his Whitman collection to the Library of Congress as an expression of his gratitude to America. No doubt book-collection attracts more than its fair share of nut cases; but the best bookmen are better than other people.

I cannot explain why I had never visited an antiquarian bookshop before I was in my mid-twenties. Second-hand or used-book shops, yes—but not a proper rare-book dealer. Nevertheless, I had acquired my first two Fitzgerald firsts during my senior year at Yale: a *Gatsby* and *Tales of the Jazz Age*—$10 for the pair in the basement of a New Haven textbook shop. When Mr. Wyllie sent me to my first antiquarian shop, it was the best one in America—certainly the best one for me: Seven Gables at 3 West 46th Street, New York City. The shop was on the third floor, and there was no sign outside. If you didn't know where it was, you obviously didn't belong there. Since this institution perished in 1978 and is not even a memory for many bookmen, it is appropriate for me to record some recollections of the two partners who encouraged me and who operated something that was at once a shop, a club, a seminar, and a reference library. Michael Papantonio was the English-literature partner, and John S. Van E. Kohn was the American-literature partner, although there was overlap.

Mike was born in 1907 and left school at sixteen to work for the Brick Row Bookshop. It is misleading to state that he was "self-educated." Mike was educated from knowing books. He knew things that he could not have learned in classrooms. After operating a shop under his own name from 1937 to 1943, he formed the partnership with John Kohn in 1946. John—a year older than Mike—graduated from Williams College and then took an M.A. at Harvard. His classroom years did not impair his bookmanship. He opened the Collectors' Bookshop in 1935. John died in 1976, after Seven Gables issued its 30th-anniversary catalogue. Mike died two years after. The feast was over. The partners had made no plans for the continuation of the business because they recognized that no one else could continue it. Seven Gables was a name and a location; John and Mike were the institution.

I was closer to John because of my American literature bias, although he was not enthusiastic about my authors. Nonetheless, he found books for me and put them aside until I came in. It gave him pleasure to see a collector's reaction to an exciting book. I am sure that he adjusted the prices downward to what he thought I could afford during my student days. In the Fifties you could buy a good book at Seven Gables for $10; for $100 you could acquire treasures. Our only serious arguments resulted from my conviction that I had a duty to instruct him that his prices for twentieth-century authors were too low. For his part, John tried to protect me from my folly and occasionally declined to exercise what he regarded as my foolish bids. When the galley proofs of *The Great Gatsby* came up at Parke-Bernet in 1971 I sat next to him to make sure that he would not drop out before the bidding reached what he regarded as the recklessly high figure of $2,600.

Mike regarded collectors of modern American literature with dismay and "took care" of me when John was out; but he found my copy of the rare *Colonial and Historical Houses of Maryland* with its foreword by Fitzgerald. It was impossible, even for an inexperienced kid, not to recognize the scope of his knowledge and the respect that was accorded by scholars. Yet I did not fully appreciate Mike's stature until I went to some of the London dealers with him: it was as though I was with the Duke of New York.

It would be a falsification for me to claim that I was on intimate terms with John or Mike. We were friends, and I was the recipient of their benefactions. Admission to the club did not require affluence. On a given day the place was populated with millionaires and hungry students—some of whom hoped for a luncheon invitation. The shop had a code of ethics that governed relations with collectors. Mike personally collected early American bindings, a field he selected because it would not put him in competition with his customers. He presented his superb collection to the American Antiquarian Society. John collected Edna St. Vincent Millay, Robert Frost, and E. A. Robinson. He assured me that none of his collections was first-rate because he did not take home the best items that came into the shop.

Seven Gables generated more scholarship than most English departments. All that was required was the courage to risk one's life in the elevator. The reputation of a rare-book shop may be distorted by its catalogues. The Seven Gables catalogues are not especially impressive because Mike and John knew who wanted a book—and to whom they wanted to sell it. They did not have to catalogue their best stock. I have before me as I write this the first Seven Gables catalogue (identified as Number 22) issued in 1946. The items range from $3.50 for Rupert Brooke's *In Remembrance* to $300 for *Lyrical Ballads*.

The Seven Gables American literature catalogues were mostly John's work—certainly the catalogues devoted to first books which were his personal and professional enthusiasm. Between 1936 and 1972 John produced six first-books catalogues—four before the war at his Collector's Bookshop and two for Seven Gables. The latter two listed 621 items, plus a supplementary list of 48. These substantial undertakings were primarily motivated by John's scholarly desire to establish a record of the bibliographical data he had crammed into his mind. They were only partly profit-motivated. The final catalogue, *More First Books by American Authors* (1972), had $10 books, and most of the items were priced under $100.

Henry Wenning was the comet of the American bookselling world. He came out of nowhere—that is, without prior experience except as an unsystematic collector. After careers as a labor organizer and then in the pension field, he issued ten modern literature catalogues in New Haven, Connecticut, between 1959 and 1966. (He also produced at least three lists.) He left bookselling but came back to issue two more catalogues between 1966 and 1971. His first catalogue ranged from $3.50 for Edith Sitwell's *Street Songs* in jacket to $100 for Proust's *Letters to Walter Berry* (one of fifteen on vellum, with an original letter from Proust to Berry laid in). In between, one could have squandered $5 for Jack Kerouac's *On the Road* ("Very fine in dust jacket") or $80 for the first edition of *Ulysses* in wrappers. I heard Henry's name mentioned in a tone of disapprobation when his Catalogue Two offered "an immaculate copy in dust jacket" of *The Catcher in the Rye* for $25. This absurdly inflated price was regarded as potentially destructive to sound collecting practices because it would encourage speculators to drive up prices. The same catalogue offered Faulkner's *Absalom, Absalom!* in jacket for $15 and Hemingway's *To Have and Have Not* in jacket for $10.50. Henry could not bring himself to ask for $11. That was the year he provided my first *Gatsby* in jacket and allowed me to pay the $30 in two installments.

Henry's catalogues were an exciting array of what was regarded as wild overpricing and bargain prices for rarities. Catalogue Five featured 54 books by Samuel Beckett and 18 periodicals at $750 for the lot. His price of $700 for the 408-page revised typescript of Nelson Algren's *Never Come Morning* (with related material) in Catalogue Eight was regarded as bullish. Catalogue Ten, his last catalogue before his retirement, put $1,500 on a lot described as "An excellent collection of First Editions by and about Dylan Thomas, including each original work, supplemented by twenty volumes of criticism and biography and a handful of periodical publications. All books are first issues when called for, and include a number of rarities unknown to his bibliographer."

Henry and I were friends, and he provided some of my best books and letters and manuscripts—often extending credit. We disagreed about nearly everything having to do with books. I never persuaded him that I was right about my collecting principles. For instance, he would not give shelf-room to a book that was not a "first issue"—unless it was an association copy. I could not convince him of the collectibility of reprints and their textual value. He'd give them to me if I happened to be in the shop before he discarded them. Our frequent arguments clarified my thinking. The first time I visited Henry's shop we got into a disagreement about the meaning of *issue,* and we continued to disagree about it. I cannot forbear inserting a plea for the consistent and accurate use of the five terms that constitute the core vocabulary of bibliography: *edition, printing* or *impression, issue,* and *state.*

Henry in the act of acquiring stock was an extraordinary spectacle. At the report that he had arrived in the area, collectors, authors, dealers, widows, and orphans would bring out their hidden treasures. I observed him do it, but I never understood how he did it. He was scrupulous about paying fair prices, although I had the impression that anything he offered would have been happily accepted.

Important things could be said about Henry's influence on the trade as the result of his relationship with young scouts and collectors who became prominent figures in the book world. Those stories are theirs to tell. My purpose here is to acknowledge my own debts. Book collecting was never my hobby: it has been an essential part of my work. I learned by acquiring books, and Henry Wenning—more than any other dealer at the time—made it possible for me to buy material that I could not pay for.

In my student days I was required to read a pernicious Charles Lamb essay on the joys of poverty, in which he claimed that his copy of Beaumont and Fletcher gave him more pleasure because he had to wait so long before he could buy it. A serious bookman does not enjoy waiting for a book; postponement does not improve the acquisition. Delay is to be endured—not embraced. Accordingly, the strongest influence on my book-collecting life—more than Mr. Wyllie—has been Frazer Clark, the distinguished Hawthorne collector and bibliographer. We met through collecting and eventually established a publishing house to produce bibliographies and literary histories. Fraze inculcated in me the true spirit of bibliographic acquisitiveness. He was the brave one, and he plunged me into debt.

Book collecting is an expression of the collector's taste, judgment, and courage. The spending of money is a mandatory element. A life can be gauged in terms of what money is used for. Sleepers are fun, but it is just as pleasurable to pay a stiff price for a book that is worth it. I am permanently obligated to a whilom colleague who declared in a voice trembling with outrage: "No book is worth $300!" Whenever I hesitate at a purchase I hear his voice and buy. Nonetheless, all book collectors undergo the inescapable process of falling behind the market. We end up boring younger bookmen with sentences that begin: "I remember when I bought *Moby-Dick* from Seven Gables for $300. . . ." In my twenties I proclaimed that books and manuscripts were absurdly cheap. Now I am amazed at the current prices; but a collector keeps collecting. The books you regret are the ones that you fail to buy.

Just as there is no substitute for handling books, there is no substitute for studying catalogues—both current and what might be termed "classic." I have never accustomed myself to hearing my secretaries say: "There's no important mail—just book catalogues." This is the place for me to acknowledge my debt to Peter Keisogloff. Twenty-five years ago the basement of his Cleveland bookshop was stacked with Anderson Galleries and American Art Association catalogues from the Twenties and Thirties—which he let me cherry-pick. I owe much to those catalogues and to Peter.

Good book talk can be found in unpromising venues. In the Fifties Jack Neiburg operated an unprosperous shop in a Boston slum. I learned from his anecdotes about the old days. Jack tried to find books for me and was happier than I when he succeeded.

B. George Ulizio was the most extraordinary bookman I have known. I met him in 1966 in my pursuit of a bibliographic ghost: the manuscript of Stephen Crane's *Maggie,* which was incorrectly attributed to his collection. Mr Ulizio was a tough old man. His domain was the lower level of his house where he had his office, memorabilia, and books. The walls of the office had racks of liquor bottles in straw wrappings—pre-Prohibition brands I had never seen before. We spent days smoking cigars and drinking scotch while he talked about his books and his bibliophile friends. His anecdotes about book collecting involved Owen D. Young, A. Edward Newton, Morris Parrish, and A. S. W. Rosenbach—of whom Mr. Ulizio said: "He thought I was a sucker."

I do not know how Mr. Ulizio became involved in book collecting; but it probably resulted from the prevailing book boom of the Twenties, when record auction prices were regularly being made and broken. No doubt the game appealed to his highly developed sense of competition. Although his formal education had not progressed beyond grade school, he was knowledgeable in the fields of literature and American history. He was not just an acquirer. Mr. Ulizio knew the importance of the works, the provenance of his copies, and their bibliographic points.

From our conversations and the auction catalogues, I have been able to piece together an overview of Mr. Ulizio's bibliophile career. He had disposed of two libraries before I met him. His most distinguished library was the English literature collection sold at the American Art Association / Anderson Galleries in January 1931 (Sale no. 3883). This sale was touted as the most important since the legendary Jerome Kern sale of 1929. Although it included many great books, Mr Ulizio's collection did not have the depth of association material that was the strength of the Kern library. The 1,084 lots brought $60,724: an average of $56 against the Kern average of $1,165. The lots were grouped, and there were some 2,900 books in the Ulizio sale. The strength of the library lay in the 97 Dickens lots, which totaled $23,838 ($245.75 per lot). Mr. Ulizio's English library had representative groups of the late-nineteenth-century and early-twentieth-century authors then in collecting vogue: Barrie, 42 lots; Conrad, 23; Galsworthy, 31; Gissing, 24; Hardy, 49; Kipling, 110 (*Departmental Ditties* reached $925); George Moore, 22; Shaw, 55; James Stephens, 21; Stevenson, 81 (*The Pentland Rising*, $875; *New Arabian Nights*, $700); and Wilde, 24. At the time of the 1931 sale it was announced that a sale of Mr. Ulizio's American literature library would follow that year, but he cancelled it. A second Ulizio sale was held at American Art / Anderson in 1935 (no. 4194). The 344 lots of English and American literature brought only $4,625.50 ($13.45 per lot). Oliver Wendell Holmes's *History of the American Stereoscope* (the first copy ever auctioned) brought $110; and a two-page Jefferson ALS attacking Hamilton and commenting on the first New York financial panic reached $120. Washing Irving letters went begging. Mr. Ulizio brought in his books at this sale. He kept back favorite items, and he continued collecting. In the copy of *Sister Carrie* that he inscribed for Mr. Ulizio, Theodore Dreiser noted his "vigorous and forthright approach to life." Dreiser almost got it right. B. George Ulizio didn't *approach* life: he *attacked* it. Our association lasted less than four years, but he filled those years.

I did not get to England until 1966—when I was thirty-five years old. Since then I have returned more than thirty times. Before I set foot in London I had formed an epistolary relationship with Anthony Rota, who for thirty-odd years has been performing unprofitable bookish services for me. That was at a time when one still heard the rule "Follow the flag" and when British editions of American authors were omitted from bibliographies or relegated to appendices. It has been crucial that I have a source for British editions of American books—not just the firsts, but "worthless reprints." Truly some of my bibliographical projects could not have been completed without Anthony's uncomplaining conscription as my research assistant. Fred Zentner's Cinema Bookshop has provided another London resource for my work. Booksellers have been more helpful to me than librarians. Having said that, I must immediately acknowledge my debts to William Cagle of the Lilly Library, Indiana University, and to Charles Mann of Penn State University. They too know what books are for.

I do not know whether I come to London in order to buy books or buy books in order to come to London. Dr. Johnson should have said: "When a man is tired of London bookshops, he is tired of life." For three years I enjoyed the best conversation in London about books, writers, and social history. In my bibliophile paradise I have just left a bookshop or the British Library and am on my way to have tea with Jean Kennerley.

Hawthorne as a Collector's Item, 1885–1924

One indication of an author's reputation is the amounts that collectors are willing to pay for his books. Obviously, there are many limitations on this method, for literary merit and collector appeal are not always concomitant qualities. The circumstances under which a major author was published may make his books too common for the collector, whereas a minor author's books may have the combination of characteristics that makes collectors reach deep into their pockets.

Nathaniel Hawthorne is an ideal figure around which to conduct a survey of American book collecting, for he provides a combination of rarity and literary merit. Until the Melville and James revivals of the 1920s, his position as the great American novelist was not seriously challenged. In so far as such a thing can be determined, Hawthorne was the first American novelist to be collected seriously; and with the exception of sporadic interest in Cooper, the first rank of nineteenth-century American collectors did not bother with other American novelists. In addition to being eminently respectable, Hawthorne's work has great collector appeal. *Fanshawe, The Celestial Rail-Road, Time's Portraiture,* and *The Sister Years* are among the supreme rarities in American literature. Of the two carrier's addresses, there are probably not more than three copies of *Time's Portraiture* and probably not more than six of *The Sister Years. The Celestial Rail-Road* is particularly tantalizing to the collector because it exists with two imprints.

On the other hand, the first printings of Hawthorne's four romances are comparatively common—or rather, all but *The Scarlet Letter* seem more common than they really are. The first edition of *The Scarlet Letter* consisted of 2,500 copies, of which a high percentage survived because of the book's immediate success. The second edition of 2,500 copies is also a collector's item because it adds the author's

---

"Hawthorne as a Collector's Item, 1885–1924" first appeared in *Hawthorne Centenary Essays*, edited by Roy Harvey Pearce (Columbus: Ohio State University Press, 1964), pp. 387–400, 476–479. Reprinted with permission of the Ohio State University Press. For help in preparing this article, M.J.B. expressed his indebtedness to Roger E. Stoddard, C. E. Frazer Clark, Jr., Peter Keisogloff, John S. Van E. Kohn, William Runge, Marcus McCorison, Miss Jane Gatliff, the American Antiquarian Society, and the Boston Public Library.

preface. *The House of the Seven Gables, The Blithedale Romance,* and *The Marble Faun* seem quite common because no attempt was made by the publisher to distinguish between the first printings and the reprints. The first printing of *The House of the Seven Gables* consisted of 1,690 copies, but there were three more printings in 1851 of 1,690, 1,051, and 1,000 copies. The first printing of *The Blithedale Romance* comprised 5,090 copies, and there was a second printing in 1852 of 2,350. The first printing of *The Marble Faun* comprised 8,000 copies, and there were two more printings of 3,000 and 1,500 copies before the conclusion was added, and two separate printings with the conclusion of 1,000 copies each—all in 1860. Only recently has the work of the Centenary Hawthorne differentiated these concealed printings.[1] Although this new information is expected to interest collectors, the obvious fact remains that even the true first printings were too large for real competition to result over them. Of course, collectors have always been eager to acquire association copies of even common books.

In between the great rarities and the romances, there is a group of books which are rare, but not superlatively so—*Twice-Told Tales, Peter Parley's Universal History, Liberty Tree, Grandfather's Chair, Famous Old People, Biographical Stories for Children.* It is clear then, that collecting Hawthorne appeals to all purses. But this survey will of necessity concentrate on the high-spots because they are more traceable and more meaningful. In general, though, the bottom of the market will be a reflection of the top: that is, when *Fanshawe* or *Twice-Told Tales* brings whopping great prices, *The Scarlet Letter* and *The House of the Seven Gables* will also be selling high.

In Hawthorne's case, at least, collector and dealer activity is significant, for the prices of his books show a steady willingness of men to back their opinions with cash. Apart from its adherence to the laws of supply and demand, there is something lawless about collecting first printings—and this is the source of its attraction. There are sound textual arguments for collecting first printings, but few collectors are textual scholars. There are sentimental excuses for collecting first printings: this is the form in which a masterpiece first appeared in print, and indeed the genius who wrote it may have held this very copy in his hands. But one wonders whether many collectors are really persuaded by this line of thinking. It seems more likely that the serious collector is attracted primarily by the sheer challenge of the game, by the act of pitting his taste, judgment, and acquisitive instincts against those of his competitors. He is also staking his money, and that is what gives collecting its edge. Assuming that a good collector collects authors he has read and appreciates—a fair assumption—the record of Hawthorne collecting is then the record of the men who were willing to bet on their estimations of Hawthorne's enduring position in American literature. Hawthorne has had a loyal rank of brave collectors: Charles B. Foote, William Harris Arnold, George M. Williamson, J. Chester Chamberlain, Frank Maier, Stephen H. Wakeman, Owen Franklin Aldis, and W. T. H. Howe. The best of them did more than assemble libraries—they promoted Hawthorne scholarship, enlarged the canon of his work, and preserved manuscript material. Their catalogues are important reference tools—and monuments to the men.

For the purposes of this survey, 1885 may be taken as the year when the collection of American first editions first won serious attention; for in 1885, Leon and Brother issued their first bookseller's catalogue devoted to American first editions, and Beverly Chew anonymously published the first bibliography of an American author, *The Longfellow Collector's Hand-Book*.[2] Before that time, serious American collectors did not collect American literature; or if they did, they collected Americana or even poetry—but not fiction. The fact that Chew did not put his name on his Longfellow work is almost certainly meaningful. Leon and Chew each appear to have felt diffident enough to preface his volume with an *apologia*. After making a patriotic appeal for American first editions, the introduction to the Leon catalogue makes a good bibliographical case: "In the first editions the text appears fresh from the author's mind—before those changes which are apt to occur, either from recollection or as the result of unfavorable criticism." If, as has been suggested, Chew wrote the Leon introduction, his role in the rise of collecting American literature becomes quite important. In the Longfellow bibliography, Chew notes the recent interest in American first editions and "the small amount of bibliographical data obtainable in print."

The Leon catalogue listed 35 items for Hawthorne, offering all for sale except *Fanshawe*. The highest price asked was $30 for *The Gentle Boy*. *Time's Portraiture, The Sister Years,* and *The Celestial Rail-Road* were not included, although the list claimed to include "all his work published in separate form." Leon supplied Chew with his first American authors, chiefly poets.

In the Nineties, the ground was prepared for the great collections that would be formed—and scattered—in the first decade of the twentieth century. Herbert Stuart Stone compiled, in 1893, the first checklist for collectors of American literature—apart from the Leon catalogue—*First Editions of American Authors*.[3] A Harvard undergraduate at the time his book was published, Stone based his lists largely on the collections at Harvard. In the following year occurred the first important auction of a Hawthorne collection at the Foote sale.[4] The Foote catalogue listed 58 Hawthorne items which totaled $648.49, including *Fanshawe* ($155), *Peter Parley's Universal History* ($17.50), *Twice-Told Tales* ($22), *The Gentle Boy* ($34), *Grandfather's Chair* ($25), *Famous Old People* ($32), *Liberty Tree* ($25), *The Celestial Rail-Road* ($58), and *The Scarlet Letter* ($27). Though not in the same class as the Foote sale, the two auctions of Christian P. Roos's books contributed to the growing interest in Hawthorne collecting.[5] In 1897, 31 unexceptional items brought $106.77; and in 1900 a group of 34 interesting books brought $333.57, the star being *Peter Parley's Universal History* at $30.

The establishment of P. K. Foley's rare-book business in 1896 was an event of signal importance for American collecting. Foley was the greatest dealer in American literature of his time—and, perhaps, of all time—and he took an active role in assembling the collections of Aldis, Wakeman, and Chamberlain. In 1897, he published *American Authors 1795–1895*, which became the standard reference tool in the field.[6] Though it has errors, and holes—Foley was not aware of *Time's Portraiture* or of the two imprints of *The Celestial Railroad*—Foley's book is a marked improvement over Stone's and includes solid bibliographical information. His first catalogue, September 1897, included 20 Hawthorne items, of which the best was the *American Magazine of Useful Knowledge* ($10). It is curious that in Foley's first 16 catalogues, up to 1905, there are only two unusual Hawthorne items: an unbound set of what are presumably proof sheets of *The Blithedale Romance* (catalogue 3, March 1899—$3) and *The Sister Years* (catalogue 15, June 1904—$400). Probably, with customers like Wakeman, Aldis, and Chamberlain, Foley found it unnecessary to catalogue his outstanding things.

Between 1903 and 1909, Foley took an active role in building the Aldis American literature collection which was presented to Yale in 1911.[7] Considerable bibliographical information about Hawthorne was made available during the Nineties; and although these checklists were not limited in use to bibliophiles, they almost certainly reflected a growing interest in Hawthorne collecting. In 1890 John P. Anderson appended a bibliography to Moncure D. Conway's *Life of Nathaniel Hawthorne*,[8] and in the same year Louise Manning Hodgkins published her "Guide to the Study of Nathaniel Hawthorne."[9] Gardner Maynard Jones published his "Complete List of Hawthorne's Writings" in 1891;[10] and in 1897 George M. Williamson published "A Bibliography of the Writings of Nathaniel Hawthorne."[11] Luther S. Livingston, an important influence on the development of American collecting, included Hawthorne in the first of his series "The First Books of Some American Authors" in 1898.[12]

By the beginning of the twentieth century, the elements for a boom in Hawthorne collecting were available, and the centenary of his birth in 1904 brought interest to a peak.

The first important collecting event of the twentieth century was the William Harris Arnold sale in 1901, an event that has not always been recognized as having stimulated interest in American first editions by publicizing these books as investments. Arnold may have collected for the wrong reasons, but just the same he converted many people to the game. He bought his first American first edition on 16 May 1895—it is wholly typical of Arnold to have recorded the event—and by 1898 he was able to publish his *First Report of a Book Collector,* [13] in which he displayed an unusual frankness about admitting his concern with profit in collecting books. His boasting about his sleepers must have seemed in terrible taste to the rich and conservative gentlemen collectors of the time. In 1901 Arnold was ready to dispose of his collection, which the catalogue claimed was "by far the fullest collection of First Editions, of the eight authors named, that has ever been sold."[14] The prices, many of them new records, attracted great attention in the collecting world, and Arnold himself was not reluctant to publicize his success. After the sale he published an elegant catalogue giving both cost and sale prices for each item.[15] It showed that he more than doubled his money: the cost of the 709 items was $3,508.16, and the return was $7,363.17. There were 64 Hawthorne items in the Arnold sale, for which he had paid $572.45 and received $1,366.72. The Hawthorne high-spots were *Fanshawe* ($200 [$410), *Peter Parley's Universal History* ($17.50 [$100), and *The Celestial Rail-Road* ($1 [$124). A copy of *Mosses from an Old Manse,* one of two in wrappers then known, appreciated from $18 to $62. Although these were bargains by today's standards—especially since Arnold was fussy about condition—they were considered remarkable in 1901. The *Literary Collector* was so impressed by the Arnold sale that it distributed to its subscribers a list of the prices and purchasers.[16]

Interest in collecting Hawthorne reached a peak during 1904 and 1905. In 1904, the centenary of Hawthorne's birth, there were celebrations in Concord and Salem; Chamberlain organized the Grolier Club exhibition and compiled the informative catalogue;[17] and the New York Public Library had an exhibition which Victor Hugo Paltsits catalogued in the *Bulletin of the New York Public Library.*[18] In the same year the *Literary Collector* published a useful checklist, "First Editions of Hawthorne," which noted the record prices of the books.[19] Appropriately, there were two important auctions in 1904. The French-Chubbuck sale had 37 Hawthorne items which realized $1,099.75[20]—including a *Fanshawe* ($450), *Peter Parley's Universal History* ($72—the same copy had sold for $17.50 in the Foote sale), the first copy of *The Sister Years* to appear at auction ($290), and *Time's Portraiture,* 1853 ($60).

The Williamson sale in 1904[21] included 12 Hawthorne letters and 3 exciting manuscripts: "Feathertop," 20 pages ($750); "The Ancestral Footstep," 88 pages ($650); and the only surviving leaf of *The Scarlet Letter,* the title page and Table of Contents ($113). In 1908, 170 of Williamson's Hawthorne books brought $1,446.40.[22] This remarkable collection included *Fanshawe* ($300) and *The Celestial Rail-Road* ($630). But apart from these two items the prices were very modest:

the terrifically rare 1851 *Scarlet Letter* in wrappers brought $5, and dozens of books went for less than one dollar.

An interesting event of 1904–1905 was William K Bixby's purchase of 165 Hawthorne letters—"the love letters"—from Julian Hawthorne. Bixby permitted the Society of the Dofobs of Chicago to issue these letters in a privately printed edition of 62 copies in 1907.[23] In 1916 and 1917 Bixby sold auction duplicates and selections from his library, including superb Hawthorne material. The 1916 Huntington-Bixby-Church sale, billed as the greatest auction since the Hoe sale, included 53 of Bixby's Hawthorne items, which brought $1,651.50, a small total considering that it was nearly all manuscript or association material.[24] The 1917 Huntington-Bixby sale included one lot of 33 letters by and to Hawthorne and his family, which went begging at $2,000.[25] In 1918 Henry E. Huntington purchased Bixby's manuscript collection, which included 200 of Hawthorne's letters.

Luther S. Livingston's *Auction Prices of Books*[26] shows that by 1904 a great deal of choice Hawthorne material was sold on a rising market. No fewer than ten *Fanshawes* were sold at a range from $75 to $840. The list includes seven copies of *The Celestial Rail-Road* ($46–$240), six copies of *Peter Parley's Universal History* ($35–$140), ten copies of *Twice-Told Tales* ($10–$41), 13 copies of *Famous Old People* ($7.50–$76), 11 copies of *The Gentle Boy* ($11–$143), 20 copies of *Grandfather's Chair* ($11.50–$76), nine copies of *Biographical Stories for Children* ($11–$36.50), eight copies of *Liberty Tree* ($19–$48), 21 copies of *The Scarlet Letter* ($6.50–$29), five copies of *The House of the Seven Gables* ($5.50–$9), five copies of *The Blithedale Romance* ($5–$60 for a presentation copy), and 11 copies of *The Marble Faun* ($7–$11.50).

The important Hawthorne events of 1905 were the two book-length bibliographies by Nina E. Browne[27] and Wallace Hugh Cathcart.[28] Both volumes are frustrating to work with and are far from definitive, but their existence demonstrates that a high point in collector interest had been reached.

Both Wakeman and Chamberlain began collecting American first editions in 1900, the year before the Arnold sale. Chamberlain purchased Chew's American authors en bloc in 1900; and in the five years left to him, he assembled a superb collection of ten authors. When catalogued for auction in 1909,[29] there were 139 Hawthorne items which realized about $4,300, including two copies of *Fanshawe*, seven of *Peter Parley's Universal History*, *Time's Portraiture* (the 1838 and two copies of the 1853 edition), *The Sister Years*, The *Celestial Rail-Road,* and *The Sunday School Society's Gift*. The 1838 *Time's Portraiture*—the first to be sold at auction—brought $550. The *Fanshawes* brought $500 and $350; *The Celestial Rail-Road* brought $380, a new record; *Sister Years* brought $260; and *The Sunday*

School Society's Gift, one of three known copies, brought $115. Eight volumes from Hawthorne's own library realized $1,376.

Less information is available on Frank Maier than on Chamberlain or Wakeman. If Maier's Hawthorne collection was not so good as Chamberlain's or Wakeman's, it was nonetheless splendid. His library was auctioned in 1909, nine months after Chamberlain's, and brought $22,324 as against $36,484 for Chamberlain's.[30] His 121 Hawthorne items brought $1,202.30, a surprisingly low total. Perhaps the Chamberlain sale had temporarily satiated Hawthorne collectors, for many of Maier's rarities went low: *Fanshaw*—$350; *Peter Parley's Universal History*—$40; *The Sister Years*—$150; *Time's Portraiture* (1853)—$50; *The Celestial Rail-Road*—$140; *Twice-Told Tales*—$10. The condition of these books may have been against them, but it is still surprising to see dozens of desirable items going at one or two dollars—first editions of *The House of the Seven Gables* and *The Blithedale Romance,* for example, brought $1.25 each. Aldis was an active buyer at the Chamberlain and Maier sales, as was Walter T. Wallace. When Wallace's books were sold in 1920, some Hawthorne items totaled about $3,200: *The Sister Years*—$130; *The Sunday School Society's Gift*—$240; *Time's Portraiture,* 1838—$450 (these three had been bought at the Chamberlain sale); *Time's Portraiture,* 1853—$220 (the Maier copy); and two pages of the manuscript of *Time's Portraiture,* $200.[31]

Wakeman started collecting in 1900 and found it necessary to retire from business in 1904 to devote all his time to his library. During the centenary year, he had privately printed from the manuscript thirty copies of *Twenty Days with Julian and Little Bunny.* Like the good collector he was, Wakeman had one copy printed on vellum for himself. In 1909, he sold his fabulous collection—including *The Blithedale Romance, Dr. Grimshawe's Secret, The Dolliver Romance, Septimus Felton,* and Hawthorne's journals—through George S. Hellman to J. Pierpont Morgan for $165,000.[32] Of Wakeman's books, which were sold at auction in 1924, John S. Van E. Kohn has written: "This sale dispersed the greatest collection of the nine Wakeman authors ever assembled . . . no comparable collection, take it for all and all, could ever be formed again."[33] The auction catalogue prepared from Wakeman's notes by Arthur Swann has become an indispensable tool for Hawthorne scholars.[34] Wakeman's 179 Hawthorne items brought $9,770, not a high total considering the quantity of inscribed material. Wakeman had *Time's Portraiture, The Sister Years,* and both imprints of *The Celestial Rail-Road*—the only time all four have ever appeared, or will ever appear, in the same sale.

There were bargains in the Wakeman sale. Barton Currie remarks that many dealers and collectors were unenthusiastic about it—though he doesn't explain why—and that Rosenbach, Wells, and Sessler "hold aloof."[35] W. T. H. Howe was a leading purchaser, and some of his acquisitions were wonderful buys by today's standards. *Fanshaw,* the copy which had brought $410 at the Arnold sale and which Wakeman had paid $450 for, was sold to Howe for $1,025. The copy of *Twice-Told Tales* inscribed by Hawthorne as a betrothal gift to Sophia Peabody had been purchased by Wakeman from Julian Hawthorne for $450;[36] Howe paid $1,000 for it. The copy of *Time's Portraiture* that Howe paid $325 for had been purchased by Wakeman for $75. Howe bought four first editions of *The Scarlet Letter,* including Sophia Hawthorne's copy ($400—Wakeman had paid $100) and a presentation copy from Hawthorne to his sister Elizabeth ($350—Wakeman paid $125).[37] *The Sister Years* brought $250. The Fish imprint of *The Celestial Rail-Road* brought $140 and the Wilder $160—well under the $380 brought by Chamberlain's Wilder. For some reason, Hawthorne's copy of *Laws of Bowdoin College* with eight Hawthorne-Hathorne signatures went for only $27.50. It brought $1,125 five years later in the Kern sale.

The great era of Hawthorne collecting—and, indeed of the collecting of nineteenth-century American authors—closed with the Wakeman sale. Many of the treasures owned by Aldis, Williamson, Chamberlain, Maier, and Wakeman have found their way to the Morgan Library, the New York Public Library, the Huntington Library, the Yale Library, and the Alderman Library at the University of Virginia. Which is where they belong unfortunately.[38]

Postscript

After the Wakeman sale, American collecting—and Hawthorne collecting—changed. It is probably too simple to blame this change on the financial conditions of the 1930s. For one thing the old breed of collectors typified by Chamberlain and Wakeman died out with these men; for another thing, the younger collectors turned their attention to younger reputations—Melville, James, Twain, and the twentieth-century authors.

No great Hawthorne collections were dispersed during the Thirties and Forties, although some great items were sold. Two magnificent groups of material from the Hawthorne family appeared in 1931. In April seventeen lots of letters to and from Hawthorne or his family—"The Property of a Descendant of Hawthorne"—brought $5,437.85 at auction.[39] The star was a letter from Hawthorne to his sister Elizabeth, dated 1 October 1824, which sold for $900. A letter from Oliver Wendell Holmes about *The Scarlet Letter* brought $1,450. In November, 46 superb books and manuscripts owned by Miss Rebecca B. Manning brought $10,099.50.[40] The top prices were $2,200 each for the inscribed copies of *Peter Parley's Universal History* and *Mosses from an Old Manse* in wrappers. An inscribed copy of *The Scarlet Letter* brought $1,300. The books did better than the manuscripts. The highest price brought by a letter was $430 for what is apparently the earliest known Hawthorne letter: to Robert Manning, 9 December 1813. Hawthorne's fifteen-page constitution of the Pin Society sold for only $340; and the five-page constitution of the Pot-8–O Club, for $375.

The 1945 Frank J. Hogan sale had only 12 Hawthorne items, including the 9 December 1813 letter, which brought $500.[41] The 19 items in the 1960 Arthur Swann sale did not include any great pieces, but the books were distinguished by their fine condition.[42] The most recent appearance of a major Hawthorne item was in November 1963, when the manuscript of "A London Suburb"—the largest Hawthorne manuscript to appear at auction since 1904—was sold for $5,500.[43]

At least four superb Hawthorne collections have been assembled since the Twenties. The catalogue of Carroll A. Wilson's library includes some hundred Hawthorne pieces, many of which are association items.[44] Two magnificent collections, still in the process of growth, are the C. Waller Barrett collections, at the University of Virginia, and the collection of C. E. Frazer Clark, Jr. A fourth notable collection is owned by Parkman D. Howe.[45]

Notes

1. Matthew J. Bruccoli, "Concealed Printings in Hawthorne," p. 106 this book. Orig. published in *Papers of the Bibliographic Society of America* 57 (First Quarter 1963): 42–49.

2. *Catalogue of First Editions of American Authors . . . by Leon & Brother* (New York, 1885), and *The Longfellow Collector's Hand-Book* (New York, 1885). It is possible to move the date of the inception of American first-edition collecting back to 1875, the year when the *Index to American Poetry and Plays in the Collection of C. Fiske Harris* (Providence, 1875) was published. See Roger E. Stoddard's "C. Fiske Harris, Collector of American Poetry and Plays," *Papers of the Bibliographical Society of America* 57 (First Quarter 1963): 14–32.

3. Cambridge, 1893.

4. 23 November 1894; Bangs.

5. 13 April 1897; Libbie. 12 March 1900; Bangs.

6. Boston, 1897. See also C. F. H. [Charles F. Heartman], *Patrick Kevin Foley* (Book Farm, 1937).

7. See Donald C. Gallup's "Aldis, Foley, and the Collection of American Literature at Yale," *Papers of the Bibliographical Society of America* 41 (First Quarter 1948): 1–9.

8. New York, 1890, appendix pp. 1–13.

9. *Guide to the Study of Nineteenth Century Authors*, part 2 (1890), pp. 15–20—not seen.

10. *Salem Public Library Bulletin* (October 1891): 46–48—not seen.

11. *Book Buyer* (October and November 1897): 218–220, 326–327.

12. *Bookman* (September 1898): 38–43.

13. New York, 1898.
14. 30 January 1901; Bangs. The catalogue appears to have also been published as a book. Arnold's eight authors were Hawthorne, Bryant, Emerson, Holmes, Longfellow, Lowell, Thoreau, and Whittier.
15. *A Record of First Editions . . . Collected by William Harris Arnold* (New York, 1901).
16. Not seen.
17. *First Editions of the Works of Nathaniel Hawthorne* (New York, 1904).
18. "List of Books, etc. by and relating to Nathaniel Hawthorne" (July 1904): 312–322.
19. (August 1904):109–116.
20. February 1904; Libbie.
21. 1 March 1904; Anderson 274.
22. 30 January 1908; Anderson 626.
23. *Love Letters of Nathaniel Hawthorne,* 2 volumes (Chicago, 1907).
24. 29 March 1916; Anderson.
25. 26 February 1917; Anderson 1280.
26. New York, 1905, volume II.
27. *A Bibliography of Nathaniel Hawthorne* (Boston, 1905).
28. *Bibliography of the Works of Nathaniel Hawthorne* (Cleveland, 1905).
29. 16 February 1909; Anderson 725, and 4 November 1909; Anderson 777. Chamberlain's other authors were Bryant, Emerson, Holmes, Irving, Longfellow, Poe, Thoreau, and Whittier.
30. 16 November 1909; Anderson 782, and 22 November 1909; Anderson 784. Maier's other authors were Bryant, Emerson, Holmes, Irving, Aldrich, Field, and Howells.
31. 22 March 1920; American Art.
32. George S. Hellman, *Lanes of Memory* (New York, 1927), pp. 42–47.
33. *Grolier* (New York, 1859), p. 98. This volume is essential for any study of American book-collecting.
34. 28 April 1924; American Art. The priced catalogue was published as a bound book by the American Art Association in 1924. Wakeman's other authors were Bryant, Emerson, Holmes, Longfellow, Lowell, Poe, Thoreau, and Whittier.
35. *Fishers of Books* (New York, 1931), p. 277.
36. A considerable quantity of great Hawthorne material—inscribed copies, letters, and manuscripts—was peddled by Julian Hawthorne during his various financial crises.
37. Howe's library was purchased for the New York Public Library by Albert A. Berg in 1940. Some of Howe's books were exhibited in 1937 at the Lockwood Memorial Library at the University of Buffalo. See *A Catalogue of an Exhibition of . . . Nathaniel Hawthorne* (Buffalo, 1937).
38. Something must be said about the Hawthorne activities of America's greatest bookseller. Dr. A. S. W. Rosenbach does not seem to have handled a great deal of Hawthorne, but he did sell some superb things. Hearst bought a manuscript of "A London Suburb" and a Dickens manuscript for $400. Owen D. Young got a bargain when he bought 146 letters from Hawthorne to Ticknor for $3,600, even though the letters had been published

in *Letters of Hawthorne to William D. Ticknor,* 2 volumes (Newark, 1910). The manuscript of *Tanglewood Tales*—the only substantial manuscript still in private hands—was sold to Adrian Van Sinderen for $28,750.

39. 29 April 1931; American Art-Anderson 3911.

40. 19 November 1931; American Art-Anderson 3927.

41. 23 January 1945; Parke-Bernet 627.

42. 22 March 1960; Parke-Bernet 1961.

43. 6 November 1963; Parke-Bernet 2222. On 28 January 1964—after this article had been set in type—nineteen important Hawthorne items were sold at the Ribal sale (Parke-Bernet 2250) for a total of $5,860. The twenty-page manuscript of "Lichfield and Uttoxeter" brought $4,250. A four-page letter from Sophia Hawthorne to Louisa Hawthorne, with Hawthorne's postscripts, brought $375; a lot consisting of first editions of *The Marble Faun* and *Transformation,* with 2 ½-page Hawthorne letter to Bennoch about the book, brought $275. A Wilder *Celestial Rail-Road* was sold for $180.

44. Carroll A. Wilson: *Thirteen Author Collections of the Nineteenth Century . . . ,* edited by Jean C. S. Wilson and David A. Randall, 2 volumes (New York, 1950).

45. Parkman D. Howe, "Contemporary Collectors XXXVI," *Book Collector* (Winter 1963): 467–475.

George D. Smith and the Anglo-American Book Migration

George D. Smith was the greatest American bookdealer. This assessment is supported by the books he acquired and the collections he built between 1900 and 1920. Smith performed the latter function with an understanding of the needs of self-made Americans: he was one of them. In 1900 he initiated this credo in the *Literary Collector,* the journal he published:

> Autograph letters furnish an index to the writer's mind nearly always valuable and often indispensable to a comprehension of his writings. They are history, and sacred history. They cost money, but so does real estate, and in the world of letters, autographs are building lots on Wall Street. . . . When the rulers of kingdoms to-day have crumbled into dust and their names forgotten of the people, the memory of a maker of a great collection will be a household word in the mouths of thousands. This is the royal road to fame.

Greatness may be the product of many factors, but it is always the result of timing. Great books make brave buyers. Brave buyers make great sales. From 1914 to 1919 more superb British libraries were dispersed than ever before or since. Smith bought and resold books that had never been seen in America, thereby encouraging collecting and stimulating the transatlantic rare-book trade—as well as providing the consigners with more money than they would have received in his absence. Yet he is now scarcely known to bookmen. The initials G.D.S., once a defiant boast, are forgotten.

Smith merits a biography; the only account of his career is Charles F. Heartman's thirty-two-page booklet *George D. Smith / G.D.S. / A Memorial Tribute to the Greatest Bookseller / the World Has Ever Known* (1945). A condensed CV will

---

"George D. Smith and the Anglo-American Book Migration" began as a paper read in 1992 at a meeting of the Bibliographical Society in London. The essay was published originally in *AB Bookman's Weekly,* 91 (14 June 1993): 2524, 2526, 2528, 2530, 2532, 2534, 2536, 2537, 2538. Reprinted with permission of Arlyn Bruccoli for the Matthew J. Bruccoli literary estate.

be useful before chronicling his London campaigns. What might be called the oral history of George D. Smith has been distorted by his turf activities: he was the owner of the Brighton racing stable and a big bettor. Since the celebrated American horse-player known as Pittsburgh Phil (d. 1905) was named George E. Smith, the reputations of the two gambling George Smiths became conflated. Subsequently Harry Strauss (1908–1941), a prolific killer for Murder, Inc., assumed the nom de mob of Pittsburgh Phil, thereby adding further nonbibliographical connotations to the Smith legend.

George D. Smith left school at thirteen in 1883 and went to work as an errand boy at the Manhattan bookshops of Wiley & Son and Dodd, Mead. Smith was not a scholar, but he appears to have been an authentic case of hypermnesia: he never forgot an important book or its points or its price. It was said that he could read a book catalogue and then recite it. His detractors insisted that Smith never read books. How many book dealers have read the volumes they buy and sell?

By the time Smith was seventeen he was in business with partners and issuing catalogues. From the start he operated on the principle that if one copy is good, two are better:

> When I was a little older I saw that prices were bound to increase and go on increasing because the demand was outgrowing the supply. It was perfectly clear to me that the dealer who had the largest stock would do the largest business, because collectors would be obliged to go to him for their books. I have never been afraid of overstocking in really rare books, and collectors have learned to think of Smith first when they were really anxious to buy. The best salesman in the world cannot sell books that he cannot deliver. The fundamental thing is to get the books.

In 1891 at age twenty-one, Smith spent $40,000 at the Brayton Ives sale, and in 1900 he bought one-third of the books at the Augustin Daly sale. The scope of Smith's activities expanded in 1911 when he purchased en bloc for Henry E. Huntington the E. Dwight Church library of English literature and Americana at a reputed price of $1.3 million. That year he also acquired the Beverly Chew collection. These acquisitions established both his most important collector relationship with Huntington and his preferred method of dealing: buy 'em all.

At the Robert Hoe sales of 1911–1912 G.D.S. established another activity that defined his career: challenging the British hegemony. The Hoe library was the most valuable to be auctioned in America and attracted the presence of Quaritch, Maggs, and other prominent European figures who did not anticipate strong native opposition. Smith—bidding mostly for Huntington, but also buying for stock—took 5,500 of the 14,588 Hoe lots, including the vellum Gutenberg Bible for Huntington at a record $50,000. He later boasted: "I had the satisfaction of having taught those English and Continental booksellers something about American sporting blood that they didn't forget for many a day."

Smith's first buying trip to England has not been determined, but he was a regular commuter between 1914 and 1920. His *aestus mirabilis* came in summer 1914. Before he arrived in London he had purchased the library of the Duke of Devonshire in bloc for Huntington at $750,000, on which Smith reportedly earned a $100,000 commission. (The official exchange rate at this time was $4.86 to the pound, but there is no way to convert the purchasing power of pre-Great War pounds.) The transaction was negotiated in New York by Montagu Barlow of Sotheby, Wilkinson, and Hodge, acting for the duke. The *London Times* referred to the Devonshire purchase as constituting "a small portion of his library consisting of the Caxtons and the Kemble collection of plays." There were 25 Caxtons—including the first and second editions of *Game and Playe of the Chesse,* the *Hystoryes of Troye,* Higden's *Polychronicon,* the first and second editions of *The Mirrour of the Worlde,* and an uncut *Dictes or Sayenges of the Philosophres.* There were more than 7,500 plays. The Shakespeare volumes included the 4 folios and 57 quartos.

Among the manuscripts were the earliest known complete text of the Chester Mystery Cycle (1591), *Misogonus* (1577), and Bale's *King Johan* (ca. 1538). A spokesman identified as "the manager at Quaritch's," presumably E. H. Dring, commented that "Americans generally have a finer appreciation of old books than Englishmen." However, the *London Times* editorialized:

> To a certain extent only can books, however beautiful, be considered as valuable works of art. There are fortunately enough *incunabula* all over the world, in public and private possession, to show us what early printed books are like. They are not always of striking typographical merit; and even when they are masterpieces of the printer's skill their beauty is not of a kind which elevates or soothes. The finest type, the fairest paper, the tallest copy can never, like some Attic vase, "tease us out of thought." The art of printing is at best a subsidiary art, and to appraise a book solely for its form or for its date is a perversity. The grotesque importance attached to pieces of paper is nowhere better illustrated than in the prices paid by collectors of postage stamps, but the sums realized by printed books are often hardly less fantastic; even when CAXTON printed a classic, like CHAUCER, the true Chaucerian would probably prefer to read his author from a modern and more accurate text. Only a very few old books possess a spiritual value, and their worth is then something more than all the millionaires in the world can combine to give it. The few

manuscripts, such as the Laurentian manuscript of SOPHOCLES, which may preserve in its purest form the text of a great writer, cannot be assessed in terms of parchment or calligraphy. CAXTON's books have no spiritual value. Neither have they, however rare and well preserved, even when they are unique, any value as works of art comparable with that of great pictures. When a Rembrandt perishes by fire the world is spiritually poorer for the loss, but by the destruction of a library of Caxtons the world after all loses little beyond a rarity. When a number of Caxtons is merely transported from one side of the globe to another no one has lost anything.

During June and July 1914 there were 11 manuscript and book auctions at Sotheby's—including the Pembroke, Huth, and Arthur sales. Smith was in London by the time of the Earl of Pembroke's Wilton House library sale on 25–26 June, which marked his first London triumph. He took 97 of the 211 lots, spending £14,850 of the £38,936 total. (Smith was evidently buying mainly for stock; two years later he sold part of his Pembroke acquisitions to Huntington for $15,000.) Smith's Pembroke purchases included *The Book of St. Albans* (£1,800), the Caxton *Cicero* (£1,050), the Caxton *Dictes or Sayenges* £1,050), and a 15th-century Dutch translation of the Latin *Speculum* (£1,200). The chief competition was between Smith and Quaritch, who spent £10,273 for 42 lots. For the next five years G.D.S. and Quaritch would dominate the Sotheby's sales.

On the first day of the Pembroke sale Smith informed the *New York Times* correspondent:

> I tried hard to buy the entire library at private sale. . . . In fact, I was negotiating for the entire library up to within five minutes of the time the sale started. . . .
>
> There was only a difference of about $50,000 between my final offer [reported as $200,000] and the sum for which they were willing to sell the whole library.
>
> . . . You see, the English are not accustomed to closing big deals as quickly as we do on the other side. They seemed nervous and afraid of making a mistake. . . .
>
> I am going to get more than half of the collection, and just what I want, too. I secured more than half of today's items. I lost only three good books, with which exceptions I obtained practically the cream of the collection so far. I got many bargains. A lot of them I bought at far below what I had expected to give. I believe I lost nothing by failing to buy the library en bloc, as I am getting the best part of it cheaper.

After the Pembroke sale Smith told the *New York Times:* "I'm rather sorry I didn't get the whole shooting match. It would have caused such a howl to go up there. . . . I get a lot of fun out of my business. The squeal of the English is highly amusing, as when I acquired the Devonshire library."

Smith obviously relished the role of Super Yank. From 8 July to 21 July 1914 he took over the Palm Court at Selfridge's for "the choicest little lot of books ever exhibited to London by America." The printed catalogue lists 5 items from the Hoe Library; 17 from the Pembroke Library—including *The Book of St. Albans* and 4 Caxtons; 6 items of Thackerayana—including the manuscript of *The Rose and the Ring;* and one lot of 89 Horatio Nelson items relating to the Nile and Trafalgar battles.

Although he acted by cable at earlier Huth sessions, Smith's first appearance at the Huth sales seems to have been for the fourth portion (I-L), which commenced 7 July 1914 and continued for three more days. He bought 244 of 671 lots, spending £7,500 of the total £18,700. Again Smith and Quaritch divided the treasures. Smith secured a presentation copy of *Sejanus* for £900; but he was underbidder on the star book, the Shakespeare source work *The True Chronicle of King Leir* (1605). When Smith hesitated at £2.300, the auctioneer applied "polite goads": "When you've turned it into dollars, Mr. Smith, it does not make many, after all." Nonetheless Smith was underbidder when it went to Quaritch's Edmund Dring for £2,400. (Smith had earlier acquired a copy of the *Leir* for Huntington in the Church library.) The London *Daily Telegraph* account of the Huth sale described Smith as "The Quaritch of America" and referred to his purchases as "American loot."

Smith vs. the Ring

Five days later Smith was the largest buyer at the Arthur Sale (15–17 July). This library was strong in 19th-century English literature, and there were no big numbers; but Smith took 286 of the 850 items, spending £3,900 of the £7,545 total. The assumption that he was brave with Huntington's money and primarily an agent is corrected by Smith's work sheets for the Arthur sale, which reveal that few of these purchases went to Huntington. After the Arthur sale Smith gave an interview to the *New York Sun* London correspondent in which he stated the he "came to London with the avowed intention of breaking up what he calls 'the London book ring'":

> They invited me to become a member of their association, but I refused, and I have succeeded in breaking up the ring. The only independent buyer in London is Mr. Quaritch, who purchases on commission for the British

Museum and similar organizations. My high prices caused the rest of the dealers to lose heart and they do not know yet what I am capable of.

The ring—a conspiracy of bidders to defraud consigners—was legal in Britain until 1927. Smith's en bloc purchases were the best way to beat the ring. Certainly, the consigners' knowledge of the ring operations facilitated Smith's pre-auction en bloc acquisitions.

The *Sun* article reported in July 1914 that Smith had spent more than $500,000 since arriving in London. It is impossible to find evidence for Smith's charges about ring operations from the marked 1914 Sotheby's catalogues; they show that Smith and Quaritch (a sometimes ringer) gorged at the feast. Nonetheless, it was accepted that the leading London dealers, including Maggs, Edwards, Sabin, Dobell, Pickering & Chatto, Spencer, and Tregaskis formed rings. It was also believed that the English dealers engaged in "trotting the American"—that is, running up the bidding short of buying.

On 18 July 1914 the *New York Times* devoted an editorial to Smith's London activities—without naming him—which treated him as an economic indicator:

> . . . an American dealer who has been paying out a large fortune for books in London this Summer, in auction rooms and elsewhere, seems to have discovered a veritable rare book trust or "ring," as he prefers to call it, which he has been "beating" in the familiar American way, by high bidding. According to the cable dispatches he has secured for distribution among the wealthy collectors of this country a large number of books which are not likely to lose their value, although the time must come with all such luxuries when the limit is reached and future sales are likely to be made at reduced prices.
>
> The chief importance of this dealer's transactions to those of his fellow countrymen who care nothing about the value collectors place upon rarity is the indication of his faith in the continuance of American prosperity and the ability of moneyed Americans in the near future to pay high prices for luxuries. Probably he has bought enough at comparatively low prices, because of his watchfulness and energy, to enable him to dispose of them at sufficiently large profits to make the holding of the more expensive treasures for better times no great burden to bear. But those better times, according to his notion, must be much nearer than the croakers are willing to admit. He is assuredly no pessimist.

The American economy was strong in the summer of 1914. Exports were booming; the Dow-Jones Industrial Average was at 81; per capita income had risen to $335; and the dollar was strong against the pound.

The Arthur sale was the last major auction during the 1914 season; but Smith was active at the Sotheby's manuscript sales on 21 and 23–24 July—acquiring 22 unpublished letters from Increase and Cotton Mather to Sir William Ashurst, treasurer of the Society for the Propagation of Faith (£750), as well as much of the Robert Louis Stevenson manuscript material sold by Lloyd Osbourne.

The Archduke Franz Ferdinand was assassinated at Sarajevo on 28 July 1914; there were no major London book sales in 1915. Early in 1916 Smith sold Huntington all of the books in his catalogue titled *Monuments of Early Printing . . . 1460–1500*. Of the 136 incunables in Smith's catalogue, 74 were from the Pembroke sale—supporting Smith's claim that he had not acted strictly as Huntington's agent. G.D.S. insisted that he bought great books whether or not he had a commission.

Smith's dealings with Huntington—which can be accurately described as a collaboration—ranged across the possible collector-dealer relations. Smith bid for Huntington on straight commission; Smith bought books for stock which he resold to Huntington; Smith acquired libraries en bloc and granted Huntington first refusal or the right of cherry-picking; Smith acquired libraries en bloc for Huntington and bought the duplicates for stock or sold the duplicates on behalf of HEH; Smith bought books at the Anderson Galleries sales of Huntington surplussage.

Whatever the basis of a particular transatlantic deal, the results were to transfer great books to the Huntington library and to redistribute great British libraries in America.

Smith's influence on the transatlantic trade during this era was prodigious. He inspired American collectors and he drove up prices on both sides of the Atlantic. Yet Smith's many detractors claimed that he drove out collectors who were afraid to meet his prices. They also charged him with violating auction ethics because he bid on books he had consigned; moreover, it was alleged that he was a silent partner in the Anderson Galleries, operated by his friend Mitchell Kennerley. His defenders asserted that he single-handedly maintained the value of great books—that his attendance could make an auction.

Despite the slaughter in France, the fifth Huth sale was held in July 1916. Smith was there; but he gave a restrained performance, taking 49 lots and spending only £3,348. In August 1916 Smith made a second great English en bloc purchase—the Britwell Americana for a reported £60,000. The deal was made with Barlow the day before the Sotheby auction was scheduled to commence; this coup was the occasion of Smith's remark that the American dealers who had come to London for the Britwell sale "had a nice sea voyage, anyway." The acquisition included 13 incunables and a collection of the major and minor *Voyages* of

Theodore De Bry in Latin and German. Smith claimed that he had bought the Britwell collection for himself but would offer it to Huntington; in the event, the entire Britwell Americana went to Huntington, who disposed of the duplicates in New York at a 1917 Anderson auction.

The collaborative activities of Smith and Huntington stimulated the American book market and brought fresh blood into the game. Smith was a principal buyer at the Huntington duplicate sales, and he relished the opportunities to rebuy and resell the same books. A seller with only one customer is restricted to a small field. "The Old Man"—as Smith referred to Huntington—came first, but Smith also bought for Henry C. Folger, Herschel V. Jones, John C. Crawford, Theodore N. Vail, J. P. Morgan, Mortimer Schiff, J. A. Spohr, Cortland Bishop, and Joseph Widener.

In May 1917 G.D.S. made his third great en bloc English purchase for Huntington: the Bridgewater House library. Again acting through Sotheby's, Smith closed the deal by cable from New York. The price was reported as over £200,000 for more than 4,000 books (exclusive of pamphlets), 200 illuminated manuscripts and other manuscripts, and 10,000 documents and letters. The treasures included the 15th-century Ellesmere Chaucer—the best manuscript of *The Canterbury Tales;* the 14th-century illuminated manuscript of Gower's *Confessio Amantis;* the manuscript for the *Treatise of Venery;* at least three Caxtons; the second known copy of Q1 *Titus Andronicus;* and the Eliot Indian Bible.

Huntington disposed of 206 Bridgewater items at the Anderson Galleries in New York during 1918. Among the surplussage was Henry Lawes's dedication copy of *Comus,* and the masque commissioned by the Earl of Bridgewater in 1634 for an entertainment at Ludlow Castle in Shropshire celebrating his presidency of the Council of Wales. Smith bought it at Anderson for $9,200 in 1918, sold it to H.V. Jones, and bought it again at Anderson in 1919 for $14,250. Smith was a relatively benign presence at the July 1917 Huth sale; Quaritch was the major buyer. But Smith's 72 purchases of the 855 lots included 8 of the 9 "Portolanos" (medieval manuscripts with charts indicating harbors or ports)—three of which broke £1,000.

The seventh Huth sale, July 1918, was unspectacular. The 1,122 lots elicited few 3-digit prices and only one 4-digit price. Smith acquired 203 lots—including the top item, *Caxton's Royal Book* at £1,800—spending only £8,155 of the £30,118 total. A letter from Huntington to Smith after the 1918 Huth sale suggests that "the Old Man" was concerned that the dealer was over-extended: "I am very glad to see that you are going to sell your valuable string of horses, and I think that by so doing *you will be able to keep in the book business.* If you should have succeeded in the horse business, you have been a wonder, for I think that there is hardly one in a hundred keeping at it who do not go 'dead broke' before they turn up their toes." (One of the horses Smith sold was the two-year-old Purchase who subsequently defeated Sir Barton and became the champion American three-year-old.)

The British economy was in trouble after the war; and the exchange rate became favorable to Americans as the pound dropped from $4.85 to $3.36 in 1919. But contrary to predictions, the London and New York book trades boomed after the Armistice. Smith did not attend the March 1919 Sotheby's sale of Lord Mostyn's early English plays, of which the press stated that "so many 16th-century rarities of the first water have never before appeared in an English sales-room within the compass of two days." There were 380 quartos. In *Anatomy of an Auction* Arthur and Jane Freeman have identified this sale as "ringed," with the conspirators investing £11,000. Bidding by cable Smith spent £18,500 of the "amazing" £50,597 total, and Quaritch (who abstained from this ring) spent about £11,000. Smith's trophies included Medwall's *Fulgens and Lucrece* (previously known only from two leaves at the British Museum, £3,400); the unique copy of Wager's *Inough Is as Good as a Feast* (£2,600); and two copies of *Gammar Gurton's Needle* (£1,000 and £1,200).

The July 1919 Huth sale was dull. Smith took some 120 lots, but there were no star items. (Smith did not attend the October Ruxley Lodge ring festival.) Before the Britwell Court sales commenced at Sotheby's on 15 December 1919, Smith's offer of $1 million for the entire library was declined. At the first sale of *Books of Airs, Ballads, Catches, Madrigals, Songs & Other Music*, he took 85 of the 166 lots, but there were no major items. The second sale, 16 December, was Smith's strongest day since the Hoe sale. He took 83 of the 108 lots, spending £84,705 of the £110,356 total—the new record for a single-day auction, and four times the previous record for the Pembroke sale. Quaritch paid £21,500 for 18 items.

The top item was number 85: *Venus and Adonis* (the only known copy of the 1599 fourth edition), with *The Passionate Pilgrim* (one of three known copies of the 1599 first edition), and with Davies & Marlow's *Epigrammes and Elegies* (1598?—one of two or three copies known). The three works were bound together in a volume that measured 4 $^{14}/_{16}$" x 3". Barlow was in the rostrum and started the bidding at £2,300. Dring of Quaritch's, bidding for Henry C. Folger, called even thousands; and Smith raised each Dring bid by £100. Smith won it for Huntington at £15,100—the highest price up to that time for a single volume at auction. The price triggered cheering for the first time at a Sotheby book sale. Smith informed the London *Daily Chronicle* that he had been prepared to go to £30,000: "The books are not bought on behalf of any syndicate, but by me to sell again. America is buying up all the rare books in the world that are to be found for sale, because the collectors there have tons of money. Where there used to be 40 there are now 300. . . . I bought up the Duke of Devonshire's library complete, and I do not suppose it will be the last good thing England will lose."

Smith's other Britwell purchases included the Heber collection of broadsides and ballads (88 pieces, £6,400); Caxton's *The Moral Proverbs of Cristyne* (£2,100); *The Hye Way to the Spyttell Hous* (only known copy, £1,280); Caxton's *The Cordyale* (£1,900); Wynkyn de Worde's *The Gospells of Dystaves* (the only complete copy known, £1,880); Greene's *Quip for an Upstart Courtier* (the only known copy of the earliest edition, £1,200); Howard's *Songes and Sonnettes* (second edition, £2,400); *The Paradise of Dainty Devises* (£1,700); the Shakespeare *First Folio* (£2,300); the *Third Folio* (£2,400); the Q1 *Much Adoe about Nothing* (£2,200); the Q1 *Richard the Third* (£2,000); Sidney's *Arcadia* (£1,000); the only known copies of three Skelton titles (£1,780); and Caxton's *The Dictes or Sayenges* (£2,900).

His claim that he bought principally for himself at the Britwell sale is substantiated by a 12 November 1919 letter from George Watson Cole, Huntington's librarian, to Dring of Quaritch's, explaining that "in view of the highest prices expected he [Huntington] has been scared out. . . . There is certainly a limit beyond which American Collectors will not go, notwithstanding the prevailing idea on your side that they stand ready to pay any price for a book of which there are only one or two copies." This document invites speculation that Dring had attempted to lure Huntington away from Smith. If Cole was accurately reporting the words of one of the world's richest men, then Smith was not just showing the flag at Britwell—he was supporting the market. During the period of Smith's London ascendancy he was often the only American bidder in the sales room: A. S. W. Rosenbach never competed against Smith in London.

Smith's last major en bloc purchase was the "Ancient & Celebrated" Arbury Hall library of Sir Francis Newdigate-Newdegate, rich in Shakespeariana and Elizabethan literature. The Sotheby's sale was scheduled for 22–23 January 1920. A copy of the catalogue survives with this message in Smith's hand: "*HEH* very fine lot and many very *important rare Early* English. Have checked this and I will cable bids on my return. Am trying to buy privately. Will examine books before leaving." Two weeks before the sale Smith acquired the entire catalogue of 362 items for $150,000. Huntington exercised first refusal on some 50 items, including two incunables and 42 English books printed before 1640—among them the only known copies of Greene's *Pandosto* (1588) and Loks's *Sundry Christian Passions* (1593), and one of the two known copies of Lodge's *Rosalynd* (1598). The remainder of the Newdigate-Newdegate books were auctioned at Anderson after Smith's death.

On 4 March 1920 Smith died of a heart attack in his store at 8 East 45th Street. He was 50. According to Heartman he died while arguing with a purveyor of suspect Washingtoniana. The New York obituaries accurately identified George D. Smith as "America's greatest rare book dealer" and "the Napoleon of book buyers." The *London Times* reported the death of "the secondhand bookseller, whose name and 'operations' of recent years have somewhat overshadowed the fame of much abler booksellers in both hemispheres."

Smith died intestate. For the next five years his rich stock was plundered. But that is another story.

Bookman

Charles Elliot Frazer Clark, Jr., 1925–2001

Frazer Clark was born in the year *The Great Gatsby* was published. All the lights were green for him until he ran out of Cadillacs.

Charles Elliot Frazer Clark, Jr., built the most comprehensive privately owned collection of Nathaniel Hawthorne (30,000 items). He founded and edited the *Nathaniel Hawthorne Journal.* He co-founded the Nathaniel Hawthorne Society. He compiled the standard Hawthorne descriptive bibliography. He co-founded the Book Club of Detroit. He served as president of the Friends of the Detroit Public Library and was a member of the Clements Library Associates Board of Governors at the University of Michigan. He assembled a serious Ernest Hemingway Collection. He co-founded the *Fitzgerald/Hemingway Annual.* He co-founded Bruccoli Clark Publishers.

We were partners for more than thirty years. I cannot remember when the partnership began: we were partners before we signed the papers. I could never have done my publishing work without Fraze, and some of my scholarly endeavors would not have succeeded without his encouragement.

Fraze was the son of Col. C. E. Frazer Clark, a public school administrator, and Lucy Huffman Clark. He lived all his life in Michigan, except for military service and college. After entering the University of Michigan miscast as an engineering student, he volunteered for the army in 1943 and was in the 87th Infantry Division. Fraze enjoyed recounting that when he was captured at the Battle of the Bulge he persuaded his captor to surrender to him. Coming from anyone else, this claim would defy credence; but he had the Kraut's pistol. Fraze always understood the uses of evidence.

"Bookman: Charles Elliot Frazer Clark, Jr., 1925–2001" was published originally in the *Dictionary of Literary Biography Yearbook: 2001,* edited Matthew J. Bruccoli (Detroit: Bruccoli Clark Layman / Gale, 2002), pp. 305–310. © Gale, a part of Cengage Learning, Inc. www.cengage.com/permissions.

In 1951 Fraze graduated from Kenyon College, where Prof. Denham Sutcliffe introduced him to the writings of Nathaniel Hawthorne; Wayne State University awarded him an M.A. in 1957 for his thesis, "Nathaniel Hawthorne, the Artist, a Self-Portrait." During his young manhood he had his poems privately printed, a work that is much rarer than *Fanshawe*. After college Fraze worked for marketing firms in Detroit. I never really understood what he did—apart from taking clients out to lunch and writing memos consisting of one-sentence paragraphs—but he was successful at it and subsequently became a partner in his own firm, Paramarketing. His choice of profession seems puzzling, for he regarded the academic life with envy. The decision was almost certainly determined by financial considerations; pedagogical poverty did not appeal to him. The university world lost a superb chairman-dean-provost when Fraze went for the money. Even so, he became a dedicated scholar who out-published most of the tenured loafers. I was never able to persuade him that he was worth the whole damn bunch of them put together.

Fraze married Margaret Ann Swanson, a commercial artist, in 1953; they had two sons, C. E. Frazer Clark III and Douglas Alexander Clark. Marge was an exemplary bookman's consort and designed most of Fraze's privately published publications. They were very happy together.

Frazer Clark's real life began in 1951 when he found a Hawthorne sleeper in Charles S. Boesen's Detroit bookshop. Let him tell it:

> He [Karl Boesen] quoted me from his copy of *Merle Johnson* the "points" identifying the first edition of *The Scarlet Letter*, and this reminded him that the copy of *The Scarlet Letter* he had on his shelf originally belonged to Merle Johnson, having been a part of the Bandler Collection and the estate of Gabriel Wells, which Karl was handling. Karl had made me curious, and partly for this reason, and partly to satisfy him, I took his copy of *The Scarlet Letter* off the shelf, carefully removed it from the slipcase that protected it, and began examining it. On the front pastedown endpaper I found an inscription to Mr. Boesen and he said, "Yes, that's the hand of James T. Fields, Hawthorne's publisher," at which he explained the importance of this as an association copy, hence much more valuable. This was why he had priced the book at $45.00, an increase over what Gabriel Wells had originally asked in the catalogue of the collection. I proceeded with my examination, turning past the ads inserted between the front pastedown endpaper and the free endpaper. I was interested to find on the free endpaper, the signature, "Nath Hawthorne." When I called this to Mr. Boesen's attention he seemed stunned. He couldn't believe it. He reached for the book to see for himself. Incredible as it was, this inscription, hidden behind the ads, had escaped discovery. Karl explained that

since the book had presumably been thoroughly described in the previous dealer catalogues, he hadn't bothered to really recheck the item carefully himself. The extent of the Bandler-Wells Library he was handling made this procedure necessary. The book was sent to Arthur Swann at Parke-Bernet in New York for authentication and appraisal. Swann reacted immediately by calling to suggest that this copy would bring a big price and should be put up at auction. Karl said he would think about it and had Swann return the book. I was there when the book came in and, on opening it, Karl proceeded to explain to me his view on what he called "the right of first refusal." As the discoverer, I had, according to Karl, the right to purchase the book at the price marked in it at the time, $45.00. Finding my first rare Hawthorne was accidental; buying my first Hawthorne was accidental; buying my first Hawthorne first edition was an act of pure avarice. On Mr. Boesen's part, the whole affair was a matter of supreme generosity for which I am lastingly grateful. That I am a Hawthorne collector is entirely Charles Boesen's responsibility.

In the spring of 1962 when I was running the *Centenary Edition of the Works of Nathaniel Hawthorne* at Ohio State University, we received a letter from a correspondent who identified himself as a Detroit business man, offering access to his Hawthorne collection. My colleague, to whom the letter was delivered, discarded it. When he mentioned it to me, I recovered it and replied. (Clark's Rule #1.) It proved to be the most important letter I ever wrote: in addition to the career rewards, it generated most of my laughter for the next thirty years.

I went to Detroit to examine the Clark books. (Rule #2.) It was a collection of high–spots: nothing with textual-bibliographical significance. But I was impressed by his ambition to build a major collection and his eagerness to learn how to do it properly. At that time Fraze was employed by a marketing firm with the unlikely name of Jam Handy and was handling either the Westinghouse account or the General Electric account in Columbus, Ohio. He had both of them after he organized Paramarketing; only Fraze could have juggled two competing clients. His regular trips to Columbus provided him with opportunities to observe the operation at the Hawthorne factory. Fraze was a fast learner. When he saw the Hawthorne that Hyman Kritzer and I were assembling at OSU, Fraze immediately understood the rationale for an author collection as a research resource. I taught him relatively little about bibliography; he was a born bookman.

Fraze began expanding his display collection into the best Hawthorne research collection. His prize acquisition was the dispatch case that Hawthorne used as American Counsel in Liverpool, which contained Hawthorne's Salem Custom-House stencil. Fraze's friends speculated that he had stenciled his flesh with it; but his wife denied it. Fraze was the best book-acquirer I have known. He always paid attention. (Rule #4.) He never gave up. He loved the pursuit. When we took scouting trips together he acquired books for my collections that I would not have been able to get on my own. He once casually handed me the dedication copy of Lucius Beebe's *Corydon*—dedicated to James Gould Cozzens. At that time some dealers still required Americans to apologize for being Americans. I was no good at it; I learned to go to the nearest pub and wait for Fraze. If there were books I needed in the shop, he got them for me. He knew how to deal with clients, and everybody—except his family and me—was a client. While Fraze was acquiring his Hawthornes, he helped me to get my Fitzgeralds. He procured books that I would have missed, and he stiffened my resolve in the auction room. The important items that I stupidly failed to get were lost when he wasn't with me. (Rules #6–7.)

Most book collectors are just book buyers or acquirers. They don't do anything with their books—except possibly look at them—because they never learn what to do with them. Fraze knew what he was doing and why he was doing it. He compiled the standard primary bibliography of Hawthorne, which he could not have done without the Clark Collection: see the CEFC locations in *Nathaniel Hawthorne: A Descriptive Bibliography*. Fraze regarded himself as the temporary custodian of his books and was endlessly generous in sharing his possessions with students and researchers.

Certain academic types fastidiously refer to "mere [always with that condescending qualifier] collectors' items" and "mere collectors." Fraze did more for Hawthorne and for American literature than entire English departments. He was a first-rate scholar: not merely the best Hawthorne bibliographer, but a serious literary historian. After Fraze died, a pretty good Hawthorne scholar said that Fraze did the "grunt work" on Hawthorne. That remark was presumably meant as a compliment, but the speaker did not understand that Fraze did the hard work that professors couldn't do because they lacked his commitment, determination, and bookmanship. Fraze claimed that the most essential attribute of a bookman was paying attention. (Rule #4.) Hawthorne was not a sporadic interest, not his hobby. His Hawthorne work was a full-time career—along with two other full-time careers. Fraze did it with his own money; he never had a grant or a sabbatical. What you spend your money on is the test of what you believe in. The books you buy are what you are. Fraze was always ready to back his book judgment with his checkbook. Although he was never wealthy, Fraze spent as though he were rich. The important thing was to get the books. Along the way he invented a new kind of arithmetic. A checkbook was a lethal weapon in Fraze's hands.

Fraze discovered, acquired, and preserved books and manuscripts for his collection; he also located lost material in institutions. We discovered the "lost" manuscript of *Transformation* after the Hawthorne specialists assured us that it had not survived. It wasn't lost or even misplaced; they hadn't looked for it in the right place. We found it badly catalogued in the British Library, where the staff were annoyed because we were behaving like Americans.

Here is how Fraze operated. When he heard that Roger Butterfield had acquired early American newspapers from a New England institution—which no doubt regarded them as "surplussage"—Fraze bought all the copies of the papers from Salem, Boston, and other cities in the area. They filled a room in his house. After Fraze separated the issues he needed, he swapped or donated the rest. Working with this archive Fraze identified unrecorded printings of Hawthorne's early writings and reviews of his books, as well as data on the Hawthorne and Manning families. Some *mere* collector.

The lesson of Fraze Clark's achievements as a bookman is that the rewards of bookmanship are books. Do it for love. Realize that the bitch may break your heart and your bankroll; but get the books.

The collection of a completist—the collection built for the bibliographical research—is a damn bad investment. The speculators want the high-spot items that everyone else wants. Fraze expected to place all his Hawthornes in one institutional library. With great difficulty he arranged for his collection to be shared by the Essex Institute and the House of the Seven Gables, both in Salem. It is doubtful that he got back what he had spent on Hawthorne. If he had bought stocks instead of books, he would have left a handsome estate. If he had restricted himself to big-ticket high-spots, he would have made a profit. But he wanted to assemble a permanently usable research collection—and did it. Fraze died broke—without his books and far from an antiquarian bookshop.

Fraze began collecting Hemingway in 1966 because pickings were slim in the Hawthorne field—collectors need to collect—and because Hemingway was shelved near Hawthorne in bookshops. Seeing the Hemingways and paying attention, Fraze concluded that very good stuff was still available. He began buying. In three years he acquired about two hundred items, including twenty inscribed copies; ten letters—including three detailed letters to Charles Poore, editor of the *Hemingway Reader;* and nine proofs, dummies, or review copies. He had Hemingway's *Who's Who in America* questionnaire, a *3 & 10* and an *in our time,* and five numbers of the Oak Park High School *Tabula.*

I introduced Fraze to Hemingway's sister Sunny who had early family letters. Fraze understood that although she was comfortably fixed, Sunny wanted outside funds for a stained-glass window in the Petoskey, Michigan, Episcopal Church. Fraze paid for the window in return for the letters. He became Sunny's warm friend and rescued artifacts from the Hemingway Walloon Lake home, including

Grace Hemingway's piano. Fraze continued to acquire Hemingway into the early Seventies, but he probably regarded this collection as an act of infidelity. Hawthorne was his true love. The Clark Hemingway collection is now at the University of Maryland Library.

From my school years on I wanted to become a publisher, but it would not have been possible without Frazer Clark. He had the connections, and he had the courage to take risks. We didn't have the necessary capital, so we had to borrow it or find backers. The crucial connection was Frederick Ruffner, with whom Fraze had formed a friendship through their activities in the Friends of the Detroit Public Library and the Book Club of Detroit. While Fred was building his Gale Research operation into the largest reference-book publisher in America, he asked Fraze's advice about rare-book-related projects; and Fraze involved me as a Gale consultant. We began producing bibliographies for Gale. The first volume with the Bruccoli Clark / Gale Research imprint was my 1971 checklist of Ross Macdonald. At the same time Fraze and I began publishing limited editions, which were mostly produced by his friend Leonard Bahr at the Adagio Press. We were advised in our early publishing projects by Vernon Sternberg—the best publisher I have ever known. The first of the Bruccoli Clark collector's editions was James Dickey's *Exchanges* in 1971. We published Robert Coover, James Gould Cozzens, Reynolds Price, James Jones, and Louis Auchincloss in the series. Most of these pricey editions lost money. When we graduated to publishing facsimiles of the manuscripts of American classics—*The Red Badge of Courage, The Great Gatsby, F. Scott Fitzgerald's Ledger,* and *Huckleberry Finn*—we lost more money. Fraze never complained about my editorial disasters. He was happy to be publishing important books.

He developed a theory of economics based on the necessity for keeping money in circulation. Money in the bank was useless to him. Fraze needed to live on the brink of financial disaster, which provided the spur for his successful deals. He always believed that the next deal would make him solvent. For a long time it worked—until his health failed. Fraze once bought the entire stock of a bookstore on Friday and sold it on Saturday—after cherry-picking it.

Even Fraze's failures were exciting. For years he tried to make a workable plan to connect rare-book dealers by teletype so that books could be readily located for collectors. That was before web sites, netscapes, and dot coms.

The *Dictionary of Literary Biography* was our most important and enduring project. It led to all the other books with the Bruccoli Clark and Bruccoli Clark Layman imprints. In November 1975 Fred Ruffner summoned us to a boat ride in Fort Lauderdale. In addition to the Gale people, there were two outside advisors, a rare-book librarian and an English professor. Fred asked the group to evaluate the feasibility and utility of a multi-volume reference of "books about writers' lives." The two advisors strongly advised against the project, warning that it was too ambitious and could not be published on schedule. When they were done Cassandra-ing, Fraze asked Fred how soon he wanted the first volume and how many volumes were required in the first year. Then Fraze and I went off by ourselves and roughed out an editorial plan and a production schedule. After the boat docked, I went to the hotel and slept while Fraze had an arithmetic meeting with Fred. He didn't need me for that. When Fraze woke me, Fred had authorized us to prepare sample entries and tables of contents for the early *DLB* volumes. We got the go-ahead in 1977; and *DLB 1: The American Renaissance in New England* was published in 1978. This remembrance of Frazer Clark is in the 301st volume of the *Dictionary of Literary Biography.*

Our worst disappointment was *America's Library,* a series of volumes providing reliable texts for the masters of American literature, to be published by Harcourt Brace Jovanovich. We worked hard on this project in 1979 and had great expectations for it; but Bill Jovanovich was persuaded to kill *America's Library* after HBJ had announced it. He was wrong. Somebody else did it. Bill described Fraze as "an American type"—meaning that he combined confidence, ambition, and shrewdness with a certain quality of naivete.

It sometimes worried me that Fraze didn't have any enemies; but he regarded grudges as a waste of energy. His policy was to keep the pigeons unwary, and then pluck 'em—preferably without letting them know they'd been taken. His appearance was deceptively innocent: he dressed Detroit and spoke fluent Detroitese. Fraze seemed uncomplicated and easy-going; yet he always cut the deck and counted the cards.

The most important work in our lives we did together between 1971 and 1981. Anything was possible when I had Fraze. He was my luck.

Part 5

On Libraries and Librarians

"Research libraries are too important to be run by administrators who do not understand that the books matter more than anything else: more than committees."

      M.J.B., introduction, *The Joseph M. Bruccoli Great War Collection in the University of Virginia Library* (Columbia, S.C.: MJB, 1999)

Mere Collectors' Items

It took Kent State University 55 years to acquire its first half-million books. You are adding volumes now at the rate of 78,000 per year—at which rate you will double your holdings by 1974. These splendid figures are overshadowed by the truly exciting fact that Kent is not acquiring just books—but great books. In the process Kent is becoming great.

In 1970 Kent State University will open its new library which will cost 9½ million dollars for the building alone without a book in it. If 9½ million for the warehouse, how much for the books? 9½ million more? 20 million? 90 million? The best answer is that a university never spends enough on books. Some universities, like Kent, spend more money on books because they believe in them—which is to say that they believe in themselves and their rendezvous with excellence.

A university is never better than its library—for a university is a collection of books surrounded by people using them. Few universities have matched Kent's bold assault on greatness through its library resources, and I am here to congratulate those of you who have helped—and to disabuse any of you who still cling to the superannuated notion that great books are the special privilege of a few old and powerful institutions. This destructive notion is still held in certain younger or smaller or undistinguished institutions. When I came to the university with which I am temporarily associated[1] in 1961, it had neither a rare-book curator nor a rare-book room—and when I questioned this I was firmly told by a senior colleague, a man who had written books and presumably researched them elsewhere, "Good God, this isn't Yale!" He was right. It wasn't Yale. It wasn't even Kent State University.

It is a truth of academic life now that every university that seeks distinction must make its library the key element in that quest. Not only must there be millions of books in the general stacks—there must also be millions of dollars worth

---

"Mere Collectors' Items" was originally an address Matthew J. Bruccoli gave at the 7 November 1968 ceremony in honor of the Kent State University Libraries' addition of a 500,000th volume. The address was published as number 4 of the Kent State University Libraries Occasional Papers, 1969. Reprinted with the permission of the Kent State University Libraries.

of great books in its special collections. Great books attract great scholars and great scholars attract good students.

What is a great book? A great book is a hard-to find—usually rare and expensive—research item: including, of course, manuscripts. These are the books that ignorant observers are in the habit of scornfully labeling *mere collector's items*. The idea behind this foolish appellation is that these *mere collectors' items* are of no use beyond exhibition purposes. To this I intolerantly reply that I have never seen a *mere collectors' item*—that is, I have never seen a useless great book. I will admit that there are certain classes of books that I do not use in my own work, and about which I do not have a great deal of enthusiasm—such as fine bindings, illustrated volumes, or fore-edge paintings. But other scholars do use these *mere collectors' items*.

There can be no question at all about the scholarly importance of books that are rare and valuable because of their texts. And no question at all about the importance of original letters and manuscripts. Therefore there can be no question at all about the propriety of institutions of higher learning—including tax-supported institutions—investing their funds in these books.

Indeed, it can be demonstrated that great books are sound investments—not just in terms of distinction, but in terms of money. Between 1952 and 1966 the average price of American common stocks went up fourfold, but the prices of modern literature went up five times; the prices of Americana six and a half times; and the prices of science and medical books ten and a half times. Newton's *Principia* went from $500 to $6,200. Darwin's *Origin of Species* went from $45 to $600. Joyce's *Ulysses*—100 signed copies—was originally sold at $30 in 1922; it is now a $2,500 book, and of the original 100 about half are now in institutions. There are two points contained in these figures: 1) rare book prices are moving with the economy; and 2) rare books are getting rarer. If ever the law of supply and demand had a clear application, it is in the case of great books. Whereas before World War II most great books were bought by private collectors, today at least 60 percent of the great books sold each year are bought by libraries. And of the remaining 40 percent, a certain amount is acquired by grateful alumni who intend to donate the books to their colleges. Books attract books: to them that have shall be donated.

Books cost more this year than they did last year. But next year they'll cost even more—and there will be a diminished supply. It is not too late to start building great collections. As Kent State University is demonstrating, now is a good time. Remember that the really great material is going into institutions—and once there, a great item is there forever. Put it another way: If you're energetic and brave you'll have one chance at a really great book or manuscript. One chance to shower distinction on your university. In 1933 A. S. W. Rosenbach cataloged the manuscript of Stephen Crane's *The Red Badge of Courage* at $11,000—which was a strong price because Dr. Rosenbach did not believe that the depression should hurt book prices. It was subsequently bought by C. Waller Barrett, who donated it to the University of Virginia. If that manuscript came up at auction today, and I were given the assignment of purchasing it for a university, my bid would be $250,000—and worth every penny of it.

Let us see what could have been done with one thousand dollars in 1945–1946. It could have been put in the bank at 1 percent, or it could have been invested in a university endowment, which at that time were normally earning 2 percent or 3 percent. Or it could have been shrewdly invested in General Motors common stock. In 1946 $1,000 would have bought 14 shares of GM at $71, and if left alone this would now be 56 shares at $88 plus $3,264 in dividends—for a total of $8,192: more than 8-fold growth in 22 years. That same $1,000 in 1945–1946 would have bought this portfolio of great books:

Stephen Crane's *Maggie* for $275—worth today $1,900. This book is not yet at Kent.

Herman Melville's *The Whale* for $575—worth today $3,000. Not yet at Kent.

Ernest Hemingway's first two books, *3 Stories and 10 Poems* and *in our time*, $200 for the pair—worth today $1,600. Both of these books have just been acquired by Kent.

That $1,000 worth of books would be worth $6,500 today.

Or this portfolio of great books:

Nathaniel Hawthorne's *Fanshawe* for $375—worth $4,000 today. Not yet at Kent.

One of the 50 copies of Stephen Crane's *Black Riders* for $80—worth today $500. Not yet at Kent.

The manuscript of Hawthorne's "Jonathan Cilley" with a Hawthorne letter about this essay for $575—worth today $7,500. Not at Kent.

This $1,030 worth of material would be worth $12,000 today.

In 1946 Kent could have used a thousand dollars to buy a complete collection of all the first printings of William Faulkner and F. Scott Fitzgerald—with ample money left over to buy a presentation copy of Hemingway's *The Torrents of Spring* for $30, a copy of *Prufrock* for $35, and a copy of *The Bridge* for $37. In fact, the 30 volumes of Faulkner and the 16 volumes of Fitzgerald might have been assembled with care for $500 in 1945. They would be worth today about $8,000—an increase of 1,600 percent or twice that of GM. By the way, Kent has an impressive Faulkner collection—purchased in 1962.

But the real difference between the GM investment and the book investment is that the books would have been used for 22 years. Not locked away in a vault and not just put on display from time to time as a sort of academic status symbol. But used by scholar-teachers to learn and teach that in its first printing of *Maggie* the heroine has a speech and an additional encounter in the climactic chapter that ends with her suicide—or that there were many significant changes between *The Whale* and *Moby-Dick,* including the fact that Melville added the epilogue in which the reader learns that Ishmael has survived the sinking of the *Pequod.*

For serious scholarship nothing can replace the actual first printing, the actual autograph letter, the actual manuscript. Only with these can a scholar verify his text and be sure that he is explicating the author's words: not some typesetter's blunder, not some editor's fancied improvements. Only with these can he identify the author's revisions of his own work. Only with these originals can the scholar check for cancelled leaves, watermarks, colors of inks, colors of paper, pin-holes, and worm holes. Microfilm or Xerox won't do for thorough work. It has been predicted that soon all the major libraries in the country will be computerized so that a scholar at any library will be able to get instant information about the location of books he needs. Then he will go to the books—as scholars have always gone to the books. When 1984 comes a lot of scholars will be coming to Kent.

Having great library resources provides another benefit: great libraries not only attract good people; they also expose bad people. The ways in which a faculty uses its library is a sensitive gauge of that faculty's competence. Just as vampires are repelled by a crucifix, so are frauds repelled by research material. For example, let us say that a university had in its special collections for years unpublished material by an American poet and that during these same years it had on its staff a professor who was a specialist in this poet and taught classes on this poet, and that further this professor never made any use of his university's material—then that university would know that it had a Count Dracula on its hands. The blood he was sucking was the students' blood and ultimately the taxpayers' blood. It was not a waste for the library to have bought this material; the only waste of money was in paying the fraud's salary. Active scholars make good teachers because they are always expanding their knowledge and because they share—directly and indirectly—their research with their students. They are learning; they are extending the boundaries of knowledge; so their students get something special from them. The frauds, loafers, and incompetents can only communicate to their students the conviction that scholarship does not matter.

As a specialist in American literature I must, of necessity, focus my comments about the state of American scholarship on my field. But I would remind you that in 1964 the late John Cook Wyllie noted that 90 percent of all the scholars who ever lived were still alive. *All* the scholars who ever lived—not just literary scholars. We can therefore anticipate great work during our century in all fields, and much of this work will be done in libraries.

In American literature I estimate that at most 20 percent of the basic—repeat, *basic*—work has been satisfactorily done. We do not have reliable bibliographies for most of our authors. We do not have editions of the letters for many of our classic authors. The biographies are too often 19th-century exercises in piety. Until 1961 we did not have a definitive edition for *any* American author. Now, ten definitive editions of 19th-century American authors are being supported by the Modern Language Association's Center for Editions of American Authors—and at least six more editions have been organized with local backing. If all of them meet the standards of textual work established by Professor Fredson Bowers, they will never have to be done over again. An encouraging start, but no more than a start. Much basic work is needed for our 20th-century giants, for Faulkner, Hemingway, Dreiser, Fitzgerald, Wolfe, O'Neill, Mencken, Eliot, Frost, Stevens, Williams, Pound. This work will be done with books: it can only be done with books; it will always be done with books.

At some point in this century scanning machines will be "reading" the books and feeding the words directly into computers which will collate texts and make concordances. But mark well that the machines will be using books. The machines are going to make scholarship—all scholarship—better and faster. They will be able to store information into computer banks: we can look forward to a true National Union Catalogue, to an inventory of every imprint in American publishing, to comprehensive catalogues of manuscripts and letters. The machines will take scholarship out of its present mewling infancy. But mark well that the machines will be using books.

The miracle of the Kent State University Library is chronicled in its card catalogue. But there are some high spots that must be cited. In the past two years you have bought three entire bookstores—one of which had 650,000 pounds of books; you have bought a Spinoza collection, a hare-boiled fiction collection, a Stephen Crane collection, a *3 Stories and 10 Poems,* an *in our time,* a *Moby-Dick,* a Hawthorne collection, a group of Library of Congress Copyright Deposit copies—including Emerson's *Nature,* a group of authors' first books, a beat collection, *The Deerslayer,* the history of the Lewis and Clark Expedition, Boswell's *Life of Johnson,* Calvin's *Institution of Christian Religion,* Crevecoeur's *Letters from an American*

Farmer, the 1806 first American edition of the Koran. Not coincidentally, *The Serif* has become a distinguished library journal.

The season of Thanksgiving approaches. I recommend that all of you who are associated with Kent State University as staff, student, parent, or tax-payer include in your thanks this year your excellent library staff and the enlightened administration that have created the miracle of Kent. Your librarian has instinct and taste; but he could not have done his great work without the support of President White, the Board of Trustees, and the university community. Together you are not just building a great library—you are building a distinguished university—and the bricks are *mere collectors' items.*

Note

1. By the time of this address in 1968 Bruccoli had decided to resign from the Ohio State University Department of English that he had joined in 1961. He accepted a professorship in the English Department at the University of South Carolina in 1969. Ed.

Where They Belong

The Acquisition of the F. Scott Fitzgerald Papers

The F. Scott Fitzgerald Papers have made the Princeton University Library a shrine for pilgrims who just want to see or touch them, as well as for scholars. This material is the most frequently consulted archive in a library that also houses the papers of John Foster Dulles and Adlai Stevenson, and includes in its collections letters and other manuscripts of Woodrow Wilson.[1] Given Fitzgerald's love for his college, Princeton is the inevitable repository for his papers. They almost did not get there. The nine-year history of their acquisition is worth tracing because of its admonitory message, and because the received account is inaccurate.

That F. Scott Fitzgerald accumulated one of the richest archives in American literature is miraculous. At a time when no one would have placed a wager on his chances for immortality, he preserved his manuscripts, typescripts, proofs, correspondence, and memorabilia during the course of a disorganized, peripatetic life: the manuscripts and the revised galley proofs in which he restructured *The Great Gatsby;* the seventeen stages of *Tender Is the Night;* manuscripts, typescripts, and edited tear sheets of stories; scrapbooks; correspondence with Hemingway and other literary figures; a collection of books inscribed to him. Fitzgerald scholarship has been so thorough because he was such a good curator.

At his death in December 1940 Fitzgerald left a small insurance policy and less than $1,000 in cash and possessions. The common-place remark that he died with his books out of print is untrue. The truth is sadder: All nine of his titles were available, but they weren't selling. Scribners still had copies of the 1925 second printing of *The Great Gatsby* in the warehouse. His last royalty check in 1940 was for $13.13 for forty copies.

Since Zelda Fitzgerald required expensive psychiatric treatment and their daughter Frances Scott (known as Scottie) was attending Vassar, the executor of

---

"Where They Belong: The Acquisition of the F. Scott Fitzgerald Papers" was first published in the *Princeton University Library Chronicle* 50 (Autumn 1988): 30–37. Reprinted with permission of Arlyn Bruccoli for the Matthew J. Bruccoli literary estate.

the estate, Judge John Biggs, tried to raise capital on Fitzgerald's papers and library.[2] Biggs, Princeton Class of 1918, had been Fitzgerald's roommate and collaborator on the *Princeton Tiger*. He published two novels with Scribners and became a United States Circuit Court Judge. Although he is reported to have remarked that Fitzgerald left the estate of a pauper and the will of a millionaire,[3] Biggs managed the estate without fee for eight years to provide an income for Zelda Fitzgerald. His benefactions were motivated by his sense of duty combined with affection and sympathy. He had no recognition of his friend's literary stature and was baffled when the Fitzgerald revival came.

Item eight of Fitzgerald's will covered the disposition of his books:

> I give, devise and bequest unto my daughter, Frances Scott Fitzgerald, all my family silverware, portraits, pictures, and all special and valuable books, short stories or other writings which I may have written, or all books of value which I may have collected or purchased to be used and controlled by her until my wife Zelda Fitzgerald shall regain her sanity and in that event the same shall become the property of Zelda Fitzgerald and any portion thereof that she does not desire to keep may be sold or otherwise disposed of by her, and in the event she shall die without regaining her sanity, then the above described property shall be the sole and separate property of my daughter, Frances Scott Fitzgerald.

Zelda Fitzgerald had never been declared legally insane; therefore the books became her sole property. The will nowhere specifically mentions Fitzgerald's own manuscripts and correspondence, and Biggs construed "other writings which I may have written" to include the manuscripts and other papers. (The other provision in the will that could apply to the papers is item 11, bequeathing "all the rest and residue of my property" to his wife and daughter "in equal portions.")

The only published account of Princeton's negotiations for the Fitzgerald Papers is David A. Randall's *Dukedom Large Enough*,[4] the memoirs of the head of Charles Scribner's Sons rare book department and director of the Lilly Library at Indiana University. Randall is rightly regarded as one of the greatest American bookmen, but he was known as a man who enjoyed a good story. According to his published account, he was introduced by Maxwell Perkins to Judge Biggs, who asked whether $750 was a fair offer for Fitzgerald's papers and library. Randall responded that whoever made that offer was "either a fool or a knave, if not both" and offered $3,750 sight unseen. He was prevented from consummating the deal because Perkins regarded it as a conflict-of-interest situation: Fitzgerald had been a member of the Scribner literary family, and the main concern was to raise money for his widow and orphan.

The $750 offer had come from Princeton. "When I pointed out to the then librarian Julian Boyd, that in my opinion, the heirs were being robbed," Randall wrote, "I was reminded tartly that Princeton was not a charitable institution, nor was its library established to support indigent widows of, and I quote, 'second-rate, Midwest hacks' just because they happened to have been lucky enough to have attended Princeton—unfortunately for Princeton."[5] Boyd was a Jefferson scholar who had no enthusiasm for Fitzgerald's work. In 1941 the manuscripts of contemporary authors were regarded by many librarians as mere collectors' items rather than scholarly resources; but that year Boyd had announced a program for a "systematic approach" to preserving contemporary literary records at Princeton.[6] However, there was bad blood between Boyd and Randall resulting, according to Randall, from his successful endeavor "to force-feed Princeton into obtaining Ray Stannard Baker's notable Woodrow Wilson collection" and other disagreements over acquisitions for the Morris L. Parrish Collection of English Literature.

The verifiable history of the Fitzgerald Papers begins on 12 March 1941 when Perkins wrote Biggs that he had asked Randall what value Fitzgerald's manuscripts would have: "He thought not much, but around a couple of hundred dollars each."[7] This was before Randall had seen the material. The first documented contract with Princeton came when Boyd reported to Biggs that Perkins had told poet Allen Tate about Fitzgerald's manuscripts. Boyd wrote: "If they are to be sold, we would like to have the privilege of considering their purchase."

Eleven months elapsed before Biggs informed Zelda and Scottie on 27 March 1942 that Randall had examined the books and papers and "thinks the whole thing can be sold to the Library of Princeton University for about $1,000." At this time Scottie was in her last semester at Vassar, and Zelda was living with her mother in Montgomery, Alabama. Citing item eight of the will but tactfully passing over the question of Zelda's sanity ("Therefore you and Scottie have the disposition of this property"), Biggs recommended the sale to Princeton. Zelda replied accepting Biggs's advice, but Scottie refused to sell ("if that library were worth $.50 or $10,000 I couldn't bear to part with it") and offered to buy the books and manuscripts from her mother.

Biggs and Harold Ober—Fitzgerald's agent who was contributing to a fund for Scottie's education—were nonplussed by her unreasonable behavior in rejecting $1,000. After the estate was settled, there was about $15,000 to provide for Zelda. Since the papers were actually Zelda's property under the will, Biggs decided to conclude the deal with Princeton, proposing to Scottie that she retain the books she wanted. But in May 1942 Biggs was advised by Lester W. Roth, a member of the law firm representing Fitzgerald's interests in California: "The executor can't sell the property, because he holds it only for the purpose of passing it on to the named legatees." Accordingly, negotiations were suspended until the property could pass to Zelda. At this time Scottie wrote to Biggs withdrawing her objections to the sale and bequeathing to him "my iron bed + text books, not to be sold or disposed of or loaned to friends, and an income of twenty cents and four mills every two and a third weeks until you are sixty, at which time you are to receive my tommy gun and straight backed chair and a trust fund yielding 44 cents a year providing you eat your broccoli every Tuesday."

In January 1943 Biggs deposited the books and manuscripts at Princeton for safekeeping and examination. Boyd reminded Biggs in March that Princeton was still interested in making the purchase for $1,000 but wanted the correspondence included. Scottie had removed the letters for use in a biography of her father that she hoped to write. She informed Biggs that they were too valuable to throw in and expressed concern about making personal letters available to the public by placing them in a library. Biggs was dismayed when Scottie informed him in June 1943 that she had destroyed certain of the letters: "The letters I threw out had *no* bearing *whatever* on Daddy—I am not trying to conceal anything about him— they were in no way interesting, that I promise. . . . The letters may belong to the estate, but the personal lives of people who are still very much alive do not belong to the estate, or to me."

The matter rested for a year and a half until Boyd wrote Biggs in 1945 offering $750 for the manuscripts and books—exclusive of the letters—following the judge's trip to Princeton. An additional $100 was to be paid for what Boyd described as "the notebooks." The library's rough inventory of the material was provided. Biggs referred the offer to Perkins, who consulted Randall: "I am quite sure that I can certainly do better for you," Randall stated. Boyd informed Biggs that he would not be able to "justifiably revise" his offer. On 30 April 1945 Biggs reported to Boyd that Randall had offered to sell the manuscripts, books, and letters for $3,500 less 20 percent commission or to buy them outright for Scribners at $1,500. (It is not clear whether Randall expected to break up the material for resale.) Zelda had by then given all of the material to Scottie, who had the sole decision over its disposition.

Willard Thorp, a distinguished professor of English at Princeton, had become involved in the transaction as Boyd's advisor and negotiator. Thorp was determined to bring the Fitzgerald archive to Princeton; his correspondence with Boyd indicates his concern to prevent the librarian from breaking off negotiations in response to what Boyd regarded as extortion. On 21 June 1945 Boyd sent Biggs a stiff letter declining to meet Randall's $2,800 figure ($3,500 less $700), which he noted was not a firm offer. Boyd expressed his conviction that the current "highly inflated" prices of books and manuscripts would not hold and suggested that Biggs invite offers from Yale and Harvard: "Princeton is quite willing to meet this kind of competition." Boyd sent a copy of this letter to Thorp with a two-page memo, authorizing him to go to $1,500, which was Randall's firm figure, and adding that "I am really very anxious to buy the papers, especially the correspondence, in spite of all my obtuseness to Fitzgerald's greatness. . . . Consequently don't make the mistake of thinking that I am not enthusiastic about the papers—I only lack enthusiasm about Fitzgerald as an artist and perhaps even there I shall be educated in time." Boyd further authorized Thorp to tell Biggs that "Randall is on public record as being inimical to Princeton" and was using the Fitzgerald papers to make Princeton pay more than they were worth.[8]

In response to Boyd's letter of 21 June, Randall wrote an angry letter to Biggs guaranteeing a payment of $2,250 if he could not sell the collection on commission within a year: "In my opinion, Princeton should pay at least $2,500 for it." On 2 July Boyd—prompted by Thorp—wrote Biggs agreeing to meet Randall's $2,500 figure. During his summer vacation Boyd attempted to read *Tender Is the Night* "thoughtfully and prayerfully" at Thorp's urging, but turned with relief to Gibbon. In August Biggs reported to Thorp that Scottie and Zelda had accepted the $2,500 offer "subject to a bill of sale the conditions of which are to be worked out." Biggs then proposed that Princeton restrict access to the letters dealing with Zelda's illness and to items *ejusdem generis* (of the same kind). The sale was not concluded, and there is no explanation for the suspension of the correspondence.

Meanwhile the first stage of the Fitzgerald revival was launched. During the summer and autumn of 1945 *The Crack-Up* and the *Portable F. Scott Fitzgerald* were well received, and reprints of *The Great Gatsby* were published by New Directions, Bantam, and the Armed Services Editions. In 1945 some fifty reviews and critical articles about Fitzgerald appeared. Moreover, American literary manuscript values were undergoing a postwar appreciation, and the Fitzgerald papers became increasingly valuable. Nothing happened on the Princeton front until Boyd wrote Biggs in August 1946—a year later—suggesting a plan for restricting the sensitive material. Three days later Biggs reported to Boyd that Zelda had returned to Highlands Hospital and was unable to execute a bill of sale. It was agreed that the material would be left at the library for "classification" until she recovered. When Zelda Fitzgerald perished in a fire at the hospital on 10 March 1948, the transaction had not been concluded.

As the result of Thorp's urging and of the rapid increase of critical interest in Fitzgerald, Princeton became anxious to close the deal. In November 1948 Boyd reminded Biggs that the matter was still unsettled; Biggs promised to talk to Scottie about it "at once." There is no extant follow-up correspondence. Boyd wrote Scottie in June 1949 expressing his eagerness to conclude negotiations. During the Autumn of 1949 Scottie and Boyd tried to arrange a Princeton meeting, which took place in December; at that time the matter was presumably settled, for on 9 January 1950 Princeton sent her a bill of sale at $2,500. Scottie responded on 21 May 1950:

> I'd like to *give* all the manuscripts, papers, letters, etc. to Princeton, with a very few restrictions such as we discussed before. But—I'd like to keep the books, + the scrapbooks + photograph albums + the ledger containing the diary, leaving you only those books by Daddy himself. . . .
>
> I enclose a carbon copy of the section of my father's will which turned up among some papers in Wilmington + which is partly responsible for my decision. I do not think the wishes of the dead should be respected in every case but in the matter of the scrapbooks I was delighted to find a good excuse to back up my reluctance to part with them.[9]

Boyd expressed suitable gratitude and drafted a deed of gift in June.[10]

On 18 November 1950 Scottie came to Princeton to select the books she wanted to retain and signed the deed of gift. The ceremony was commemorated by a photograph of Boyd, Scottie, and her husband that subsequently appeared on the cover of the *Princeton Alumni Weekly*[11]—the periodical F. Scott Fitzgerald was reading when he suffered his fatal heart attack.

Notes

1. According to Alexander P. Clark, former curator of manuscripts. I acknowledge the generous assistance of Mr. Clark and of university archivist Earle E. Coleman.

2. Fitzgerald's will was executed in Tryon, North Carolina, on 17 June 1937. It appointed Biggs and Maxwell Perkins as his executors, but Perkins resigned because of a possible conflict-of-interest situation.

3. Scottie Fitzgerald included these words in the dedication of *The Romantic Egotist* (New York: Scribners, 1974) to Judge Biggs as "the very incarnation of the words, 'Family Friend.'"

4. David A Randall, *Dukedom Large Enough* (New York: Random House, 1969), pp. 253–255.

5. Ibid., pp. 253–255. This Biggs-Randall correspondence does not substantiate Randall's testimony that he offered immediate payment of $3,750. Another error in Randall's published account is his comment that Fitzgerald's reputation was so low that he "had even been dropped from the current edition of Merle Johnson's inclusive book collector's *vade mecum, American First Editions*, and it was pretty impossible to get lower than that." If there are degrees of impossibility, a lower level is to have never been included in Johnson—which is the case for Fitzgerald.

6. Julian Boyd, "The Princeton Archives of American Letters," *Princeton University Library Chronicle* (June 1941): 133–136.

7. All the letters cited are in the care of the Manuscript Division of the Department of Rare Books and Special Collections, Princeton University Library, or in the University Archives. The Fitzgerald Estate files were given to Princeton by Judge Biggs's son, John Biggs III, Class of 1951.

8. Five days after Boyd's letter to Biggs, Scottie—now married to navy officer Samuel J. Lanahan, Princeton '41, and working at the *New Yorker*—wrote to the judge offering to buy everything from her mother for $1,500. No response to her letter survives.

9. This document has not been found. Since Fitzgerald's executed will does not refer to the scrapbooks, the will Scottie refers to was probably an earlier will.

10. Not even Randall was able to accept the growth in the literary and monetary value of Fitzgerald's papers. On 7 June 1965 he told me a version of his dealings with Boyd in which he put his offer at $5,000. Randall was incredulous when I remarked that the archive was probably worth five million dollars. If my estimate was bullish in 1965, it is conservative in 1988. What would the manuscript of *The Great Gatsby* now bring at auction?

11. *Princeton Alumni Weekly* (9 February 1951).

John Cook Wyllie

The proper fulfillment of John Cook Wyllie's greatness was impeded by his refusal to recognize his greatness: he did not know how extraordinary his mind was. Wyllie did not achieve the high reputation accorded to lesser librarians and bibliographers because he cared nothing for personal credit; he routinely gave away his ideas and discoveries. Wyllie's career inspires admiration and regret among those who worked with him because he accomplished so much but left so little of his mind on paper.

Wyllie was a double anachronism, joining old allegiances with an awareness of future requirements. One of those professionals who are described by amateurs as eccentric, he was a self-reliant man of principle who was too busy to be eccentric. Consistently truthful, he expressed apparently contradictory positions. Thus he was a generous benefactor of scholars and a dedicated preserver of research material who had reservations about promiscuous publication. "The frequent tooting of the tin horn of productive research is nothing more than the outward and visible sign of an inward and spiritual degeneration." This attitude no doubt influenced his reluctance to publish his work, which he regarded as work in progress. Accordingly, his 1960 Rosenbach Lectures were never prepared for publication.

Like many other great librarians he did not possess a library-school degree; his formal training in librarianship was limited to one summer at the University of Chicago. There was nothing about books that he could have learned from library schools or schools of information science or schools of media arts. He was a born bookman; working as a librarian enabled him to devote his life to gathering books, preserving books, editing books, generating books, reviewing books, and facilitating the use of books. He functioned as an educator—not just as a librarian.

Addressing the Association of Colleges and Reference Libraries in 1948, Wyllie admonished the group that "the mixture that still exists today of the librarian

---

"John Cook Wyllie" was published originally in *American Book-Collectors and Bibliographers, First Series,* edited by Joseph Rosenblum, volume 140 of *Dictionary of Literary Biography* (Detroit: Bruccoli Clark Layman / Gale Research, 1994), pp. 327–341. © Gale, a part of Cengage Learning, Inc. Reproduced by permission. www.cengage.com/permissions.

and the bibliophile is unfortunately a dying phenomenon." He defined rare books as the "unexpendable parts of a library's collection":

> One of the chief reasons for the need of rare book rooms in our university libraries today is the locust-like descent of great swarms of people on our collections. The locusts fall into two general categories: the student and the so-called trained librarian. Out of deference to the stated objectives of this association I pass over one of these categories lightly, but I will not forbear lamenting to this select group the wretched state of a profession, formerly one of dignity and character, which has so far fallen from the graces of the liberal arts and the natural sciences as to set up what can only be called trade schools. It is a dirty bird that fouls its own nest. You will forgive my bitterness if you have ever seen a class mark on a Ratcliffe binding, or if you have seen the Gaylord brand on a Zaehnsdorf inlay, or a punched page of an illuminated manuscript. Here surely are the marks of the beast....
>
> Most books, it is true, find their chief end in the noble function of being read, but the man who says that a book is only for reading is to me a pervert of the same order and only of a different kind of man who says that a woman is only for sleeping with. Of course there are a great many books that are good only for reading, and some that are not good even for that, just as I dare say there are all kinds of women, but there is something in seeing a Gutenberg Bible or a first folio of Shakespeare or a Grolier binding or a Kelmscott Chaucer that has nothing at all to do with reading a book.

He believed that the chief responsibilities of a rare-books and manuscripts curator were to acquire research material to protect it from the atrocities of librarianship, and to make it usable by scholars.

Wyllie devoted his life's work to the University of Virginia, and it was his secret guilt that he was not an authentic Virginian. The son of the Rev. William Wyllie and Mabel Cook Wyllie, Episcopal Church missionaries, he was born in Palatka, Florida, on 26 October 1908. It may be a clue to Wyllie's character that he was a "missionary kid"—one of a group that has disproportionately distinguished itself in American life. He grew up in Santo Domingo, where he was educated by tutors, and briefly attended two Virginia preparatory schools, Christchurch and St. Christopher's. In 1925 he was denied admission to the University of Virginia because he lacked necessary high-school credits. After a year at Lane High School in Charlottesville, he entered the University in 1926 and graduated with a B. A. in English in 1929. As an undergraduate he worked—paid and unpaid—for the library when it was located in the Rotunda.

After graduation Wyllie continued to work for the library while taking every advanced course offered by the English department, but he never took another degree. Having decided that the University was placing too much emphasis on graduate degrees, he declined to participate in what he regarded as a trend away from learning to diploma mills. Wyllie did not enjoy teaching in the classroom, but he was preceptor to a chain of students and colleagues. His preferred pedagogical technique was to initiate a project and then turn it over to someone else.

Wyllie was appointed assistant reference librarian in 1929; he was in fact the only reference librarian. In 1933–1934 he went, almost without funds, to Europe to visit libraries, binderies, and bookshops. Gerald Langford, Wyllie's graduate-school friend, has written that "on that trip to England, he picked up a copy of the 1636 edition of Kingsmill Long's translation of John Barclay's *Argenis,* which he gave me, with the suggestion that it would make a good Ph.D. dissertation subject for me, which indeed it did."

Upon his return Wyllie became curator of the Virginia Collection. When the Alderman Library opened in 1938 Wyllie was appointed director of the Division of Rare Books and Manuscripts. He created the rare-book division by examining every volume in the general stacks. At the Alderman Library dedication the first major gift to the new library was announced: the Tracy M. McGregor Library. McGregor had assembled a collection of 12,500 items dedicated to American history and had attempted to recruit Wyllie as his private librarian; after the collector's death the trustees of the McGregor Fund presented his library to the University of Virginia, at least partly in recognition of McGregor's respect for Wyllie's abilities. Housed in the McGregor Room, this collection includes more than 2,000 Mather items.

After the army, navy, and marines turned him down because he was nearsighted, Wyllie joined the American Field Service as an ambulance driver in 1941—before Pearl Harbor. He served with the British Eighth Army in North Africa, where he was the last man out of Tobruk and "heard the bagpipes at El Alamein." He received a field commission from the British, then returned to America and enlisted in the air corps. In 1944 he was communication chief for U.S. air-ground communication in Burma; in 1944–1945 he was an air-ground combat liaison and communications officer in China. Wyllie received a second field commission in the air corps and was discharged with the rank of first lieutenant, having been decorated by the British, American, and Chinese governments. The Legion of Merit citation read:

> For exceptionally meritorious service from 8 April 1943 to date as Senior Officer of an American Air-Ground Liaison Team operating with the Chinese 57th and Temporary 6th Division. Lt. Wyllie exhibited great courage and resourcefulness in establishing and maintaining observation posts in the most forward areas available from which he directed the extremely effective close air

support of his unit which was credited with being one of the most contributing factors in the success of the Chinese Mission. When the 57th Division was relieved he immediately requested a new assignment to a forward area and proceeded to join the Temporary 6th Division where he continued to operate with great success making an enviable record and bringing great credit on the Military Service of the United States.

Wyllie was appointed Curator of Rare Books in 1946. When he married in 1949 he took a wife from the Alderman Library staff. He and the former Evelyn Dollens had two daughters, Elizabeth and Jane, who is a librarian. In 1956 he became university librarian, a promotion he accepted unenthusiastically because he felt that he could not work at the Alderman under any librarians other than his predecessors Harry Clemons and Jack Dalton; if he were to remain he would have to accept the librarianship. High administrative rank did not gratify Wyllie because he preferred books to committee work, yet he functioned effectively on an extraordinary number of committees. In 1966 he was appointed Director of Libraries of the University of Virginia system with responsibility for all the libraries in the University of Virginia system. In this post he founded the Science and Technology Library at the University. The library at Clinch Valley College in Wise, Virginia, which he helped establish, was named for him in 1969.

John Cook Wyllie was five feet, ten inches tall with close-cut, wiry hair. His suits and ties were sprinkled with ashes. Wyllie was embarrassed by displays of emotion or self-revelation; but his close friends testified to his periods of doubt. During the war years he wrote, "Fact is in its simplest terms that I don't know what I want but have to depend upon my instincts to prevent me from getting it, and I can always in the last analysis count on my following the line of most resistance." He spent nothing on himself, except for two packs of cigarettes a day; he did not drink and was indifferent to food. Whatever spare money he had was spent on books which he gave to the Alderman. He was wholly unpretentious. As Curator of Rare Books in the 1950s he did not have a proper office; his desk was in a passageway behind bookcases, surrounded by piles of books. He frequently returned to the library after dinner. Many nights were spent with what he called "the book machine"—his system for processing gifts and acquisitions. Although he did not give the impression of being under pressure, Wyllie routinely worked on several projects at once and disliked time-wasting interruptions. He carried a book to read when he might be compelled to wait.

The mind of a scholar-librarian-educator is gauged by the books in his life. Wyllie was unostentatiously omnibibliophilic. There were nearly thirty books by his bed the night he died—all of which he was reading: Allen, *Love in the*

Making; Aiken, *Collected Criticism;* Adams, *John James Audubon;* Martinez, *Memoirs of a Medico;* Chekhov, *The Seagull and Three Sisters;* Deutscher, *Stalin;* Durrell, *Clea;* Eifert, *Louis Jolliet;* Freud, *Dictionary of Psychoanalysis;* Fromm, *May Man Prevail; The Hazlitt Sampler;* Heimann, *History of Economic Doctrines;* Hobhouse, *Liberalism;* Hume, *An Enquiry Concerning Human Understanding;* Knapp, *A History of War and Peace, 1939–1965;* Labaree, *The Boston Tea Party;* Matthiessen, *American Renaissance;* Maxwell, *Ring of Bright Water;* Nucete-Sardi, *Aventura y tragedia di Don Francisco de Miranda;* Price, *A Generous Man;* Price, *A Long and Happy Life;* Quer, *The Physiology of Plants;* Shannon & Weaver, *The Mathematical Theory of Communication;* Tyler, *Anthropology;* Wade, *Slavery in the Cities, The South 1820–1860;* Wagenknecht, *John Greenleaf Whittier;* Waxell, *The Russian Expedition to America;* Wheare, *Legislatures.*

A university is an assemblage of books surrounded by people using them. Wyllie was highly receptive to technological developments; but his principal concern was in extending the use of the library to all classes of readers and researchers. When William Faulkner arrived at the University of Virginia as a writer in residence in 1956, there were not enough copies of his books in the Alderman stacks to meet the new demand; Wyllie placed a supply of uncatalogued Faulkner paperbacks in the library.

A librarian is best judged by his bookmanship and by the books and collections he builds or acquires. Wyllie's chief contribution to scholarship and librarianship was his work as Curator of Rare Books, which provided his chief gratification. During his tenure as head of rare books—with or without the title—the Alderman Library acquired the Tracy W. McGregor Library and the C. Waller Barrett Library of American Literature. He was partially or wholly responsible for the acquisition of these collections by gift or purchase:

Wilbur Cortez Abbott Collection of Seventeenth-Century English History
    and Literature (especially related to Oliver Cromwell);
Armed Services Editions Collection;
Samuel Bemiss Collection of Incunabula and Classics;
Joseph M. Bruccoli Great War Collection;
James Branch Cabell Papers;
Warren Chappell Collection;
Elizabeth Cocke Coles Collection of Virginiana;
Philip K. Crowe Collection (books about Ceylon);
John Dos Passos Papers;
William Faulkner Collection of Linton R. Massey;
Library of the Garnett Family of Elmwood (Essex County, Virginia);

Douglas H. Gordon Collection of French Renaissance Literature;
T. Catesby Jones Collection of Early Twentieth Century European Graphic Art;
Edward L. Stone Collection on the Development of Printing;
Thomas W. Streeter Railroad Collection;
Marvin Tatum Collection of Contemporary Prose and Poetry;
Mrs. Robert Coleman Taylor Collection of First Editions of American Best Sellers;
Alfred Lord Tennyson Collection (of which the core was previously known as the Templeton Crocker Tennyson Collection);
Trollope Family Collection;
Victorius Evolution Collection;
Virginiana Collections;
Isaac Walton Collection;
Steven Watts Collection of Type Specimen Books;
James Madison Collection;
Alexander MacKay-Smith Collection (printed scores, primarily of eighteenth-century music);
Stephen McClellan Aviation Collection;
American Sheet Music Collection (part of which is called the Lynn T. McRae Collection);
Oscar Ogg Collection of Typography, Book Design, and Book Illustration;
Sabine Hall Library of Landon and Robert Wormeley Carter;
Sadleir-Black Collection of Gothic Novels;
Marion duPont Scott Collection of Sporting Books.

Wyllie's achievements as a collection builder were impeded by a puny budget and by his attitudes toward money. He was not stingy; but he did not comprehend how other people were motivated by money. He was personally indifferent to money—apart from providing for his family—and probably regretted the necessity of accepting any salary from the university. He declined consulting fees from libraries and other academic institutions because he believed that it was his duty to make his abilities available. Wyllie nurtured the conviction that dealers were insufficiently sensitive to the honor of donating material to the university. Great collections went elsewhere because he would not purchase anything for the library unless the funds were in hand. Adequate amounts were never in hand; in 1955 the total budget for rare-book and manuscript purchases was fifteen thousand dollars: ten thousand dollars from the McGregor Fund and five thousand dollars from the state. During the 1950s and 1960s when the University of Texas was omnivorously paying big money for collections and other institutions were attempting to compete, Wyllie felt that such conduct bordered on indecency. His achievements in collections development resulted from his ability to convince potential donors of the value of the University of Virginia and its library.

Wyllie's integrity as well as his technique in acquiring material are demonstrated by his response to James Branch Cabell's offer to donate some of his manuscripts to the Alderman Library and sell the rest of his papers elsewhere:

> There is a Calvinist streak in me requiring me to admit that these manuscripts ought not to be dispersed. In the interest simply of future Cabell scholarship, I would rather the entire batch go to Bill Jackson at Harvard or Jim Babb at Yale (Either one can put his hands on more money than I can) than that the manuscripts should be scattered from hell to breakfast with us getting some.
>
> If you scatter the manuscripts there will be some disorganized flurries of notoriety at the wrong time in American literary history. But if you will just see to it that the manuscripts are kept together where they can be got at when the time comes for the real flowering of your literary fame, then you will have done something both for yourself and for American literature. I sadly admit that, unless I read the literary portents incorrectly, we will both long since have been underground when this day comes. But I have no shadow of a doubt that it will come, and for me to be a silent party to the dispersal of the manuscripts is to do less than justice to my own critical acumen.
>
> I admire your work and yet am hardheaded enough to know that its special bouquet is not for the present generation's mass market, where the prices are made. What would you think about getting yourself a professional appraisal and then letting us try to find donors for half that sum? You could check the accuracy of the appraisal and the reality of your own interest by putting one of the manuscripts up at public auction in New York and letting us see if we could buy it in.

The Cabell Papers came to the Alderman Library through the generosity of the author's brother.

It is pardonable that most collectors are not bibliographers. It is unforgivable that some bibliographers are not collectors. But it is a capital offense for an alleged rare-books curator not to be a bookman. Wyllie formulated this code for his own bookmanship: "If you ask me why I looked for bookstores and libraries when I was in Cairo and Liverpool, my only answer is that I went to Cairo and Liverpool to look for libraries and bookstores. . . . I don't really claim to be a collector myself. I am only a keeper and admirer of other people's collections. Ownership of a book for most people like myself is a fugitive and transitory affair, lasting only a few years or decades. It takes a real book collector . . . to confer something of an immortality on their ownership."

During his term as book editor for the *Richmond News Leader* Wyllie trained the editors to retain the array of printed material the paper received, which he fetched back to the university. He instructed the dubious journalists that even the "nut mail" constituted a record of the time that would be unrecoverable unless preserved. Wyllie's all-embracing acquisitions policy was not shared by some of his associates who claimed that "John's junk" was not worth the expense of cataloguing. His rationale extended to the rare-book stacks, which were populated with what lesser curators described as duplicate copies. Wyllie recognized that what appeared to be duplicates were not necessarily duplicates. Accordingly, he developed techniques for differentiating concealed printings on the basis of typographical evidence. For this purpose he bought the first Hinman Collator outside the Folger Library. He may have originated the technique for using gutter measurements to identify impressions; and he was able to reconstruct the binding process for a printing from the thread colors in the copies. Wyllie's interest in cancels was connected with his work on differentiating printings; his 1953 article on "The Forms of Twentieth-Century Cancels" was the first published attempt to describe post-1825 examples.

Wyllie dismayed conventionally trained librarians by shelving later printings and editions of key works in his rare-book stacks. He believed that the proper function of bibliography is to construct the biography of a book and that books embody their own histories. He addressed the Grolier Club on the topic of "Second Editions"; characteristically he did not keep a copy of his remarks. Wyllie preserved everyone's work except his own.

In dedicating *The New Sabin* (1974) to Wyllie, Lawrence S. Thompson explained that he was "a sort of apostle of the rare book in America. His breviary was Joseph Sabin's *Dictionary of Books Relating to America,* and he dreamed of expanding it to a point at which it would dwarf the *National Union Catalogue* in sheer bulk. He printed for very limited distribution six entries of a type which he conceived to be the ideal Sabin."

Wyllie was foremost a bookman, but he experimented with methods for applying technology to bibliographical research. In 1960 he rigged a television camera with a reading stand in order to transmit images of pages to other libraries at the university; in 1966 he collaborated with nuclear scientist W. Reed Johnson to reproduce watermarks by beta-ray photography and apply this technique to the Jefferson papers. Addressing the Bibliographical Society of America in 1964—

before the computer revolution—he forcefully called for new approaches to bibliographical work:

> With eighty-five percent of the collectors who have ever lived still alive today, and with ninety-five per cent of the bibliographers who have ever lived still stalking the land, how do we create the conditions to get the two populations into useful juxtaposition for this presumably desirable heat transfer? How do we bring about the set of circumstances that will put great collections to great uses? How can great needs be supplied with great means? . . .
>
> My suggestion is that the Society form a Council on Bibliographical Research and Development, and that this Council be handed as much money as can be scratched up and charged with finding as much more as it can, while it develops an approved dossier of research proposals to offer the eleemosynarily inclined. . . .
>
> My only point, and I have now labored it enough, is that we are living in an age of machines, and we ought to learn to use them. The age is also one of corporate research, so I repeat my lugubrious warning, with what cheerfulness I can summon, that the great and solitary heroes like Bradshaw and de Ricci are gone, and we must all soon follow.

From 1952 to 1962 Wyllie was book editor for the *Richmond News Leader,* producing what was regarded as the best newspaper book page in the South. He wrote hundreds of reviews, which were characterized by clarity and disdain for literary chitchat. Reviewing B. H. Liddell Hart's edition of the *Rommel Papers* (18 May 1953), Wyllie drew upon his experiences with the Eighth Army to expose the historian's pomposity and carelessness, concluding:

> It makes me a little mad for a stuffed shirt like Liddell Hart to have got his front feet in Rommel's trough. When Rommel is talking about the Blitzkrieg in France, Liddell Hart says Oh yes, he himself had invented it in 1920, and had a better name for it—the "expanding torrent."
>
> Nuts to us both, Mr. Liddell Hart. I invented this system of annotation before 1920 and I still call it "scratching my own back."

After attending a William Faulkner press conference at the 1955 National Book Awards ceremony, Wyllie wrote (31 January 1955):

> He is a small man, shy, sincere, nothing of the smart-aleck. He gets clothes-dummy frozen before banked cameras or a press gang, thaws readily in a group of two or three people if one of them has a kind or an understanding word. The two Oxfords (Mississippi and England) are strong in him: rough edges of

the country-store philosopher and the sophisticated reserve of the housebroken British; a Mississippi accent in Swinburnian rhythms, but too faint to hear unless you listen intently.

His eyes are black, his hair white. The sharp forward, ferret taper of his face and the fixed public stare give him a zoo-like appearance, something between a chicken and a fox, but he is handsome even in his mask. He carries a red bandanna handkerchief that he tucks up his left sleeve. His public voice is an inaudible inexpressive monotone. As a public speaker he is a total loss but what he writes to speak is golden. . . .

This interviewer came away puzzled, but with an undiminished respect for Faulkner, and for his own part, still believes Faulkner was right to be obscure, believes now that Faulkner moves under intense artistic compulsions, hovering between sophisticated coma and savage convulsion, of which your interviewer has only a dim and unsatisfactory comprehension.

Here, at all events, is a fleeting impression of the most influential, the most original, and the most vilified novelist living, each of whose works has enriched all his others. Hemingway (Faulkner's closest rival in contemporary literary fame) has been too personal to support followers, too attractive not to produce imitators, but Faulkner has been sinking deep roots, while Hemingway has only been blooming and fading.

Wyllie denied that he was a man of letters, but a good case can be made for his literary qualifications. He wrote forceful prose that effectively expressed his critical judgments. His style was direct, almost journalistic, for he wrote against deadlines and had little opportunity to revise. Just as he was appalled by ostentatious or pretentious conduct, he eschewed fancy writing. He read widely in literature, history, and biography and drew upon his extensive knowledge in his writings.

The earliest scholarly publication on which Wyllie's name appears in *A Spenser Bibliography for 1928–1930,* which he and Randolph W. Church—later the Virginia State Librarian—compiled and mimeographed in 1931. The parodic title page provides an indication of Wyllie's unsolemn approach to academic endeavors.

Dumas Malone said that Wyllie "knew more than any other living man about the slaves of Thomas Jefferson"; and his work grew to more than 950 file cards. Not a pious idolater of Jefferson, Wyllie pursued this subject because of the allegations that Jefferson had sired slave children; however, Willie found no evidence to support this claim. Wyllie also accumulated some seventy-five thousand citations for all reported Jefferson texts—in print or manuscript—which he made available to the Princeton University Jefferson Papers project. Wyllie's unpublished identification of the paper stocks purchased by Jefferson was undertaken to facilitate the dating of his writings.

What the Alderman Library staff refers to as the "Wyllie File" consists of seventy-two card trays containing some seventy-nine thousand three-by-five-inch cards and slips, mostly in his hand. The majority of the cards index the *University of Virginia's Alumni Bulletin* and other university publications; but four trays hold more than four thousand cards with his notes on secondary Poe publications.

Wyllie's 1954 translation of Andres Bello's *A Georgic of the Tropics,* the first English translation of the 1826 poem, does not carry his name; the "Translator's Foreword" is signed J.C.W.

As a bibliographer Wyllie was chiefly interested in the identification of typefaces, the subject of his Rosenbach Lectures at the University of Pennsylvania in 1960 under the title "Three Illustrated Lectures on Type Faces Used in Books." His techniques for "fingerprinting" individual pieces of type from a font led him to question the accepted publication history of the *Bay Psalm Book* dated 1640. Wyllie suspected that what is held to be the first book printed in North America was actually printed in London:

A) The type used for this *Bay Psalm Book* was used only for that book and a Harvard commencement broadside—and for no other surviving work printed in North America.

B) This identical type was used in England before and *after* 1640.

Wyllie concluded that the 1640 *Bay Psalm Book* and the Harvard broadside were printed in England. He did not deny that a psalm book could have been printed in Cambridge, Massachusetts; but he contended that the volume dated 1640, which stipulates no printer or place of publication, was not printed in the Bay Colony. Because the same type was in use at the London shop of Isaac Jaggard, printer of the *First Folio* (1623) and Shakespeare quartos, Wyllie suspected that certain quartos dated before 1620 had been printed later.

In his Rosenbach Lectures Wyllie also revealed that although the Carter and Pollard disclosures about the Wise fabrications were correct, their typographical evidence was flawed. Carter and Pollard claimed that the pamphlets printed from kernless type were later than 1883, but Wyllie was able to identify kernless type in English printing of the 1870s.

Most bookmen or bibliographers are specialists; Wyllie, in addition to his work in typography and Virginia history, had an extraordinary range of research activities. But he was not a hobbyist, because he had no hobbies. Although he did not publish a book-length work of scholarship, he worked hard and seriously on his simultaneous research projects, intending to complete them in his retirement. He ran out of time.

Like all serious men, Wyllie disliked committee meetings, but he was an effective organizer of scholarly groups and projects. Wyllie was a founding member of the Albermarle County Historical Society and of the Virginia Place Name Society; he was an active member of other Virginia local-history organizations. It is difficult to rank his activities, but one of Wyllie's more significant endeavors was his role in the Bibliographical Society of the University of Virginia, of which he was a founding member, secretary-treasurer from 1947 to 1962, and treasurer from 1963 to 1968. He wrote or edited fifty-three numbers of the *Secretary's News Sheet* during those years.

The activities of the Bibliographical Society of the University of Virginia and the library were closely connected, and Wyllie assisted the launching of Fredson Bowers's *Studies in Bibliography*. Wyllie also reorganized the University of Virginia Press and was superintendent of the press from 1947 through 1949. He directed the McGregor Room Seminars (renamed the Peters Rushton Seminars) in Literature and Criticism and wrote most of the program notes.

Much of Wyllie's time was expended on editing other people's work and arranging for its publication or in organizing cooperative projects. After the death of Robert J. Turnbull, Wyllie salvaged the work in progress on Turnbull's *Bibliography of South Carolina, 1563–1950*, which was published in six volumes by the University of Virginia Press. He also edited and arranged the posthumous publication for Robert H. Webb's translations of Aristophanes. He supervised the Virginia Imprint Series and compiled in 1946 the first volume, *Preliminary Checklist of Abingdon, 1807–1876*. He encouraged Roger P. Bristol to undertake the Index to Evans's *American Bibliography* and helped to start the *Supplement to Evans*. In 1968, the year of his death, he initiated the Microfilm/Publications project, funded by the National Historical Publications and Records Commission, that produced microfilm and guides for research collections at the university. He served on the advisory boards for *The Papers of Thomas Jefferson* and *The Papers of James Madison*. He served on the boards of the Ellen Bayard Weedon Foundation and the William Faulkner Foundation.

There were book people in and out of Virginia for whom the most notable thing about the Alderman Library was the presence of John Cook Wyllie. When he received the Algernon Sidney Sullivan Award, a high honor bestowed by the University of Virginia, the citation written by Harry Clemons, the tenth university librarian, stated: "The full story of his generous and self-sacrificing efforts is known to no one else, and has been forgotten by him."

John Cook Wyllie suffered a heart attack at the end of his normal fourteen-hour workday and died on 18 April 1968. His death pauperized the University of Virginia libraries and the world of books.

References

[Randolph W. Church], *John Cook Wyllie, 1908–1968: A Very Personal Remembrance* (Privately printed, 1972).

"John Cook Wyllie 1908–1968," *AB Bookman Weekly* (27 April 1970): 1439–1440. Tributes by Sol M. Malkin, C. Waller Barrett, Matthew J. Bruccoli, and Robert K. Black.

J.E.M., "John Cook Wyllie," *Proceedings of the American Antiquarian Society* (16 October 1968): 236–238.

Dumas Malone, "John Cook Wyllie," *The Century Association Year-Book 1973* (New York, 1973), pp. 371–372.

Jesse C. Mills, "Detective in the Book World," *Graphic Arts Review* (May 1960): 7–8, 46–48.

Research Libraries without Reference Books

DISCLAIMER: These observations on libraries and librarianship are not aimed at school libraries, public libraries, or small-college libraries. My targets are the book-enemy library administrators at putative research institutions and the information science faculties who have produced a self-slain profession.

A culture has been defined as a lot of people who know the same things—and feel the same way about them. Specifically, a lot of people who have read the same books and have had their minds formed by them. That doesn't happen online.

The process of using reference books is educational. Their usefulness and usability derive from their organization, connections, and even style. Samuel Johnson's *Dictionary* is still read for the pleasure of exposure to his mind and expression. Nobody consults Wikipedia for literary enjoyment or intellectual stimulation. Using a database doesn't teach anything about the research process. The information science practitioners base their case for electronic/digital sources on the utility of the quick fix—a term from the "drug culture." Online gratification is temporary and incomplete, but habit-forming.

Reference books are readable. Web sites are not intended to be read. Reference volumes are organic: the reader holds the whole thing and has a sense of its connectedness. Web sites or databases are fragmentary: the user sees pieces of information on the screen. Information is not enough. Connections must be made. A good reference book provides what you are looking for—organized for utility; a database offers more than you need—or know how to use.

The form in which a reference text is encountered may determine what use is made of it—and how it influences a student-researcher. Reference books can be annotated and retained for life. The marked copy becomes a record of the owner's

---

"Research Libraries without Reference Books" was delivered as a speech at the annual Charleston Conference of librarians, vendors, and publishers, 9 November 2007. It was originally published in *The Necessity of Reference Books in the Digital Age* (Columbia, S.C.: privately printed, 2008), pp. 1–5. Reprinted with permission of Arlyn Bruccoli for the Matthew J. Bruccoli literary estate.

intellectual activity. Not so with a screen. My response to the redundant testimonies to the convenience of online information obviating the need for reference books—and the need to own them—is that I live and work surrounded by my reference books. I like owning them. They comfort me.

There was a time in my lifetime when students were routinely introduced to the monumental one-man reference works, which moved us to a recognition of the capacity of one person to influence his country, his time, and his culture through the power of his mind and learning. Dr. Johnson compiled and wrote his 40,000-entries dictionary with the help of several copyists, and it took him eight years.

Noah Webster spent twenty years compiling his 70,000-entries dictionary with the assistance of his son, who copied the manuscript. Working with a computer now they might be able to do it faster—but probably not much faster and certainly not better—and go directly online. The results would be uninspiring data dumps. It may be objected that it is not the function of a reference book to glorify its author. Nonetheless, it is good for students, scholars, and teachers to be reminded that what person had done, person can do. We need culture heroes, and the world of learning provided them.

The best reference books are not impersonal or anonymous. They carry the authority of the scholars responsible for them. A catalogue may not be just a list: the *Catalogue of Crime* carries the authority of Jacques Barzun. I am told that librarians don't care about the authority for a web site. I am told that the web-site producers oppose bylines, claiming that uncredited entries have something to do with the democratization of information. When all data is equal, it is equally untrustworthy. The real reason for suppressing or concealing credit is to enable online entrepreneurs to sell and resell the same information.

Enduring reference books are expressions of the mind and genius of their begetters. It is unlikely that there can be impersonal reference books outside of the sciences—certainly not in literature, history, and the arts. The tens of thousands of editorial decisions required establish the book's character and reveal the mind behind it. Definitions depend on the definer. Even chronologies have personality; the act of selection is personal.

The defenders of reference books often make their cases on sentimental or antiquarian grounds. The major reference works—especially those known to scholars and researchers by the names of their makers (Bartlett, Sabin, Greg, Child, Hoyle, Roberts, Burke, Grove, Brewer, Evans) or those identified by their acronyms (*OED, DNB, LHUS, STC, DLB, DAB, CBEL*) are now regarded as moss-covered monuments. Yet they are inspirational monuments of learning, research, and scholarship. When a reference book perishes, it leaves an emptiness.

The value of a library's reference room is the product of the selection of the books and their placement. Students and researchers learn from seeing books that are shelved near each other. The books they need to know about are the ones they didn't know about. That doesn't happen on a screen. Thomas Carlyle declared in support of the London Library that "A collection of books is the best of all Universities; for the University only teaches us how to read the book: you must go to the book itself for what it is."

Web sites do not serve the function of libraries, which have historically been centers of intellectual, cultural, and even social life. The impact of the Library of Congress and British Museum reading rooms is immeasurable. Now erstwhile research libraries are emptying of books and users and turning into something else. We are threatened with cultural destitution. It was once confidently remarked that if all of the buildings at Harvard—except the Widener Library—were destroyed, Harvard would still be Harvard. But the Widener is presently depopulated, although the Houghton Library still draws researchers because there are kinds of research that require the authority of the real thing. Consulting scanned manuscripts on the screen is like kissing through a screen door; furthermore, the trustworthiness of the scanned image depends on the scanning and the scanner. You don't know whether you have examined the complete document on screen until you have verified it against the real thing. A convenience is just that: a substitute. A "virtual library" is not a library; neither is a "universal library."

The databases are eroding the concept of learning for its own sake. College and university libraries are becoming libraries without reference books—as well as libraries without researchers. As library purchase orders for reference books steadily diminish and their prices rise to compensate for reduced sales, publishing for libraries is becoming a self-indulgent activity. Certain reference books will survive, at least temporarily, by being simultaneously printed and digitized. But many, probably most, of what have been regarded as "standard reference books" will vanish from the shelves. Database users talk about "hits"; reference books require and reward more extended use. There is probably something wrong with someone who checks a date, a name, or a title and then closes the reference book. The organization, design, and layout of a reference book are functional. Reference books have the reputation for being typographically dull. Now that they are in danger of superannuation there is a life-and-death need for them to be redesigned to enhance their functionality. But they will still be books.

The research libraries will survive as long as students come in to use them as libraries because their teachers have assigned book projects. Many university teachers would have trouble finding the library. They are at least as culpable as librarians for the emptying of libraries: empty of books and empty of students using books. Library administrators embrace opportunities to convert book space to bookless space. At the Thomas Cooper Library the Student Success Center has replaced the Z stacks: many of the books about books, the bibliographies, and the publishing histories have been transferred to offsite storage. It doesn't matter how fast these books can be delivered to the library: they cannot be seen and handled by students where they are stored. Double-think librarians claim that providing students and researchers with out-of-library resources is a great improvement in library service.

Reference books are not perishing alone. All forms of print on paper are endangered. The National Endowment for the Arts 2007 report, *To Read or Not to Read,* is a grim document, revealing that America is becoming a nation of non-readers. NEA Chairman Dana Gioia concludes, "Whatever the benefits of newer electronic media, they provide no measurable substitute for the intellectual and personal development initiated and sustained by frequent reading."

I grieve for the whilom libraries that have abandoned their historic function of print preservation. The administrators have eagerly—even gleefully—capitulated to the powers of ignorance and illiteracy. Nelson Baker's *Double Fold* has documented that librarians have been assiduous print and book destroyers. Now they are happily converting their de-booked libraries into Starbucks clones and internet cafes while boasting about the resulting increased traffic of patrons playing video games, watching telly, and engaging in self-inflicted online brain damage.

Libraries are as good as their books. Without a plenitude of books—especially reference books—it isn't a library.

AFTERWORDS: The meeting of librarians for which this paper was prepared included sessions on "weeding collections." Books are not weeds.

Part 6

On Other Writers

"Literature belongs to the people who read it—most of whom reside off campus. Indeed, literature is too important to be left entirely in the hands of professors and critics."

"We have never had so many great writers that we can discard one because his aims and standards are unfashionable."

M.J.B., foreword, *The O'Hara Concern:
A Biography of John O'Hara* (1975).

"The Light of the World"

Stan Ketchel as "My Sweet Christ"

In his preface to *The Fifth Column and the First Forty-nine Stories* (1938) Ernest Hemingway indicates that "The Light of the World" has been undervalued: "Reading them over, the ones I liked the best . . . and a story called 'The Light of the World' which nobody else ever liked."[1] As late as 1955 he was still concerned about "The Light of the World," according to A. E. Hotchner:

> Ernest cautioned me that the story was not as simple as it looked. He told me to think of it as a love letter to a whore named Alice who tipped the scales at 210. He said it was a story of illusion; that no one can really distinguish between how one was at a particular time in the past and how one is at the moment.[2]

Hemingway was right: the story is first-class Hemingway and merits more respect than it has received. The reason why it has been underrated and generally misunderstood is that the meaning of the story depends on the irony of Stan Ketchel as a Christ figure; but few readers know enough about Ketchel (or Ketchell) to work out the meanings of the story.[3]

Stan Ketchel, "The Michigan assassin," was the flamboyant middleweight champion between 1908 and 1910, when he was murdered. Born Stanislaus Kiecal (possibly Kaical or Klecal) in Grand Rapids, Michigan, in 1886 or 1887, Ketchel had his first recorded professional fight was in 1903 at age sixteen or seventeen—by which time he had been a hobo and a bouncer in the mining camps of Montana. Between 1903 and 1910 he fought sixty-three bouts, winning forty-four by knock-outs. Ketchel won the title in 1908, lost it the same year to Billy Papke, and regained it the same year. His most famous bout came in 1909 when he fought Jack Johnson, the Negro heavyweight champion, in California

---

"'The Light of the World:' Stan Ketchel as 'My Sweet Christ'" was published originally in the *Fitzgerald/Hemingway Annual 1969*, pp. 125–130. Reprinted with permission of the NCR Corporation. Bruccoli's "Stan Ketchel and Steve Ketchel: A Further Note on 'The Light of the World'" was published in the *Fitzgerald/Hemingway Annual 1975*, pp. 325–326.

amid considerable White Hope feeling. This fight became the source of legends and myths, some of them created by Ketchel's eccentric manager, Wilson Mizner. It is clear that Ketchel was heavily outweighed; his normal fighting weight was around 155, and Johnson was a 200-pounder. It has been alleged that the scales were rigged to reduce the official weight difference. *Nat Fleischer's The Ring Record Book and Boxing Encyclopedia* gives 170¼ vs. 205½.[4] Ketchel was knocked out in the twelfth after having floored Johnson in the same round. The generally accepted account is that there was an agreement between Ketchel and Johnson that they would put on an exhibition—even though the fight was billed as a title-bout—and that Ketchel tried to double-cross Johnson by knocking him out in the twelfth. Mizner claimed that the whole thing, including the two knock-downs in the twelfth, was fixed. Another version is that there was an agreement to coast the first ten rounds for the benefit of the movie cameras, after which the real fight would begin. Johnson—a notoriously unreliable man—reportedly told Dumb Dan Morgan, a boxing figure, that Ketchel did in fact knock him down. Since Johnson was also a notoriously vain man, his admission that Ketchel knocked him down is difficult to dismiss. All accounts, then, except Mizner's, agree that Ketchel—who was a savage puncher—actually did knock down Johnson, who outweighed him by thirty to fifty pounds and who is considered the greatest defensive boxer in the heavyweight division.[5] A high-liver and big-spender, Ketchel—who may have included opium among his dissipations—was burned out by 1910, when he was twenty-three or twenty-four, and went to a farm near Conway, Missouri, to recover his vigor. There he was shot by a farmhand named Walter Hurtz whom he rebuked for beating a horse. Goldie Smith, a servant on the farm, claimed that she was Hurtz's wife and that Hurtz was defending her honor; and it was generally accepted that the quarrel was over Goldie. Hurtz was really named Walter Dipley and was not married to Goldie under any name. They were tried as accomplices in a scheme to rob Ketchel and were both given long sentences.[6]

In addition to punching power and ring courage, Ketchel had a heroic appetite for women. He had a reputation for being extremely sentimental as well as having a passion for literature. Jim Tully, the hobo writer, is supposed to have called Ketchel the best-read man he ever knew—which takes in considerable territory, since Tully also knew H. L. Mencken.[7]

The title phrase, "The Light of the World," occurs twice in the New Testament. In the Sermon on the Mount (Matthew 5:14) Christ addresses the believers as "the light of the world"; but the reference Hemingway probably had in mind is the episode of the woman taken in adultery (John 8:2–12): "I am the light of the world; he that followeth me shall not walk in darkness, but shall have the light of life." Carlos Baker suggests that the title is derived from Holman Hunt's painting, "I Am the Light of the World." A copy of this painting was in a scrapbook Hemingway's mother made for him.[8]

In "The Light of the World" two whores claim Ketchel as their savior, the light of their world which at the time includes a hostile bartender, a homosexual, Indians, a nasty lumberjack, five whores, and two boys of seventeen and nineteen who are passing through. That Ketchel was in no way a Christ figure is revealed by the facts of his life, but the problem is that he might have been a savior to the whores. Any reading of this story depends on which of four options the reader takes: neither whore slept with Ketchel; both did; Peroxide did; Alice did. My reading is based on the interpretation that Alice is telling the truth and that she was somehow enlightened by knowing him.

Ketchel's name is first mentioned by the "shy man" who says, "Cadillac is where Steve Ketchel came from and where Ad Wolgast is from." The statement is half right. Ad Wolgast—lightweight champion from 1910 to 1912 and almost certainly the model for Ad Francis in "The Battler"—was born in Cadillac; but Ketchel was born in Grand Rapids. The blond whore whom the narrator calls Peroxide immediately states that Ketchel was shot by his father: "Yes, by Christ, his own father." This is false, and so the connection between the deaths of Christ and Ketchel is false; nevertheless, nobody contradicts her, even though the facts about Hurtz-Dipley were well known. The only challenge to Peroxide's statement comes from the homosexual cook who asks if Ketchel's first name wasn't Stan, not Steve. This is a difficult point: although Stanislaus Kiecal fought as Stan Ketchel, he seems to have preferred being addressed as Steve. Instead of showing that neither whore knew Ketchel, the Steve references could indicate at least one of them is pretending to a false intimacy with him. Peroxide continues to boast of her intimacy with Ketchel: "I loved him like you love God. . . . Oh, my God, what a man he was. . . . I hope to God they don't have fighters like that now. He was like a god. . . . My soul belongs to Steve Ketchel." This is the free-wheeling speech of a whore, but it is clear that Ketchel is being deified. Along with these remarks she states that Johnson, "that black son of bitch from hell," knocked out Ketchel with a surprise punch when Ketchel turned to look at her—which does not accord with any account of the fight. If anyone threw a surprise punch, it was Ketchel. Peroxide's story is weakest here, for she has to contradict herself and explain that she went to the coast "just for that fight."

Alice, the 350-pound whore with the nice voice, then calls Peroxide a liar, saying that Peroxide never knew Ketchel, but that she did, and that he said to her,

"You're a lovely piece, Alice." This is true, "to Jesus and Mary true," says Alice crying. They match insults, with Alice getting the better of it as she says in her "sweet lovely voice" that Peroxide has had venereal disease whereas she is clean.

At this point the narrator is becoming interested in the logistics of sleeping with Alice, and his friend takes him out *to walk in darkness*—away from whatever light there is in the railway station.[9]

Although Alice fails to prove that she did know Ketchel, she is clearly more convincing than Peroxide. She avoids Peroxide's clichés and "stagey" speech—"my true, wonderful memories." Alice's emotion seems honest as she is moved to tears, and her voice is sincere. If we believe Alice—as I submit we must—then we have a story about a waste land partially redeemed by a false savior. As Tom asks, "What the hell kind of a place is this?" The distance between Stan Ketchel and Jesus Christ is absurd; nevertheless, for Alice-in-waste-land who believed in Ketchel there is some light. Significantly, her first words in the story are, "Oh, my Christ. . . . Oh, my sweet Christ." For Peroxide there is no light, for she falsifies her belief in the Ketchel-savior.

The total meaning of "The Light of the World" depends on the narrator's response to this exposure to corruption and partial salvation. Although he is not named, the narrator here undergoes the same initiation as Nick Adams in "The Battler" (1924) or "The Killers" (1927). He encounters a form of evil and leaves, presumably to analyze the experience later. But "The Light of the World" departs from the Nick stories in that here the boy–young man is attracted to Alice, who is both lost and saved through her faith in Ketchel. Nonetheless, her savior will not work for the narrator. "Tom saw me looking at her and he said, 'Come on. Let's go.'"

Notes

1. Hemingway wanted to place "The Light of the World" first in *Winner Take Nothing* (New York: Scribners, 1933) but was dissuaded by Maxwell Perkins. Hemingway compared the story with one of his favorite works, Maupassant's "La Maison Tellier." Since these stories have little in common apart from whores, it must be assumed that Hemingway's comparison indicated his respect for the merits of "The Light of the World"—see Carlos Baker, *Hemingway: The Writer as Artist* (Princeton: Princeton University Press, 1963), p. 140.

2. Sleeve of *Ernest Hemingway Reading* (Caedmon TC 1185; 1965). One band on this record, "Saturday Night at the Whorehouse in Billings, Montana," gives Hemingway's experiences with the real 258-pound Alice; but since he also recounts his impossible experiences with Mata Hari, these collections must be dismissed as a joke. It is to be noted that Alice's weight fluctuates in these reports.

3. Baker sees the story as humorous. Philip Young in *Ernest Hemingway: A Reconsideration* (University Park: Pennsylvania State University Press, 1966) correctly sees it as an initiation story. William Bysshe Stein ("Love and Lust in Hemingway's Stories," *Texas Studies in Literature and Language* [Summer 1961]) reads the story as presenting a travesty of Christian love which damns the narrator. The best readings are Joseph DeFalco's (*The Hero in Hemingway's Stories* [Pittsburgh: University of Pittsburgh Press, 1963]) and Sheridan Baker's (*Ernest Hemingway* [New York: Holt, Rinehart and Winston, 1967]) which see Ketchel as Christ-substitute. But no critic has conflated the facts of Ketchel's career with what is said about him in the story.

4. New York: Ring, 1953. My thanks to Mr. Fleischer for answering questions.

5. Alvah Johnson in *The Legendary Mizners* (New York: Farrar, Straus and Young, 1952) discusses these theories about the Ketchel-Johnson fight and has considerable information about Ketchel.

6. *New York Times* (16 October 1910): 1

7. Alexander Johnston, *Ten—And Out!* (New York: Ives Washburn, 3rd revised edition, 1947).

8. Baker, *Ernest Hemingway: A Life Story* (New York: Scribners, 1969), p. 606.

9. There are interesting connections between "The Light of the World" and "A Clean, Well-Lighted Place." The stories were written at roughly the same time and were coupled in *Winner Take Nothing* and *The Fifth Column and the First Forty-nine Stories* (New York: Scribners, 1938). In both, artificial illumination is contrasted with spiritual light, and it might be said that "The Light of the World" presents a dirty, partly-lighted place. See Daniel Barnes, "Ritual and Parody in 'A Clean Well-Lighted Place'" (*Cithara* [May 1966]) and Nicholas Cannady, Jr., "Is There Any Light in Hemingway's 'The Light of the World'?" (*Studies in Short Fiction* [Fall 1965]).

Thomas Wolfe's
"The Four Lost Men"

Commencing in 1929 the House of Scribner published Thomas Wolfe in untrustworthy texts, which have been perpetuated in uncorrected reprints and inaccurate resettings. Critical editions of his work are necessary, starting with the short stories and long stories. We don't know what or even whom we are reading when we read a Wolfe story now. Francis Skipp's edition of *The Complete Short Stories of Thomas Wolfe* (New York: Scribners, 1987) lacks editorial or textual notes. The editorial history of the published stories is unusually obscure because the textual evidence is incomplete. There is an abundance of manuscript and typescript in the Wisdom Collection at the Houghton Library but almost no proofs of stories.[1] Wolfe was not a painstaking proofreader—when he bothered with proofs. Moreover, it is probable that the Scribners editors were reluctant to run the risk of having him rewrite his stories in proof.

The familiar criticism of Thomas Wolfe is that he was deficient in sense of form: that his novels and stories are loosely organized or even unstructured and include unnecessary material. The terms "self-indulgent" and "undisciplined" have been freely applied to his published work. This influential charge interferes with the proper evaluation and understanding of his work. At its most pernicious, it provides an alibi for the failure to publish trustworthy Wolfe texts.

Wolfe's short stories and long stories that were published during his lifetime were routinely edited and pruned by somebody else to meet the space requirements of magazines. A twenty-thousand- to thirty-thousand-word Wolfe manuscript would be published in a five-thousand-word version. Wolfe did not always bother to vet these truncations. The surviving story manuscripts and typescripts permit scholars to recover Wolfe's intentions for these lost works: lost because they were not published as he wrote them. . . .[2]

This essay was published originally as the introduction to *The Four Lost Men: The Previously Unpublished Long Version, Including the Original Short Story,* edited by Arlyn and Matthew J. Bruccoli (Columbia: University of South Carolina Press, 2008), pp. ix–xxi. The introduction was written by M.J.B. Reprinted with the permission of the University of South Carolina Press.

Wolfe's long stories have been misleadingly categorized as novelettes or short novels; such labeling legitimizes criticism of their structure. The long twenty-thousand- to thirty-thousand-word narratives were usually written as pieces of a vast gestating multivolume work and were not intended by Wolfe for separate magazine publication. Sometimes they started as short stories and outgrew the commercial form. Maxwell Perkins salvaged material from Wolfe's stockpile of manuscripts for publication in *Scribner's Magazine*—as with "A Portrait of Bascom Hawke" and "The Four Lost Men."

Perkins referred to Wolfe's "dithyrambs"—alluding to the early Greek narrative choral odes for the worship of Dionysus, god of wine and intoxication. This joke makes the point that much of Wolfe's writing is rhetorically expansive—inspired by his excitement with language.

F. Scott Fitzgerald got it right and wrong. He wrote Perkins about *Look Homeward, Angel* in 1930: "John Bishop told me he [Wolfe] needed advice about cutting ect, but after reading this book I thought that was nonsense. He strikes me as a man who should be let alone as to length, if he has to be published in five volumes.[3] Right. But in 1937 Fitzgerald started an argument with Wolfe about "leaver-outers" and "putter-inners" by urging him to emulate "the novel of selected incidents." Wolfe responded to this bad advice:

> . . . your argument is simply based upon one <u>way</u>, upon one method instead of another. And have you ever noticed how often it turns out that what a man is really doing is simply rationalizing his own way of doing something, the way he has to do it, the way given him by his talent and his nature into the only inevitable and right way of doing everything—a sort of classic and eternal art form handed down by Apollo from Olympus without which and beyond which there is nothing?[4]

Wolfe's Story Publications, 1932–1935

There is no record of Wolfe trying to publish stories before 1932. "The Angel on the Porch"—which was not written as a story—was plucked by Perkins from *Look Homeward, Angel* and published in *Scribner's Magazine* (August 1929). Wolfe's next story publication, "A Portrait of Bascom Hawke," in the April 1932 *Scribner's*, was not written as a stand-alone story. Perkins removed it from the manuscripts for *Of Time and the River* and entered it in the *Scribner's* short-novel prize contest; it was the co-winner with John Hermann's "The Long Short Trip." "The Web of Earth" was also published by *Scribner's* in 1932. When Wolfe needed money in 1933, he tried to write sellable magazine stories. Elizabeth Nowell, who became his story agent-editor that year, stated, "Wolfe had no idea of what constituted a salable short story. With the exception of 'The Web of Earth,' his stories had been picked out of his vast mass of manuscript by Perkins, accepted in rough draft by *Scribner's Magazine,* then reworked (and lengthened in the process) by Wolfe, and finally cut and edited by Alfred Dashiell."5 "The Four Lost Men" did not undergo this prepublication process.

Little is known about Wolfe's working relationship with Dashiell, editor of *Scribner's.* Few pieces of their editorial correspondence survive. But there is an important letter to Dashiell about the magazine text of "The Four Lost Men":

Dear Fritz: I'm sorry for the delay but here are the proofs of The Four Lost Men—all I've been able to do to it. I've worked all day on it, but I can't make my head work well today—its' worn out and won't work for me—I feel as if I'm taking a big chance with this and have never felt so uncertain about a mss. But I can't do any more now; so will send it on.

I would appreciate it if you or Miss Buckles did this for me: on galley 2 towards bottom where father says "The first vote I ever cast for President. . . . I cast in 1872 for . . . . . U.S. Grant"—will you please verify all these dates for me? I think I am right about them, but I want the year and the Candidate to be right—in each case the vote should be for the Republican candidate of that year.

Again, Max asked me to cut out references to whores and brothels in reference to Our Presidents, etc. But I notice on galley seven a direct referent "—did they not carry . . . . . Garfield, Arthur, Harrison and Hayes . . . . . the intolerable burden of their savage hunger into the kept and carnal nakedness of whores"6

If you want to keep this as is, its O.K. with me, but I think you will find that I cut it out of the mss. and wrote a new phrase. If you want to see that, look at mss. again. Please look over such corrections as I have made to see if you approve—if not restore to original. I'm awfully sorry to be so late and not to have done more—I'm tired, but my head is too tired to work for me. Be sure to see that the type-written insertion goes in where indicated on Galley 4—
Yours with thanks,
Tom Wolfe7

Nowell explains:

> There was also the constant difficulty of too great length: Wolfe never wrote a story under the usual limit of five thousand words in his entire life, with the exception of the brief episodes which were lifted virtually untouched from his books, such as "The Sun and the Rain" and "The Far and the Near." His stories naturally came out somewhere between ten and thirty thousand words.8

Nowell did not place "The Four Lost Men." She probably began marketing Wolfe's stories with "Boom Town." That is, making them marketable by cutting and editing them. Twenty-two Wolfe stories were published in magazines during 1932–35. Fourteen were collected in *From Death to Morning*. Perhaps all were excerpted from novels in progress; ten also appear in novels.

Composition and Publication of "The Four Lost Men"

"The Four Lost Men" grew out of Wolfe's research for the character Joe Barrett or Lindau, based on Aline Bernstein's father, actor Joseph Frankau, for *The Good Child's River*. Wolfe consulted the *Encyclopædia Britannica* for the background on 1881, the year of her birth, which was the year of President Garfield's murder. Wolfe's pocket notebook for September-December 1931 includes biographical data on Garfield, Arthur, Hayes, and Harrison. This material probably triggered Wolfe's memory of his father's political declamations, which inspired "The Four Lost Men."

Like W. O. Gant, W. O. Wolfe was born in Pennsylvania and claimed a role in the Battle of Gettysburg. He came south in his young manhood. His loyalty to the Republican Party and his denunciation of the Democrats may have been inspired by his sense of being an outsider in the Reconstruction South and by the satisfaction he took in opposing the local Democratic establishment. Hayes, Garfield, and Harrison failed to carry North Carolina.

> Garfield, Jas. Abram (1831–1881)
> B. Log cabin frontier town, Orange, Cuyahoga County, Ohio.
> Walks across country to Cleveland aet. 16—works on lake schooner for canal boatmant.
> Works way through school as teacher, carpenter, farmer—studies at West. Reserve Eclectic Inst. At Hiram—Goes to Williams—returns to Hiram as principal, enters political life, anti-slavery man—enlists—lt. colonel—then, Brigadier—then maj. Gen'l—gallantry at Shiloh and Chickamauga.
> Year 1874—one of trouble—Reconstruction, Credit Mobilier, Salary Grab, Greenback issue.
> On July 2, 1881 on way to Wms. College commencement shot in Wash. Rwy. Station by Guiteau.

> Arthur, Chester Alan (1830–1886).
> B. Fairfield, Vt.—Oct. 5, 1830—son of Irishman who came to Vt. From Canada.
> Enters Union College in 1848 as Soph.—1853 enters law office NY City.

Known as defender of glaring negro cases—1855 gets decision that negroes entitled to ride as whites on st. r'ways.

Quartermaster Gen'l of N.Y. state troops in War—1862 resumes practice—1871 appointed collector of customs for port of NY by Pres. Grant—Office noted for abuse of "spoils systems"—Gen. Arthur makes no reforms.

In 1877 Hayes tries to oust him—In 1878 he is removed—Becomes V. Pres. And Pres. On death of Garfield.

In spite of public fear makes honest pres.—vetoes spoils appropriation of 18 mills. For bigger over little states (1881).

North Pacific, South Pac., Asch Top. And St. Fe completed in his admin. Wash. Monument—Feb. 21, 1885, dies 1886.

Hayes (1822–1893)

B. In Delaware, Ohio Oct 4, 1822.

Goes to Harvard Law School practices in Cincinnati—enlists—becomes brig. & maj. Gen'l.

Goes to Congress—in 1868 becomes gov. of Ohio—to 1872. In 1875 again elected. 1876 becomes cand. for pres. Against Tilden. Hayes declared elected 8 to 7 by commission.

Policy of pacification in South—Ends carpetbag govts. Withdraws troops. Attempts civil service reforms, able and honest.

Harrison, Benj. (1833–1901)

B. North Bend near Cincinnati, Ohio—log school house—Miami University—studies law in law office—aet. 21 goes to Indianapolis, soon leading lawyer.

Enlists in Civil War, breveted brig. gen'l.

Then resumes legal profession—elected U.S. Senator 1881—nominated for pres. 1888—defeats Grov. Cleveland.

Passage of McKinley Tariff Bill and Sherman Silver Bill of 1890—

Suppression of Louisiana Lottery—enlargement of navy—civil service reform—arbitration of Bering Sea fur trade with Britain.

Revival of trade—defeated by Cleve. 1892 because of strikes—labor unions against Tariff party.[9]

Hayes, Garfield, Arthur, and Harrison were the four Republican presidents who followed Grant during the Reconstruction and post-Reconstruction periods. (Democrat Grover Cleveland served terms before and after Harrison.) All were Civil War generals—the last ones to serve as presidents. All were self-made men. Garfield was the last president born in a log cabin. Benjamin Harrison was the grandson of President William Henry Harrison, but his family was not affluent. All were Ohio-bred, although Harrison achieved his success in Indiana. All were presidents whose terms were not marked by egregious scandals—apart from the disputed Hayes-Tilden election. None was a great or distinguished president.

Given Wolfe's customary use of character sources in his fiction, it is to be expected that he drew on actual boarders for Mr. Helm. The Old Kentucky Home guest register for 1907 is signed by Mrs. and Mr. Philip Helm of New Orleans. Philip Leopold Helm (d. 1938) was a letter carrier. He had no connections with a New Orleans bank, and it is not known whether he spoke with a German accent. The guest register for 1906 includes an entry for "Mrs Mr. Moses New Orleans." In 1906 Elkin Moses was cashier at the Equitable Life Assurance Society in the Hibernia Bank Building. Nothing further is known about his business life. (This register page has the smeared ink signature "Tom W" at the bottom. Wolfe was not yet six years old.) Mr. Helm of "The Four Lost Men" is possibly an amalgam of Philip Helm and Elkin Moses. Or Wolfe may have combined Helm and Moses with an invented character.

The manuscript evidence . . .[10] establishes that Wolfe wrote a short version of "The Four Lost Men." He then enlarged it to twenty-one thousand words; but he used the original, shorter version for the *Scribner's Magazine* short story. The setting copy and proofs are not extant. Wolfe acceded to Perkins's request that the reference to the presidents as brothel frequenters be deleted for magazine publication. Consequently, in both *Scribner's* and *From Death to Morning* they do a great deal of anticipatory waiting outside houses, but the reader is not told what they are waiting for.

Two characters in the long version, Helms and McKeithan, are missing in the magazine and book texts. The previously unpublished version includes the story line for Helms's ruin resulting from the New Orleans bank failure. There is no evidence that Wolfe wrote any of the manuscript material more than once: no rewriting, copying, or cutting on the manuscript pages. Presumably Wolfe developed the long version from the short one, adding material about the boarders and W. O. Gant's death because he intended to incorporate it into "The Hills Beyond Pentland," eventually abandoned. As published in *Scribner's*, "The Four Lost Men" is much as Wolfe originally wrote it. Forty-seven pages (6–35 and most of 37–54) of the total seventy-two were added to expand the story for the unpublished "Hills Beyond Pentland"; but after page 54, except for bowdlerization (two pages' worth), the addition of one page, and reordering of a few paragraphs, the *Scribner's* story is close to the long typescript.

"The Four Lost Men" typescript has two cover pages. One identifies it as part of "The Hound of Darkness," Wolfe's unfinished saga of nighttime America.

"The Hound of Darkness" became the prologue for "The Hills Beyond Pentland," the fictionalized history of Wolfe's mother's people he worked on during 1932–1933.[11] The other cover page alters the title from "The War in April" to "The Four Lost Men." Wolfe's 8 February 1934 report on the work accomplished during his Guggenheim Fellowship year describes the 1933 *Scribner's* magazine stories:

> There is one final thing about these pieces and their relation to the book. All of them, with the exception of The Four Lost Men, belong to the first book of a series, that is to the manuscript which Mr. Perkins now has, which will probably be called Time and the River, and which will be published this year. The Four Lost Men belongs to a second book of a series which will be called The Hills Beyond Pentland, of which I now have about 200,000 words in typed manuscript.[12]

When "The Four Lost Men" appeared in the February 1934 *Scribner's*, Wolfe wrote to Robert Raynolds: "I am glad you liked the last piece in *Scribner's*. Perkins liked it, too, and says the time will come when every one will know what it's about, which seems plain enough to me now, but I think some people may be puzzled by it now."[13]

The stories in *From Death to Morning* were selected by Perkins for publication in *Scribner's* to support Wolfe between *Look Homeward, Angel* and *Of Time and the River*. Publishers were not generous with advances during the Thirties. While Wolfe was in Europe during March through July 1935, Perkins assembled *From Death to Morning* and apparently had it set in galleys. Wolfe, who was brooding about what he regarded as Perkins's high-handed editorial interference with *Of Time and the River*, was concerned that the collection would be published without his final approval.

> Finally, you must not put the manuscript of a book of stories in final form until after my return to New York. If that means the book of stories will have to be deferred till next spring, then they will have to be deferred, but I will not consent this time to allow the book to be taken away from me and printed and published [referring to the publication of *Of Time and the River*] until I myself have had time to look at the proofs, and at any rate to talk to you about certain revisions, changes, excisions, or additions that ought to be made. I really mean this, Max.[14]

Some thirteen hundred words were cut from "The Four Lost Men" between *Scribner's* and *From Death to Morning*, all the substantial cuts occurring in the last third of the story. Only a few words were added—which was unusual for Wolfe. . . .[15]

The timing for production and publication of *From Death to Morning* was very tight. Wolfe was in New York between 4 and 27 July 1935, while he was writing his speech for the Colorado Writers' Conference, published as *The Story of a Novel* in 1936. He returned to New York from the West during the last week of September, when proofs for the story volume were ready. Wolfe's marked *From Death to Morning* galleys do not survive, but he was never a painstaking proofer. He worked on the book proofs with Scribners editor John Hall Wheelock, who had handled the proofing for *Look Homeward, Angel* and *Of Time and the River*. On 18 October Wheelock reported to Wolfe, "All the proofs of 'From Death to Morning' are in the printer's hands. . . . If there are any corrections you wish to make, they can be made in page proof, which I hope to have to-morrow."[16] Copies of the book were ready by 29 October 1935, the day Wolfe inscribed one for Aline Bernstein.

From Death to Morning, the only collection of Wolfe's stories published during his lifetime, was on sale 14 November 1935. The seventy-five hundred copies of the first printing sold out; it was reprinted in 1935, and copies were remaindered. William Heinemann published a London edition in 1936.[17]

Scribners didn't know how to promote Wolfe's first collection of stories. The prepublication catalogue copy emphasized their humor and revealed that "The Four Lost Men" "is based on a memory." True enough. It is about time and memory: Wolfe's memory, the narrator's memory, his father's memory, and American memory. Referring to the narrator's father, the typescript employs the phrase "sorrow of irrecoverable memory,"[18] followed by "sorrowful time and memory," "sorrow of time and memory," and "sorrowful acceptance of time and memory." The jacket flap copy calls attention to "some of the five and six page stories which for economy and precision of style are unsurpassed." The reviews of the collection were unenthusiastic—except for those by Wolfe's friends Hamilton Basso in the *New Republic* ("gains its chief distinction from those pages of dithyrambic declamation")[19] and Clayton Hoagland in the *New York Sun* ("a sustained flight of lyricism").[20] In a mixed *New York Herald Tribune Books* notice that reviewed Wolfe's height as well as his stories, Ferner Nuhn cited "The Four Lost Men" as "most original in conception."[21] Wolfe reacted to Nuhn in the inscription for the copy of *From Death to Morning* he presented to Henry Volkening, a former New York University colleague:

> I'm a little sad as I write you this. I've just read the first review of this book—in next Saturday's Herald-Tribune—which pans it and sees little in it except a man six foot six creating monstrous figures in a world of five feet eight.—I do not think this is true, but now I have a hunch the well known "reaction" has

set in against me, and that I will take a pounding in the book.—Well, I am writing you this because I believe that as good writing as I have ever done is in this book—and because my faith has always been that a good thing is indestructible and that if there is good here—as I hope and believe there is—it will somehow survive.—This is a faith I want to have, and that I think we need in life—and that is why I am writing you this—not in defense against attacks I may receive—but just to put this on record *in advance* with you, who are a friend of mine.—So won't you put this away—what I have written—and keep it—and if someday it turns out I am right—won't you take it out and read it to me?

Yours—

Tom[22]

Howard Mumford Jones (the *Saturday Review of Literature*) and R. P. Blackmur (*Southern Review*) denounced the formlessness of the stories. Jones: "violates the simplest principles of construction. 'The Four Lost Men,' for example, begins as a prose rhapsody about a young man in wartime, continues as a realistic transcript of the elder Gant's conversation regarding presidential elections, and concludes as a Wolfian prose poem about life, death, war, and time."[23] Blackmur: "Form, we might say, is the only sanity—the only principle of balanced response—possible to art."[24]

The London *Times Literary Supplement* unsigned review of the British edition got it right:

> There is, at his best, something of incantation in his descriptive, exhortatory passages, recreating not only sights and smells but a whole emotional attitude to all that he has known and felt in teeming, seething American living and in his own being.
>
> No one story in this collection is so characteristic as "The Four Lost Men," in which recalling his father's words about four figures of the past, he identifies himself with them:

> *Had they not, as we, then turned their eyes up and seen the huge starred visage of the night, the immense and lilac darkness of America in April? Had they not heard the sudden, shrill, and piping whistle of a departing engine? Had they not waited, thinking, feeling, seeing the immense mysterious continent of night, the wild and lyric earth, so casual, sweet, and strange familiar, in all its space and savagery and terror, its mystery and joy, its limitless sweep and rudeness, its delicate and savage fecundity? Had they not the visions of the plains, the mountains, and the rivers flowing in the darkness, the huge pattern of the everlasting earth and the all-engulfing wilderness of America?*

Admittedly such writing must either succeed or fail completely. It is either magnificent or nonsense. In our view it is often the one; the depth of feeling behind saves it from ever becoming the other.[25]

Literary crimes are collaborations. The proper recognition of Thomas Wolfe's genius and the correct judgment of his work continue to be impeded by the circumstances of his publication. This statement applies to most of his long or short stories. The blame for the bad published texts of Wolfe adheres to him because he was not a painstaking reviser-polisher and proofer. Indeed, study of his work in progress indicates that Wolfe was more concerned with getting it all down than with publication. But blame attaches to the editors and publishers who did not serve him well. The proofreading standards at 597 Fifth Avenue were relaxed. Probably the task was impossible to perform properly while Wolfe was alive and writing. Since then Wolfe scholars have given scant attention to his texts. Most of his published work—lifetime and posthumous—exists in unreliable or suspicious editions.

Notes

1. The only marked story galley proof I have seen is for "The Web of Earth"—which is heavily edited in an unidentified nonauthorial hand.

2. The ellipses replace a description of *The Four Lost Men: The Previously Unpublished Long Version*, edited by Arlyn and Matthew J. Bruccoli. It is described as not an "ideal text" but as "a lightly emended version of the long typescript that Wolfe developed from the short typescript intended for inclusion in a planned book, never completed, 'The Hills Beyond Pentland.'" Ed.

3. F. Scott Fitzgerald to Maxwell Perkins, 1 September 1930. *The Sons of Maxwell Perkins: Letters of F. Scott Fitzgerald, Ernest Hemingway, Thomas Wolfe, and Their Editor*, edited by Matthew J. Bruccoli with Judith S. Baughman (Columbia: University of South Carolina Press, 2004), p. 120.

4. Ibid., p. 257.

5. Elizabeth Nowell, *Thomas Wolfe: A Biography* (Garden City, N.Y.: Doubleday, 1960), p. 223.

6. See *Scribner's Magazine* (February 1934): 108: "the intolerable burden of all the pain, joy, hope, and savage hunger that a man can suffer, that the world can know?"

7. Wolfe to Alfred Dashiell, late 1933. *To Loot My Life Clean: The Thomas Wolfe-Maxwell Perkins Correspondence*, edited by Matthew J. Bruccoli and Park Bucker (Columbia: University of South Carolina Press, 2000), p. 123.

8. *Thomas Wolfe: A Biography*, p. 233.

9. *The Notebooks of Thomas Wolfe*, edited by Richard S. Kennedy and Paschal Reeves (Chapel Hill: University of North Carolina Press, 1970), volume 2, pp. 563–565.

10. The ellipses replace a reference to the "The Manuscripts and Typescripts" chapter in *The Four Lost Men*, edited by Bruccoli and Bruccoli, pp. 55–60. After having examined the archive of Thomas Wolfe papers at the Houghton Library at Harvard University that

"includes nearly 800 pages of manuscript (holograph) and 240 of typescript (or carbon copy) identified or recognizable in the catalogue notations as the short story or novelette 'The Four Lost Men,'" Arlyn Bruccoli demonstrates that Wolfe wrote a short version of "The Four Lost Men" for *Scribner's Magazine* prior to the expanded version edited by the Bruccolis and published in 2008. Ed.

11. This work was not the same as *The Hills Beyond*—the volume of short pieces assembled by Edward Aswell in 1941.

12. Wolfe to Henry Allen Moe, 8 February 1934. *To Loot My Life Clean*, p. 120.

13. Wolfe to Robert Raynolds, 2 February 1934. *The Letters of Thomas Wolfe*, edited by Elizabeth Nowell (New York: Scribners, 1956), p. 405.

14. Wolfe to Maxwell Perkins, 12 August 1935. *To Loot My Life Clean*, p. 172.

15. The ellipses replace a cross-reference to "The Four Lost Men: Substantive Variants between Previously Published Versions." Ed.

16. Wolfe to John Hall Wheelock, 18 October 1935. *To Loot My Life Clean*, p. 184.

17. Carol Johnston, *Thomas Wolfe: A Descriptive Bibliography* (Pittsburgh: University of Pittsburgh Press, 1987), pp. 49–59.

18. Page- and line-number references to the Bruccolis' *Four Lost Men* text are omitted here. Ed.

19. Hamilton Basso, review of *From Death to Morning*, by Thomas Wolfe, *New Republic* (1 January 1936): 232.

20. Clayton Hoagland, review of *From Death to Morning*, by Thomas Wolfe, *New York Sun* (14 November 1935): 26.

21. Ferner Nuhn, review of *From Death to Morning*, by Thomas Wolfe, *New York Herald Tribune Books* (17 November 1935): 7.

22. Henry Volkening, "Tom Wolfe: Penance No More," *Virginia Quarterly Review* (Spring 1939): 215. See *Thomas Wolfe's Friendship with Henry Volkening*, edited by Arlyn Bruccoli and Matthew J. Bruccoli ([Akron, Ohio]: Thomas Wolfe Society, 2005).

23. Howard Mumford Jones, review of *From Death to Morning*, by Thomas Wolfe, *Saturday Review of Literature* (30 November 1935): 13.

24. R. P. Blackmur, review of *From Death to Morning*, by Thomas Wolfe, *Southern Review* (Spring 1936): 897–899.

25. "American Incantation," unsigned review of *From Death to Morning*, by Thomas Wolfe, *Times Literary Supplement* (21 March 1936): 241.

Out of Life

John O'Hara's Character Creation

Sometime before 6:45 P.M. on 14 February 1933 William ("Birdsie") Richards shot himself with a .32 caliber revolver in his home at the Zerbey Apartments on Arch Street in Pottsville, Pennsylvania. He was 27 years, 6 months old. The death certificate gave his occupation as surveyor, but his real occupation seems to have been gambling. His wife, whom he had recently married, attributed his suicide to financial worries.

This obscure tragedy had an enduring influence on American literature. It became the source for Julian English's appointment in Samarra; and it provided John O'Hara with his method for character creation. O'Hara always refused to make a public identification of Julian English's original. In his 1953 introduction to the Modern Library edition of *Appointment in Samarra* he wrote:

> Nobody ever guessed Julian English right. The quick readers thought they knew because of superficial resemblances between Julian English and some living men (me included), such as financial and social backgrounds, drinking habits, clothes. The truth is that the basic Julian English was from the wrong side of the tracks and never wore a buttoned-down collar in his tragic life. Under cumulative and finally unbearable pressure he killed himself. That's all I'll say about that.

The only lead to Birdsie Richards that O'Hara provided was in a 1962 letter to Gerald Murphy—himself the model for F. Scott Fitzgerald's Dick Diver:

> In the case of Julian English, the guy in real life was a fellow named Richards, who was definitely not country-club, but had charm and a certain kind of native intelligence, and who, when the chips were down, shot himself. I

"Out of Life: John O'Hara's Character Creation" was published originally as "Out of Life" in the *John O'Hara Journal* 1 (1978): 18–28. Reprinted with permission of Arlyn Bruccoli for the Matthew J. Bruccoli literary estate.

took his life, his psychological pattern, and covered him up with Brooks shirts and a Cadillac dealership and so on, and the reason that the story rings so true is that it is God's truth, out of life.[1]

This technique—compounding the psychological pattern of an actual person with accurate details from other lives—served O'Hara for fourteen novels over the next thirty-six years.

One of the simplistic critical views of O'Hara's work holds that he practiced the roman à clef—that he simply disguised real people who could be recognized by anyone who knew them. As is demonstrated by the connection between Birdsie Richards and Julian English, John O'Hara's method for creating characters involved considerably more than changing names.

O'Hara correctly held that the art of fiction is chiefly the art of creating characters. Great novels are remembered for the characters; and everything in the work contributes to the effectiveness of the characters. As O'Hara explained in his letter to Murphy, "Long, long before I start writing a novel I have learned all I can about the principal characters. I have determined, to my own satisfaction, what they would do in any and all circumstances. And I am pretty generally right. Why? Because they are all real people, people who are living or who have lived. I use the psychological pattern of real people, then I put them in different locations and times, and cover them up with superficial characteristics, etc."

John O'Hara was not a practicing literary critic and did not publish a body of critical essays—a circumstance which has led critics to compare him to a musician who could play only by ear. The rather prominent O'Hara ears came in for a good deal of attention from reviewers who were always willing to concede that O'Hara had a sharp ear for speech. That was what reviewers were supposed to say. The unwritten rules of book reviewing also required the recognition of his eye for detail; but it became obligatory to cite the needless use of detail for its own sake. Answering O'Hara's critics forces one into the awkward position of promulgating the self-evident: that his fiction was always under his control, that he was a skilled technician, that he had developed and refined his own body of critical principles. He didn't write masterpieces by accident.

O'Hara attempted to formulate his thinking about his craft in three lectures he gave at Rider College in Trenton, N.J., in 1959 and 1961. Although he thought well enough of these lectures at the time to have planned publication, they remained unpublished until they posthumously appeared in *"An Artist Is His Own Fault"* (1977).

The main concern of the Rider lectures was with character creation and the use of dialogue and detail to reinforce characterization. This is how O'Hara created Joe Chapin of *Ten North Frederick*: "In that instance I took a real person whose life was rather dramatically changed by an episode that made a tremendous change in his mode of living. The episode occurred when my real-life person was a grown man, and a man set in his ways. Now what I, the novelist, did was to pretend that the dramatic episode—over which, by the way, he had no control—had never occurred. What kind of man would this be, how would he have turned out, if the episode had not occurred? From then on I wrote pure fiction."[2] The real-life figure was Franklin Delano Roosevelt. The novelist set himself the problem of imagining what Roosevelt would have been like if he had not been crippled, and then moved him to Gibbsville. O'Hara provided no clues to the connection between Chapin and Roosevelt because the connection does not matter to the reader. Joseph B. Chapin is not Franklin Delano Roosevelt. *Ten North Frederick* derived from the author's analysis of the psychology of a real person, but it is not about that person. It is not a roman à clef. O'Hara wrote only one roman à clef—*Butterfield 8* in which Gloria Wandrous is a fictionalized Starr Faithfull.

In *From the Terrace* the psychological pattern for Alfred Eaton came from Anthony Eden, whom O'Hara never met. Here again, the novel does not depend in any way on the reader's identification of Eden. The name echo was just an authorial private joke and was not intended as a clue. O'Hara was writing fiction out of life. When he achieved "God's truth" it was because the truth was in the character.

O'Hara's theory and practice required that the psychological truth of his characters be reinforced by social accuracy—and he did this better than anyone. He believed that the key element in this process is dialogue. A writer who can't be trusted to get his characters' speech right can't be trusted for anything else. Character emerges from speech—a rule that O'Hara learned as a boy and had confirmed by his reading of Ring Lardner. Dialogue must be right in terms of a character's social-economic-educational background. One wrong word can destroy the characterization for a reader—who may not necessarily be aware of just what is wrong. It is enough for the reader to sense a false note and therefore hold reservations about the characterization. Like Lardner, O'Hara learned *hard*. He noticed, for example, that upper-class women never said "half-dollar." He noticed what he called the "elegant resistance of the objective pronouns" by educated people who said "Mary went with she and I" because they had been drilled to avoid "Me and her went with Mary." However, O'Hara knew that real speech can't be duplicated in print, that it would be unreadable if it were transcribed. He admitted that his superbly real dialogue was artificial, as all art is artificial. His achievement was in conveying a controlled impression of vocabulary, grammar, and speech rhythms. F. Scott Fitzgerald paid O'Hara this compliment in his *Notebooks:* "The queer slanting effect of the substantive, the future imperfect, a matter of intuition or ear to O'Hara, is unknown to careful writers like Bunny

[Wilson] and John [Peale Bishop]."³ However, Fitzgerald's assessment is incomplete: it was not just "a matter of intuition or ear." O'Hara's dialogue was under his control. So closely interwoven were characters and speech for O'Hara that toward the end of his life he would imagine two faces and write dialogue for them until their characters emerged—only then deciding whether the story was worth completing.

Related to the details of accurate speech are other social details which O'Hara properly insisted were significant details. As with speech, even the wrong details must be deliberately wrong and therefore meaningfully right. O'Hara expected an attentive reader to recognize that there is something fraudulent about a character who wears a miniature hunting horn instead of a collar pin with a business suit. Details function as characteristics. You are what you own—or what owns you.

One of O'Hara's favorite characterizations was the automobile. At Rider College he explained:

> In the twenties if you said a man owned a Franklin you would not be talking about the kind of man who owned a Buick, although some Buicks cost the same amount of money as some Franklins. The Franklin-owner would not be wearing an Elk's tooth nor a Rotary Club button. He might wear a Masonic pin, but not a Shriner's. The Franklin-owner was more likely to be a tennis player than a golfer, a doctor than a real estate agent, a college man than a non–college man, and a much more independent thinker than the Buick owner. He would also be likely to own more securities than the Buick owner, whose money would be tied up in personal enterprises. Now why is all this so important to the novelist? It is important because character is so important; it would be out of character for a Buick type man to own a Franklin; it would not be quite so much out of character for a Franklin man to own a Buick. In any case, the novelist has told the reader that Jones owns a Franklin; therefore Jones will behave as a Franklin-owning Jones will behave. And if he behaves in a way that is out of character, either the novelist has been wrong in providing him with a Franklin, or he, the novelist, must explain and make credible the acts that are not in character for the Franklin-owning Jones.⁴

Here is an actual case of car-characterization, from Pottsville, that amused O'Hara while it reinforced the connection between character and detail:

> In my town there was a man who had a prosperous business. . . . Mr. Sizing, as I shall call him, worked very hard six days a week. He owned a comfortable house on the best street in town. He was married and he had a son. For six days a week he was always at the laundry, and he and his wife never

went out socially. On the seventh day, however, Mr. Sizing would drive his car to a roadhouse which was conducted by the leading madam of our part of the country, and he would spend all day Sunday at the roadhouse. . . . The car was a handsome yellow Stutz Bearcat.

It was completely out of character for a hard-working businessman to own a Stutz Bearcat. But it was not out of character for a man who spent every Sunday at a roadhouse that was conducted by the leading madam. The fascinating part of it all for me, who was already determined to be a writer, was that Mr. Sizing was in appearance more like a man who would spend his time in a roadhouse than he was the hard-working businessman.[5]

Note well that O'Hara was utilizing cars as characterizers—not simply as class symbols. It is revealing that he placed the example of the Franklin in the Twenties, for many characterizers O'Hara worked with so deliberately no longer function. The Franklin is gone, and the Buick means nothing now. Critics have expressed impatience with O'Hara's details, charging that they have no relevance—or, at best, only private meaning for the writer. O'Hara's reply to people who questioned his material was: "You don't notice much, do you?" O'Hara noticed; and he expected his good readers to notice. Nonetheless, O'Hara himself classified his details of social verisimilitude as both significant and superficial. His characters—not their possessions—carry his novels. But his characters are buttressed by accurate speech and meaningful detail.

To be sure, there will always be readers for whom certain kinds of material are meaningless, no matter who writes about them. That is the way literature works. The same readers who are bored or baffled by O'Hara's details may respond complexly to details in, say, the fiction of Bernard Malamud or Saul Bellow. Detail does more than reinforce characterization: it certifies the world of fiction. Nevertheless, O'Hara became increasingly wary about "social history" as it was—sometimes patronizingly, he felt—applied to his work. He acknowledged that "every great writer of fiction was a social historian."[6] But at Rider College O'Hara denied that he was a social historian and insisted that the social history in his novels was incidental to the art of fiction. Social history in a novel is important when the novel requires it. Gratuitous or nonfunctional social history damages a work of art. "If the social history part does not relate to his characters, the author is converting himself into historian or journalist."[7] O'Hara's uneasiness about the implications of the designation "social historian" as it applied to him notwithstanding, he was American literature's best social novelist. O'Hara said this of himself: "I saw and felt and heard the world around me and within my limitations and within my prejudices I wrote down what I saw and felt and heard. I tried to keep it mine and when I was most successful it was mine."[8]

The O'Hara canon resulted from the circumstance that in 1905 a boy was born in Pottsville who would notice and retain more than other people—and he would be compelled to make it his, and ours, by making it into fiction. John O'Hara was a born writer in the sense that all great writers are born writers, but Pottsville made him the kind of writer he became. He was the son of a near-legendary doctor in a small city with an elaborate social structure. (Surely, the myth that John O'Hara's fiction was a response to the pain of a deprived childhood no longer has to be rebutted.) Moreover, he was both sensitive and sentimental—conditions he tried to control with an objective style that opaque critics have categorized as hard-boiled. Although he left in 1928, his memories returned always to Schuylkill County, his "Pennsylvania Protectorate." Gibbsville—with Jefferson, Mississippi, and Altamont, North Carolina—became one of the three most fully achieved communities in American fiction. His best work was not limited to Gibbsville—which is not the case with Faulkner's Jefferson or Wolfe's Altamont—but O'Hara's Gibbsville fiction has a recognizable emotional quality that differentiates it from his other work. It is a sense of the permanence of the past and the validity of the feelings associated with its people.

It can be argued that most of O'Hara's best work draws upon what he called "The Region"—an area within a 30-mile radius of Pottsville. Lykens became Lyons; Minersville became Collieryville; Tamaqua became Taqua; Cressona became Fair Grounds; Frackville became Mountain City; Schuylkill Haven became Swedish Haven. Surprisingly, only *Appointment in Samarra* and *Ten North Frederick* are set in Gibbsville; two novels, *Ourselves to Know* and *The Lockwood Concern*, are set elsewhere in The Region. There are five other Pennsylvania novels that take place outside The Region: *A Rage to Live*, *From the Terrace*, *The Farmer's Hotel*, *Elizabeth Appleton*, and *Lovey Childs*. Even so, O'Hara's work with The Region is impressive. Sixty-two of his 402 published stories are set in The Region—including "The Doctor's Son," "Imagine Kissing Pete," "A Family Party," "The Cellar Domain," "The Bucket of Blood," "Fatimas and Kisses," and "Yostic." It may not have been coincidental that the first story he published in 1960 after a decade of self-imposed exile from the short story was "Imagine Kissing Pete," one of his strongest novellas. There were probably Gibbsville stories that demanded to be written, that literally gave him no peace until they were written.

O'Hara began publishing short stories in 1928, but he did not develop the concept of Gibbsville (which was named for his friend, the *New Yorker* writer Wolcott Gibbs) until 1931, when he wrote an unpublished entry for the *Scribner's Magazine* short novel contest. This lost novelette established the background for O'Hara's first novel, *Appointment in Samarra* (1934), in which "Gibbsville" first saw print. Perhaps five years were needed for the development of Gibbsville because it was more than a locale; it was a community. Sherwood Anderson's Winesburg, Ohio was little more than a convenience for the author, allowing him to collect a group of stories. But Gibbsville and The Region provided O'Hara with a framework of social and personal interrelationships that he would enlarge for thirty-five years. Much more than geography was involved.

When he dealt with The Region O'Hara drew upon a bank account of people and memories. O'Hara distrusted all figures of speech, but this metaphor works because the account accumulated interest. His memories became more usable after thirty of forty years. Writing out of life, O'Hara wrote fiction that was true to life—or even truer than life because it was structured and ordered. The aim of the godlike author is to improve on God. The good writer always knows that he is distorting and simplifying and rearranging. If he knows exactly what he is doing the result is called art. But behind the technique and the observation and the discipline there must be the enduring emotions generated by the material. It is the function of realism or naturalism, no less than of any other literary method, to involve the reader in an emotion. The only way the writer can move the reader is by evoking an authentic emotion.

Sometime after 1957, when the O'Haras built "Linebrook," their Princeton home, he began an article about his study and bath. A comment on the size of the tub started O'Hara's memory flow:

> A man in my hometown drowned in the bathtub, and I still remember, as his epitaph, the drearily repetitious jokes about his dying a clean death. In fact all I remember about Mr. Halberstadt is that he had two attractive daughters, Mary and Imogene; that he drove a Maxwell; and that he died in the tub. I do remember that the Halberstadts had a big tree in front of their house, in the center of the sidewalk, and you had to walk around it. I happen to be a great lover of trees and I wish to give the Halberstadts full credit for not disturbing this tree, which I think was a horse chesnut, but I am not able to say whether it was Mr. Halberstadt or his wife who was the dendrophile. Now that I have thought it over and taken myself back fifty years, I incline to the belief that the tree was an oak. If there is anyone who lived in the 1600 block on Mahantongo Street, Pottsville, Pa., and remembers the tree in front of the Halberstadts', I would be glad to hear from him, or her.
>
> The Halberstadt girls were like Norma and Constance Talmadge in that Nim Hal was, like Norma, the prettier, but Mary Hal, like Constance, was the cuter. There was always a bunch of girls on their porch: Elizabeth Fox, Peggy Mould, Margaretta Archbald, Sara Shay, Lucetta Ibach. If there had been a Junior League in Pottsville, they would have been in it.[9]

O'Hara's memory provided a configuration of details and emotions: the man who drowned, his car, his house, a favorite tree, his daughters, a group of girls (one of whom O'Hara loved desperately) on the porch—culminating with an assessment of the social position of the girls. The details and emotions are not just associated; they inseparably reinforce each other. O'Hara's feelings about Pottsville were not nostalgic: see Hemingway for nostalgia. O'Hara's memories—and the way they became memories—made him the kind of realist he was. Writing became for him an obligation to preserve—not to report, not to record—but to preserve the integrity of experience. Jimmy Malloy, O'Hara's persona, explains in *Sermons and Soda-Water*:

> After I became reconciled to middle age and the quieter life I made another discovery: that the sweetness of my youth was a persistent and enduring thing, as long as I kept it at the distance of years. Moments would come back to me, of love and excitement and music and laughter that filled my breast as they had thirty years earlier. It was not nostalgia, which only means homesickness, nor was it a wish to be living that excitement again. It was a splendid contentment with the knowledge that once I felt things so deeply and well that the throbbing urging of George Gershwin's "Do It Again" could evoke the original sensation and the pictures that went with it: a tea dance at the club and a girl in a long black satin dress and my furious jealousy of a fellow who wore a yellow foulard tie. I wanted none of it ever again, but all I had I wanted to keep. . . . "When Hearts Are Young" became a personal anthem, enduringly sweet and safe from all harm, among the protected memories. In middle age I was proud to have lived according to my emotions at the right time, and content to live that way vicariously and at a distance. I missed almost nothing, escaped very little, and at fifty I had begun to devote my energy and time to the last simple but big task of putting it all down as well as I knew how.[10]

That was the O'Hara concern.

Notes

1. *Selected Letters of John O'Hara*, edited by Matthew J. Bruccoli (New York: Random House, 1978), pp. 401–403.

2. *"An Artist Is His Own Fault": John O'Hara on Writers and Writing*, edited by Bruccoli (Carbondale and Edwardsville: Southern Illinois University Press / London and Amsterdam: Feffer and Simons, 1977), p. 27.

3. *The Notebooks of F. Scott Fitzgerald*, edited by Bruccoli (New York and London: Harcourt Brace Jovanovich / Bruccoli Clark, 1978), p. 162.

4. *"An Artist Is His Own Fault,"* pp. 14–15.

5. Ibid., pp. 15–16.

6. Ibid., p. 106.
7. Ibid., p. 29.
8. From Don A. Schanche's notes.
9. "*An Artist Is His Own Fault,*" pp. 130–131.
10. "Imagine Kissing Pete," *Sermons and Soda-Water* (New York: Random House, 1960), pp. 71–72.

Focus on *Appointment in Samarra*

The Importance of Knowing
What You Are Talking About

> I feel I have a duty to get down as much of what I know as I can.
> John O'Hara, as quoted in "Special Report,"
> *Newsweek* (13 June 1963): 57

John O'Hara is what he called Hemingway in 1950, "the most important author living today."[1] Although he did not specifically analyze the importance of Hemingway in the review of *Across the River and Into the Trees,* he particularly praised Hemingway for "pre-paper discipline"—which "means, first of all, point of view" or "the expression of an attitude." O'Hara's work has a controlled, uninvolved point of view—which is one of the reasons he is regarded as hard-boiled—as well as the competence and clarity he admired in Hemingway; but his real importance comes from a commitment Hemingway also had: the duty to tell how it was. "The United States in this century is what I know, and it is my business to write about it to the best of my ability, with the sometimes special knowledge I have. The Twenties, the Thirties, and the Forties are already history, but I cannot be content to leave their story in the hands of the historians and the editors of picture books. I want to record the way people talked and thought and felt, and to do it with complete honest and variety" (*Sermons and Soda-Water,* 1960).

There are more elegant stylists, more profound thinkers, more sensitive spirits. There is no working writer who matches O'Hara's importance as a social historian. When the next century wants to know how Americans lived between 1920 and 1940, it will find what it wants to know in O'Hara. It will find the names of

"Focus on *Appointment in Samarra:* The Importance of Knowing What You Are Talking About" was published originally in *Tough Guy Writers of the Thirties,* edited by David Madden (Carbondale and Edwardsville: Southern Illinois University Press / London and Amsterdam: Feffer and Simons, 1968), pp. 129–136. Reprinted with permission of David Madden.

things—the right names—but it will also find accurate analyses of the social structure and characters who are both real and representative. The stories and people may not always fall within the individual reader's experience, but it is difficult to believe that O'Hara's wide knowledge and deep commitment to the truth would permit him to falsify his material.

There are subjects—such as the labor movement and national politics—O'Hara has never tried to study in depth. Despite the gaps in his coverage, he has a much broader scope than his competitors—think of James T. Farrell, Louis Auchincloss, John P. Marquand. His closest competitor is James Gould Cozzens, whose commitment to history is modified by his philosophical-ethical concerns. Social history has not been widely admired in American literature, and the second-rate practitioners, such as Henry James and Edith Wharton, have been overrated because they were not reliable observers. Indeed, most influential critics seem to feel that social history belongs to a lower order of endeavor called reportage. Note the of-course and to-be-sure way these chaps admit that John O'Hara does have a sharp ear before they move on to his crudeness. Critics like authors who make them look good. Since O'Hara writes fiction that does not require—or permit—brilliant explication, the critics picket him.

John O'Hara's first novel, *Appointment in Samarra* (1934), employs techniques of tone and point-of-view, materials, and language found in the *Black Mask* school; but it is more ambitious and varied. Historically, it is considered tough or hard-boiled today partly because it was so labeled by its reviewers. Jamesian R. P. Blackmur put O'Hara in the school of Hemingway, James M. Cain, and Benjamin Appel—the school of pointless toughness—and charged that *Appointment in Samarra* was actually distorted and unrealistic (*Nation* [22 August 1934]: 220–221). Genteel Henry Seidel Canby was so upset by the dirty language and "water closets" that he was inspired to write one of his triumphantly opaque reviews in which he cited "incident recorded only because it happens" and characters without any meaning "except a sociological importance." This review is worth reading. It concludes: "It makes one long for the good old days of the Restoration when in a literature equally thin, equally without values, equally unrepresentative of what was happening in a society at large, and far more wittily erotic, one encountered sometimes a *Millimaunt* and felt the saving presence of a beauty that certainly never waved its wings over Gibbsville" (*Saturday Review of Literature* [18 August 1934]: 53, 55).

Appointment in Samarra has certain resemblances to two other novels published in 1934, Dashiell Hammett's *The Thin Man* and Cain's *The Postman Always Rings Twice*—uninvolved viewpoint, economical style, accurate speech, dirty words, frank sex. But it is much closer to F. Scott Fitzgerald's *Tender Is the*

Night in its interest in character deterioration and in money. *Appointment in Samarra* is a long way from both James T. Farrell's *The Young Manhood of Studs Lonigan* and Henry Roth's *Call it Sleep*. It is not a Depression novel, although the action takes place in 1930 and some of Julian English's troubles are financial. O'Hara has cited Sinclair Lewis and Fitzgerald as the chief literary influences on this novel—and he has discounted any significant influence of Hemingway (*Appointment in Samarra* [Modern Library, 1953]). Hammett, Raoul Whitfield, and Paul Cain—all of whom had published their best work by 1934—are not on the list of secondary influences, which includes Galsworthy, Tarkington, Owen Johnson, Hemingway, Lardner, and Dorothy Parker. Raymond Chandler, the best social observer to come out of *Black Mask,* did not publish his first detective story until 1933.

If there is a connection between O'Hara and the *Black Mask* school, it comes from a shared obligation to the first generation of American naturalists. Although O'Hara does not seem to have been directly influenced by Crane, Norris, or Dreiser, his work reflects their interest in documentary verisimilitude, social stratification, sexual force, and the unpretty aspects of American life—and Crane's perspective on the fate of his characters. O'Hara is a determinist, but he is happily free from the cosmic theorizing and nature-questing of the pioneer naturalists. His characters' lives are controlled by forces they cannot themselves control: by social position—which is not just environmental—and appetite. Their possessions—the things they spend their money and mortality on—are the symbols of their bondage to deterministic forces. O'Hara's genius for meaningful cataloguing of the objects and systems of environment is striking, but he also exhibits a certain commitment to simple hereditary determinism. In *Appointment in Samarra* there is the obvious possibility that Julian's suicide may not be unrelated to his grandfather's. The metaphor of the title obviously says that Julian's fate was determined, though it is left to the reader to assess the influence of the several forces which operate on Julian. As I have indicated, heredity in *Appointment in Samarra* must include such things as the social position and family traditions one inherits at birth. Being born on a certain street to certain parents with certain memberships and being early impressed with the knowledge that one will be expected to attend certain schools where one will join—or be able to join—certain organizations, after which one will honor certain family obligations and marry into a certain social level: these are as deterministic in O'Hara as a family taint of idiocy is in Zola. Always in O'Hara there is the money; and inherited money is better than new money.

The neat theory that O'Hara's work stems from his poor boy's pain at being excluded from Pottsville, Pennsylvania, society has been widely—gleefully—

accepted along with the joke about "let's all take up a collection and send John O'Hara to Yale." These wound-and-bow analyses are supposed somehow to discredit his work, although the childhood wounds—preferably sexual—of other writers are deemed respectable. However, the story of O'Hara's socially deprived youth, at least as commonly interpreted, is not true. For the record, he has written, "In 1918, in a store on Chestnut Street in Philadelphia, my old man bought me a pair of riding boots for $55.00 and the first pair of wing-tip brogues I had ever seen, for $26.50. He paid cash, and we didn't have to thumb it home. That didn't last but don't say it never happened."[2] The anti-O'Hara school would of course claim that this statement—especially the last sentence—exposes his over concern with the thing he is denying. It is possible, even probable, that as a Catholic, O'Hara experienced prejudice and exclusion, which is not the same as making him the little match boy. Religious bias is covered in his work—notably in *Appointment in Samarra*—but it is hardly a preoccupation. To say that O'Hara writes as an outsider is too simple because so much of his work depends on inside information.

Edmund Wilson has stated that the cruel side of social snobbery is O'Hara's main theme (*The Boys in the Back Room*, 1941). It is one of his themes, but not his chief one. However, snobbery—interpreted as all the machinery of social conduct and social stratification—is his main subject. The main theme within this subject is not the cruelty of exclusion, but the futility and tragedy of the waste of life within the social system. In *Ten North Frederick*, a minor character sums up what he has learned about the system: "The safest way to live is first, inherit money. Second, marry a woman that will cooperate with you in your sexual peculiarities. Third, have a legitimate job that keeps you busy. Fourth, be born without a taste for liquor. Fifth, join some big church. Sixth, don't live too long." There is authorial irony here, of course, for these are rules for a safe, happy, and futile life. But they really are good rules for a safe life in society. It is worth noting that of the six rules, four concern things we normally do not control and which have social consequences: inherited wealth, sexual peculiarities, alcoholism, and life-span; and the other two involve social relationships. The job is not for income or satisfaction, and the church is not for religion.

O'Hara has been tagged a hard-boiled writer partly because of his realistic treatment of the rougher aspects of life, and mostly because of his detachment from his characters—or what has been described as his sardonic attitude toward them. It is said that he is indifferent to their fates and refuses to judge them. It is even said that he hates his rich people, in which case he cannot be detached at all. True, he is interested in the underworld and its show-business fringes—for example, Al Grecco and Ed Charney in *Appointment in Samarra*. But he is much more interested in the middle and upper classes—the Flieglers and the Englishes—because they are more complicated. The rich are different; and the richer they are, the more different they are. Like Fitzgerald, O'Hara is impressed by the charm and grace the rich can achieve; and like Fitzgerald, O'Hara is disappointed by what these privileged people actually do with their lives. It is also true that O'Hara shares an interest in the varieties of sexual conduct with the hard-boiled writers—and is more explicit about it. But his scope is wider, his ambition greater. When he describes people in bed, he is trying to show that most people do and say the same things, or that some people do not.

O'Hara's work is free from the deliberate shock element found in hard-boiled detective fiction—the detailed beatings and the descriptions of bullet-holes in foreheads; the exaggerated indifference of the protagonists to pain, even their own; the matter-of-fact inventories of alcoholic consumption; the refusal to display emotion. Where O'Hara does cover the same ground—Julian's or Luther's drinking, for example—he makes it part of the bigger job of showing how the character lived, how the drinking was part of social rituals. Critics have complained that O'Hara supplies needlessly elaborate case histories for minor characters in *Appointment in Samarra*—that there is too much about Al Grecco for his importance in the novel—but these biographical sketches are clear indications that the novel was intended as a sociological study as well as a character study. O'Hara is interested in the man who had the appointment in Samarra; in fact the social organization of Samarra determines the nature of the appointment.

What has been assumed to be O'Hara's indifference to his characters—his hard-boiled attitude—has been confused with his disciplined authorial point of view. He is not an intrusive author, and he does not get emotionally involved with his characters. This is not to say that he does not approve and disapprove of them. He thinks Dr. William Dilworth English is a choice son-of-a-bitch, and the reader knows that he does. O'Hara's procedure is to tell as much as he can about his characters' histories and then to let them reveal themselves through their behavior and speech while he avoids open judgment on them. That O'Hara offers no judgment does not mean that there is no judgment. The very acts of selecting material, of inventing characters, of having them act, of creating speech—all involve judgment. He does not instruct us in how he wants us to feel about Julian, but it is clear that O'Hara is not without feelings about him. The novel shows us that Julian is weak and self-indulgent, but not wholly contemptible and certainly not vicious. He is doomed by forces of character and circumstance he cannot cope with; and because he does not merit his doom, he deserves pity. But only a little pity because there is nothing in particular to admire about him. There have been complaints that he is a surface characterization, that O'Hara fails to make the reader understand Julian, that we never really know why he commits suicide. That is what O'Hara intended. The novel is not superficial: Julian is a superficial human being. He is not a tragic character and was not intended as one. *Appointment in Samarra* is a sociological novel, not a psychological novel.

When O'Hara does openly comment, it is clear that his controlled handling of his material conceals the fact that he is a sentimental man who can be very sentimental about sex, love, and marriage. It may be that O'Hara's uninvolved point of view is his tactic for disciplining his sentimentality, a sentimentality that has become more apparent in his recent work—"Imagine Kissing Pete," for example. In *Appointment in Samarra*, when Julian and Caroline have intercourse after he has failed to apologize to Harry Reilly, O'Hara does comment: "It was the greatest single act of their married life. He knew it, and she knew it. It was the time she did not fail him." If Julian's reaction to Caroline's refusal to keep their lovemaking date at the country club seems extreme, the point is that this time she fails him again when he desperately needs reassurance. Julian fails Caroline, of course, but he needs her more than she needs him. The English marriage is contrasted with the Fliegler marriage, which opens and closes the novel. Luther and Irma do not fail each other. If Julian can be considered the victim of one particular thing, he is the victim of Caroline's bitchiness. In her grieving for Julian, she recognizes that she would have failed Julian again, that it is better for both of them that he killed himself. "But this time she knew she would not have come back this afternoon, and he had known it, and God help us all but he was right. There was nothing for him to do today.... There, that was settled. Now let the whole thing begin again."

O'Hara's plain style adds to the impression that he is a hard-boiled writer. His prose moves; it is clear and exceptionally readable—which in some quarters counts against him—but it lacks the grace of Fitzgerald's prose. To be sure, O'Hara has a good ear, and his dialogue includes words that used to upset people. His writing is uncomplicated and notably bare of simile and metaphor. Allegory he eschews along with ambiguity and ambivalence. He creates no white whales; but he has an unsurpassed skill with his kind of symbols, which are the names of things. That Julian is a Cadillac dealer is appropriate and meaningful. The characters may not always understand what their possessions reveal about them, but O'Hara does. He knows what he is talking about.

You may not like what he writes about, but "don't say it never happened."

Notes

1. *New York Times Book Review* (10 September 1950): 1. I do not extend the rest of his sentence to O'Hara: "the most outstanding author since the death of Shakespeare." This

review has occasioned a good deal of jibing at O'Hara for hyperbolic misjudgment of a poor novel; but the review is clearly not a rave notice of *Across the River and Into the Trees*, which he obviously considered weak Hemingway. It is a defense of Hemingway's career.

2. "Don't Say It Never Happened," *New York Herald Tribune Books* (18 April 1962): 3. Surprisingly, it is "a store."

A Reopening of the *By Love Possessed* Case

If you doe not like him, surely you are in some manifest danger not to understand him.

Heming and Condell, preface to the
Shakespeare First Folio (1623)

Forty years ago, in 1957, a master work of the American novel was published by James Gould Cozzens. The initial marketplace and critical success of *By Love Possessed* was followed by attacks intended to destroy the reputations of the author and this novel; but Cozzens was insulated from the pain of critical rejection by his contempt for his detractors. He knew how good he and his novels were. More than most great writers, he wrote for himself, meeting his own exacting standards. Nevertheless, professionals write to be published and read, and Cozzens regretted that potential readers were being turned away by attacks that were only partly responses to literary concerns.

Cozzens's novels commencing with *The Last Adam* (1933) provided "a new acquist of true experience" for grown-ups. He insisted that what matters in a novel is what the author intends and what the reader sees; most criticism was dismissed by him as exercises in finding what isn't there. Cozzens's position on literary fame was: "If a book's good, don't worry; it'll outlast any amount of partisan malice and stupid criticism; while if it isn't any good, what right has it to outlast anything? In my own case, I was and am happy to let it go at that—we'll wait and see." A reopening of the *By Love Possessed* case—which is the James Gould Cozzens case—is overdue.

"A Reopening of the *By Love Possessed* Case" was published originally as the untitled introduction to the 1998 Carroll and Graf edition of James Gould Cozzens's 1957 novel. Reprinted with permission of Arlyn Bruccoli for the Matthew J. Bruccoli literary estate. The standard Cozzens biography is Bruccoli's *James Gould Cozzens: A Life Apart* (New York: Harcourt Brace Jovanovich, 1983); the standard Cozzens bibliography is Bruccoli's *James Gould Cozzens: A Descriptive Bibliography* (Pittsburgh: University of Pittsburgh Press, 1981).

James Gould Cozzens (1903–1978) published his first novel, *Confusion* (1924), during his sophomore year at Harvard and left college to become a full-time writer. In 1927 he married Bernice Baumgarten, who came to be regarded as the best literary agent in New York. *Michael Scarlett* (1928), an historical novel set in Elizabethan England, and two Cuban novels, *Cockpit* (1928) and *The Son of Perdition* (1929), were later disavowed by Cozzens.

The major phase of Cozzens's career commenced in 1931 when he was twenty-eight, with *S.S. San Pedro,* a novelette about a disaster at sea, followed by *The Last Adam* (1933), an examination of a small Connecticut town and its doctor. At that time the Cozzenses purchased a farm in Lambertville, New Jersey, where he stayed home and wrote—eschewing the literary life in New York. By the Thirties Cozzens had identified the central theme of his fiction: deontology, the ethics of duty, which he developed with increasing complexity in the rest of his fiction. *Castaway* (1934), an experimental novel set in a department store after an unspecified disaster, was the only departure from his realistic social novels: *Men and Brethren* (1936) about an Episcopal minister; *Ask Me Tomorrow* (1940) about a young American writer in Europe; and *The Just and the Unjust* (1942) about a murder trial in a country town. Three of these novels were Book-of-the-Month-Club selections—Bernice Baumgarten served her client well—but none was a best-seller; nor did Cozzens receive the critical attention accorded Hemingway, Faulkner, or Steinbeck.

The war removed Cozzens from his reclusive life; he enlisted in the Army Air Force in 1942 and rose to major on the staff of General H. H. Arnold, chief of the Air Force. *Guard of Honor,* published in 1948, was the surprise winner of the Pulitzer Prize—which Cozzens regarded as an embarrassment. Set at a Florida air base, *Guard of Honor* is the best American novel of World War II.

With *By Love Possessed* in 1957 Cozzens briefly became a literary celebrity. He described his novel as concerned with "the underlying, everlasting opposition of thinking and feeling, with life's simple disaster of passion and reason, self-division's cause."[1] It was an immediate success: the number-one best-seller from September 1957 to March 1958 (replacing *Peyton Place* and yielding to *Anatomy of a Murder*); the Book-of-the-Month-Club main selection; the record paperback advance to that time; a *Reader's Digest* condensation; and a lucrative movie deal. There is no way to estimate how many copies were read, but the word-of-mouth response was strong enough to keep *By Love Possessed* on the *Publishers Weekly* best-seller list for nine months.

When *By Love Possessed* was published, Cozzens unwisely cooperated with *Time* for a cover story, which portrayed him as an anachronistic crank. Cozzens's irony—a staple of his speech and writing—provided the *Time* writers with opportunities to ridicule him, through malice or opacity. But the most influential of the early reviews were strongly receptive. John Fischer, editor of *Harper's,* headed his article "Nomination for a Nobel Prize" and declared: "If your great-grandchild should ever want to find out how Americans behaved and thought and felt in the mid-years of this century, Cozzens's major novels probably would be his most revealing source."

The opposition charged Cozzens with anti-Semitism, anti-Catholicism, emotional deficiency, misanthropy, misogyny, snobbery, conservatism, and stylistic crimes against inattentive readers. His objective revelations of the vanity of human wishes upset readers accustomed to reassuring messages about the nobility of human nature. Cozzens's reliance on irony of style, irony of tone (concerned detachment or pitying aloofness), and irony of observation puzzled or offended general readers and ill-equipped critics. He admitted that he indulged his fondness for rhetorical irony: "Those wise doubts about irony and 'experiment' always, in my experience, get mislaid when I have pen in hand and the shooting-off-of-my-face is going good. I weaken. I tell myself or my typewriter that one more little irony won't do us any harm." Cozzens wrote for fit readers. He expected that there were enough of them.

The liberals' vehemence against *By Love Possessed* in the second Eisenhower term was partly generated by Julius Penrose's disquisitions on intolerance, which were assumed to be the author's personal pronouncements: "a rabble of professional friends of man, social-worker liberals, and practitioners of universal brotherhood—the whole national horde of nuts and queers—will come at a run to hang me by the neck until I learn to love." Outraged readers did not understand the function of Penrose's rhetoric, despite Cozzens's instructions: "the well-known habit of the finished phrases, in their level precision almost rehearsed-sounding, the familiar deliberately mincing tones that mocked themselves with their own affectation." All readers of *By Love Possessed* should have no difficulty in recognizing the pervading irony that Penrose, the dominant intelligence in the novel, is also its most steadfast lover.

Much of the novel is written in Cozzens's clear, unadorned prose; but he held that the simple truth may not be the entire truth in writing. When necessary to reveal a character's thought process or to probe the determinants of behavior, Cozzens matched style with meaning. Such passages call attention to themselves; but they are not deliberately opaque, or fancy for the sake of opulence. Cozzens's elaborate sentences are precise. He was a much more careful writer than Faulkner, whose extravagances are admired.

Among the noticeable stylistic characteristics of *By Love Possessed* are long sentences; parenthetical constructions; sentence parallelisms; unfamiliar words; unacknowledged quotations from the classics of English literature (often from Shakespeare[2]); the device of following a formal statement with a clarifying or deflating colloquialism; polyptoton (repetition of a word in different cases or inflections: "result's result"); inverted word order; not unfunctional double negatives; the technique of defining a word by its use or providing alternatives; and periodic sentences in which meaning becomes clear only at the end of the sentence. In certain instances the style mocks the content as well as itself.

The requirements of Cozzens's style are balanced by the complex clarity of the novel's structure. *By Love Possessed* is tightly planned, spanning forty-nine hours of clock time—3 P.M. Friday to 4 P.M. Sunday—during which the novel confirms Judge Dealey's dictum that "Whatever happens, happens because a lot of other things have happened already." Yet *By Love Possessed* is not restricted to forty-nine hours; by means of flashbacks Cozzens documents the process of causality underlying present occurrences. The epigraph on the title page alerts the reader that time is of the essence. Cozzens was a master of simultaneity—providing a sense of what else is happening at the same time and how the separate events converge. No American novelist surpasses him in the control of time and causality. Malcolm Cowley identified Cozzens as "the greatest architect in contemporary American fiction."

The angriest denunciation of *By Love Possessed* was by Dwight Macdonald in the January 1958 *Commentary*—four months after the novel's publication. The magazine was at the time programmatically liberal, but Macdonald concentrated on Cozzens's putative crimes of style. The article was hailed by the liberal-academic establishment. There was no challenge to Macdonald by Cozzens's whilom advocates. Cozzens made no public response; he regarded Macdonald's jeremiad as inspired by resentment of the novel's success, invoking Dr. Johnson: "Criticism enlarged by rage and exclamation." Having experienced the rewards of fame, Cozzens resumed his writing life apart from the literary life.

In 1964 Cozzens published his only collection of short stories, *Children and Others;* there are superb stories in the volume, but the form did not interest him. His thirteenth novel, *Morning Noon and Night* (1968), is a rare excellent American novel about a businessman. Although a Book-of-the-Month-Club selection, it was a critical and sales failure. There was no Cozzens comeback. James Gould Cozzens did not write another novel before his death in 1978.

For the Record

Much literary reputation-making results from friendship or enmity. It is proper and natural to praise our friends and damn our enemies—who do the same for us. Yet civilians—the readers for whom fiction is intended—have no way of knowing whether a review or introduction represents the judgment of friend, foe, or innocent bystander. Critical bias is not necessarily personal; critics frequently form literary judgments on what they take to be an author's sociopolitical ideas.

I cannot claim the honor of James Gould Cozzens's friendship. He insisted that he had no friends. I never met him; that's the way he wanted it. But I published four books by him (two posthumously); we corresponded and talked on the phone about these projects during the last years of his life. Everything that I learned about his work, everything that he wrote, reinforced my respect for Jim and my animosity toward his detractors. I wrote this in 1983: "Such was James Gould Cozzens, whose force of mind was formidable, whose veneration for truth was inflexible, whose dedication to the craft of literature was uncontaminated by fashions. His novels have a safe place of proper stature among the sound achievements in American literature."

Appendix

The use of difficult words in *By Love Possessed* irritated readers and reviewers; but James Gould Cozzens did not regard it as an imposition for the reader to consult a dictionary. Sixty-odd words in a 570-page novel is not an outrageous proportion. He stated to Frederick Bracher, who wrote *The Novels of James Gould Cozzens* (1959):

> The charge, stated or implied, that I look up hard words to impress the boobs I think I can answer by pointing out that normally no boob would so much as try to read beyond a first page of mine. Sometimes the long word will be the one right word and I don't scruple to use it—if the reader doesn't know it, it's time he learned; but such words, if bunched together as some critics bunched them, don't I think really indicate that I'm a lover of long words for their own sake. The elaborations, where I attempted them, were of course directed at the kind of reader I normally do have. With him, I can count on a good meeting of the minds. He is likely to find the sort of mild relish that I myself find in the notes of irony or even sarcasm that fancy or high-falutin phrasings of bold unfancy facts can strike. Still I confess that tongue-in-cheek stuff comes pretty close to the weakness Fowler describes as Polysyllabic Humor, and I ought to watch it. I will. . . .[3]

Notes

1. From Fulke Greville's *The Tragedy of Mustapha* (1609): "What meanest nature by these diverse laws? / Passion and reason self-division cause."

2. The three section titles are unstipulated stage directions from Shakespeare. "Drums Afar Off" (*Coriolanus*) and "A Noise of Hunters Heard" (*The Tempest*) were, Cozzens

said, "picked for sound rather than any special implication." "Within the Tent of Brutus" (*Julius Caesar*) refers to the pre-battle confrontation between Cassius and Brutus.

3. The ellipsis at the conclusion of the Cozzens quotation acknowledging the accusation that he deliberately used "hard words" indicates a deletion by the editor of a list of fifty-eight difficult words, including definitions with page references to the novel, provided by M.J.B. for "the convenience of readers." Ed.

Raymond Chandler and Hollywood

A pre-occupation with words for their own sake is fatal to good film making. It's not what films are for. It's not my cup of tea, but it could have been if I'd started it twenty years earlier.
                    Chandler to Dale Warren (7 November 1951)

I am not interested in why the Hollywood system exists. . . . I am interested only in the fact that as a result of it there is no such thing as an art of the screenplay, and there never will be as long as the system lasts, for it is the essence of this system that it seeks to exploit a talent without permitting it the right to be a talent. It cannot be done; you can only destroy the talent, which is exactly what happens—when there is any talent to destroy.
                    Chandler, "Writers in Hollywood" (1945)

Most writers in Hollywood are employees. . . . As an individual I refuse to be an employee, but of course I am only an individual.
                    Chandler, "Critical Notes" (1947)

Raymond Chandler occupies a canonized position among twentieth-century detective novelists. Along with Dashiel Hammett and James M. Cain, he was one of the big three of hard-boiled fiction; but Chandler has always enjoyed special attention. His style has been justly admired, and he has been accorded considerable serious critical consideration. Indeed, he has been regarded as almost a major writer in some quarters—especially in Europe. Such a judgment is not an absolute distortion, for Chandler clearly merits respect. He, as much as anyone else, took a subliterary American genre and made it into literature. Hammett did it first, but Chandler did it better.

"Raymond Chandler and Hollywood" was published originally as the afterword to Chandler's *The Blue Dahlia: A Screenplay,* edited by Matthew J. Bruccoli (Carbondale and Edwardsville: Southern Illinois University Press / London and Amsterdam: Feffer and Simons, 1976). Reprinted with permission of the Southern Illinois University Press.

The genre he worked in was the hard-boiled detective story, which flourished in the late Twenties and Thirties in the pulp magazines or "dime novels"—especially in *Black Mask* under the editorship of Capt. Joseph Shaw. Here Chandler began publishing in 1933 as a forty-five-year-old unemployed oil company executive. These detective stories as written by Hammett, Cornell Woolrich, Carroll John Daly, George Harmon Coxe, Frank Gruber, Horace McCoy, and Erle Stanley Gardner had certain common elements in addition to the detective hero (sometimes a policeman, sometimes a private eye, sometimes a civilian): a great deal of violence and an attempt to write tough dialogue. Frequently the results were close to self-parody. The heroes absorbed endless beatings and were often too hard-boiled to believe. The most serious flaw of the school was the tendency of the speech to exaggerate toughness into something unrealistic. How much of the eat-nickels-and-spit-dimes dialogue can be blamed on the influence of Hemingway remains a moot point. Chandler not only made his dialogue believable, he even gave it style. As a writer who had failed as a poet before World War I, he possessed a concern with words, a feeling for good writing, and an obvious pleasure in striking metaphors or similes. But, more than any other element, it was his conception of his hero that distinguished his work from that of other "Boys in the Black Mask." Chandler's Philip Marlowe is not a thug; he is complex and highly intelligent. Marlowe is the Los Angeles knight imposing a little justice on a corrupt world, handling problems that the agents of the law are too busy, too dumb, or too crooked to deal with.[1] A loner, he makes a bare living while serving his personal code of honor and duty. Philip Marlowe is not greatly different from Hammett's Sam Spade, who appeared in *The Maltese Falcon* (1930) nine years before *The Big Sleep*. Nevertheless, there is the difference that Marlowe is more idealistic and less cynical than Spade, acutely sensitive beneath his tough manner: the anti-romantic romantic hero. It has become a critical commonplace that the private-eye figure—particularly Marlowe—was a response to the corruption of the Twenties and the social injustice of the Thirties. However, it is not necessary to seek politico-socio causes for Marlowe's concern with honor and justice, which were moral concerns for Raymond Chandler. He was not political, and his work included no political ideas apart from his distrust of power. Remember, Chandler lived in England from age eight to age twenty-four (1896–1912) and received a public school education at Dulwich College. Chandler/Marlowe's code is that of the Edwardian-Georgian gentleman. His hero is an English gentleman transplanted to one of the bizarre colonies, setting an example for the natives.

Raymond Chandler published his first novel, *The Big Sleep,* in 1939, when he was fifty-one years old. In 1944—at age fifty-six—he commenced as a screenwriter at Paramount for $1,750 per week. Between 1944 and 1951 he worked on at least seven screenplays for Paramount, Warner Brothers, MGM, and Universal. Chandler was mostly involved with Paramount and in 1945 signed a three-year contract with that studio calling for two scripts a year, for which he received a $50,000 annual guarantee whether or not he delivered the scripts. His Hollywood agent was H. N. "Swanie" Swanson (who also represented F. Scott Fitzgerald, William Faulkner, and John O'Hara). In addition to handling Chandler's services, Swanson also sold six of his novels to the movies—only one of which Chandler worked on.

Chandler's seven years on the payrolls of the studios were largely unsatisfactory, although he earned a great deal of money. In 1947, for example, Universal paid him $100,000 for writing the screenplay version of *Playback*—which was never produced. Although Chandler respected the potential of the movies, he was unable to work comfortably under the mandatory collaborative system. As late as 1948 Chandler called the movies "the only original art the modern world has conceived,"[2] but he disliked most of the people he had to work with, and feuded with his collaborators. He was further annoyed to see his own books butchered by other screenwriters. The only classic movie made from his work, Howard Hawks's *The Big Sleep*, did not involve Chandler.[3]

The earliest movie versions of Chandler's novels were strange attempts to superimpose characters created by other writers on Chandler's plots: *The Falcon Takes Over* (1941) combined *Farewell, My Lovely* with Michael Arlen's "Falcon"; and *Time to Kill* (1942) combined *The High Window* with Brett Halliday's Michael Shayne. Chandler's first screenwriting job at Paramount teamed him with Billy Wilder on James M. Cain's *Double Indemnity* (1944). He disliked both Wilder and the finished product, although the movie was a great success and received an Academy Award nomination for best screenplay. Chandler then collaborated on a pair of undistinguished projects: *And Now Tomorrow* (1944), a sentimental movie about a deaf girl and her doctor; and *The Unseen* (1945), a spooky suspense job. Meanwhile RKO remade *Farewell, My Lovely* as *Murder, My Sweet* (1945) without Chandler, a superior movie directed by Edward Dmytryk, in which Dick Powell was the first Philip Marlowe.

Late in 1944 Paramount had a crisis: Alan Ladd was about to be recalled by the army, and there was no script ready for him.[4] John Housman's account of how *The Blue Dahlia* was written includes the characteristic elements of Raymond Chandler's personality and work, which may be summarized by the concept of *honor*. In completing this screenplay he did the honorable thing, and honor is what *The Blue Dahlia* is about. Johnny Morrison lives by the code of the hard-boiled Los Angeles knight ("Down these mean streets a man must go who is not himself mean, who is neither tarnished nor afraid . . . if he is a man of honor in one thing, he is that in all things"), the agent of justice functioning apart from the law. It does not occur to Johnny Morrison / Alan Ladd to seek police assistance. His wife has been murdered, and he is obligated to do something about it. She was unfaithful and was responsible for the death of their child in a drunken car accident; nevertheless she was his wife. This sense of honor is even shared by Eddie Harwood, Helen Morrison's lover. A fugitive murderer, Harwood—well played by Howard da Silva—now an elegant quasi-racketeer, is troubled with guilt over his broken marriage to Joyce (Veronica Lake) and recognizes Johnny Morrison's moral superiority. Harwood's gangster partner, Leo, sees these conflicts in him and warns: "Just don't get too complicated, Eddie. . . ."

John Houseman's account of the evolution of the plot can be supplemented from Chandler's letters. Chandler did in fact know at the start who the murderer of Helen Morrison was supposed to be: Buzz Wanchek. But at that time the conduct of servicemen in movies had to be cleared with Washington; and the Navy Department ruled that Wanchek, a wounded hero, could not be the murderer. Bad for morale; disrespect for the service. Therefore Chandler was required to abandon the plot rationale of his screenplay. In June 1946 he complained to James Sandoe, a crime literature specialist:

> Yes I'm through with The Blue Dahlia, it dates even now. What the Navy Department did to the story was a little thing like making me change the murderer and hence make a routine whodunit out of a fairly original idea. What I wrote was a story of a man who killed (executed would be a better word) his pal's wife under the stress of a great and legitimate anger, then blanked out and forgot all about it; then with perfect honesty did his best to help the pal get out of a jam, then found himself in a set of circumstances which brought about partial recall. The poor guy remembered enough to make it clear who the murderer was to others, but never realized it himself. He just did and said things he couldn't have done or said unless he was the killer; but he never knew he did them or said them and never interpreted them.[5]

Hence the absurd trick-shooting scene—supposedly proving that Buzz could not have shot Helen Morrison. Another departure from Chandler's original intention comes at the close of *The Blue Dahlia*. The script ends with the three war buddies looking for a bar after Joyce Harwood drives away: "Did somebody say something about a drink of bourbon?" But in the print of the movie that was released, Buzz and George walk away leaving Johnny with Joyce in a promissory happy-ever-after finish.

Director George Marshall has responded to John Houseman's memoir—mostly substantiating it, but challenging Houseman's statement that he tried to rewrite the screenplay as he shot it:

> When the treatment was handed to me exactly as written on yellow foolscap paper, I was so impressed by the material and the quality of writing I remarked to an associate (maybe John himself), that in all the years I had been making films, I had finally found a story which was so beautifully written I could shoot it right from the treatment. . . . Why would I want to re-write something which I had thought so perfect at the beginning? Surely because the material had been put into the script form would be no reason for destroying its inherent value.[6]

The only piece of rewriting that Marshall claims is the scene in which Leo and his thug have kidnapped Johnny Morrison. In the movie version—but not in the screenplay—Leo's toe is broken during the brawl. The injury actually occurred to actor Don Costello while the scene was being shot, so Marshall had to revise the rest of the scene to accommodate Costello/Leo's broken toe. Chandler was not available for this chore because he was at home completing the screenplay. Marshall fully endorsed Chandler's complaints about the Navy Department tampering with the plot.

Although Marshall denies that he tampered with the dialogue, Chandler reported otherwise in a letter to Sandoe:

> It is ludicrous to suggest that any writer in Hollywood, however obstreperous, has a "free hand" with a script; he may have a free hand with the first draft, but after that they start moving in on him. Also what happens on the set is beyond the writer's control. In this case I threatened to walk off the picture, not yet finished, unless they stopped the director putting in fresh dialogue out of his own head. As to the scenes of violence, I did not write them that way at all. . . . The broken toe incident was an accident. The man actually did break his toe, so the director immediately capitalized on it.[7]

Whatever else Marshall may or may not have done to the screenplay, this letter goes a good way toward putting Chandler's complaints against Marshall in perspective. The rights of the matter seem to be that the director had an injured actor and an incommunicado writer, so he improvised lines and action to accommodate the accident and kept shooting. Nevertheless, Chandler objected to even this emergency revision. It appears, then, that what disturbed him was the place of the writer in the movie-making system—which was subservient to the director. Once the camera starts rolling, the movie becomes the director's movie. Chandler understood this and resented it: "There is no such thing as an art of the screenplay."[8]

George Marshall's assessment of the responsibilities of a movie director are instructive for outsiders who tend to lament what this director or that director does to a screenplay by an admired author:

A director's function is to make as good a film as possible. He must be the guiding force on the stage. He must be able to translate the words as written in the script into a visually entertaining painting, always hoping that it will be the best thing he has ever done. Unfortunately, there are times when the words as written do not fit the people who are to say them. Casting problems have forced the producer to use artists of lesser ability than the ones originally chosen. There are also times when the set does not fit the action called for in the script, so new words are written to overcome the problem; or an injury, as described in the Blue Dahlia. A director must be a master of all trades and he had better well have an answer, and a damn good one, when the problems arise.[9]

Chandler was not proud of *The Blue Dahlia*, feeling that the plot change and the incompetent performance of "Miss Moronica Lake" had damaged it. He complained to Sandoe: "The only times she's good is when she keeps her mouth shut and looks mysterious. The moment she tries to behave as if she had a brain she falls flat on her face. The scenes we had to cut out because she loused them up! And there are three godawful close shots of her looking perturbed that make me want to throw my lunch over the fence"[10] (30 May 1946). Nevertheless *The Blue Dahlia* was a success. It grossed over $2,750,000—a lot of money in those days. Chandler received his second Academy Award nomination for the screenplay, but the Award went to Muriel and Sydney Box for *The Seventh Veil.* The critical reception was predictably mixed. Bosley Crowther of the *New York Times* praised it as entertainment ("a honey of a rough-'em-up-romance"); John McCarten ridiculed it in the *New Yorker;* and John McManus of *PM* found it wanting in relevance. The best review came from James Agee in the *Nation* (8 June 1946): "The picture is as neatly stylized and synchronized and as uninterested in moral excitement as a good ballet; it knows its own weight and size perfectly and carries them gracefully and without self-importance; it is, barring occasional victories and noble accidents, about as good a movie as can be expected from the big factories."

The Blue Dahlia is a good—but not a great—movie; certainly not in the same class with *The Big Sleep*. Probably the chief problem is in the casting. Alan Ladd and Veronica Lake are unconvincing, although Ladd's work later improved. But some of the blame for the weakness of the movie belongs to Raymond Chandler. Apart from the problem of the Navy-dictated plot change, the plotting is still weak. Joyce Harwood is not integrated into the action. She picks up Johnny Morrison in her car on a rainy night for no reason and feels an instantaneous commitment to him for no reason. There is no explanation for her behavior toward him before she learns of the murder of Helen Morrison—except, possibly, elective affinity. She is the mandatory Hollywood love interest. Boy must find Girl, whether he needs her or not; and Chandler did not show any originality in handling this requirement.

Chandler never returned to his novel after he converted it into this screenplay. Since the working draft of the novel has not been found, we can only speculate about whether *The Blue Dahlia* was originally conceived as a Philip Marlowe vehicle.

While Chandler was working on *The Blue Dahlia*, *The Big Sleep* was made at Warner Brothers with Humphrey Bogart as a superb Marlowe. In 1946 Chandler had his first opportunity to work on one of his novels, when MGM teamed him with Steve Fisher on *The Lady in the Lake*. Chandler disliked everything about the project—especially his collaborator—and withdrew, refusing screen credit. This experimental "camera eye" movie was directed by Robert Montgomery, who also played the off-screen Marlowe. The idea was that the camera would serve as the narrator and would therefore photograph only what Marlowe could see. Then in 1947 Fox remade *The High Window*—again without Chandler's participation—as *The Brasher Dubloon* with George Montgomery as the fourth Marlowe.

After abortive jobs on *The Innocent Mrs. Duff* (Paramount, 1946) and *Playback* (Universal, 1947?)—both unproduced—Chandler received a choice assignment in 1950 to work with Alfred Hitchcock at Warner Brothers on Patricia Highsmith's *Strangers on a Train*, but this project turned into another failure from Chandler's point of view. Here is Hitchcock's report of the collaboration:

> Our association didn't work out at all. We'd sit together and I would say, "Why not do it this way?" And he'd answer, "Well, if you can puzzle it out, what do you need me for?" The work he did was no good and I ended up with Czenzi Ormonde, a woman writer who was one of Ben Hecht's assistants. When I completed the treatment, the head of Warner's tried to get someone to do the dialogue, and very few writers would touch it. None of them thought it was any good.[11]

Chandler reluctantly accepted joint screen credit with Ormonde. *Strangers on a Train* was Chandler's last Hollywood writing job. After his death in 1959, two more movies were made from his novels. *The Little Sister* became *Marlowe* in 1969 with James Garner playing a quizzical Philip Marlowe. The latest Hollywood attempt to translate Chandler was an atrocious parody of *The Long Goodbye* written by Leigh Brackett and directed by Robert Altman. Elliot Gould was the sixth incarnation of Marlowe.

"There's always some lousy condition," Monroe Stahr says in *The Last Tycoon*. That Raymond Chandler worked to little purpose in Hollywood can in large part be blamed on the conditions of movie-making. But blame also attaches to Chandler, whose contempt for the professionals rendered him incapable of collaborating with them comfortably, even when he was assigned to work with the best in the business. Indeed, this contempt was hardly distinguishable from self-contempt. When he was in the position to write *The Blue Dahlia* alone, he had to anesthetize himself.

Notes

1. This view of Chandler's work has been developed by Philip Durham in *Down These Mean Streets a Man Must Go* (Chapel Hill: University of North Carolina Press, 1963).

2. "Oscar Night in Hollywood," *Atlantic Monthly* (March 1948).

3. The screenplay for *The Big Sleep* was by William Faulkner, Leigh Brackett, and Jules Furthman. There is an undocumented anecdote that at one point Faulkner sent a message to Chandler asking whether the Sternwood chauffeur had committed suicide or had been murdered, and Chandler replied that he didn't know.

4. "In less than two weeks I wrote an original story of 90 pages. All dictated and never looked at until finished. It was an experiment and for one subject from early childhood to plot-constipation, it was rather a revelation. Some of the stuff is good, some very much not."—Chandler to Charles W. Morton, 15 January 1945. *Raymond Chandler Speaking*, edited by Dorothy Gardiner and Katherine Sorley Walker (Boston: Houghton Mifflin, 1962).

5. Chandler Collection, UCLA Library.

6. Letter to Matthew J. Bruccoli, 16 December 1974.

7. 2 October 1947. Chandler Collection, UCLA Library.

8. "Writers in Hollywood," *Atlantic Monthly* (November 1945).

9. To Matthew J. Bruccoli, 16 December 1974.

10. Chandler Collection, UCLA Library.

11. François Truffaut, *Hitchcock* (New York: Simon and Schuster, 1967), pp. 142–143.

Hemingway's Pursuit of Fame

I

When Ernest Hemingway published his disappointing novel *Across the River and into the Trees* in 1950, John O'Hara's article in the *New York Times Book Review* identified him as "The most important author living today, the outstanding author since the death of Shakespeare."[1] This proclamation generated incredulity and ridicule, but it was probably accurate if "American" is inserted before "author."

Hemingway combined nonliterary fame with literary stature. Few American writers have had both: Hemingway, Mark Twain, and F. Scott Fitzgerald—who achieved it posthumously. One gauge of an American writer's stature at his death is the length and placement of the *New York Times* obituary. On 3 July 1961 the *Times* accorded Hemingway three columns with a two-column photo above the fold on the front page, five full columns on page 6, an assessment by *Times* book reviewer Charles Poore, and tributes by seventeen literary figures—including John Dos Passos, Robert Frost, and William Faulkner, who provided a Faulknerian statement that was scrambled by the compositors:

> One of the bravest and best, the strictest in principles, the severest of craftsmen, undeviating in his dedication to the believable moment the antics craft: which is to arrest for a of human beings involved in the comedy and tragedy of being alive. To the few who knew him well he was almost as good a man as the books he wrote. He is not dead. Generations not yet born of young men and women who want to write will refute that word as applied to him.

At the time of Hemingway's death literary historian Malcolm Cowley tried to convey a sense of the force of his character:

"Hemingway's Pursuit of Fame" was published originally as the introduction to *Hemingway and the Mechanism of Fame*, edited by Matthew J. Bruccoli with Judith S. Baughman (Columbia: University of South Carolina Press, 2006), xvii–xxvi. Reprinted with permission of the University of South Carolina Press.

If Hemingway had appeared on a South Sea island two centuries ago, he would have been made a chief, his toenail parings would have been burned to protect them from commoners, and after his death he would have been deified.[2]

Hemingway had enjoyed the experience of reading his obituaries while he was alive, after the false reports of his death in 1954. The news of the African plane crash and his survival made the *Times* and *New York Herald Tribune* front pages for two days. The *Trib* also provided an editorial celebrating his endurance: "It is, somehow, characteristic of Ernest Hemingway that he should walk away from two plane crashes in the heart of Africa. Death has been his familiar companion for many years—an association freely accepted, even courted by the author, as if the dark shadow by his side threw his own abounding vitality into higher relief."[3]

Hemingway was easily the most famous writer in the world at the time of his suicide. His reputation and stature have fluctuated during the forty years since his death, but there has been no major reappraisal. Hemingway's work has withstood the depredations of political correctness, feminism, deconstruction, and postmodernism. He is the most recognizable American writer. He photographed well, and he provided a ready subject for caricatures. People who have never read his books—or any books—identify his face as that of "some kind of writer." Hemingway was famous for being famous. Archibald MacLeish, his on-and-off friend wrote of him:

> And what became of him? Fame became of him.
> Veteran out of the wars before he was twenty:
> Famous at twenty-five: thirty a master—[4]

This tribute characteristically exaggerates Hemingway's war record: he was a World War I veteran by courtesy, having been wounded distributing chocolate and tobacco while serving with the Red Cross.

Hemingway's extra-literary activities made the practice of authorship respectable to civilians who were suspicious of writing as an occupation for grown men. At the same time he may have damaged the profession of authorship by providing readers with a distorted model for how writers were supposed to live and work: writers who didn't emulate Hemingway were regarded as minor figures or hobbists or sissies. Many would-be writers wanted to be writers so that they could live like Hemingway.

Hemingway's fame was not a spontaneous response to his books. He deliberately cultivated and manipulated his public images. Ernest Hemingway's best-invented character was Ernest Hemingway—really a cluster of characters: hunter, fisherman, soldier, aesthetician, patriot, military strategist, yachtsman, drinker, womanizer, gourmet, sportsman, philosopher, naturalist, intellectual, anti-intellectual, traveler, war correspondent, boxer, big-game hunter—and author. In each of these roles he projected the authority of the professional: the man who knows the right way to do it and can do it correctly, the man who knows the true gen and the inside dope; the writer with the "built-in, shock proof, shit detector."[5] More than any other American writer, he became identified with his characters. His fiction was read as autobiography: Jake Barnes, Frederic Henry, and Robert Jordan were assumed to be Hemingway—or at least to have been based on him. He was not scrupulous about correcting the false connections between his life and his fiction—apart from denying that he had suffered Barnes's penile wound.

Although Hemingway complained about invasions of his privacy and interference with his working time, he was available to journalists and photographers. He pal-ed around with gossip columnists. The camera loved him: Hemingway with large dead animals, Hemingway with large fish, Hemingway with bullfighters, Hemingway with beautiful women, Hemingway in war, Hemingway in glamorous places, Hemingway with famous men. The extraordinary element of his self-generated celebrity is that everything he did apart from writing seemed to have something to do with literature. Other writers were rebuked for self-indulgence or irresponsibility—by critics and by Hemingway—when they left their desks; but it was somehow understood that Hemingway was fishing, hunting, boozing, wenching, and brawling for the eventual enrichment of American literature. He wrote forcefully and convincingly about the value of literature and the force of his commitment to it.

The *Pilar* provides a gauge of his incremental fame. Hemingway's fishing boat was thirty-eight feet long when he bought it in 1934; at the time of his death it had grown into a legendary vessel, along with the *Constitution*, the *Cutty Sark*, and the *Isle de France*.

> A country, finally, erodes and the dust blows away, the people all die and none of them were of any importance permanently, except those who practiced the arts, and these now wish to cease their work because it is too lonely, too hard to do, and is not fashionable. A thousand years makes economics silly and a work of art endures forever, but it is very difficult to do now and it is not fashionable.[6]

Hemingway's testimonies about his dedication to his craft take the form of boasting. For him the profession of authorship was a blood competition. In 1949 he analyzed his achievements and ambitions for his publisher, Charles Scribner III:

Am a man without any ambition, except to be champion of the world, I wouldn't fight Dr. Tolstoi in a 20 round bout because I know he would knock my ears off. The Dr. had terrific wind and could go forever and then some. But I would take him on for six and he would never hit me and would knock the shit out of him and maybe knock him out. He is easy to hit. but boy how he can hit. If I can live to 60 I can beat him. (MAYBE)

For your information I started out trying to beat dead writers that I knew how good they were. (Excuse vernacular) I tried for Mr. Turgenieff first and it wasn't too hard. Tried for Mr. Maupassant (won't concede him the de) and it took four of the best stories to beat him. He's beaten and if he was around he would know it. Then I tried for another guy (am getting embarrassed or embare-assed now from bragging; or state-ing) and I think I fought a draw with him. This other dead character.

Mr. Henry James I would just thumb him once the first time he grabbed and then hit him once where he had no balls and ask the referee to stop it.

There are some good guys nobody could ever beat like Mr. Shakespeare (The Champion) and Mr. Anonymous. But would be glad any time, if in training, to go twenty with Mr. Cervantes in his own home town (Alcala de Henares) and beat the shit out of him. Although Mr. C. very smart and would be learning all the time and would probably beat you in a return match. The third fight people would pay to see. Plenty peoples.

But these Brooklyn jerks are so ignorant that they start off fighting Mr. Tolstoi. And they announce they have beaten him before the fight starts. They should be hung by the balls until dead for ignorance. I can write good and I would not get into the ring with Mr. T. over the long distance unless I and my family were not eating.

In the big book I hope to take Mr. Melville and Mr. Doestoevsky, they are coupled as stable entry, and throw lots of mud in their faces because the track isn't fast. But you can only run so many of those kind of races. They take it out of you.

Know this sounds like bragging but Jeezoo Chrise you have to have confidence to be a champion and that is the only thing I ever wished to be.[7]

Hemingway got away with his braggadocio because his readers believe him. Why they wanted to believe him is unclear.

II

[. . .][8] Hemingway's life and career were driven by his need for self-dramatization. When he wasn't writing for publication, he compulsively dispatched hundreds—

probably thousands—of letters shaping and augmenting the Hemingway legends. [. . .] He was able to project the image that the time or occasion required. In the Twenties he was contemptuous of noble causes and patriotism; during the early Thirties he was apolitical; during the Spanish Civil War he was an anti-fascist activist; during World War II he was a patriot. These modulations did not hurt sales of his books. Eventually the bruiser became the sage who appeared on the cover of *Wisdom*.

Those seeking consistency in Hemingway's roles will find it most clearly in "The Man of Letters." When he discoursed on writing he did it with what Fitzgerald identified as "the authority of success."[9] His early detractors portrayed him as "a dumb ox"; but while they were writing term papers, Hemingway was taking tutorials with Ezra Pound, James Joyce, and Gertrude Stein. While they were editing their college literary magazines, he was editing the *transatlantic review* with Ford Madox Ford and being published by William Bird, Robert McAlmon, and Ezra Pound. Hemingway's comments on the craft and standards of literature document his wide reading, high requirements, literary intelligence, and contempt for critical fashions.

Hemingway's practice of literary criticism was always personal. It was also a form of vendetta. Thus his moving response to the death of Joseph Conrad provided an opportunity to denigrate T. S. Eliot: "If I knew that by grinding Mr. Eliot into a fine dry powder and sprinkling that powder over Mr. Conrad's grave Mr. Conrad would shortly appear, looking very much annoyed at the forced return and commence writing I would leave for London early tomorrow morning with a sausage grinder." That wisecrack does not disclose Eliot's literal capital crimes—which included being more admired than Hemingway in 1924—but it delivers the message that Hemingway was ready to kill for the sake of literature. Other long-term grudge fights were with Gertrude Stein, Waldo Frank, and, intermittently, William Faulkner—whose offenses included winning the Nobel Prize before Hemingway.

With the exception of the Stein feud, which she triggered by ridiculing him in *The Autobiography of Alice B. Toklas* (1933), Hemingway's feuds were one-sided. F. Scott Fitzgerald, who was the target of Hemingway's ridicule, alive and dead, observed in his notebooks that "Ernest would always give a hand to a man on a ledge a little higher up."[10] Hemingway consistently extolled Tolstoy, Turgenev, Stendhal, Joyce, and Pound—none of whom constituted competition or made claims for his influence on Hemingway.[11]

Much of Hemingway's literary criticism consists of blurbs and reading lists. He did not write a book review after 1925. He maintained distrust and contempt for critics—especially those of the academic persuasion. In *Green Hills of Africa*

(1935) he identified critics as "All angleworms in a bottle, trying to derive nourishment from their own contact and from the bottle."[12] Yet he forcefully asserted that the profession of literature was a fit endeavor for serious men—and few women. His standards were masculine: good writers had balls; bad writers were sissy boys; his detractors were fairies, lesbians, or virgins of both sexes.

The range of books and authors endorsed by Hemingway is characteristic of his stance as an anti-intellectual intellectual: from high culture to sports-writing, from Ezra Pound and Archibald MacLeish to Jimmy Cannon and Red Smith. He was not a promiscuous blurber. Some of his endorsements—for MacLeish, Pound, Josephine Herbst, John Herrmann, and George Plimpton—were in part acts of friendship; others were apparently unsolicited responses to novels he admired: W. C. Heinze's *The Professional,* C. S. Forester's *Beat to Quarters,* Nelson Algren's *The Man with the Golden Arm.*

The element Hemingway most admired in fiction was the accuracy that resulted from the writer's knowledge of the way it was, based on observation and experience, accurately reported. The word *truly* echoes throughout his nonfiction and fiction. He subscribed to Maxwell Perkins's dictum that "the utterly real thing in writing is the only thing that counts."[13] The getting-it-right test permeates his own work, as well as his judgments on other authors. Worthless books were written by fakers who didn't know what they were writing about.

III

Hemingway's rejection of political causes and writers who professed them was manifest before the Spanish Civil War. During the early Thirties when leftist orthodoxy was a requirement for literary merit and intellectual respectability, Hemingway sneered at the political converts and conformists. He insisted that political doctrines had nothing to do with enduring literature. *To Have and Have Not* (1937) ridicules the proletarian school of fiction and its practitioners, but most of the fellow-travelers didn't get it. They wanted to read it as a Steinbeckian sermon and claim Hemingway as a fellow fellow-traveler. During the Spanish Civil War he wrote pro-Loyalist statements, public letters, and introductory material for publications affiliated with the Communists. Josephine Herbst, who was in Spain with Hemingway, diagnosed the war's pull on him: "He wanted to be the war writer of his age and he knew it and went toward it."[14] The party-liners fancied that they had a proselyte; but Hemingway was a noncommunist anti-fascist. He did not sell out to the leftist critical establishment to refurbish his literary position, which had been bruised by denunciations of *Death in the Afternoon* (1932) and *Green Hills of Africa* (1935) as decadent and irrelevant in the Depression.

Hemingway maintained his complex honesty and suspicion of organizations. He divided the world into two categories: Insiders (us) and Outsiders (them). His writings provided readers with membership in the Insiders Club. As the ultimate Insider he was determined to obtain the real dope about the Spanish Civil War and use it. But Hemingway's emotional involvement with the international brigades and their volunteers penetrated his writings during the war. The combination of war and adultery in Madrid influenced his didactic play *The Fifth Column* (1938). But the zealots who had celebrated his Loyalist activities in Spain were outraged by *For Whom the Bell Tolls* (1940). Alvah Bessie's attack in *The Heart of Spain* (published by the Veterans of the Abraham Lincoln Brigade in 1951) indicates the extent of Hemingway's influence on public perception of that war:

> It was felt that Hemingway's talent and the personal support he rendered to many phases of the loyalist cause were shockingly betrayed in his work "For Whom the Bell Tolls" in which the Spanish people were cruelly misrepresented and leaders of the International Brigade maliciously slandered. The novel in its total impact presented an unforgivable distortion of the meaning of the struggle in Spain. Under the name and prestige of Hemingway, important aid was given to humanity's worst enemies.[15]

IV

Hemingway's introductions, forewords, and prefaces are about Hemingway. The work he is ostensibly discussing provides an occasion for him to demonstrate his expertise in that field. His claims are sometimes embarrassing. A writer is his own fault. He is also the fault of readers who expect or require writers to be romantic or glamorous or self-destructive figures. Celebrity writers learn that they can get away with almost anything; and this realization spoils or ruins many of them. Hemingway gave the customers what they wanted and thereby cultivated the Hemingway legend.

The self-legendizing process in these personal writings functioned through style and language that depart from the controlled prose and understatement of Hemingway's books. Here the writing sometimes resembles parody Hemingway—what James Gould Cozzens called "that dreadful 'simplicity' of style."[16] It is even oracular, as in the nature-mysticism of "On the American Dead in Spain": "This spring the dead will feel the earth beginning to live again. . . . And as long as all our dead live in the Spanish earth, and they will live as long as the earth lives, no system of tyranny ever will prevail in Spain." Hemingway used sarcasm in his opinion pieces to attack and destroy the opposition. The targets are the fools and the weaklings themselves, as well as their thinking and conduct. His weapon of choice was the ad hominem wisecrack.

Hemingway claimed that his influence on American prose was "only a certain clarification of the language which is now in public domain." There was more to it: he opened serious fiction to material that had been relegated to subliterary status. He customarily assessed writers in the terminology of sports: "Imagine not being able to get your fastball by Truman Capote or dropping a close decision to some Brooklyn Tolstoy." [. . .] Hemingway was probably the only writer who could have persuaded Americans who had never witnessed a bullfight that bullfighting was an ethical and aesthetic spectacle. More than any other writer, Ernest Hemingway influenced what American writers were able to write about and the words they used.

[. . .] By the Fifties—probably earlier—his efforts to maintain his legends and roles had subverted his creative powers. He continued to write, but his work was self-indulgent and read like imitation Hemingway. John O'Hara diagnosed the malady of Hemingway's fame in a 1960 letter to William Maxwell:

> We have in Hemingway the most important writer of our time and the most important writer since Shakespeare. That is the statement I made in the famous Sunday Times review of ACROSS THE RIVER AND INTO THE TREES. The various circumstances that have made him the most important are not all of a purely literary nature. Some are anything but. We start with a first-rate, original, conscientious artist, who caught on because of his excellence. The literary and then the general public quickly realized that a great artist was functioning in our midst. Publicity grew and grew, and Hemingway helped it to grow, not always deliberately but sometimes deliberately. He had an unusual, almost comical name; he was a big, strong, highly personable man. He associated himself, through his work, with big things: Africa, Italy, Spain, war, hunting, fishing, bullfighting, The Novel, Style, death, violence, castration, and a teasing remoteness from his homeland and from the lit'ry life. All these things make you think of Hemingway, and each and all of them add to his importance, that carries over from one writing job to another. I have a theory that there has not been a single issue of the Sunday Times book section in the past twenty years that has failed to mention Hemingway; his name is a synonym for writer with millions of people who have never read any work of fiction. Etc., etc. He is the father image of writing as FDR was of politics.
>
> Now this has not all been good for Hemingway, and Lord Acton's remark about power can be applied here, substituting acclaim for power. It is not good for any artist if he does not keep on working as, for example, Picasso has kept

on working. The test of the man, and possibly of the artist, is what he does after he gets the Nobel prize. Hemingway, I'm afraid, has not done well in that test. It is not only that he has rested on his laureate; he might have done better to have rested. I am told, but I do not quite believe it, that he has several novels in a bank vault. I believed it for a while—until I saw the Life pieces.[17] I now believe that he has been wasting his time, which would be okay if he had decided to quit, to decide that he wanted to write no more, and stuck to that decision. But there is a cheapness about Hemingway that I deplore. He likes to get favorable mention in Leonard Lyons's column, which is cheapness at the cheapest, and extremely costly to the man who is willing to settle for it. Hemingway can't stand the quiet of retirement, and he can't stand the company of the ass-kissers with whom he deliberately surrounds himself. They don't realize that you can't win with Hemingway. He will give you an argument on anything, and he hates you just as much for arguing with him as he does for agreeing with him; and yet he can't reject the toadies. He comes to New York, makes an ass of himself with Earl Wilson and Toots Shor, then hurries away to what? To watch bullfighting and, later, to write about what is to me the most disgusting spectacle in modern sports-entertainment. But the worst spectacle in the Life pieces was not the bullfighting itself but the collapse of Ernest Hemingway, artist and man.[18]

For most of his professional life Ernest Hemingway was an undiagnosed manic-depressive—with alcoholism, which deteriorated his ability to control that condition. There is a polygenetic predisposition for manic-depressive illness (bipolar disorder), and it carries a high prevalence of suicide: there were four suicides in the Hemingway family. Manic-depression usually kicks in between fifteen and the late twenties, and it can be triggered by post-traumatic stress. Hemingway was nineteen when he was wounded in World War I; but he was already an ardent self-fabulist. [. . .] After a certain point in the Thirties he may not have known when he was improving on the Ernest Hemingway saga.

Notes

1. *New York Times Book Review* (10 September 1950): 30–31.
2. "One Man's Hemingway," *New York Herald Tribune Book Review* (9 July 1961): 3, 15.
3. *Herald Tribune* (26 January 1954): 16.
4. Archibald MacLeish, *Years of the Dog, Actfive and Other Poems* (New York: Random House, 1948), p. 53.
5. George Plimpton, "The Art of Fiction: Ernest Hemingway," *Paris Review* (Spring 1958): 60–89.

6. Ernest Hemingway, *Green Hills of Africa* (New York: Scribners, 1935), p. 109.

7. 6 and 7 September 1949; *Selected Letters,* edited by Carlos Baker (New York: Scribners, 1981), p. 673.

8. The bracketed ellipses in this essay represent omission of references by M.J.B. to illustrative items included in his *Hemingway and the Mechanism of Fame,* the volume to which this essay is the introduction. Otherwise, M.J.B.'s observations about Hemingway have been faithfully retained. Ed.

9. *The Notebooks of F. Scott Fitzgerald,* edited by Bruccoli (New York and London: Harcourt Brace Jovanovich / Bruccoli Clark, 1978), #1915.

10. Ibid., #1819.

11. A monograph on the Hemingway/Pound connection is needed.

12. Hemingway, *Green Hills of Africa,* p. 21

13. 30 August 1935. *The Only Thing That Counts: The Ernest Hemingway / Maxwell Perkins Correspondence, 1925–1947,* edited by Bruccoli with Robert W. Trogdon (New York: Scribners, 1996), p. 224.

14. "The Starched Blue Sky of Spain," *Noble Savage* (Spring 1960): 93.

15. Alvah Bessie, *The Heart of Spain* (New York: Veterans of the Abraham Lincoln Brigade, 1951), p. vi.

16. 18 May 1964. *Selected Notebooks: 1960–1967,* edited by Matthew J. Bruccoli (Columbia, S.C., and Bloomfield Hills, Mich.: Bruccoli Clark, 1984), 83.

17. "The Dangerous Summer," *Life* (5, 12, 19 September 1960).

18. 23 September 1960. *Selected Letters of John O'Hara,* edited by Bruccoli (New York: Random House, 1978), pp. 348–349.

PUBLICATIONS BY MATTHEW J. BRUCCOLI

Books Written by Bruccoli

"'A handful, lying loose': A Study of F. Scott Fitzgerald's Basil Duke Lee Stories." Master's thesis, University of Virginia, 1956.

James Branch Cabell: A Bibliography. Part II, *Notes on the Cabell Collections at the University of Virginia.* Charlottesville: University of Virginia Press, 1957.

"The Composition of *Tender Is the Night:* A Study Based on the Manuscripts." Ph.D. dissertation, University of Virginia, 1961.

The Composition of "Tender Is the Night": A Study of the Manuscripts. Pittsburgh: University of Pittsburgh Press, 1963.

F. Scott Fitzgerald Collector's Handlist. Columbus, Ohio: Fitzgerald Newsletter, 1964.

Raymond Chandler: A Checklist. Kent, Ohio: Kent State University Press, 1968.

Checklist of F. Scott Fitzgerald. Columbus, Ohio: Charles E. Merrill, 1970.

Kenneth Millar / Ross Macdonald: A Checklist. Detroit: Bruccoli Clark / Gale Research, 1971.

F. Scott Fitzgerald: A Descriptive Bibliography. Pittsburgh: University of Pittsburgh Press, 1972.

John O'Hara: A Checklist. New York: Random House, 1972.

Apparatus for F. Scott Fitzgerald's "The Great Gatsby" [Under the Red, White, and Blue]. Columbia: University of South Carolina Press, 1974.

The O'Hara Concern: A Biography of John O'Hara. New York: Random House, 1975. Reprinted, with new afterword, "Appendix: O'Hara and *The New Yorker,*" and "*New Yorker* Rejections." Pittsburgh and London: University of Pittsburgh Press, 1995.

Ring W. Lardner: A Descriptive Bibliography. With Richard Layman. Pittsburgh: University of Pittsburgh Press, 1976.

"The Last of the Novelists": F. Scott Fitzgerald and "The Last Tycoon." Carbondale and Edwardsville: Southern Illinois University Press / London and Amsterdam: Feffer and Simons, 1977.

Compiled by Jennifer Hynes and Judith S. Baughman. First published, Columbia: University of South Carolina Press, 2008. Reprinted with permission.

John O'Hara: A Descriptive Bibliography. Pittsburgh: University of Pittsburgh Press, 1978.
Scott and Ernest: The Authority of Failure and the Authority of Success. New York: Random House; London: Bodley Head, 1978.
Raymond Chandler: A Descriptive Bibliography. Pittsburgh: University of Pittsburgh Press, 1979.
Supplement to F. Scott Fitzgerald: A Descriptive Bibliography. Pittsburgh: University of Pittsburgh Press, 1980.
James Gould Cozzens: A Descriptive Bibliography. Pittsburgh: University of Pittsburgh Press, 1981.
Some Sort of Epic Grandeur: The Life of F. Scott Fitzgerald. New York: Harcourt Brace Jovanovich; London: Hodder and Stoughton, 1981. Revised edition, London: Cardinal, 1991; New York: Carroll and Graf, 1993. Second revised edition, Columbia: University of South Carolina Press, 2002.
James Gould Cozzens: A Life Apart. New York, San Diego and London: Harcourt Brace Jovanovich, 1983.
Ross Macdonald / Kenneth Millar: A Descriptive Bibliography. Pittsburgh: University of Pittsburgh Press, 1983.
Ross Macdonald. San Diego, New York, and London: Harcourt Brace Jovanovich, 1984.
Nelson Algren: A Descriptive Bibliography. With Judith Baughman. Pittsburgh: University of Pittsburgh Press, 1985.
The Fortunes of Mitchell Kennerley, Bookman. San Diego, New York, and London: Harcourt Brace Jovanovich, 1986.
F. Scott Fitzgerald: A Descriptive Bibliography. Revised edition, Pittsburgh: University of Pittsburgh Press, 1987.
James Dickey: A Descriptive Bibliography. With Judith S. Baughman. Pittsburgh: University of Pittsburgh Press, 1990.
Fitzgerald and Hemingway: A Dangerous Friendship. New York: Carroll and Graf; London: Deutsch, 1994. Reprinted, Columbia, S.C.: Manly, 1999.
Reader's Companion to F. Scott Fitzgerald's "Tender Is the Night." With Judith S. Baughman. Columbia: University of South Carolina Press, 1996.
Classes on F. Scott Fitzgerald. Columbia: Thomas Cooper Library, University of South Carolina, 2001. Reprinted, Columbia, S.C.: Manly, 2004 [2001 on title page].
Classes on Ernest Hemingway. Columbia: Thomas Cooper Library, University of South Carolina, 2002.
Joseph Heller: A Descriptive Bibliography. With Park Bucker. New Castle, Del., and Pittsburgh: Oak Knoll Press and University of Pittsburgh Press, 2002.

Books Edited by Bruccoli

Introductions and other material by Bruccoli are noted.
The American, by Henry James. Boston: Houghton Mifflin, 1962.

The Sea-Wolf, by Jack London. Includes introduction. Boston: Houghton Mifflin, 1964.

Stephen Crane: 3 Stories of Peacetime. Includes introduction. Kingsport, Tenn.: Kingsport Press, 1965.

[Textual editor]. *Plagued by the Nightingale,* by Kay Boyle. Carbondale and Edwardsville: Southern Illinois University Press, 1966.

[Textual editor]. *Save Me the Waltz,* by Zelda Fitzgerald. Carbondale and Edwardsville: Southern Illinois University Press / London: Feffer and Simons, 1967. Reprinted, New York: New American Library, 1968.

[Textual editor]. *Palimpsest,* by H[ilda] D[oolittle]. Carbondale and Edwardsville: Southern Illinois University Press / London and Amsterdam: Feffer and Simons, 1968.

The Profession of Authorship in America, 1800–1870, by William Charvat. Includes preface. Columbus: Ohio State University Press, 1968. Reprinted, with postscript, New York: Columbia University Press, 1992.

Fitzgerald/Hemingway Annual 1969. Washington, D.C.: NCR Microcard Editions, 1969. Credited articles: "'The Light of the World': Stan Ketchel as 'My Sweet Christ,'" pp. 125–130, and "A Lost Book Review [by Hemingway]: *A Story-Teller's Story,*" pp. 71–75.

[Textual editor]. *Year before Last,* by Kay Boyle. Carbondale and Edwardsville: Southern Illinois University Press / London: Feffer and Simons, 1969.

Ernest Hemingway, Cub Reporter: Kansas City Star Stories. Includes preface. Pittsburgh: University of Pittsburgh Press, 1970.

Fitzgerald/Hemingway Annual 1970. With C. E. Frazer Clark, Jr. Washington, D.C.: NCR Microcard Editions, 1970. Credited articles: "Editorial," p. 265; "Fitzgerald's List of Neglected Books," pp. 229–230; "Francis Macomber and Francis Fitzgerald," p. 223; "A Note on Jordan Baker," pp. 232–233; "'Oh, Give Them Irony and Give Them Pity,'" p. 236; review of *Islands in the Stream,* by Ernest Hemingway, pp. 245–246; "Six Letters to the Menckens from F. Scott Fitzgerald," pp. 102–104; and "'Sleep of a University'—an Unrecorded Fitzgerald Poem," pp. 14–15.

[Textual editor]. *The Boy in the Bush,* by D. H. Lawrence and M. L. Skinner. Carbondale and Edwardsville: Southern Illinois University Press / London and Amsterdam: Feffer and Simons, 1971. Reprinted, London: Heinemann, 1972.

Ernest Hemingway's Apprenticeship: Oak Park, 1916–1917. Includes introduction. Washington, D.C.: NCR Microcard Editions, 1971.

Fitzgerald/Hemingway Annual 1971. With C. E. Frazer Clark, Jr. Washington, D.C.: NCR Microcard Editions, 1971. Credited articles: "Boulevardier Ghost," p. 312; "Fitzgerald's Ledger," pp. 3–31; "Fitzgerald's Marked Copy of *This Side of Paradise,*" pp. 64–69; "F. Scott Fitzgerald's Hollywood Assignments, 1937–1940," with Jennifer McCabe Atkinson, pp. 307–308; "Lost Hemingway Review Found," translated by James Franklin, pp. 195–106; "Ole Anderson, Ole Andreson, and Carl Andreson," pp. 341–342; and "Preface to *This Side of Paradise,*" pp. 1–2.

F. Scott Fitzgerald in His Own Time: A Miscellany. With Jackson R. Bryer; includes foreword. Kent, Ohio: Kent State University Press, 1971. Reprinted, New York: Popular Library, 1974.

Profile of F. Scott Fitzgerald. Includes preface and "*Tender Is the Night*—Reception and Reputation," pp. 92–106. Columbus, Ohio: Charles E. Merrill, 1971.

As Ever, Scott Fitz— : Letters between F. Scott Fitzgerald and His Literary Agent Harold Ober, 1919–1940. With Jennifer McCabe Atkinson; includes introduction. New York and Philadelphia: Lippincott, 1972; London: Woburn Press, 1973.

F. Scott Fitzgerald's Ledger: A Facsimile. Includes introduction. Washington, D.C.: Bruccoli Clark / NCR Microcard Editions, 1972.

Weeds, by Edith Summers Kelley. Includes introduction. Carbondale and Edwardsville: Southern Illinois University Press / London and Amsterdam: Feffer and Simons, 1972. Reprinted, New York: Popular Library, [n.d.].

Bits of Paradise: 21 Uncollected Stories by F. Scott and Zelda Fitzgerald. With Scottie Fitzgerald Smith; includes preface. London: Bodley Head, 1973; New York: Scribners, 1974. Reprinted, New York: Pocket Books, 1976.

Chandler before Marlowe: Raymond Chandler's Early Prose and Poetry, 1908–1912. Includes preface. Columbia: University of South Carolina Press, 1973.

The Chief Glory of Every People: Essays on Classic American Writers. Includes preface. Carbondale and Edwardsville: Southern Illinois University Press / London and Amsterdam: Feffer and Simons, 1973.

Fitzgerald/Hemingway Annual 1972. With C. E. Frazer Clark, Jr. Washington, D.C.: NCR Microcard Editions, 1973. Credited articles: "Hemingway Broadcast," p. 423; "Malcolm Lowry's Film Treatment for *Tender Is the Night,*" p. 337; review of *Edmund Wilson: A Bibliography,* by Richard David Ramsey, pp. 409–410; and review of *The Nick Adams Stories,* by Ernest Hemingway, pp. 397–398.

The Great Gatsby: A Facsimile of the Manuscript, by F. Scott Fitzgerald. Includes introduction. Washington, D.C.: Bruccoli Clark / Microcard Editions, 1973.

Hemingway at Auction, 1930–1973. With C. E. Frazer Clark, Jr.; includes compilers' note. Detroit: Bruccoli Clark / Gale Research, 1973.

The Devil's Hand, by Edith Summers Kelley. Includes afterword. Carbondale and Edwardsville: Southern Illinois University Press / London and Amsterdam: Feffer and Simons, 1974. Reprinted, New York: Popular Library, 1976.

Fitzgerald/Hemingway Annual 1973. With C. E. Frazer Clark, Jr. Washington, D.C.: Microcard Editions, 1974. Credited articles: "Bruccoli Addenda," pp. 339–346; "Discussion at the Paris Conference," with Morrill Cody et al., pp. 77–81; "Donald Ogden Stewart: An Interview," pp. 83–89; "An Unrecorded Hemingway Public Letter," pp. 227–229; and "Ways of Seeing Hemingway," pp. 197–207.

The Romantic Egoists: A Pictorial Autobiography from the Scrapbooks and Albums of F. Scott and Zelda Fitzgerald. With Scottie Fitzgerald Smith and Joan P. Kerr. New York: Scribners, 1974. Reprinted, Columbia, S.C.: Bruccoli Clark, 1984; Columbia: University of South Carolina Press, 2003.

Fitzgerald/Hemingway Annual 1974. With C. E. Frazer Clark, Jr. Englewood, Colo.: Microcard Editions, 1975. Credited articles: "Bruccoli Addenda II," pp. 275–283; and "Interview with Allen Tate," pp. 101–113.

Fitzgerald/Hemingway Annual 1975. With C. E. Frazer Clark, Jr. Englewood, Colo.: Microcard Editions, 1975. Credited articles: "Bruccoli Addenda," pp. 337–339; "Fitzgerald's St. Paul Academy Publications: Possible Addenda," pp. 147–148; "'How Are You and the Family Old Sport?': Gerlach and Gatsby," pp. 33–36; and "Stan Ketchel and Steve Ketchel: A Further Note on 'The Light of the World,'" pp. 325–326.

The Blue Dahlia: A Screenplay, by Raymond Chandler. Includes afterword. Carbondale and Edwardsville: Southern Illinois University Press / London: Feffer and Simons, 1976; London: Hamish Hamilton / Elm Tree Books, 1976.

The Cruise of the Rolling Junk, by F. Scott Fitzgerald. Includes introduction. Bloomfield Hills, Mich., and Columbia, S.C.: Bruccoli Clark, 1976.

Pages: The World of Books, Writers, and Writing. With C. E. Frazer Clark, Jr.; includes prefatory note. Detroit: Gale Research, 1976.

Some Champions: Sketches & Fiction by Ring Lardner. With Richard Layman; includes introduction. New York: Scribners, 1976. Reprinted, New York: Collier Books, 1992.

"An Artist Is His Own Fault": John O'Hara on Writers and Writing. Includes introduction. Carbondale and Edwardsville: Southern Illinois University Press / London and Amsterdam: Feffer and Simons, 1977.

Conversations with Writers [I]. With others. Detroit: Bruccoli Clark / Gale Research, 1977. Credited interviews: "Vance Bourjaily," pp. 2–23; "James Dickey," pp. 24–45; "William Price Fox," pp. 46–80; "Mary Welsh Hemingway," pp. 180–194; "Ring Lardner, Jr.," pp. 196–215; "Wallace Markfield," pp. 216–236; and "Donald Ogden Stewart," pp. 238–250.

First Printings of American Authors: Contributions toward Descriptive Checklists. Volume 1, with others. Detroit: Bruccoli Clark / Gale Research, 1977. Author of "Raymond Chandler 1888–1959," pp. 63–65; "Robert Coover 1932– ," pp. 69–70; "James Gould Cozzens 1903– ," pp. 71–74; "Hart Crane 1899–1932," pp. 75–77; "Stephen Crane 1871–1900," pp. 79–82; "James Dickey 1923– ," pp. 93–95; "Irvin Faust 1924– ," p. 127; "F. Scott Fitzgerald 1896–1940," pp. 131–134; "George V. Higgins 1939– ," p. 187; "James Jones 1921– ," pp. 193–195; "Edith Summers Kelley 1884–1956," p. 215; "Wallace Markfield 1922– ," p. 241; "Kenneth Millar [John Macdonald, John Ross Macdonald, Ross Macdonald] 1915– ," pp. 259–263; "John O'Hara 1905–1970," pp. 285–289; "Eugene O'Neill 1888–1953," pp. 291–296; and "Kurt Vonnegut, Jr. 1922– ," pp. 395–397.

Fitzgerald/Hemingway Annual 1976. Englewood, Colo.: Information Handling Services, 1977. Credited articles: "'Ballet Shoes': A Movie Synopsis," pp. 2–7, and "Bruccoli Addenda," pp. 251–253.

Conversations with Writers II. With others. Detroit: Bruccoli Clark / Gale Research, 1978. Credited interviews: "Stanley Ellin," pp. 2–20; "James T. Farrell," pp. 22–45;

"Irvin Faust," pp. 46–72; "Barbara Ferry Johnson," pp. 74–93; and "Anita Loos," pp. 124–140.

First Printings of American Authors: Contributions toward Descriptive Checklists. Volume 2, with others. Detroit: Bruccoli Clark / Gale Research, 1978. Author of "Zelda Fitzgerald 1900–1948," p. 163.

First Printings of American Authors: Contributions toward Descriptive Checklists. Volume 3, with others. Detroit: Bruccoli Clark / Gale Research, 1978. Author of "Sheilah Graham," pp. 137–138.

F. Scott Fitzgerald's Screenplay for Three Comrades by Erich Maria Remarque. Includes afterword. Carbondale and Edwardsville: Southern Illinois University Press / London and Amsterdam: Feffer and Simons, 1978. Reprinted, New York: Popular Library, 1979.

Just Representations: A James Gould Cozzens Reader. Includes introduction. Carbondale and Edwardsville: Southern Illinois University Press / New York and London: Harcourt Brace Jovanovich, 1978.

The Notebooks of F. Scott Fitzgerald. Includes introduction. New York and London: Harcourt Brace Jovanovich / Bruccoli Clark, 1978.

Selected Letters of John O'Hara. Includes introduction. New York: Random House, 1978.

First Printings of American Authors: Contributions toward Descriptive Checklists. Volume 4, with others. Detroit: Bruccoli Clark / Gale Research, 1979. Author of unsigned entries.

Fitzgerald/Hemingway Annual 1978. With Richard Layman. Detroit: Bruccoli Clark / Gale Research, 1979. Credited articles: "Lipstick: A College Comedy," pp. 2–35, and "The Perkins/Wilson Correspondence about Publication of *The Last Tycoon*," pp. 63–66.

James Gould Cozzens: New Acquist of True Experience. Includes introduction. Carbondale and Edwardsville: Southern Illinois University Press / London and Amsterdam: Feffer and Simons, 1979.

The Naked City: A Screenplay, by Malvin Wald and Albert Maltz. Carbondale and Edwardsville: Southern Illinois University Press / London and Amsterdam: Feffer and Simons, 1979.

The Price Was High: The Last Uncollected Stories, by F. Scott Fitzgerald. Includes introduction, "$106,585." New York: Harcourt Brace Jovanovich / Bruccoli Clark; London: Quartet, 1979.

San Francisco: A Screenplay, by Anita Loos. Carbondale and Edwardsville: Southern Illinois University Press / London and Amsterdam: Feffer and Simons, 1979.

Two by O'Hara: "The Man Who Could Not Lose," an Original Screen Story, and "Far from Heaven," a Melodrama, by John O'Hara. Includes foreword. New York and London: Harcourt Brace Jovanovich / Bruccoli Clark, 1979. Reprinted, Franklin Center, Pa.: Franklin Library, 1979.

Correspondence of F. Scott Fitzgerald. With Margaret M. Duggan; includes introduction. New York: Random House, 1980.

Fitzgerald/Hemingway Annual 1979. With Richard Layman. Detroit: Bruccoli Clark / Gale Research, 1980. Credited articles: "Bennett Cerf's Fan Letter on *Tender Is the Night:* A Source for Abe North's Death," pp. 229–230; review of *Hokum,* by Morris McNeil and apparently Ernest Hemingway, pp. 427–428; and "Zelda Fitzgerald's Lost Stories," pp. 123–126.

Poems, 1911–1940, by F. Scott Fitzgerald. Bloomfield Hills, Mich., and Columbia, S.C.: Bruccoli Clark, 1981.

Selected Notebooks: 1960–1967, by James Gould Cozzens. Includes introduction. Columbia, S.C., and Bloomfield Hills, Mich.: Bruccoli Clark, 1984.

A Time of War: Air Force Diaries and Pentagon Memos, 1943–45, by James Gould Cozzens. Includes introduction. Columbia, S.C., and Bloomfield Hills, Mich.: Bruccoli Clark, 1984.

The New Black Mask Quarterly. Number 1, with Richard Layman. San Diego: Harcourt Brace Jovanovich, 1985.

The New Black Mask Quarterly. Number 2, with Richard Layman. San Diego: Harcourt Brace Jovanovich, 1985. Uncredited interview with Elmore Leonard, pp. 1–12.

The New Black Mask Quarterly. Number 3, with Richard Layman. San Diego: Harcourt Brace Jovanovich, 1985. Uncredited interview with Donald E. Westlake, pp. 1–15.

New Essays on "The Great Gatsby." Includes introduction. Cambridge, New York, et al.: Cambridge University Press, 1985.

Conversations with Ernest Hemingway. Includes introduction. Jackson and London: University Press of Mississippi, 1986.

The New Black Mask Quarterly. Number 4, with Richard Layman. San Diego: Harcourt Brace Jovanovich, 1986.

The New Black Mask Quarterly. Number 5, with Richard Layman. San Diego: Harcourt Brace Jovanovich, 1986. Uncredited interview with William Haggard, pp. 1–20.

The New Black Mask Quarterly. Number 6, with Richard Layman. San Diego: Harcourt Brace Jovanovich, 1986.

The New Black Mask Quarterly. Number 7, with Richard Layman. San Diego: Harcourt Brace Jovanovich, 1986. Uncredited interview with Ed McBain, pp. 1–11.

The New Black Mask Quarterly. Number 8, with Richard Layman. San Diego: Harcourt Brace Jovanovich, 1987.

A Matter of Crime: New Stories from the Masters of Mystery & Suspense. Volume 1, with Richard Layman. San Diego: Harcourt Brace Jovanovich, 1987.

A Matter of Crime: New Stories from the Masters of Mystery & Suspense. Volume 2, with Richard Layman. San Diego: Harcourt Brace Jovanovich, 1987. Uncredited interview with Joe Gores, pp. 1–16.

F. Scott Fitzgerald: Inscriptions. Includes introduction. Columbia, S.C.: Matthew J. Bruccoli, 1988.

A Matter of Crime: New Stories from the Masters of Mystery & Suspense. Volume 3, with Richard Layman. San Diego: Harcourt Brace Jovanovich, 1988. Uncredited interview with George V. Higgins, pp. 1–13.

A Matter of Crime: New Stories from the Masters of Mystery & Suspense. Volume 4, with Richard Layman. San Diego: Harcourt Brace Jovanovich, 1988.

Hardboiled Mystery Writers: Raymond Chandler, Dashiell Hammett, Ross Macdonald. With Richard Layman. Volume 6 of *Dictionary of Literary Biography Documentary Series.* Detroit: Bruccoli Clark Layman / Gale Research, 1989. Reprinted as *Hardboiled Mystery Writers: Raymond Chandler, Dashiell Hammett, Ross Macdonald: A Literary Reference* (New York: Carroll and Graf, 2002).

Vladimir Nabokov: Selected Letters, 1940–1977. With Dmitri Nabokov. San Diego, New York, and London: Harcourt Brace Jovanovich / Bruccoli Clark Layman, 1989.

The Short Stories of F. Scott Fitzgerald. Includes preface. New York: Scribners, 1989. Preface reprinted in *Babylon Revisited,* by Fitzgerald (Norwalk, Conn.: Easton Press, 1989).

F. Scott Fitzgerald Manuscripts. 18 volumes, includes introductions. New York: Garland, 1990–1991. *The Great Gatsby,* 1 volume, 1990; *The Beautiful and Damned,* 2 volumes, 1990, edited and introduced by Alan Margolies; *The Last Tycoon,* 3 volumes, 1990; *This Side of Paradise: The Manuscripts and Typescripts,* 2 volumes, 1990; *Tender Is the Night: The Melarky and Kelly Versions,* 2 volumes, 1990; *Tender Is the Night: The Diver Version,* 5 volumes, 1991; *The Vegetable, Stories, and Articles,* 3 volumes, 1991.

The Sun Also Rises: A Facsimile Edition, by Ernest Hemingway. 2 volumes, includes introduction. Detroit: Manly/Omnigraphics, 1990.

Facts On File Bibliography of American Fiction, 1919–1988. 2 volumes, with Judith S. Baughman; includes series introduction and editors' note. New York: Manly / Facts On File, 1991.

The Great Gatsby, by F. Scott Fitzgerald. Volume 1 of *The Cambridge Edition of the Works of F. Scott Fitzgerald.* Includes introduction, textual apparatus, explanatory notes, and seven appendices. Cambridge, New York, et al.: Cambridge University Press, 1991. Text reprinted, with new introduction by Bruccoli and "Winter Dreams." London and Sydney: Scribners, 1991; London: Abacus, 1992. Text reprinted, with new preface and notes by Bruccoli. New York et al.: Collier Books / Scribner Classic, 1992. The 18th printing [2000] adds "Foreword to the Seventy-fifth Anniversary Edition: F. Scott Fitzgerald, *The Great Gatsby,* and the House of Scribner" by Bruccoli.

Zelda Fitzgerald: The Collected Writings. Includes preface. New York: Scribners; New York and Toronto: Macmillan, 1991. Reprinted as *The Collected Writings: Zelda Fitzgerald* (London: Little, Brown, 1992; London: Abacus, 1993). Reprinted as *The Collected Writings of Zelda Fitzgerald* (Tuscaloosa and London: University of Alabama Press, 1997).

Gibbsville, PA: The Classic Stories, by John O'Hara. Includes fifty-three stories and introduction. New York: Carroll and Graf, 1992. Republished with forty-two stories, New York: Carroll and Graf, 2004.

Ring around the Bases: The Complete Baseball Stories of Ring Lardner. Includes introduction. New York: Scribners, 1992. Reprinted, Norwalk, Conn.: Easton Press, 1996.

Reprinted, with a newly discovered story, Columbia: University of South Carolina Press, 2003.

Babylon Revisited: The Screenplay, by F. Scott Fitzgerald. Includes afterword. New York: Carroll and Graf, 1993.

The Love of the Last Tycoon: A Western, by F. Scott Fitzgerald. Volume 2 of *The Cambridge Edition of the Works of F. Scott Fitzgerald.* Includes chronology, introduction, facsimiles, inventory of drafts, and textual apparatus. Cambridge, New York, and Melbourne: Cambridge University Press, 1993. Text reprinted, with new preface and notes by Bruccoli, New York et al.: Scribner, 1993. Text reprinted, with new preface and notes by Bruccoli, London: Little, Brown, 1994; London: Abacus, 1995.

F. Scott Fitzgerald: A Life in Letters. With Judith S. Baughman; includes introduction and "A Brief Life of Fitzgerald." New York: Simon & Schuster / Touchstone, 1994; London: Penguin, 1998.

Modern African American Writers. With Judith S. Baughman. New York: Manly / Facts On File, 1994.

Modern Classic Writers. With Judith S. Baughman. New York: Manly / Facts On File, 1994.

Modern Women Writers. With Judith S. Baughman. New York: Manly / Facts On File, 1994.

Tender Is the Night: A Romance, by F. Scott Fitzgerald. Includes explanatory note. London: Samuel Johnson, 1995.

Fie! Fie! Fi-Fi! A Facsimile of the 1914 Acting Script and the Musical Score, book and lyrics by F. Scott Fitzgerald, music by D. D. Griffin, A. L. Booth, and P. B. Dickey. Includes introduction. Columbia: University of South Carolina Press for the Thomas Cooper Library, 1996.

F. Scott Fitzgerald on Authorship. With Judith S. Baughman; includes introduction, "The Man of Letters as Professional." Columbia: University of South Carolina Press, 1996.

Main Street, by Sinclair Lewis. Includes introduction. New York: Carroll & Graf, 1996.

The Only Thing That Counts: The Ernest Hemingway / Maxwell Perkins Correspondence, 1925–1947. With Robert W. Trogdon; includes introduction. New York: Scribners, 1996.

Tender Is the Night, by F. Scott Fitzgerald. "Centennial Edition"; includes introduction with note on the text. London: Everyman, 1996.

American Expatriate Writers: Paris in the Twenties. Volume 15 of *Dictionary of Literary Biography Documentary Series.* With Robert W. Trogdon; includes introduction. Detroit: Bruccoli Clark Layman / Gale Research, 1997.

The Bad and the Beautiful, by Charles Schnee. Carbondale and Edwardsville: Southern Illinois University Press, 1998.

Dictionary of Literary Biography Yearbook: 1997. With George Garrett. Detroit: Bruccoli Clark Layman / Gale Research, 1998. Credited articles: "Novels for Grown-Ups," pp. 182–184, in "The James Gould Cozzens Case Reopened"; "Public Domain and the

Violation of Texts," pp. 193–195, in "Reader's *Ulysses* Symposium"; and "William R. Emerson" (1923–1997), p. 367.

The Rich Boy and Other Stories, by F. Scott Fitzgerald. Includes introduction. London: Phoenix, 1998.

Butterfield 8, by John O'Hara. Includes introduction. London: Prion, 1999

Crux: The Letters of James Dickey. With Judith S. Baughman; includes introduction. New York: Knopf, 1999.

Dictionary of Literary Biography Yearbook: 1998. Detroit: Bruccoli Clark Layman / Gale Group, 1999. Credited articles: "Charley" [tribute to Charles Mann], pp. 258–259, and "The Great Modern Library Scam," pp. 117–118.

Pal Joey, by John O'Hara. Includes introduction. London: Prion, 1999.

Dictionary of Literary Biography Yearbook: 1999. Detroit: Bruccoli Clark Layman / Gale Group, 2000. Credited article: "Joseph and George" [tribute to Joseph Heller and George V. Higgins], pp. 389–390.

F. Scott Fitzgerald's "The Great Gatsby": A Documentary Volume. Volume 219 of *Dictionary of Literary Biography.* Includes introduction. Detroit: Bruccoli Clark Layman / Gale Group, 2000. Reprinted as *F. Scott Fitzgerald's "The Great Gatsby": A Literary Reference* (New York: Carroll and Graf, 2000).

O Lost: A Story of the Buried Life, by Thomas Wolfe. With Arlyn Bruccoli; includes introduction. Columbia: University of South Carolina Press, 2000.

To Loot My Life Clean: The Thomas Wolfe–Maxwell Perkins Correspondence. With Park Bucker. Columbia: University of South Carolina Press, 2000.

Trimalchio: A Facsimile Edition of the Original Galley Proofs for "The Great Gatsby," by F. Scott Fitzgerald. Includes afterword and postscript. Columbia: University of South Carolina Press in Cooperation with Thomas Cooper Library, 2000.

Before Gatsby: The First Twenty-six Stories, by F. Scott Fitzgerald. With Judith S. Baughman; includes introduction and "Textual and Editorial Policy." Columbia: University of South Carolina Press, 2001.

Dictionary of Literary Biography Yearbook 2000. Detroit: Bruccoli Clark Layman / Gale Group, 2001. Credited articles: "The Books of George V. Higgins: A Checklist of Editions and Printings," pp. 293–312; "Hemingway Salesmen's Dummies," pp. 319–320; and "Interview with Virginia Spencer Carr," pp. 257–264.

Dictionary of Literary Biography Yearbook 2001. Detroit: Bruccoli Clark Layman / Gale Group, 2002. Credited articles: "Charles Elliot Frazer Clark, Jr. (1925–2001)," pp. 305–310, and "F. Scott Fitzgerald: A Descriptive Bibliography, Supplement (2001)," pp. 399–425.

The Last Romantic: A Poet among Publishers: The Oral Autobiography of John Hall Wheelock. With Judith S. Baughman; includes introduction. Columbia: University of South Carolina Press, 2002.

Catch as Catch Can: The Collected Stories and Other Writings, by Joseph Heller. With Park Bucker; includes foreword. New York: Simon & Schuster; London: Scribner, 2003.

Dictionary of Literary Biography Yearbook 2002. With George Garrett. Detroit: Bruccoli Clark Layman / Thomson / Gale, 2003. Credited articles: "The Extension of Copyright," pp. 502–504; "The Hemingway/Fenton Correspondence," pp. 282–299; "Hyman Kritzer: Acquisitions Man," p. 439; "Interview with Barney Rosset," pp. 132–137; "Interview with Derek Robinson," 345–351; and "Interview with Joe Gores," 339–344.

F. Scott Fitzgerald's "Tender Is the Night": A Documentary Volume. Volume 273 of *Dictionary of Literary Biography.* With George Parker Anderson; includes introduction. Detroit: Bruccoli Clark Layman / Thomson / Gale, 2003.

Conversations with F. Scott Fitzgerald. With Judith S. Baughman; includes introduction. Jackson: University Press of Mississippi, 2004.

Conversations with John le Carré. With Judith S. Baughman; includes introduction and chronology. Jackson: University Press of Mississippi, 2004.

The Easiest Thing in the World: The Uncollected Fiction of George V. Higgins. Includes editor's note. New York: Carroll and Graf, 2004.

James Gould Cozzens: A Documentary Volume. Volume 294 of *Dictionary of Literary Biography.* Includes introduction. Detroit: Bruccoli Clark Layman / Thomson / Gale, 2004.

The Sons of Maxwell Perkins: Letters of F. Scott Fitzgerald, Ernest Hemingway, Thomas Wolfe, and Their Editor. With Judith S. Baughman; includes preface and introduction. Columbia: University of South Carolina Press, 2004.

Hemingway and the Mechanism of Fame: Statements, Public Letters, Introductions, Forewords, Prefaces, Blurbs, Reviews, and Endorsements. With Judith S. Baughman; includes introduction and chronology. Columbia: University of South Carolina Press, 2005.

Thomas Wolfe's Friendship with Henry Volkening: The Documents. With Arlyn Bruccoli; includes introduction. [Akron, Ohio]: Thomas Wolfe Society, 2005.

John O'Hara: A Documentary Volume. Volume 324 of *Dictionary of Literary Biography.* Includes introduction, "The Way It Was." Detroit: Bruccoli Clark Layman / Thomson / Gale, 2006.

This Side of Paradise, by F. Scott Fitzgerald. Includes introduction. New York: Signet Classics, 2006.

John O'Hara's Hollywood. Includes introduction. New York: Carroll and Graf, 2007.

The Four Lost Men: The Previously Unpublished Long Version, Including the Original Short Story, by Thomas Wolfe. With Arlyn Bruccoli; includes introduction. Columbia: University of South Carolina Press, 2008.

Into the Modern, 1896–1945. Volume 3 of *Encyclopedia of American Literature.* Revised and augmented from the first edition prepared by Carl Rollyson; with George Parker Anderson and Judith S. Baughman. New York: Facts On File, 2008. Author of the introduction, pp. ix–xi; *"All the Sad Young Men"* (as Morris Colden), p. 7; *"Appointment in Samarra,"* p. 13; "Babylon Revisited," pp. 19–20; "The Basil Duke Lee Stories" (as Colden), p. 21; "Boni and Liveright" (as Colden), p. 27; *"Butterfield 8"* (as

Colden), p. 32; "The Chicago Renaissance" (as Colden), p. 44; "Cozzens, James Gould," 48–51; *"The Crack-Up,"* p. 51; "The Diamond as Big as the Ritz" (as Colden), pp. 61–62; "The Doctor's Son" (as Colden), p. 63; "Fitzgerald, F. Scott," pp. 95–99; "Fitzgerald, Zelda Sayre" (as Colden), p. 100; *"Flappers and Philosophers"* (as Colden), p. 100; "Fuchs, Daniel" (as Colden), p. 106; "Gibbsville, Pennsylvania" (as Colden), p. 109; *"The Great Gatsby,"* p. 114; "Harcourt, Brace" (as Colden), pp. 123–124; "Hard-Boiled Fiction" (as Colden), p. 124; "The Jazz Age" (as Colden), p. 149; *"The Just and the Unjust"* (as Colden), p. 155; "Kelley, Edith Summers" (as Colden), p. 158; *"The Last Adam"* (as Colden), p. 167; "The Last of the Belles" (as Colden), p. 167; *"The Last Tycoon / The Love of the Last Tycoon,"* pp. 167–168; "The Lost Generation" (as Colden), p. 181; "May Day" (as Colden), p. 190; *"Men and Brethren"* (as Colden), p. 193; "The Modern Library" (as Colden), p. 200; *"New York Herald Tribune"* (as Colden), p. 209; "O'Hara, John," pp. 221–224; "One Trip Abroad" (as Colden), p. 230; "Perkins, Maxwell E." (as Colden), p. 236; "The Rich Boy" (as Colden), p. 258; "Charles Scribner's Sons" (as Colden), pp. 272–273; "Simon and Schuster" (as Colden), p. 277; *"S. S. San Pedro"* (as Colden), p. 285; "Stewart, Donald Ogden" (as Colden), p. 294; *"The Story of a Novel"* (as Colden), p. 295; *"Tales of the Jazz Age"* (as Colden), p. 299; *"Taps at Reveille"* (as Colden), p. 299; *"Tender Is the Night,"* pp. 301–302; *"This Side of Paradise,"* p. 303; *"The Web and the Rock"* (as Colden), pp. 322–323; "Winter Dreams," p. 343; and *"You Can't Go Home Again"* (as Colden), p. 354.

The Magical Campus: University of North Carolina Writings, 1917–1920, by Thomas Wolfe. With Aldo P. Magi; includes preface. Columbia: University of South Carolina Press, 2008.

Student's Encyclopedia of American Literary Characters. 4 volumes. With Judith S. Baughman. New York: Manly / Facts On File, 2008. Author of the introduction, pp. lvii–lviii; "Daisy Fay Buchanan," pp. 386–387; "Nick Carraway," pp. 387–388; "Jay Gatsby," pp. 389–390; "Monroe Stahr," pp. 390–391; "Nicole Diver," pp. 393–395; "Richard (Dick) Diver," pp. 395–396; "Amory Blaine," pp. 396–397; "Lew Archer," pp. 809–810; and "James Malloy," pp. 972–973.

F. Scott Fitzgerald in the Marketplace: The Auction and Dealer Catalogues, 1935–2006. With Judith S. Baughman; includes introduction and overview. Columbia: University of South Carolina Press, 2009.

Contributions to Books Edited or Written by Others

"Ancient History," pp. 26–31, with Robert Immerman. *Observatory,* edited by Neil H. Hertz. New York: Bronx High School of Science, 1949.

More Traditional Ballads of Virginia; Collected with the Cooperation of Members of the Virginia Folklore Society, edited by Arthur Kyle Davis, Jr.; editorial assistance by Bruccoli, George Walton Williams, and Paul Clayton Worthington. Chapel Hill: University of North Carolina Press, 1960.

"Hawthorne as a Collector's Item, 1885–1924," pp. 387–400. *Hawthorne Centenary Essays,* edited by Roy Harvey Pearce. Columbus: Ohio State University Press, 1964. Reprinted as "Appendix," pp. 374–390, in *Hawthorne at Auction, 1894–1971,* edited by C. E. Frazer Clark, Jr. (Detroit: Bruccoli Clark / Gale Research, 1972).

"Focus on *Appointment in Samarra:* The Importance of Knowing What You Are Talking About," pp. 129–136. *Tough Guy Writers of the Thirties,* edited by David Madden. Carbondale and Edwardsville: Southern Illinois University Press / London and Amsterdam: Feffer and Simons, 1968.

"'A Might Collation': Animadversions on the Text of F. Scott Fitzgerald," pp. 28–50. *Editing Twentieth Century Texts: Papers Given at the Editorial Conference, University of Toronto, November 1969,* edited by Francess G. Halpenny. Toronto: University of Toronto Press, 1972.

"Stephen Crane as Collector's Item," pp. 153–173. *Stephen Crane in Transition: Centenary Essays,* edited by Joseph Katz. DeKalb: Northern Illinois University Press, 1972.

"A Mirror for Bibliographers: Duplicate Plates in Modern Printing," pp. 190–195. *Readings in Descriptive Bibliography,* edited by John Bush Jones. Kent, Ohio: Kent State University Press, 1974. Revision of essay published in *Papers of the Bibliographical Society of America* 54 (Second Quarter 1960): 83–88.

"Bruccoli Addenda," pp. 247–249, and "The Feather Fan," pp. 3–8. *Fitzgerald/Hemingway Annual 1977,* edited by Margaret M. Duggan and Richard Layman. Detroit: Bruccoli Clark / Gale Research, 1977.

"On F. Scott Fitzgerald and 'Bernice Bobs Her Hair,'" pp. 219–223. *The American Short Story,* edited by Calvin Skaggs. New York: Dell, 1977.

"Kenneth Millar," pp. 122–124. *Dictionary of Literary Biography Yearbook: 1983,* edited by Mary Bruccoli and Jean W. Ross. Detroit: Bruccoli Clark / Gale Research, 1984.

"Recollections of an ASE Collector," pp. 23, 25–28. *Books in Action: The Armed Services Editions,* edited by John Y. Cole. Washington, D.C.: Library of Congress, 1984.

"The Bestseller Lists: An Assessment," pp. 38–39. *Dictionary of Literary Biography Yearbook: 1984,* edited by Jean W. Ross. Detroit: Bruccoli Clark / Gale Research, 1985.

"Packaging Papa: *The Garden of Eden,*" pp. 79–82. *Dictionary of Literary Biography Yearbook: 1986,* edited by J. M. Brook. Detroit: Bruccoli Clark Layman / Gale Research 1987.

Unsigned entries. *First Printings of American Authors: Contributions toward Descriptive Checklists.* Volume 5, edited by Philip B. Eppard. Detroit: Bruccoli Clark Layman / Gale Research, 1987.

Colden, Morris P. [pseud.] "All in the Family: Writers Related to Writers," pp. 41–43; "First Books—Famous and Forgotten—by Well-Known American Writers," pp. 153–158; "Writing under Cover: American Literary Pseudonyms," pp. 159–162; "'Without Whom . . .': Book Dedications," pp. 177–182; "Writing Close to Life: Romans à Clef," pp. 183–186; "Literary Cons: Hoaxes, Frauds, and Plagiarism in

American Literature," with David A. Plott, pp. 187–194; and "The Profession of Authorship: Authors/Publishers/Editors/Agents," pp. 195–200. *American Literary Almanac: From 1608 to the Present; An Original Compendium of Facts and Anecdotes about Literary Life in the United States of America,* edited by Karen L. Rood. New York: Bruccoli Clark Layman / Facts On File, 1988.

"O'Hara, John Henry," pp. 480–482. *Dictionary of American Biography, Supplement Eight, 1966–1970,* edited by John A. Garraty and Mark C. Carnes. New York: Scribners / London: Collier Macmillan, 1988.

"John O'Hara's Pottsville Journalism," pp. 192–196, and "A Tribute" [to Charles E. Feinberg], p. 217. *Dictionary of Literary Biography Yearbook: 1988,* edited by J. M. Brook. Detroit: Bruccoli Clark Layman / Gale Research, 1989.

Introduction, pp. vii–xi. *The Sun Also Rises,* by Ernest Hemingway. Norwalk, Conn.: Easton Press, 1990.

"Conversations with Rare Book Dealers I: An Interview with Glenn Horowitz," pp. 184–192. *Dictionary of Literary Biography Yearbook: 1990,* edited by James W. Hipp. Detroit: Bruccoli Clark Layman / Gale Research, 1991.

"Getting It Right: The Publishing Process and the Correction of Factual Errors—with Reference to *The Great Gatsby,*" pp. 40–59. *Essays in Honor of William B. Todd,* edited by Dave Oliphant, compiled by Warner Barnes and Larry Carver. Austin: Harry Ransom Humanities Research Center, University of Texas at Austin, 1991. Revised and separately published, Columbia, S.C.: [n.p.], 1994.

"A Tribute" [to Fletcher Markle], p. 279, and "Working with Fredson Bowers," pp. 248–253. *Dictionary of Literary Biography Yearbook: 1991,* edited by James W. Hipp. Detroit: Bruccoli Clark Layman / Gale Research, 1992.

"Camden House: An Interview with James Hardin," with James W. Hipp, pp. 187–192. *Dictionary of Literary Biography Yearbook: 1992,* edited by Hipp. Detroit: Bruccoli Clark Layman / Gale Research, 1993.

"B. George Ulizio," with Dean H. Keller, pp. 282–288; and "John Cook Wyllie," pp. 327–341. *American Book-Collectors and Bibliographers, First Series,* edited by Joseph Rosenblum. Volume 140 of *Dictionary of Literary Biography.* Detroit: Bruccoli Clark Layman / Gale Research, 1994.

"James Gould Cozzens," p. 28. *American Decades: 1950–1959,* edited by Richard Layman. Detroit: Manly / Gale Research, 1994.

"A Tribute" [to Albert Erskine], pp. 279, 284, and "A Tribute" [to William Ober], p. 297. *Dictionary of Literary Biography Yearbook: 1993,* edited by James W. Hipp. Detroit: Bruccoli Clark Layman / Gale Research, 1994.

"Conversations with Rare Book Dealers II: An Interview with Ralph Sipper," pp. 193–199. *Dictionary of Literary Biography Yearbook: 1994,* edited by James W. Hipp. Detroit: Bruccoli Clark Layman / Gale Research, 1995.

"The Arts," pp. 19–74, and "Media," pp. 291–330, both with Arlyn Bruccoli. *American Decades: 1920–1929,* edited by Judith S. Baughman. New York: Manly / Gale Research, 1996.

"Conversations with Publishers III: An Interview with Donald Lamm," pp. 198–201, and "The Practice of Biography IX: An Interview with Michael Reynolds," pp. 235–240. *Dictionary of Literary Biography Yearbook: 1995,* edited by James W. Hipp. Detroit: Bruccoli Clark Layman / Gale Research, 1996.

"Foreword: Why Read Fitzgerald?" p. v. *A Young Reader's Guide to F. Scott Fitzgerald,* by Harriett S. Williams. Columbia: Fitzgerald Centenary Committee of the University of South Carolina in Cooperation with the South Carolina Department of Education and South Carolina ETV, 1996.

"C. E. Frazer Clark, Jr.," pp. 23–29. *American Book Collectors and Bibliographers, Second Series,* edited by Joseph Rosenblum. Volume 187 of *Dictionary of Literary Biography.* Detroit: Bruccoli Clark Layman / Gale Research, 1997.

"Editorial," pp. 285–286, and "Falsifying Hemingway," pp. 228–230. *Dictionary of Literary Biography Yearbook: 1996,* edited by Samuel W. Bruce and L. Kay Webster. Detroit: Bruccoli Clark Layman / Gale Research, 1997.

Foreword, pp. vii–viii; "Earnings," pp. 63–64; "Editing Fitzgerald's Texts," pp. 64–65; "Fitzgerald, Frances Scott (Scottie) (1921–1986)," pp. 80–81; and "Fitzgerald, Francis Scott Key (1896–1940)," pp. 81–84. *F. Scott Fitzgerald A to Z: The Essential Reference to His Life and Work,* by Mary Jo Tate. New York: Manly / Facts On File, 1998. Reprinted—and F. Scott Fitzgerald entry enlarged—in *Critical Companion to F. Scott Fitzgerald: A Literary Reference to His Life and Work,* by Tate (New York: Facts On File, 2007).

Introduction, pp. vii–xvii. *By Love Possessed,* by James Gould Cozzens. New York: Carroll and Graf, 1998.

Introduction, pp. iii–iv. *The Joseph M. Bruccoli Great War Collection in the University of Virginia Library,* compiled by Edmund Berkeley, Jr. Columbia, S.C.: MJB, 1999.

"Fitzgerald as Studied," pp. 169–194, and "Fitzgerald's Eras," pp. 85–102. *F. Scott Fitzgerald,* by Judith S. Baughman. Volume 1 of *Literary Masters.* Detroit: Manly / Gale Group, 2000.

"What Bowers Wrought: An Assessment of the Center for Editions of American Authors," pp. 237–244. *The Culture of Collected Editions,* edited by Andrew Nash. Houndmills, Basingstoke, Hampshire, UK: Palgrave Macmillan, with the Institute of English Studies, University of London, 2003.

"What Maxwell Perkins Really Did for *Look Homeward, Angel,*" pp. 221–230. *Look Homeward and Forward: Thomas Wolfe, an American Voice across Modern and Contemporary Culture,* edited by Agostino Lombardo, Mario Faraone, Monica Melloni, and Igina Tattoni. [Rome, Italy]: Casa Editrice Università degli Studi di Roma La Sapienza, 2003.

"Get It and Keep It," pp. 59–60. *Charleston Conference Proceedings 2003,* edited by Rosann Bazirjian and Vicky Speck; Katina Strauch, series editor. Westport, Conn., and London: Libraries Unlimited, 2004.

Introduction, pp. ix–xiv. *The Matthew J. and Arlyn Bruccoli Collection of F. Scott Fitzgerald at the University of South Carolina: An Illustrated Catalogue,* compiled by Park

Bucker. Columbia: University of South Carolina Press Published in Cooperation with the Thomas Cooper Library, 2004.

Introduction, pp. xi–xv. *The Joseph M. Bruccoli Great War Collection at the University of South Carolina: An Illustrated Catalogue,* compiled by Elizabeth Sudduth. Columbia: University of South Carolina Press Published in Cooperation with the Thomas Cooper Library, 2005.

"Foreword: The Way It Was," pp. xiii–xviii. *Windows of the Heart: The Correspondence of Thomas Wolfe and Margaret Roberts,* edited by Ted Mitchell. Columbia: University of South Carolina Press, 2007.

Statement, p. 250. *George, Being George: George Plimpton's Life as Told, Admired, Deplored, and Envied by 200 Friends, Relatives, Lovers, Acquaintances, Rivals—and a Few Unappreciative Observers,* edited by Nelson W. Aldrich, Jr. New York: Random House, 2008.

Periodical Appearances

"A Collation of F. Scott Fitzgerald's *This Side of Paradise.*" *Studies in Bibliography* 9 (1957): 263–265.

Unsigned articles and notes. *Fitzgerald Newsletter,* no. 1 (Spring 1958)–no. 40 (Winter 1968).

"'Hutzpa,' 'Chuzpa'—'Gall, Nerve.'" *American Speech* 33 (October 1958): 230.

"Textual Variants in Sinclair Lewis's *Babbitt.*" *Studies in Bibliography* 11 (1958): 263–268.

"An American Classic: F. Scott Fitzgerald Novel 25 Years Old in April." *Richmond News Leader,* 1 April 1959, p. 13.

"Twentieth-Century Books." *Library Trends* 7 (April 1959): 566–573. Reprinted separately, Urbana: University of Illinois Library School, 1959.

Review of *Sorrow Laughs,* by Harry Bloom. *Saturday Review,* 3 October 1959, p. 23.

Review of *Dissertations in American Literature, 1891–1955,* by James Woodress. *William and Mary Quarterly,* Third Series, 16 (October 1959): 614.

Review of *Daniel Defoe, Citizen of the Modern World,* by John Robert Moore, and *Bibliography of American Editions of Robinson Crusoe to 1830,* by Clarence S. Brigham. *William and Mary Quarterly,* Third Series, 17 (January 1960): 122–123.

"A Mirror for Bibliographers: Duplicate Plates in Modern Printing." *Papers of the Bibliographical Society of America* 54 (Second Quarter 1960): 83–88.

"Bibliographical Notes on F. Scott Fitzgerald's *The Beautiful and Damned.*" *Studies in Bibliography* 13 (1960): 258–261.

"*Tender Is the Night* and the Reviewers." *Modern Fiction Studies* 7 (Spring 1961): 49–54.

Review of *Robert Nathan, a Bibliography,* by Dan H. Laurence. *Papers of the Bibliographical Society of America* 55 (Third Quarter 1961): 265–266.

"Imposition Figures and Plate Gangs in *The Rescue,*" with Charles A. Rheault, Jr. *Studies in Bibliography* 14 (1961): 258–262.

"Hidden Printings in Edith Wharton's *The Children.*" *Studies in Bibliography* 15 (1962): 269–273.

"Concealed Printings in Hawthorne." *Papers of the Bibliographical Society of America* 57 (First Quarter 1963): 42–49.

"Notes on Ring Lardner's 'What of It?'" *Papers of the Bibliographical Society of America* 57 (First Quarter 1963): 88–90.

Review of *James Branch Cabell,* by Joe Lee Davis. *American Literature* 35 (May 1963): 253–254.

"States of Salinger Book." *American Notes & Queries* 2 (October 1963): 21–22.

"A Further Note on Lardner's 'What of It?'" *Papers of the Bibliographical Society of America* 57 (Third Quarter 1963): 377.

"A Further Note on the First Printing of *The Great Gatsby.*" *Studies in Bibliography* 16 (1963): 244.

Review of *F. Scott Fitzgerald,* by Kenneth Eble. *American Literature* 35 (January 1964): 549–550.

Review of *The Letters of F. Scott Fitzgerald,* edited by Andrew Turnbull. *American Literature* 36 (March 1964): 101–102.

"Ring Lardner's First Book." *Papers of the Bibliographical Society of America* 58 (First Quarter 1964): 34–35.

"States of *Fanshawe.*" *Papers of the Bibliographical Society of America* 58 (First Quarter 1964): 32.

"Five Notes on Ring Lardner." *Papers of the Bibliographical Society of America* 58 (Third Quarter 1964): 297–298.

"Negative Evidence about 'The Celestial Rail-Road.'" *Papers of the Bibliographical Society of America* 58 (Third Quarter 1964): 290–292.

"Material for a Centenary Edition of *Tender Is the Night.*" *Studies in Bibliography* 17 (1964): 177–193.

"F. Scott Fitzgerald's First Book Appearance." *Papers of the Bibliographical Society of America* 59 (First Quarter 1965): 58.

"Cora's Mouse." *Papers of the Bibliographical Society of America* 59 (Second Quarter 1965): 188–189.

"A Sophisticated Copy of *The House of the Seven Gables.*" *Papers of the Bibliographical Society of America* 59 (Fourth Quarter 1965): 438–439.

Letter about "A Cheer for Princeton." *Princeton Alumni Weekly* 66 (8 February 1966): 3.

"A Third Printing of *Maggie* (1896)," with Joseph Katz. *Stephen Crane Newsletter* 1 (Fall 1966): 2–3.

"An Unrecorded Review of *Maggie.*" *Stephen Crane Newsletter* 1 (Fall 1966): 4.

"A Colonial Edition of *Great Battles of the World,*" with Joseph Katz. *Stephen Crane Newsletter* 1 (Winter 1966): 3–4.

Review of *F. Scott Fitzgerald and the Craft of Fiction,* by Richard D. Lehan. *American Literature* 39 (March 1967): 122–123.

Review of *Stephen Crane: From Parody to Realism,* by Eric Solomon. *Stephen Crane Newsletter* 1 (Spring 1967): 5–6.

"The Heinemann *War Is Kind,*" with Joseph Katz. *Stephen Crane Newsletter* 1 (Summer 1967): 6.

"A Source for Sartoris?" *Mississippi Quarterly* 20 (Summer 1967): 163.

"Maggie's Last Night." *Stephen Crane Newsletter* 2 (Fall 1967): 10.

"Toward a Descriptive Bibliography of Stephen Crane: 'Spanish-American War Songs,'" with Joseph Katz. *Papers of the Bibliographical Society of America* 61 (Third Quarter 1967): 267–269.

"Notes on the Destruction of *The Scarlet Letter* Manuscript." *Studies in Bibliography* 20 (1967): 257–259.

"Ernest Hemingway as Cub Reporter." *Esquire* 70 (December 1968): 207, 265.

Review of *Stephen Crane: A Biography,* by R. W. Stallman. *Stephen Crane Newsletter* 3 (Winter 1968): 9–10.

Review of *Ernest Hemingway: A Comprehensive Bibliography,* by Audre Hanneman. *American Literature* 40 (January 1969): 571–572.

"'The Wonders of Ponce': Crane's First Puerto Rican Dispatch." *Stephen Crane Newsletter* 4 (Fall 1969): 1–3.

"Scholarship and Mere Artifacts: The British and Empire Publications of Stephen Crane," with Joseph Katz. *Studies in Bibliography* 22 (1969): 277–287.

"Robert Barr's Proofs of *The O'Ruddy.*" *Stephen Crane Newsletter* 4 (Spring 1970): 8.

Letter to the editor about John Cook Wyllie, 1908–1968. *AB Bookman's Weekly,* 27 April 1970, p. 1440.

"Report on CEAA Auction." *CEAA Newsletter* 3 (June 1970): 15.

"An Unrecorded Parody of Stephen Crane." *Stephen Crane Newsletter* 4 (Summer 1970): 7.

"A Few Missing Words." *PMLA* 86 (September 1971): 587–589.

"James Upton: Hawthorne in the Salem Custom-House—an Unpublished Recollection." *Nathaniel Hawthorne Journal 1971,* pp. 113–115.

"A Lost Hawthorne Manuscript: 'Buds and Bird-Voices.'" *Nathaniel Hawthorne Journal 1971,* pp. 155–158.

"William Harris Arnold and His Hawthorne Collection." *Nathaniel Hawthorne Journal 1971,* pp. 204–207.

"The Interdependence of Rare Books and Manuscripts: The Scholar's View," with Claude M. Simpson, Jr., and William H. Goetzmann. *Serif* 9 (Spring 1972): 3–22.

"A Further Note on the *Galena Guide.*" *Serif* 9 (Fall 1972): 47.

"British Resources for the Study of American Literature." *Journal of American Studies* 6, no. 3 (1972): 354–356.

"The SCADE Series: Apparatus for Definitive Editions." *Papers of the Bibliographical Society of America* 67 (Fourth Quarter 1973): 431–435.

"A Great Neck Friendship." *New York Times,* 7 November 1976, section 21, pp. 3, 16.

"'An Instance of Apparent Plagiarism': F. Scott Fitzgerald, Willa Cather, and the First *Gatsby* Manuscript." *Princeton University Library Chronicle* 39 (Spring 1978): 171–178.

Letter to the editor. *Papers of the Bibliographical Society of America* 72 (First Quarter 1978): 143–144.

"Out of Life." *John O'Hara Journal* 1, no. 1 (1978): 18–28.

"Epilogue: A Woman, a Gift, and a Still Unanswered Question." *Esquire* 91 (30 January 1979): 67.

"The Mystery of Ross Macdonald." *Saturday Night* 99 (January 1984): 38–45.

"Addenda to Bruccoli, *Raymond Chandler:* Chandler's First American Publication." *Papers of the Bibliographical Society of America* 78 (Third Quarter 1984): 360–361.

"Portrait of the Writer as Liar." Reviews of *Along with Youth: Hemingway, the Early Years*, by Peter Griffin, and *Hemingway, a Biography*, by Jeffrey Meyers. *National Review* 38 (31 January 1986): 58, 60.

"The Mysterious Mitchell Kennerley" [excerpts from *The Fortunes of Mitchell Kennerley, Bookman*]. *Publishers Weekly*, 2 May 1986, pp. 24–28.

"Mitchell Kennerley: He Loved, Books, Money and Women" [excerpts from *The Fortunes of Mitchell Kennerley, Bookman*]. *AB Bookman's Weekly*, 1 September 1986, pp. 645, 646, 648, 650, 651, 653, 654.

"Addenda to Bruccoli, *Nelson Algren*." *Papers of the Bibliographical Society of America* 82 (September 1988): 367–369.

"Where They Belong: The Acquisition of the F. Scott Fitzgerald Papers." *Princeton University Library Chronicle* 50 (Autumn 1988): 30–37.

"Debts." *Private Library*, 4th series, 4 (Winter 1991): 132–145.

"From the Diary of James Gould Cozzens," editor and introduction. *Yemassee* 1 (Spring 1993): 46.

"George D. Smith and the Anglo-American Book Migration." *AB Bookman's Weekly*, 14 June 1993, pp. 2524, 2526, 2528, 2530, 2532, 2534, 2536, 2537, 2538.

"American Writers in Paris," with Robert W. Trogdon. *Ex Libris 1997–1998* (University of South Carolina Division of Libraries and Information Systems, 1998): 22–24.

Hemingway's note on Fitzgerald's missing the Lyon train, editor; "James Dickey: Letters from France," editor; anecdote about James Jones in Paris, author. *Paris Review*, no. 150 (Spring 1999): [26]; 336; [355].

"Notes on *The Great Gatsby*." *Metropolitan Opera Playbill*, December 1999, [pp. 45–46].

"Gettysburg" from *O Lost*, editor and introduction. *Paris Review*, no. 153 (Winter 1999): 14–33.

"Address by Dr. Matthew J. Bruccoli upon Receiving the Thomas Cooper Medal for Distinction in the Arts and Sciences." *Ex Libris 1998–1999* (University of South Carolina Division of Libraries and Information Systems, 1999): 34–36.

"The Joseph M. Bruccoli Great War Collection." *Ex Libris 1999–2000* (University of South Carolina Division of Libraries and Information systems, 2000): 32–36.

"'Yr Letters Are Life Preservers': The Correspondence of Ezra Pound and Ernest Hemingway," "Literary Sketches: John Hall Wheelock," editor. *Paris Review*, no. 163 (Fall 2002): 96–124, 220–237.

"John Hall Wheelock's Work on Thomas Wolfe's Proofs." *Thomas Wolfe Review* 26, nos. 1–2 (2002): 23–32.

"The Profession of Authorship in Twenty-First-Century America." *American Studies in Scandinavia* 37, no. 1 (2005): 1–15.

"The *Paris Review* Years" and "'Die of Sheer Joy with My Head on the Manuscript'" [interviews with Mary Lee Settle]. *Appalachian Heritage* 34 (Winter 2006): 90–95, 96–97.

Review of *Look Homeward, Angel: A Story of the Buried Life*, with Arlyn Bruccoli. *Thomas Wolfe Review* 30, nos. 1–2 (2006): 144–146.

"The End of Books and the Death of Libraries." *Against the Grain* 19 (February 2007): 70–74.

"The Love Poems of James Gould Cozzens with Notes by Matthew J. Bruccoli." *Yemassee* 14 (Spring 2007): 43–47.

"Convictions—Lessons for Library Benefactors." *Against the Grain* 19 (June 2007): 68–69.

"What Do You Do with Them?" *Against the Grain* 19 (November 2007): 68, 70.

"The DLB at Thirty." *Against the Grain* 20 (February 2008): 72.

"Dust Jackets" [letter to the editor]. *Times Literary Supplement*, 4 April 2008, p. 6.

["James Dickey."] *James Dickey Newsletter* 25 (Fall 2008): 15–16.

Exhibition Catalogues Compiled or Introduced by Bruccoli

An Exhibition of Books, Manuscripts, and Letters: Nathaniel Hawthorne, 4 July 1804–19 May 1864, at the Main Library, Ohio State University, Marking Hawthorne Day, 15 May 1964. Columbus: Ohio State University, 1964.

Stephen Crane, 1871–1971: An Exhibition from the Collection of Matthew J. Bruccoli. Columbia: Department of English, University of South Carolina, 1971.

F. Scott Fitzgerald and Ernest M. Hemingway in Paris: An Exhibition at the Bibliothèque Benjamin Franklin in Conjunction with a Conference at the Institut d'Études Américaines, 23–24 June 1971, 1, place de l'Odéon, Paris, France. With C. E. Frazer Clark, Jr. Bloomfield Hills, Mich., and Columbia, S.C.: Bruccoli Clark, 1972.

Introduction, p. [8]. *An Exhibition of 100 Significant Books Acquired by the Kent State University Libraries during Hyman W. Kritzer's Tenure as Director of University Libraries, 1966–1983,* compiled by Dean H. Keller. Kent, Ohio: Kent State University Libraries, 1983.

Introduction, pp. [5–6]. *High Spots from the Collections of Matthew J. Bruccoli in the Kent State University Libraries: An Exhibition, 12 September–28 November 1988,* compiled by Dean H. Keller. Kent, Ohio: Kent State University Libraries, 1988.

F. Scott Fitzgerald, 21 December 1940–21 December 1990. An Exhibition at the Thomas Cooper Library, the University of South Carolina. [Columbia, S.C.]: Thomas Cooper Society, 1991.

F. Scott Fitzgerald Centenary Exhibition, September 24, 1896–September 24, 1996: The Matthew J. and Arlyn Bruccoli Collection, the Thomas Cooper Library. Includes preface and "Scottie Fitzgerald, 1921–1986." Columbia: University of South Carolina Press for the Thomas Cooper Library, 1996.

"Foreword: Joseph M. Bruccoli and the Great War Collection," pp. 4–5. *The Great War 1914–1918: An Exhibition Drawn from the Joseph M. Bruccoli Great War Collection at the University of Virginia and from Other Collections, November 1997–January 1998*, compiled by Patrick Scott. Columbia: Thomas Cooper Library, University of South Carolina, 1997.

150 Years of the American Short Story: An Exhibition Prepared by William R. Cagle and Matthew J. Bruccoli. Bloomington: The Lilly Library, Indiana University, 1998.

James Gould Cozzens: An Exhibition from the Bruccoli Collection, September–November 2000. Columbia, S.C.: Thomas Cooper Library, 2000.

Hemingway and the Thirties: A Symposium and Exhibition from the Speiser and Easterling-Hallman Collection. With Patrick Scott; includes "Ernest Hemingway: The Thirties," pp. 7–9. Columbia: Thomas Cooper Library / University of South Carolina, 2001.

"Great War Songs," p. [5]. *Songs of the Great War: An Exhibition, University of South Carolina Libraries, November 11, 2002.* Columbia, S.C.: Joseph M. Bruccoli Great War Collection, [2002].

Preface, p. 3. *The Joseph Heller Papers: An Exhibition,* compiled by Patrick Scott. Columbia: Department of Rare Books and Special Collections, Thomas Cooper Library, University of South Carolina, [2002].

22 Collections: An Exhibition from the Matthew J. and Arlyn Bruccoli Collections in the Thomas Cooper Library, University of South Carolina. Includes "Matthew and his goddam books" and "Postscript: Thoughts Generated by Proofing This Text." Columbia, S.C.: Thomas Cooper Library, 2005.

Preface, p. [3]. *Fredson Bowers and His Legacy: A Centennial Exhibition.* Columbia: Thomas Cooper Library, University of South Carolina, December 2005–January 2006.

"Massachusetts' Best Novelist," pp. 2–6. *George V. Higgins: A Retrospective Exhibition, Thomas Cooper Library, University of South Carolina, November 9, 2006–January 15, 2007,* exhibition and catalogue by Jeffrey Makala. Columbia, S.C.: Thomas Cooper Library, 2006.

Scottie Fitzgerald: The Stewardship of Literary Memory: An Exhibition from the Matthew J. & Arlyn Bruccoli Collection of F. Scott Fitzgerald, Thomas Cooper Library, University of South Carolina, October–December 2007, exhibition curated by Jeffrey Makala. Columbia: Thomas Cooper Library / University of South Carolina, 2007. Includes CD of Bruccoli interview with Scottie Fitzgerald Smith.

Other, Including Keepsakes with Material by Bruccoli, Pamphlets, and Audio and Video Appearances

Rise Lurid Stars, by Walt Whitman. Coeditor and coprinter with M[ichael] L[azare]. New Haven, Conn.: Bruccoli and Lazare, 1953. Broadside.

Mere Collectors' Items. Kent, Ohio: Kent State University Libraries, 1969. Keepsake.

Introduction, pp. 4–9. *The Author's Intention: An Exhibition for the Center for Editions for American Authors. The Folger Shakespeare Library, Washington, D.C., 14 February–10 March 1972.* Columbia, S.C.: Center for Editions of American Authors, 1972. Pamphlet.

Introduction, p. 1. *Recovering and Preserving the Author's Intention.* Columbia, S.C.: Center for Editions of American Authors, 1972. Pamphlet.

[Editor]. *A Cub Tells His Story,* by John O'Hara. Includes preface. Iowa City: Windhover Press / Bruccoli Clark, 1974. Pamphlet.

"Lost American Fiction," p. 1. *1978 Lost American Fiction Catalog and Backlist.* Carbondale and Edwardsville: Southern Illinois University Press, 1978. Advertising flyer.

"Scottie as the Daughter of . . . ," pp. 12–13. *In Memoriam: Frances Scott Fitzgerald Smith, 1921–1986.* [N.p.]: Anne Nevin Chamberlin et al., [1987]. Keepsake.

"A Certain Splendid Memory," p. 4. In program for *The Cat's Whiskers (Love, among Other Things),* by Frances Scott Fitzgerald Smith. Montgomery, Ala.: Auburn University at Montgomery, 1988.

"An Introduction to F. Scott Fitzgerald's Fiction." *Modern American Literature—Eminent Scholar/Teachers Series.* Detroit: Omnigraphics, 1988. Video recording.

"The Profession of Authorship in America." *Modern American Literature—Eminent Scholar/Teachers Series.* Detroit: Omnigraphics, 1988. Video recording.

"Understanding F. Scott Fitzgerald's *The Great Gatsby.*" *Modern American Literature—Eminent Scholar/Teachers Series.* Detroit: Omnigraphics, 1988. Video recording.

Introduction, p. [1]. *Celestial Eyes—from Metamorphosis to Masterpiece,* by Charles Scribner III. [N.p.]: Matthew J. Bruccoli, Charles Scribner III, and Peter Shepherd, 1991. Essay and introduction reprinted in *Metropolitan Opera Playbill,* December 1999, pp. 8–10, 12, 14, 16, 18, 20. Keepsake.

"Afterword: How Coradal-Cugat Came to Columbia," p. [7]. *Francis Coradal-Cugat.* Columbia: McKissick Museum, University of South Carolina, 1994. Keepsake.

[Editor]. *F. Scott Fitzgerald, 24 September 1896 to 21 December 1940: 24 September 1996 Centenary Celebration.* [Tributes from well-known writers.] Includes preface. Columbia, S.C.: Thomas Cooper Society, Thomas Cooper Library, 1996. Keepsake.

"Bruccoli's Response," pp. 11–15. *Remarks at the Opening of the F. Scott Fitzgerald Centenary Exhibition and in Recognition of the Matthew J. and Arlyn Bruccoli Collection, 29 September, 1996,* introduction by Donald J. Greiner and "For Matt Bruccoli" by Frederick Busch. Columbia: Thomas Cooper Library, University of South Carolina, 1997. Keepsake. Reprinted, p. 124, in "F. Scott Fitzgerald Centenary Celebrations,"

Dictionary of Literary Biography Yearbook: 1996, eds. Samuel W. Bruce and L. Kay Webster (Detroit: Bruccoli Clark Layman / Gale Research, 1997).

Statement, p. [3]. *Memorandum of agreement made this twenty-third day of September 1919 between F. Scott Fitzgerald . . . and Charles Scribner's Sons . . . [on] a work entitled: This Side of Paradise.* Columbia, S.C.: Bruccoli Clark Layman, 1998. Keepsake.

[Editor]. *Dear Bill: Letters to His Publisher,* by James Gould Cozzens. Includes headnote and notes. Columbia: Thomas Cooper Library, University of South Carolina, 2000. Keepsake.

Introduction, pp. 3–4. *An Annotated Chapter from "O Lost": A Story of the Buried Life [by] Thomas Wolfe,* edited with, and with explanatory notes by, Arlyn Bruccoli. Columbia: University of South Carolina Press, 2000. Pamphlet.

[Editor]. *"Picture yourself in my place,"* by F. Scott Fitzgerald. Includes editor's note. [Columbia]: Thomas Cooper Library, University of South Carolina, 2004. Keepsake.

Getting It Wrong: Resetting The Great Gatsby. Columbia, S.C., 2005. Pamphlet.

[Compiler]. *On Literary Biography: Twenty-one Statements.* Includes statement by Bruccoli, p. 4. Columbia, S.C. Bruccoli Clark Layman, Dictionary of Literary Biography, 2005. Keepsake.

[Editor]. *Welcome to the New Citizens,* by John O'Hara. Includes afterword, "The Way It Was." Columbia, S.C.: Bruccoli Clark Layman, 2006. Keepsake.

The Big Read, National Endowment for the Arts. Member of Readers Circle and panelist on audio CD recordings: "F. Scott Fitzgerald's *The Great Gatsby*" (2006), "Ernest Hemingway's *A Farewell to Arms*" (2006), and "Dashiell Hammett's *The Maltese Falcon*" (2007).

[Editor]. *The Paroxide Blonde,* by Scottie Fitzgerald. Includes afterword. Columbia, S.C.: The Matthew J. and Arlyn Bruccoli Collection of F. Scott Fitzgerald, 2007. Keepsake.

"Research Libraries without Reference Books," pp. 1–5. *The Necessity of Reference Books in the Digital Age.* [Columbia, S.C.]: The Print Conservancy, 2008. Includes essays by Richard Layman and Joel Myerson. Pamphlet.

Series Editorships

The Centenary Edition of the Works of Nathaniel Hawthorne. Volume 1, *The Scarlet Letter,* 1962; Volume 3, *The Blithedale Romance and Fanshawe,* 1964; Volume 2, *The House of the Seven Gables,* 1965; associate textual editor with Fredson Bowers; Volume 4, *The Marble Faun; or, The Romance of Monte Beni,* 1968; Volume 5, *Our Old Home: A Series of English Sketches,* 1970, general coeditor with William Charvat, Roy Harvey Pearce, and Claude M. Simpson. Columbus: Ohio State University Press, 1962–1970.

The Charles E. Merrill Program in American Literature. General editor with Joseph Katz. 107 volumes. Columbus, Ohio: Merrill, 1968–1972. Includes *Merrill Checklists,* 23 volumes; *Merrill Guides*, 18 volumes; *Merrill Handbooks*, 2 volumes; *Merrill Literary Texts*, 10 volumes; *Merrill Profiles*, 6 volumes; *Merrill Standard Editions*, 13 volumes; *Merrill Studies*, 35 volumes.

Pittsburgh Series in Bibliography. 34 volumes to date. Pittsburgh: University of Pittsburgh Press, 1969–2002; New Castle, Del., and Pittsburgh: Oak Knoll Press and University of Pittsburgh Press, 2002– .

Lost American Fiction. 29 volumes. Carbondale and Edwardsville: Southern Illinois University Press / London and Amsterdam: Feffer and Simons, 1972–1980.

Screenplay Library. 8 volumes. Carbondale and Edwardsville: Southern Illinois University Press / London and Amsterdam: Feffer and Simons, 1976–1982.

Conversations. Editorial director. 3 volumes. Detroit: Bruccoli Clark / Gale Research, 1977–1978.

First Printings of American Authors: Contributions toward Descriptive Checklists. 5 volumes. Detroit: Bruccoli Clark / Gale Research, 1977–1987.

Dictionary of Literary Biography. Editorial director with Richard Layman. 400 volumes to date. Detroit: Bruccoli Clark Layman / Gale Research, 1978– .

Album Biographies. 5 volumes. San Diego, New York, and London: Harcourt Brace Jovanovich, 1982–1985.

Understanding Contemporary American Literature. 80 volumes to date. Columbia: University of South Carolina Press, 1985– .

Contemporary Authors: Bibliographical Series. Editorial director with Richard Layman. 2 volumes. Detroit: Bruccoli Clark Layman / Gale Research, 1986.

Eminent Scholar/Teachers. Editorial director with Richard Layman. 32 videos. Detroit: Omnigraphics, 1988.

Encyclopedia of American Business History and Biography. Editorial director with Richard Layman. 9 volumes. New York: Bruccoli Clark Layman / Facts On File, 1988–1994.

William Shakespeare Series. Editorial director with Richard Layman. 5 videos. Detroit: Omnigraphics, 1988.

Author to Author. Editorial director with Richard Layman. 5 videos. Detroit: Omnigraphics, 1990.

Cambridge Edition of the Works of F. Scott Fitzgerald. Founding editor. 2 volumes. London and New York: Cambridge University Press, 1991–1993.

Facts On File Bibliography of American Fiction. Editorial director with Richard Layman. 4 volumes. New York: Manly / Facts On File, 1991–1993.

Understanding Contemporary British Literature. 25 volumes to date. Columbia: University of South Carolina Press, 1991– .

Twentieth-Century American Decades. Editorial director with Richard Layman. 9 volumes. Detroit: Manly / Gale Research, 1994–1996.

Twentieth-Century Culture. Editorial director with Richard Layman. 5 volumes. Detroit: Manly / Gale Research, 1994–1996.

American Eras. Editorial director with Richard Layman. 8 volumes. Detroit: Manly / Gale Research, 1997–1999.

Gale Study Guides. Editorial director with Richard Layman. 30 volumes. Detroit: Manly / Gale Research, 2000–2002.

History in Dispute. Editorial director with Richard Layman. 21 volumes. Detroit: Manly / Gale Research, 2000–2005.

World Eras. Editorial director with Richard Layman. 10 volumes. Detroit: Manly / Gale Research, 2001–2004.

Joseph M. Bruccoli Great War Series. 8 volumes to date. Columbia: University of South Carolina Press, 2006– .

Journal Editorships

Fitzgerald Newsletter. 40 issues. Charlottesville, Va., and Columbus, Ohio: F. Scott Fitzgerald Society, Spring 1958–Winter 1968. Also contributed "Checklist" to each issue. Collected in *Fitzgerald Newsletter,* editor. Washington, D.C.: NCR Microcard Editions, 1969.

CEAA Newsletter. 7 numbers. Center for Editions of American Authors. Columbia: Department of English, University of South Carolina, July 1969–November 1975.

Fitzgerald/Hemingway Annual. 11 volumes. Washington, D.C.: NCR Microcard Editions, 1969–1972. Washington, D.C.: NCR Microcard Editions; Englewood, Colo.: Information Handling Services, 1973–1975. Englewood, Colo: Information Handling Services, 1976. Detroit: Bruccoli Clark / Gale Research, 1977–1979.

Nathaniel Hawthorne Journal 1971. Consulting editor; edited by C. E. Frazer Clark, Jr. Washington, D.C.: NCR Microcard Editions, 1971.

The New Black Mask. Coeditor with Richard Layman. 8 volumes. San Diego: Harcourt Brace Jovanovich, 1985–1987.

A Matter of Crime: New Stories from the Masters of Mystery and Suspense. Coeditor with Richard Layman. 4 volumes. San Diego and London: Harcourt Brace Jovanovich, 1988–1989.

F. Scott Fitzgerald Collection Notes. Editor. 9 numbers. Columbia: Thomas Cooper Library, University of South Carolina, September 1995–11 November 2004.

INDEX

Abraham Lincoln Brigade, 283
Absalom, Absalom! (Faulkner), 163
"Absolution" (Fitzgerald), 10
Across the River and Into the Trees (Hemingway), 256, 284
Acton, John Emerich Edward Dalberg, 284
Adams, Franklin P., 20
Adams, J. Donald, 49
Adventures of Huckleberry Finn (Clemens), 194
Agee, James, 274
Aiken, Conrad, 29
Alderman Library, University of Virginia, 214–218
Aldis, Owen Franklin, 169, 170, 174
Algren, Nelson, 118, 163, 282
Allen, Hervey, 47
"Angel on the Porch, The" (Wolfe), 237
American Antiquarian Society, 162
American Art Association, 165, 166
American Authors 1797–1895 (Foley), 170
American Magazine of Useful Knowledge (Foley), 170
American Renaissance in New England, The (Mott, ed.), 195
American Tragedy, An (Dreiser), 118
America's Library, 195
Anatomy of an Auction (Freeman and Freeman), 186
Anatomy of a Murder (Voelker), 264
"Ancestral Footstep, The" (Hawthorne), 171
And Now Tomorrow (movie), 271

Anderson Galleries, 165, 166
Anderson, George, 40
Anderson, John P., 170
Anderson, Sherwood, 253
Anthony Adverse (Allen), 47
antiquarian auctions and sales of mss. and books, 179–182, 184, 186
antiquarian bookshops:; Bookspan, 139; Brick Row, 161; Collectors' Bookshop, 161; Seven Gables, 161
Apple, Benjamin, 257
Appointment in Samarra (O'Hara), xxii, 247, 252, 256–261; compared to Black Mask fiction, 257; as hard-boiled novel, 256, 257; influences on, 258
Arcadia (Sidney), 187
Argosy, 29
Arlen, Michael, 10, 271
Arnold, William Harris, 169, 170, 171, 172, 174
Arthur, Chester Alan, 238, 239, 240
Ashurse, William, 184
Ask Me Tomorrow (Cozzens), 264
Auchincloss, Louis, 194, 257
Auction Prices of Books (Livingston), 172
Authors Guild, 138
Autobiography of Alice B. Toklas, The (Stein), 281

Babbitt (Lewis), 91–96, 103; printing history of, 91; textual variations in, 91
"Babes in the Woods" (Fitzgerald), 17
"Babylon Revisited" (Fitzgerald), 76
Bahr, Leonard, 194

Baker, Carlos, 233
Baker, Nelson, 228
Baker, Stannard, 207
Barnes & Noble, 143
Barnes, Margaret Ayers, 47
Barrett, C. Waller, 108. 175, 201
Barrie, James M., 166
Barthelme, Donald, 120
Bartlett, John, 226
Barzun, Jacques, 226
Basil Duke Lee stories (Fitzgerald), 10
Basso, Hamilton, 243
Battle of the Bulge, 189
"Battler, The" (Hemingway), 233
Baughman, Judith S., xxii
Baumgarten, Sylvia Bernice, 264
Bay Psalm Book, The, 221
Bayle, John, 180
Beat to Quarters (Forester), 282
Beaumont (Francis) and Fletcher (John), 167
Beautiful and Damned, The (Fitzgerald), 5, 8; Anthony Patch in, 22–23; as best-seller, 5; Dick Caramel in, 23; early titles of, 26n5; effects of photo-offset printing on, 104; Gloria Patch in, 22–23, 24, 25; point-of-view problems in, 22–23; revisions of, 23–24; sales of (1922), 47–48; self-judgment by Fitzgerald in, 22–23
Becker, Charles, 31, 33, 124
Beebe, Lucius, 192
Beer, Thomas, 6
Belasco, David, 124
Bellow, Saul, 119, 251
Benchley, Robert, 19
Bensen, Robert Hugh, 18
Bernstein, Aline, 239, 243
Berryman, John, 30
Bessie, Alvah, 283
Bibliographical Society of Virginia, 160

Bibliography on the Writings of Nathaniel Hawthorne, A (Williamson), 170
Big Sleep, The (Chandler), 270, 271, 274, 275
Biggers, Earl Deer, 6
Biggs, John, 205, 206, 208
Biographical Stories for Children (Hawthorne), 158, 172
Bird, William, 281
Bishop, Cortland, 185
Bishop, John Peale, 30, 237, 250
Bixby, William K., 172
Black Mask, 270
Black Mask School, xxii, 257, 258; characteristics of, 270; writers in, 270
Black Riders (Crane), 201, 257
Blackmur, R. P., 257
Blithdale Romance, The (Hawthorne), 107, 168, 170, 172, 173; first printings of, 168
Blockbuster Complex, The (Whiteside), 139
Blue Dahlia (Chandler), xxii, 271, 272, 274, 275; Chandler's analysis of murderer in, 272; critical reception of, 274; ending of, 272; evolution of plot of, 272; Navy Department influence upon, 272
Bogart, Humphrey, 275
Book Expo, 141
Book of St. Albans, The, 181
Book-of-the-Month-Club, 139
Books-a-Million, 143
"Boom Town" (Wolfe), 239
Booth, Wayne C., 56
Borders, 143
Bosen, Charles S., 190
Boswell, James, 203
Bottome, Phyllis, 47
Bowers, Fredson, xv, xvi, xvii, 57, 83, 103, 107, 117, 160, 203

Boyd, Julian, 207, 208
Boyd, Tom, 10
Boys in the Back Room, The (Wilson), 259
Bradshaw, 158
Brasher Dubloon, The (movie), 275
Brewer, Ebenezer Cobham, 226
Brickell, Hershell, 46
Bridge, The (Hart Crane), 201
British Library, 193
British Museum reading rooms, 227
British ring, xxi
Bromfield, Louis, 10
Brooke, Rupert, 17, 162
Brown, Andrew, 89
Brown, Nina, 172
Bruccoli, Arlyn, xiii
Bruccoli, Joseph M., xv
Bruccoli, Mary Gervasi, xv
Bruccoli, Matthew Joseph, ix, x, xiii, xv, xvi, xvii, xviii, xix, xxi, xx, xxii, xxiii, 57; academic appointments of, xvii, xviii; on best-seller lists, 139; birth of, xv; "bookman" as label used by, xxi; on decline of line editing, 136; earliest acquisitions of Fitzgerald first editions, 161; early interest in Fitzgerald, xv; on editorial emendation, 151; education of, xv–xvi; hard-boiled detective fiction, interest in, xxii
Bruccoli/Clark/Gale Research imprint, 194
Bruccoli/Clark/Layman imprints, 194
Bryan, Joseph III, 75
"Bucket of Blood" (O'Hara), 252
Burt, Struthers, 6
Butterfield 8 (O'Hara), 249
Butterfield, Roger, 193
By Love Possessed (Cozzens), 102, 263, 265, 266, 267, 268; as best seller, 264; denunciations against, 265; Julian Penrose in, xxii; reviewers' reception of, 265, 266; style of, 266
Byrne, Donn, 6

Cabell, James Branch, 217; papers of, 217
Cain, James M., 257, 269, 271
Cain, Paul, 258
Call it Sleep (Roth), 258
Callaghan, Morley, 10
"Cameo Frame, The" (Fitzgerald), 17
Canby, Henry Seidel, 49, 257
Cannon, Jimmy, 282
Canterbury Tales, The (Chaucer), 185
Capote, Truman, 284
"Captured Shadow, The" (Fitzgerald), 124
Carlyle, Thomas, 227
Castaway (Cozzens), 264
Catalogue of Crime (Barzun), 226
Catcher in the Rye, The (Salinger), 163
Cathcart, Wallace Hugh, 172
Cather, Willa: on writing as business or art, 4
Caxton, William, 180, 187; books printed by, 180, 181, 187
Caxton's Royal Book, 185
Celestial Railroad, The (Hawthorne), 167, 169, 170, 171, 172, 173
"Cellar Domain, The" (O'Hara), 252
Centenary Edition of the Works of Nathaniel Hawthorne, xvii, xx, 83, 106, 167, 191; early editions in, 85, 86; elements of, 85; purpose of, 86
Center for Editions of American Authors (CEAA), xvii, 83, 105, 2–3; approved text of, 86; associated editions of, 87; funded editions of, 89–90; Wilson denunciation of, 87
Cerf, Bennett, 52, 141
Cervantes, Saavedra Miguel de, 280

Chamberlain, J. Chester, 169, 170, 172, 173, 174
Chamberlain, John, 30, 48, 56
Chandler, Raymond, 140, 160, 258, 269–276; Academy Award nominations of, 271, 274; attitude toward collaborative screen writing, 271; concept of hero in works of, 270; criticism of Veronica Lake by, 274; evolution of career of, 270; Hitchcock criticism of, 275; honor and justice as theme of, 271; on lack of screenwriter autonomy, 272; as leader of hard-boiled detective genre, 270; Philip Marlowe in works of, 270, 275
Chandler, Theodore, 39
Charvat, William, xvii, 132, 159; on professional writing, 3
Chase, Mary Ellen, 47
Chatto & Windus, 29
Chaucer, Geoffrey, 185
Chester Mystery Cycle, 180
Chew, Beverly, 169, 179
Children, The (Wharton), 97–100; differentiating printings of, 97
Children and Others (Cozzens), 266
Cicero (tr. Caxton), 181
Clark, C. E. Frazer III, xxiii–xxivn10, 190
Clark, Charles Elliot Frazer, Jr. xxi, 164, 175, 189–195
Clark, Douglas Alexander, 190
Clark, Lucy Huffman, 190
Clark, Mary Ann Swanson, 190
Clemens, Samuel (Mark Twain), 25, 143, 277
Cockpit (Cozzens), 264
Cohen, Octavus Roy, 6
Cole, George Watson, 187
College Humor, 7
Colonial and Historical Houses of Maryland (Swann, ed., Fitzgerald foreword in), 162

Colum, Mary, 49
Committee on Scholarly Editions (CSE), xvii, 83
"Complete List of Hawthorne's Writings" (Jones), 110
Complete Stories of Thomas Wolfe, The, 236
Composition of "Tender Is the Night": A Study of the Manuscripts, The (Bruccoli), xvi
Comus (Milton), 185
Confederacy of Dunces (Toole), 142
Confessio Amantis (Gower), 185
Confusion (Cozzens), 264
Conrad, Joseph, 50, 68, 166, 281
Conway, Moncure D., 170
Cooper, James Fenimore, 167, 203
Coover, Robert, 194
Corydon and Other Poems (Beebe), 192
Cost Books of Ticknor and Fields and Their Predecessors, 1832–1858, The (Charvat and Tryon, eds.), xvii, 84
Costello, Don, 273
Count of Darkness stories, (Fitzgerald), 63
Cowley, Malcolm, 30, 33, 35, 44, 46, 47, 48, 54, 126, 151, 266; on Hemingway's fame, 277–278; on revised edition of *Tender Is the Night,* 55
Coxe, George Harmon, 270
Cozzens, James Gould, 11, 102, 118, 192, 194, 257, 263–268; central theme in fiction of, 264; on Hemingway's simplicity of style, 283
Crack-Up, The (Fitzgerald, Wilson, ed.), 4, 30, 209
Crane, Stephen, 165, 194, 201, 203, 258
Crawford, John C., 185
Creed, Thomas, 101
Crevecoeur (Michel-Guillaume-Jean de), 203
Crowther, Bosley, 274

Cugat, Francis, 28
Currie, Barton, 173

Daly, Carroll John, 270
Darwin, Charles, 200
Dashiell, Alfred, 44, 238
Davies, John, 186
DaVinci Code, The (Brown), 133
Davis, Owen, 8, 29
De Bry, John Théodore, 184
De Ricci, Seymour Robert Rosso, 158
De Sliva, Howard, 272
De Worde, Wynkyn, 187
"Debutante, The" (Fitzgerald), 17
Decline of the West, The (Spengler), 32, 77n5
Deerslayer, The (Cooper), 203
Delihant, Cecilia (as model for Cecelia in *Last Tycoon*), 78n8
Departmental Ditties (Kipling), 166
"Diamond as Big as the Ritz, The" (Fitzgerald), 6, 7, 10
"Dice, Brassknuckles & Guitar," 10
Dickey, James, 151, 194
Dictes or Sayinges of the Philosophres (printed by Caxton), 180, 181, 187
Dictionary of Books Relating to America (Sabin), 218
Dictionary of Literary Biography, xxi, 194
Dictionary of the English Language, A (Johnson), 225
Digital Book Center, 141
Dillard, R. H. W., 135
Dinesen, Isak, 47
Directory of Literary Magazines, The, 142
Dmytryk, Edward, 171
"Doctor's Son, The" (O'Hara), 252
Dollens, Evelyn. *See* Wyllie, Evelyn Dollens
Dolliver Romance, The (Hawthorne), 173
Dos Passos, John, 12, 30, 277
Dostoyevsky, Feodor, 280

Double Fold (Baker), 226
Double Indemnity (Cain), 271
Doyle, Sir Arthur Conan, 6
"Dr. Diver's Holiday A Romance" (Fitzgerald), 43
Dr. Grimshaw's Secret (Hawthorne), 173
Dramatists Guild, 138
Dreiser, Theodore, 118, 166, 203, 258
Dring, Edmund H., 180, 187
"Drunkard's Holiday, The" (Fitzgerald), 42
Dukedom Large Enough (Randall), 206
Dulles, John Foster, 205
Dunn, Charles, 146

E. M. Fuller and William F. McGee (brokerage firm), 125. *See also* Fuller-McGee Case
East of Eden (Steinbeck), 142
E-Books, 143–144
Echoes of the Jazz Age (Fitzgerald), 32, 33
Eden, Anthony, 249
Edwards, Richard, 187
Eliot, T. S., 12, 30, 149, 201, 203
Elizabeth Appleton (O'Hara), 252
Ellesmere Chaucer, 185
Emerson, Ralph Waldo, 203
Encyclopedia Britannica, 239
Epigrams and Elegies (Davies & Marlowe), 186
Epstein, Jason, 87
Erskine, Albert, 136, 146
Esquire, 4
Essex Institute, 193
Evans, Charles, 226
Exchanges (Dickey), 194

F. Scott Fitzgerald's Ledger, 4, 5, 42, 194
Fadiman, Clifton, 49
Faithfull, Starr, 249
"Falcon" (Arlen), 271
Falcon Takes Over, The (movie), 271

"Family Party, A" (O'Hara), 252
Famous Old People (Hawthorne), 168, 172
Famous Story Magazine, 29
Fanshaw (Hawthorne), 167, 168, 169, 171, 172, 173, 174, 190, 201
"Far and the Near, The" (Wolfe), 238
Farewell My Lovely (Chandler), 271
Farewell to Arms, A (Hemingway), 147
Farmer's Hotel, The (O'Hara), 252
Farrell, James T. 257, 258
"Fatimas and Kisses" (O'Hara), 252
Faulkner, William, 6, 12, 121, 122, 163, 264, 277, 281
"Feathertop" (Hawthorne), 171
Feinberg, Charles, xvi, 160
Ferdinand, Franz (Archduke), 184
Fields, Annie (Mrs. James T. Fields), xvii, 113
Fields, James T., xvii, 112, 190
Fifth Column and the First Forty-nine Stories, The (Hemingway), 231–235, 283
First Books of Some American Authors, The (Livingston), 170
First Folio (Shakespeare), 187
First Report of a Book Collector (Arnold), 171
Fischer, John, 265
Fisher, John Hurt, 84
Fisher, Steve, 275
Fitzgerald, F. Scott (Francis Scott Key), 117, 120, 127, 146, 158, 192, 203, 247, 258, 260; break with Harold Ober, 64; compliments O'Hara, 249; on Hemingway's "authority of success," 281; impediments to reputation of, 3–4; income of, 4, 5–6, 140; last royalty check of, 205; Marxism eschewed by, 12; papers of, 105; posthumous fame of, 277; revival of, 30; self-denigration by, 9; self-assessment by, 12; "strippings" by, p. 10; tax problems of, 7; on Thomas Wolfe, 237

Fitzgerald, Scottie (Francis Scott Fitzgerald Lanahan Smith), xviii, 66, 87, 89, 205, 206, 207
Fitzgerald, Zelda Sayre, 7, 17, 20, 22, 25, 39, 63, 66, 76, 206, 207; psychiatric treatment of, 5; stories published by, 7
Fitzgerald/Hemingway Annual, 189
Foley, P. K, 170, 186
Folger, Henry C., 185, 186
Foote, Charles B., 169
For Whom the Bell Tolls (Hemingway), 283
Ford, Corey, 32
Ford, Ford Madox, 281
Forester, C. S., 282
"Four Lost Men, The" (Wolfe), xxii, 236–246; reviewers' response to, 243–244; sketches of presidents in, 239–240; sources for characters of, 241
Four Lost Men, The: The Previously Unpublished Long Version (Bruccoli and Bruccoli), 245n2
Fox, Joe, 136
France, Anatole, 25
Frankau, Joseph, 239
Frazier, Brenda, 68
Fred Zentner's Cinema Bookshop, 166
Freeman, Jane, 186
Freud, Sigmund, 3
Frisco, Joe, 124
From Death to Morning (Wolfe), 239, 241, 242
From the Terrace (O'Hara), 249, 252
Frost, Robert, 162, 203, 277
Fulgens and Lucrece (Medwall), 186
Fuller-McGee Case, 32, 125

Gale Research, 194
Galsworthy, John, 166, 258
Game and Playe of the Chesse (printed by Caxton), 180

Gammer Gurton's Needle (Stevenson), 186
Gardner, Erle Stanley, 270
Garfield, James Abram, 238, 239
Garrett, George, 142
Gentle Boy, The (Hawthorne), 169, 172
George D. Smith / G.D.S. / A Memorial Tribute to the Greatest Bookseller / the World has Ever Known (Heartman), 178
Gere, Richard, 120
Gibbon, Edward, 209
Gibbs, Wolcott, 252
Gibson, William, 84
Gingrich, Arnold, 4, 76
Gioia, Dana, 228
Gissing, George R., 166
Gollob, Herman, 136
Good-bye, Mr. Chips (Hilton), 47
Good Child's River, The (Wolfe), 239
Gospells of Dystaves, The (D'Arras), 187
Gower, John, 185
Graham, Sheilah, 64
Grand Voyages (De Bry), 184–185
Grandfather's Chair (Hawthorne), 168, 169, 172
Grattan, C. Harley, 48, 50
Gray, Gilda, 124
Gray, James, 30, 49
Great Gatsby, The (Fitzgerald), 5, 7, 8, 12, 15, 16, 117, 118, 123, 124, 125, 126 151, 161, 163, 189, 194, 205, 209; Armed Services Edition, 30; Bantam edition, 30; cluster stories in, 10; dramatization of, 29; first printing sales of, 138; Fitzgerald on mood of, 124; function of illusions in, 34; jacket of, 28; "orgastic/orgiastic future" in, 125; plan for, 27; popular songs in, 32; posthumous editions of, 30–31; promotion of, 28–29; reception of, 28, 29–30; revisions of, 27–28; revival, 30–31; sales of (1925), 48; synesthesia in 33; textual errors in, 117, 122, 123; *Tycoon/Gatsby* edition, 30; Viking Portable edition, 30
Green Hills of Africa (Hemingway), 281
Green, Robert, 187
Greg, W. W., 83, 226
Gregory, Horace, 49
Grolier Club, 158, 171, 218
Grove, George, 226,
Gruber, Frank, 270
Guard of Honor (Cozzens), 264
"Guide to the Study of Nathaniel Hawthorne" (Hodgkins), 170
Gutenberg Bible, 179, 213

Halliday, Brett, 271
Hamlet, The (Faulkner), 121
Hammett, Dashiell, 140, 160, 257, 258, 269
Handy, W. C., 32
Hanlon, Brooke, 6
Hanson, Harry, 18
hard-boiled school, 256, 259, 260, 269–270; characteristics of, 270; major writers of, 270
Harding, D. W., 51
Hardy, Thomas, 166
Harrison, Benjamin, 238, 240
Hartley, L. P., 29
Hawks, Howard, 271
Hawthorne and His Circle (Julian Hawthorne), 112
Hawthorne, Elizabeth Manning (Hawthorne's sister), 174
Hawthorne, Julian, xvii, 112, 113, 114, 172, 174
Hawthorne, Nathaniel, xxvi, 106, 167, 189, 190, 192, 194, 201, 203; Bandler Collection of, 190; booksellers of early editions of, 169, 170, 189; collectors of works by, 169, 172, 173; dispatch case of, 191; early bibliographies of,

Hawthorne, Nathaniel (*continued*) 170, 172; love letters of, 172; Salem Custom House stencil of, 191; sales of rare writings of, 170, 171, 172
Hawthorne, Sophia Peabody, 174
Hayes, Rutherford Birchard, 238, 240
Hayward, Leland, 75
"Head and Shoulders" (Fitzgerald), 5, 8
Hearst's International, 6
Heart of Spain (Bessie), 283
Heartman, Charles, F., 178
Heinemann, William, 243
Heinze, W. C., 282
Helen and Kurt Wolff Books, 120
Hellman, George S., 173
Hemingway, 9, 11, 12, 40, 43, 50, 120, 143, 146, 157, 163, 193, 194, 201, 203, 205, 232, 254, 257, 258, 264, 277–286; achievements and ambitions of, 279–280; African plane crashes of, 278; analysis of artistic decline of, 283; attitude toward critics by, 281, 282; "authority of success" of, 281; commitment to accuracy by, 282; endurance of work by, 278; on importance of art, 279; as insider, 283; as model for writers, 278; multiple public personas of, 278, 279; *New York Times* obituary, 277; Nobel Prize received by, 285; as noncommunist anti-fascist, 282; ongoing feuds of, 281; oracular style of, 283; personal approach to criticism by, 281; posthumous tributes to, 277; reaction to Cowley edition of *Tender Is the Night*, 56, 126; rejection of political causes by, 282; self-generated celebrity of, 278, 279, 280, 281
Hemingway Reader (Poore, ed.), 193
Herbst, Josephine, 282
Hergesheimer, Joseph, 6, 29, 51
Herrmann, John, 237, 282
Hibben, John Grier, 16

Higgins, George V., 133, 138
High Window, The (Chandler), 271, 275
Highsmith, Patricia, 275
"Hills Beyond Pentland, The" (Wolfe), 341, 342
Hilton, James, 47
Hinman Collator, xvi, 91, 92, 98, 106, 158, 218
History of the American Stereoscope (Holmes), 166
Hitchcock, Alfred, 275
Hoagland, Clayton, 243
Hobart, Alice Tisdale, 47
Hodgkins, Louise Manning, 170
Hoe, Robert, 172, 179
Hogan, Frank, 175
Holmes, Oliver Wendell, 166, 174
Hotchner, A. E., 231
Houghton Library, 227, 236; Wolfe mss. in, 236
"Hound of Darkness, The" (Wolfe), 241
House of Seven Gables, The (Hawthorne), 86, 107, 168, 172, 173, 193; first printings of 168
Houseman, John, 271, 272
Howard, Henry, 187
Howe, Parkman D. 175
Howe, W. T. H., 169, 174
Huffman, Lucy. *See* Clark, Lucy Huffman
Hunt, Holman, 233
Huntington, Henry E., 172, 179, 182, 184, 185, 186, 187
Huntington Library, 184
Hurtz, Walter, 232
Hye Way to the Spyttell House, The (printed by Wynkyn de Worde), 187
Hynes, Jennifer, xxii
Hystoryes of Troye (tr. Caxton), 180

"I Am the Light of the World" (painting by Holman Hunt), 233

"Imagine Kissing Pete" (O'Hara), 252, 261
in our time (Hemingway), 193, 201, 203
In Our Time (Hemingway), 157
In Remembrance (Brooke), 162
Indian Bible (Eliot trans.), 185
Innocent Mrs. Duff, The (movie, unproduced), 275
Inough Is as Good as a Feast (Wager), 186
International Brigade, 283
Irving, Washington, 166

Jakes, John, 135
James, Henry, 12, 167, 257
Jazz Age, 15, 31, 32, 48
Jefferson, Thomas, 207, 220
Jenks, Almet, 6
Johnson, Jack, 231, 232, 233
Johnson, Merle, 190
Johnson, Owen, 15, 258
Johnson, Samuel, 3, 143, 166, 225, 226, 266
"Jonathan Cilley" (Hawthorne), 201
Jones, Gardner Maynard, 170
Jones, Herschel V., 185
Jones, Howard Mumford, xvii, 244
Jones, James, 194
Jonson, Ben, 182
Josephine Perry stories (Fitzgerald), 10
Journals and Miscellaneous Notebooks (Emerson), 83
Jovanovich, William, 136, 141, 195
Joyce, James, 39, 200, 281
Just and the Unjust, The (Cozzens), 264

Kaufman, George S., 66
Keisogloff, Peter, 165
Kelland, Clarence Budington, 6
Kelmscott Chaucer, 213
Kemble, John Philip, 180
Kemble play collection, 180
Kennerley, Jean, 166

Kennerley Mitchell, 184
Kern, Jerome, 165
Kerouac, Jack, 118, 163
Ketchel, Stanley (b. Stanislaus Kiecal), xxi, 231
King Johan (Bale), 180
Kipling, Rudyard, 11, 166
Knopf, Alfred, 137
Kohn, John S. Van E., 161, 173
Koran, the, 204
Kritzer, Hyman, 191

Ladd, Alan, 271, 272
Ladies Home Journal, 6
Lady in the Lake, The (Chandler), 275
Lake, Veronica, 272, 274
Lamb, Charles, 164
Lamb in His Bosom (Miller), 47
Lanahan, S. J., 89
Langford, Gerald, 214
Lardner, Rex, 127
Lardner, Ring, 33, 39, 128, 249, 258
Last Adam, The (Cozzens), 263, 264
"Last Kiss" (Fitzgerald), 66
Last Tycoon, The (*The Love of the Last Tycoon: A Western*), 12, 30, 175; compared with other Fitzgerald novels, 70, 76; Fitzgerald's publication proposal to *Collier's*, 64–65, 70; source of plane crash scene in, 78n11; synopsis of, 67–70
Lawes, Henry, 185
Leon & Brother, 169
Leonard, Elmore, 142
Letters from an American Farmer (Crevecoeur), 203–204
Letters to Walter Berry (Proust), 163
Lewis and Clark expedition, 203
Lewis, Sinclair, xvi, 6, 19, 47, 91, 118, 133, 258
Liberal Imagination, The (Trilling), 16
Liberty, 7

Liberty Tree (Hawthorne), 168, 169, 172
Library of America, 87
Library of Congress, 227
Life of Johnson (Boswell), 203
Life of Nathaniel Hawthorne (Conway), 170
Light of Heart, The (Williams), 76
"Light of the World, The" (Hemingway), xxi, 231–235; Ad Wolgast in, 233; Jack Johnson in, 231, 232
Lightening Source, 140–141
"Lipstick" (Fitzgerald), 9
Literary Collector, 171, 178
Literary Guild, 139
Littauer, Kenneth, 64, 65, 70
Little Sister, The (Chandler), 160, 175
Livingston, Luther S., 172
Lockwood Concern, The (O'Hara), 252
Lok, Henry, 187
London book ring, 182
London Suburb, A (Hawthorne), 175
Long Goodbye, The (Chandler), 160, 175
"Long Short Trip, The" (Herrmann), 237
Longfellow Collector's Handbook, The (Chew), 169
Look Homeward, Angel (Wolfe), 145, 146, 147, 149, 237, 242, 243; early Scribner readers of ms, 146; Perkins on reorganization of, 149; principal editorial excisions of, 148
Lorimer, George Horace, 7, 75
"The Love Song of J. Alfred Prufrock" (Eliot), 201
Lovey Childs (O'Hara), 252
Lyon, Leonard, 285
Lyrical Ballads (Wordsworth and Coleridge), 162

Macdonald, Dwight, 266
Macdonald, Ross. *See* Millar, Kenneth
Mackenzie, Compton, 15, 18
MacLeish, Archibald, 282
MacMillan, H. A., 49
Maggie (Crane), 165, 201
Maggs Brothers, 179, 202
Maier, Frank, 169, 173, 174
Main Street (Lewis), 19
"Majesty" (Fitzgerald), 6
Malamud, Bernard, 251
Maltese Falcon, The (Hammett), 270
Man with the Golden Arm, The (Algren), 282
Mann, Charles, 166
Manning, Robert, 175
Mansion, The (Faulkner), 121
Marble Faun, The (Hawthorne), 107, 168, 172; first printings of, 168; significance of textual variants in, 110
Marlowe, Christopher, 12, 186
Marquand, John P., 6, 257
Marquis, Don, 6
Marshall, George, 272, 273, 274
Mary Peters (Chase), 47
Massey, Linton, xv
Mather, Cotton, 184
Mather, Increase, 184
Matthew J. and Arlyn Bruccoli Collection of F. Scot Fitzgerald, xix
Matthiessen, F. O. (Francis Otto), xvi
Maupassant, Guy de, 280
Maxwell, William, 283
"May Day," 6
Mayer, Louis B., as model for Bradogue (*Last Tycoon*), 67
McAlmon, Robert, 281
McCall's, 6
McCarten, John, 274
McCoy, Horace, 270
McKerrow, Ronald Brunlees, 157
McManus, John, 274
Medwall, Henry, 186

Melville, Herman, 30, 167, 201, 202, 280
Men and Brethren (Cozzens), 264
Mencken, H. L. (Henry Louis), 7, 19, 29, 50, 203, 232
Metro-Goldwyn-Mayer, 8, 53
Metropolitan, 6, 8
Meyer, Wallace, 146
Michael Scarlett (Cozzens), 264
Millar, Kenneth (Ross Macdonald), xxii, 194
Millay, Edna St. Vincent, 162
Miller, Caroline, 47
Miller of Old Church, The (Glasgow), 102
"Millionaire's Girl" (Zelda Fitzgerald), 8
Milton, John, 185
Mirror of the World, The (printed by Caxton), 180
Misogonus, 180
Mizner, Wilson, 232
Moby-Dick (Melville), 202, 203
Modern Language Association (MLA), 83
Montgomery, Robert, 275
Moore, George, 166
Moral Proverbs of Cristyne (printed by Caxton), 187
Morgan, Dan, 232
Morgan, J. Pierpont, 173, 185
Morley, Christopher, 6
Morning, Noon, and Night (Cozzens), 266
Mosses from an Old Manse (Hawthorne), 171, 174–175
Mostyn, Thomas, 186
Moxon, Joseph, 101
Much Adoe about Nothing (Shakespeare), 187
Muller, Julian, 136
Murder, My Sweet (movie), 271
Murphy, Gerald, 39

Murphy, Sara Wiborg (Mrs. Gerald Murphy), 39, 247, 248

Nassau Literary Magazine, 17, 25
Nat Fleischer's The Ring Record Book and Boxing Encyclopedia, 232
Nathan, George Jean, 25
Nathaniel Hawthorne: A Descriptive Bibliography (Clark), 192
Nathaniel Hawthorne Journal, xxi, 189
Nathaniel Hawthorne Society, 189
National Endowment for the Arts, 228
National Endowment for the Humanities, x, 83
National Union Catalogue, 203, 218
Nature (Emerson), 203
Neiberg, Jack, 165
Nelson, Horatio, 182
Never Came Morning (Algren), 163
New Arabian Nights (Stevenson), 166
Newton, A. Edward, 165
Newton, Isaac, 200
Nigger of the Narcissus, The (Conrad), 50
Norris, Frank, 258
Notebooks of F. Scott Fitzgerald, 11, 17, 53, 249
Nowell, Elizabeth, 237, 238, 239
Nunn, Ferner, 243

O Lost (Wolfe), xx, 145–152; as early title of *Look Homeward, Angel,* 146; literary references in, 152; University of South Carolina edition of, 145, 147, 150, 151; MJB editorial methods for, 150
Ober, Harold, 4, 5, 7, 10, 23, 39, 63, 64, 72, 207
O'Connor, Patrick, 138, 142
Of Time and the River (Wolfe), 150, 237, 242, 243

O'Hara, John, xxii, 30, 31, 33, 47, 76, 247–262; details in character creation, 249–250; fiction set in Pottsville region, 252; as hard-boiled writer, 256, 259–260
  on Hemingway's artistic decline, 283
  on Hemingway's importance, 256, 260–261n1; models for characters in fiction of, 247, 248, 249; Rider College lectures of, 248, 249, 250, 251; as social historian, 256–257; source for Gibbsville in fiction of, 252
Oil for the Lamps of China (Hobart), 47
Old Man and the Sea, The (Hemingway), 103
"On a Play Twice Seen" (Fitzgerald), 7
"On the American Dead in Spain" (Hemingway), 283
On the Road (Kerouac), 163
"One Trip Abroad" (Fitzgerald), 40
Oppenheim, E. Phillips, 6
Oprah Book Club, 142
Origin of Species (Darwin), 200
"Our April Letter," (Fitzgerald), 11
Ourselves to Know (O'Hara), 252

Paltsits, Victor Hugo, 171
Pandosto (Green), 187
Papantonio, Michael, 161
Papke, Billy, 231
Paradise of Dainty Devises (Edwards), 187
Parker, Dorothy, 258
Parrish, Morris L., 165, 207
Passionate Pilgrim, The (Shakespeare), 186
Pat Hobby stories (Fitzgerald), 72, 76
Peabody, Sophia. *See* Hawthorne, Sophia Peabody
Pentland Rising, The (Stevenson), 166
Perkins, Maxwell, xx, 4, 5, 8, 10, 25, 32, 39, 40, 42, 43, 44. 53, 63, 64, 71, 73, 120, 124, 125, 126, 127, 128, 141, 206, 208, 237; as central to Bruccoli's Fitzgerald and Hemingway scholarship, xx; cuts by, in *Look Homeward, Angel,* 147, 149; devotion of, to authors, 141; editorial manner of, 25, 121; as executor of Fitzgerald' will, 223; on the "only thing that counts," 282; policies on factual errors in *Gatsby,* 127; reputation of, 145; as role model for the collaborating editor, 120; Wolfe's debt to, 150
Peter Parley's Universal History (Hawthorne), 168, 169, 170, 171, 172, 173, 174
Peyton Place (Metalious), 264
Phipps Psychiatric Clinic, 40
Picasso, Pablo, 284
Picture of Dorian Gray (Wilde) 17, 18
Playback (Chandler), 160, 271, 275
Plimpton, George, 282
Polychronicon (Higden), 180
Poore, Charles, 56, 193, 277
"Popular Girl, The" (Fitzgerald), 7
Portable F. Scott Fitzgerald, The (Parker, ed.), 209
Portrait of Bascome Hawke, A (Wolfe), 237
Postman Always Rings Twice, The (Cain), 257
Pound, Ezra, 203, 281, 282
Powell, Dick, 271
Price, Reynolds, 194
"Princeton—The Last Day" (Fitzgerald), 17
Princeton Alumni Weekly, 49, 210
Princeton Tiger, 17, 205
Principia (Newton), 200
Principles of Bibliographical Description (Bowers), 160
Private Worlds (Bottome), 47
Profession of Authorship in America, The (Charvat, ed. Bruccoli), 84

Professional, The (Heinze), 282
Proust, Marcel, 163
"Prufrock." *See* "Love Song of J. Alfred Prufrock, The"
Public Lending Right, 138
Publishers Weekly, 5, 98
pulp magazines, 140
Purpose Driven Life, The (Warren), 133

Quaritch, Bernard, 181, 182, 185
Quip for an Upstart Courtier (Green), 187

Rage to Live, A (O'Hara), 252
Rahv, Philip, 48
Randall, David A., 206, 207, 208
Rantoul, Robert, 113
"Rationale of Copy-Text, The" (Greg), 84
Raynolds, Robert, 242
Red Badge of Courage, The (Crane), 194, 201
Red Book, 6
Red-Headed Woman (Fitzgerald), 9
Richard the Third (Shakespeare), 187
Rimbaud, Arthur, 51
Ring, Frances Kroll, 76
Robinson, E. A., 162
"Romantic Egotist, The" (orig. title of *This Side of Paradise,* Fitzgerald) 16, 17
Roos, Christian, 170
Roosevelt, Franklin Delano, 249
Rosalynd (Lodge), 187
Rose and the Ring (Thackeray), 68, 182
Rosenbach, A. S. W., 165, 174, 187, 201
Rosenbach lectures, 212, 222
Rosenthal, Herman, 31, 33, 124
Rota, Anthony, 166
Roth, Henry, 258
Roth, Lester, 208
Rothstein, Arnold, 32, 33, 124

Rowland, Henry C., 6
Ruffner, Fred, 194

S.S. San Pedro (Cozzens), 264
Sabin, Joseph, 218, 226
Sandoe, James, 272, 274
Saturday Evening Post, 3, 4, 5, 6, 7, 8, 10
Sayre, Zelda. *See* Fitzgerald, Zelda Sayre
Scarlet Letter, The (Hawthorne), 84, 85 168, 169, 171, 172, 174, 175, 190; first editions of, 167; manuscript of, 112; variants in, 102
Schiff, Mortimer, 185
Schulberg, Budd, 30, 56
Scribner, Charles, 63, 71,
Scribner, Charles, Jr. 87, 126
Scribner, Charles III, 279
Scribner Classics editions, 89
Scribners (Charles Scribner's Sons), 5, 8, 12, 28, 120, 136, 138, 146, 151, 236; Fitzgerald's 1919 contract with, 138; subsidiary rights (contractual), 138–139
Scribner's Magazine, 43, 44, 237, 238, 241, 252
Sejanus (Jonson), 182
Seldes, Gilbert, 6, 12, 48
self-publishing, 140
"Sensible Thing, The" (Fitzgerald), 10
Septimus Felton (Hawthorne), 173
Serif, The, 204
Sermons and Soda Water (O'Hara), 254, 256
Sessler, Charles, 174
Settle, Mary Lee, 141
Seven Gables bookshop, 161
Seven Gothic Tales (Dinesen), 47
Seventh Veil (movie), 274
Shakespeare, William, 25, 182, 185, 186, 187, 277, 280
Shanks, Edward, 29
Shaw, George Bernard, 25, 52, 166

Shaw, Joseph, 270
Shearer, Norma (Mrs. Irving Thalberg), 253
Shor, Toots, 285
Sidney, Philip, 187
Sister Carrie (Dreiser), 166
Sister Years, The (Hawthorne), 167, 169, 170, 171, 172, 173
Sitwell, Edith, 163
Skelton, John, 187
Skip, Francis, 236
Smart Set, The, 6, 19
Smith, George D, xxi, 178–188; *London Times* on, 181
Smith, Goldie, 232
Smith, Red, 282
Snopes Trilogy (Faulkner), 121
So Red the Rose (Young), 47
Society of the Dofobs of Chicago, 178
Something About Eve (Cabell), 104
Son of Perdition, The (Cozzens), 264
Songes and Sonnettes (Howard), 187
Sophocles (Laurentian ms.), 181
Sound and the Fury, The (Faulkner), 122
Spanish Civil War, 281, 282; International Brigade in, 283; Lincoln Brigade in, 283; Spengler, Oswald, 32
Spinoza, Benedict de, 203
Spohr, J. A., 185
Spring-Rice, Cecil, 6
Steel, Oliver, 102, 108
Stein, Gertrude, 30, 39, 281
Steinbeck, John, 142, 264
Stephens, James, 166
Sternberg, Vernon, 194
Stevens, Wallace, 203
Stevenson, Adlai, 205
Stevenson, Robert Louis, 166, 184
Stewart, Donald Ogden, 75
Stone, Stewart, 169
Story of a Novel, The (Wolfe), 150, 242
Strangers on a Train (Highsmith), 275

Strauss, Harry, 179
Street Songs (Sitwell), 163
Studies in Bibliography, 158, 160
"Sun and the Rain, The" (Wolfe), 238
Sunday School Society's Gift, The, 173
Sundry Christian Passions (Lok), 187
Sutcliff, Denham, 190
Swann, Arthur, 173, 181
Swanson, H. N., 142
Swanson, Mary Ann. *See* Clark, Mary Ann Swanson

Tabula, 193
Tales of the Jazz Age (Fitzgerald), 25, 161
Taps at Reveille, 10
Tarkington, Booth, 15, 258
"Tarquin of Cheapside" (Fitzgerald), 25
Tate, Allen, 207
Ten North Frederick (O'Hara), 248, 252, 259
Tender Is the Night (Fitzgerald), 4, 5, 8, 9, 10, 16, 30, 124, 126, 205, 209, 257; "Author's Final Version, The," 51–58; Bowers on Cowley edition of, 57–58; composition of, 39–43; Cowley's restructuring of 54–55; dominant theme in, 42; editing and publication of, 44–46; effects of FSF's drinking on, 43; first Dick Diver version, 42; Fitzgerald on "NEW" form and structure, 39; Fitzgerald on three-part structure in, 42; Francis Melarky versions, 39; influence of Zelda Fitzgerald's illness on, 40, 41, 42; reception of, 47–50; serialization of, 43; time scheme in, 61n31
Terry, George, xviii–xix
Thackeray, William Makepeace, 68
Thalberg, Irving, 67; as model for Monroe Stahr (*Last Tycoon*), 67, 68
Thin Man, The (Hammett), 257
Third Folio (Shakespeare), 187

This Side of Paradise (Fitzgerald), 5, 8, 32, 33, 35, 52, 125, 126, 138, 158; as American college novel, 15; Amory Blain in, 16, 17,18, 19; author's evaluation of, 15; as best-seller, 5; Fitzgerald on supernatural occurrences in, on, 19; preface to, 18; printings and royalties, 20; reception of, 19–20; as "a romance and a reading list," 17; sales of (1920), 47; themes of, 16; title source, 17
Thomas Cooper Library, 227
Thomas, Dylan, 163
Thorp, Willard, 208, 209
Three Comrades (Remarque), 9
Three Stories and Ten Poems (Hemingway), 157, 193, 201, 203
"Thumbs Up" (Fitzgerald), 64
"Tiare Tahiti (Brooke)," 17
Ticknor (George) & Fields (James T.), 110
Time to Kill (movie), 271
Time's Portraiture (Hawthorne), 167, 170, 171, 172, 173, 174
Titus Andronicus (Shakespeare), 185
To Have and Have Not (Hemingway), 163, 282
Tolstoy, Leo, 280
Torrents of Spring, The (Hemingway), 201
Town, The (Faulkner), 121
transatlantic review, 281
Transformation (Hawthorne), 193
Treatise of Venery (Twety), 185
Triangle Club, 17
Trilling, Lionel, 7, 11–12, 16
Trimalchio (Fitzgerald): early title of *Gatsby*, 147
Troy, William, 30, 49
True Chronicle of King Leir, 182
Tully, Jim, 232
Turgenev, Ivan Sergeevich, 280
Twain, Mark. *See* Clemens, Samuel

Twenty Days with Julian and Little Bunny (Hawthorne). 173
Twice-Told Tales (Hawthorne), 168, 169, 172, 173, 174

Ulizio, George, 165, 166
Ulysses (Joyce), 163, 200
Unseen, The (movie), 271

Vail, Theodore N., 185
Vegetable, The, 5, 7
Venus and Adonis (Shakespeare), 186
Volkening, Henry, 243
Vonnegut, Kurt, 140

Wager, William, 186
Wakman, Stephen H., 169, 170, 172, 173, 174
Wallace, Edgar, 6
Wallace, Walter T., 173
Walton, Edith, 49
"War in April, The" (Wolfe), 242
"Web of the Earth, The" (Wolfe), 237, 238
Webster, Noah, 226
Weeks, Edward, 48
Wells, Gabriel, 174, 257
Wells, H. G., 15, 18
Wenning, Henry, 163, 167
Wescott, Glenway, 30
Whale, The (Melville), 201, 202
Wharton, Edith, xvi, 30, 97
Wheelock, John Hall, 146, 151
White, Stewart Edward, 6
Whitejacket (Melville), xvi
Whiteside, Thomas, 139
Whitfield, Raoul, 258
Whitman, Walt, 160
Who's Who in America questionnaire: Hemingway copy of, 193
Widener Library, 227
Wikipedia, 225

Wilde, Oscar, 15, 18, 166
Wilkinson, Max, 64, 75
Williams, Emlyn, 76
Williams, William Carlos, 203
Williamson, George M., 169, 170, 171, 174
Wilson, Carroll A., 175
Wilson, Earl, 285
Wilson, Edmund, 4, 23, 44, 77, 125, 126, 249–250
Wilson, Harry Leon, 6
Wilson, Woodrow, 205
Winick, Eugene, 139, 140
"Winter Dreams" (Fitzgerald), 10, 34
Within This Present (Barnes), 47
Wodehouse, P. G., 6
Wolfe, Thomas, xx, xxii, 6, 12, 120, 136, 203, 236–246; on first meeting with Perkins, 146–147; Guggenheim Fellowship report by, 242; on Perkins editorial interference, 242; reaction to Fitzgerald criticism, 237; on revising "The Four Lost Men," 238
Woolrich, Cornell, 270
Work of Art (Lewis), 47

Works of Jonathan Edwards, 83
Wyllie, John Cook, xviii, xviii, 157, 161, 203, 212–223; Alderman library acquisitions by, 216–218; career at Alderman Library, 214–215; as editor and project facilitator, 223; education of, 212; on Faulkner, 220–221; on importance of physical book, 213; on Jefferson, 221–222; lectures and addresses by, 158, 212; military career, 214–215; reading passion of, 215–216; on technology, 219–220
Wyllie, Elizabeth, 215
Wyllie, Evelyn Dollens, 215
Wyllie, Jane, 215
Wyllie, Mabel Cook, 213
Wyllie, William, 213

Young Manhood of Studs Lonigan (Farrell), 258
Young, Owen D., 165
Young, Stark, 47

Ziegfeld, Florenz, 70
Zola, Émile, 258